SPAIN'S STRUGGLE FOR EUROPE

1598-1668

Gaspar de Guzman, count-duke of Olivares. An impressive portrait of Olivares
which seems to show the count-duke at the height of his powers in the mid
1630s. The man's sheer bulk and his imperious glance, which cast terror
into grandees, generals and civil servants alike, are nicely conveyed, as is
the thinning hair which eventually persuaded Don Gaspar to sport a wig.
(*Biblioteca National, Madrid*)

SPAIN'S STRUGGLE
FOR EUROPE
1598-1668

———

R.A. STRADLING

THE HAMBLEDON PRESS

LONDON AND RIO GRANDE

Published by The Hambledon Press 1994

102 Gloucester Avenue, London NW1 8HX (U.K.)
P.O. Box 162, Rio Grande, Ohio 45674 (U.S.A.)

ISBN 1 85285 089 2

A description of this book is available from
the British Library and from the Library of Congress

Typeset by The Midlands Book Typesetting Company

Printed on acid-free paper and bound in Great Britain
by Cambridge University Press

Contents

Acknowledgements

The articles reprinted here first appeared in the following places and are reprinted by kind permission of the original publishers.

1 *European Studies Review*, 9 (1979), pp. 157–94.

2 *European History Quarterly*, 14 (1984), pp. 77–91.

3 *Historical Journal*, 33 (1990), pp. 769–85.

4 *The Seventeenth Century*, 4 (1990), pp. 91–116.

5 *English Historical Review*, 101 (1986), pp. 68–94.

6 Published in Spanish as '"Los dos Grandes Luminares de la Tierra": España y Francia en la política de Olivares'. *La España del conde duque de Olivares*, ed. J.H. Elliott and A. García Sanz (Valladolid, 1990), pp. 129–60. First publication here in English.

7 *Historical Journal*, 19 (1976), pp. 1–31.

8 *English Historical Review*, 87 (1972), pp. 269–86.

9 *History*, 64 (1979), pp. 205–19.

10 *Tijdschrift voor geschiedenis*, 93 (1980), pp. 541–58.

11 *History*, 69 (1984), pp. 208–21.

12 This appears here for the first time.

Preface

The world of 'early-modern' Spanish studies has for nearly thirty years provided me with a stimulating area of research. The statement has a note of ambivalence, because this particular chapter of the historian's guild has not been noted for the fraternal warmth of its proceedings. But here is no cause to mourn; scholarly life ought to be precarious, both emotionally and intellectually. I never sought to enter one of the gentle occupations, given over to the protocols of a mutual admiration society. Disagreement - expressed candidly in public as well as private, and over both incidentals and fundamentals - is earnest of dynamism and healthy commitment to change. Yet experience tells me that friendship and collaboration between workers in the same field is possible, and perhaps all the more to be celebrated because achieved in a discipline whose more dominant (if no less life-enhancing) characteristics are competition and ephemerality.

I first went to Spain as an apprentice, and have remained an obdurate autodidact. My unrefined interest in things Hispanic arose from a Catholic background and education (of a sort). In its cultural dimension, at least, the Catholicism is still in evidence. In Spain, one was obliged to learn quickly: 'La necesidad enseña más que la universidad.' My benefactors in transmitting the necessary technical ability were student coevals and professional colleagues rather than academic tutors *stricto sensu*. In the 1960s the working environment for a foreign student lacking glamorous academic connections and social cachet was frankly inimical. Luck as well as determination was needed so as not to add to the number of Anglo-Saxons who failed to conclude (or, subsequently, to develop) their studies.

In the present collection, the introduction and conclusion, in which the important issues are re-examined and refocused, are both new. Chapter 11 - also in its debut - is a synoptic product of what will be my last archive-centred, 'scientific' enquiry into the history of the Spanish monarchy. The other chapters appear in their initial form, save for corrections of factual errors and some bibliographical additions.

I should like to record my gratitude to the undermentioned institutions which helped with research funds, as well as individuals who provided scholarly help and information, during the original preparation of the essays in this collection. In the first category are the British Academy, the Twenty-Seven Foundation of the University of London, University College, Cardiff (latterly University of Wales, College of Cardiff), and the Wolfson Foundation. In the second, M. Echevarría, Sir John Elliott, Kate Belsey, Terry Hawkes, Alberto Hauf, Harry Hearder, J.R. Jones, A.W. Lovett, Maria Peralta, Mark Pierce, Peter Thomas, Nora Temple, Richard Trewinnard, Lorraine White and Patrick Williams. My work in Spain over the years has also been assisted at various times by my friends; Gill Bird, Benito Vázquez Iglesias, Carmén Jorde Vallejo and José Ramón Pelayo Loscertales. Thanks are also due to the original publishers for permission to reprint essays; and to Martin Sheppard of Hambledon for his expert guidance in a variety of editorial and other relevant matters.

Unless otherwise stated, all books were published in London.

R.A.S.

July 1993

Illustrations

Abbreviations

AAE   Archives du Ministère des Affaires Étrangères, Paris
             CE   Correspondance Espagnole

ADV   Archivo de la Diputación Foral de Vizcaya, Bilbao

AGS   Archivo General de Simancas, Valladolid
             AEH   Ambassade de l'Espagne à La Haye
             CMC   Contaduría Mayor de Cuentas
             CJH   Consejo y Juntas de Hacienda
             E   Estado
             GA   Guerra Antigua

AHM[A]   Archivo Histórico Municipal de Alicante, Alicante

AHN   Archivo Histórico Nacional, Madrid
             E   Estado
             Hac. Hacienda

AHP[C]   Archivo Histórico Provincial de Cantabria, Santander
             CEM   Centro de Estudios Montañeses
             LAR   Archivo Municipal de Laredo

AHP[G]   Archivo Histórico Provincial de Guipúzcoa, Tolosa

AHP[O]   Archivo Histórico Provincial de Orense, Orense

AME   Archivo del Ministerio de Asuntos Exteriores, Madrid

AN   Archives Nationales de la France, Paris
             SHE   Section d'Histoire Étrangère

APR   Archivo del Palacio Real de Oriente, Madrid
             Adm   Sección Administrativa
             SH   Sección Histórica

ARB   Archives Générales du Royaume, Brussels
           SEG   Sécrétairerie d'État et de Guerre

BAE   Biblioteca de Autores Españoles

BL   British Library, London
           Add.   Additional MS
           Eg.   Egerton MS
           Harl.   Harleian MS

BPU   Bibliothèque Publique et Universitaire, Geneva [Collection
           Favre]

BN   Biblioteca Nacional, Madrid

BRB   Bibliothèque Royale d'Albert Premier, Brussels

CODOIN   Colección de Documentos Inéditos para la Historia de España

CSPD   Calendar of State Papers, Domestic

CSPV   Calendar of State Papers, Venetian

EHR   *English Historical Review*

MN   Archivo del Museo Naval, Madrid

NMM   National Maritime Museum Library, Greenwich
           PHB   Phillips Collection

Oxf. Bod. Bodleian Library, Oxford

PRO   Public Record Office, Chancery Lane, London.
           SP   State Papers

RAH   Real Academia de la Historia, Madrid [Colección Salazar y
           Castro]

Introduction

Religion and Reputation – A Universal Cause?

Firstly, my son, you must fear God; for in fearing Him is wisdom,
and, being wise, you can make no mistake.[1]

So runs the advice, concerning the essence of temporal rulership, given by
Don Quixote to Sancho, upon the latter's surprising appointment as governor
of an island. No writer of the Hispanic world in the early modern period would
have dissented from this nostrum, and most of them explicitly subscribed to it.[2]
The Habsburg kings and their councillors constantly performed the requisite
self-audit of their magisterial purity in the sense it conveyed. Apart from
regular individual self-scrutiny in the confessional, they consulted a panel
of highly-qualified clerics before embarking upon any decision which had
major ethical or religious implications. As we know from his correspondence,
Philip IV ceaselessly strove to be a God-fearing ruler, and thus to preserve
his worthiness to rule – in canonical practice, for a state of grace. The king
was ultimately responsible, but he was not alone responsible. In the critical
spring of 1647, with Mazarin's France poised to give the *coup de grace* to an
enfeebled Castile, Philip set up a junta to inquire into the reasons 'why God
should be so annoyed with the monarchy of Spain'. After due consideration
the convener of this committee, Fray Juan Martínez – the king's confessor
– reported that the main causes were decline of religion and the increase
in pride and vanity among Castilians.[3] More than forty years later Philip's
son, Carlos II, commissioned another report on the causes 'of the many grave
calamities which afflict this Monarchy'. The same conclusion was reached
and the same remedies were ordered for the revival of religious observance.[4]
Cervantes' kinsman and fellow-writer, Saavedra y Fajardo, was one of Spain's
negotiators at Munster and much inclined to peace. Yet even for him, war was

---

[1] M. de Cervantes, *The Adventures of Don Quixote*, trans. J. M. Cohen, (1950), p. 738.

[2] See the excellent survey of political literature in the early seventeenth century by
F. T. Valiente, in idem (ed.) *Historia de España Menéndez Pidal*, xxv (Madrid, 1982), pp. 21–82.

[3] *Consulta* of March, 1647, BL, Add. 28452, ff. 302–308.

[4] *Consulta* of 14 Jan. 1691, BN, 11034, ff. 146–149.

often necessary in the defence of true religion. The cross of crusade sanctioned all: 'In hoc signo, vinces.'[5].

Accordingly, during the seventeenth century the Spanish monarchy fought a stubborn rearguard action in the attempt to maintain its European hegemony. This 'Fifty Years War' (1618–68) was a phenomenon which dominated the history of the Iberian communities, and indeed of many other peoples situated in a broad geographical swathe of south-western Europe. For Spain's decision-making elites, for countless subordinate members of the Monarchy, and for thousands of their European associates and sympathisers, these apparently endless conflicts represented more than a simple power-struggle over interests and resources. Salvador de Madariaga once remarked that Habsburg Spain became a church; but 'it did not submit to the Roman Church ... It was itself a Church in that for it nationality and religion became one, and its official interests were religious, i.e., the spiritual welfare of its subjects.'[6] As a modern expert has proclaimed, with all the fervour of the recent convert – Spain was 'a power uniquely firmly committed to enforcing the Counter Reformation and the supremacy of the Catholic Faith and uniquely successful, both at home in the Peninsula and in her overseas empire, in breaking down other religions and cultures and Catholicising her subject populations'.[7] Spain's commitment to religious war might be compared to those of the indigenous American empires which its conquistadores had overthrown in the early sixteenth century. In the religion of the Aztecs, for example, the need to sustain the Sun God in his debilitating nightly struggle with the powers of darkness could only be met by the blood of living warriors. It was the task of the War God, Huitzilipochtli, to demand unceasing warfare – itself primarily a religious ritual – in order to ensure a regular supply of prisoners fit for sacrifice. War was thus, quite literally, the fuel of existence, as necessary to the community as its food and drink.[8]

There is, surely, a striking analogy to be drawn here. The silent majority of the Spanish Monarchy, its vast, amorphous, unprivileged masses, seems to have complaisantly accepted the demands of warfare. Such privations were part of the penalty of the Fall, the eternal struggle of life on earth, a condition of their environment. In contrast (if with some dissenters), the political estates viewed them more positively; primordially as a matter of conscience, and as a bid for eternal glory in the hereafter. Like many pro-Europeanists of today, their ardour was fired by an ideal: not (or not only) by the prospect of prosperity but also by the promise of an ultimate, universal and perpetual peace. This latter case was nothing less

---

[5] D. Saavedra Fajardo, *Idea de un príncipe político-christiano* BAE, 25 (Madrid, 1949), pp. 70–71.

[6] S. de Madariaga, *Spain* (1930), p. 40.

[7] J. I. Israel, *Empires and Entrepots: The Dutch, the Spanish Monarchy and the Jews, 1585–1713* (1990), p. xi.

[8] J. Alcina Franch, *Los Aztecas* (Madrid, 1989), pp. 32–34.

than that divinely-ordained and prophesied condition of things which would enable the final consummation of Christian teleology, the Second Coming. To invert the words of instruction which figured prominently in the catechism of the faithful, the word 'Universal' meant 'Catholic'. No more under Philip IV than under his grandfather and chief exemplar, Philip II, did Spain seek crude territorial conquest. In a variety of more subtle ways, it sought to bring about a more ideologically homogeneous Europe: if not one politically united, *stricto sensu*, then at least one at ease with its own soul. Its rulers rejected the grim prospect of a Europe tortured by pandemic confessional and cultural strife, riven by dynastic-nationalist rivalry.

The undertaking was one which demanded and received – as well as an astonishing acceptance of sacrifice among the ruled – an almost unwavering intensity of commitment among the rulers. The nature of this communion suggests something which cannot be fully explained by the invocation of macroeconomic or geopolitical criteria – not to mention other influential instruments of modern historical analysis. In this it was certainly not unique in historical experience, nor – perhaps more importantly – should it be regarded as culturally alien to the modern world. For all their contrast of discourse, both in the fundamentalist world of the Iranian Ayatollahs and the non-denominational world of their (alleged) cultural opposites in Washington, the role of a supportive godhead located at the incorruptible kernel of policy is a palpable one. In terms of prolonged international confrontations - to attempt the broadest possible context of definition – Spain's struggle in the seventeenth century resembled the Crusades, the French Revolutionary Wars, and the wars of dialectical ideology earlier in our present century (also, as it happened, a fifty year struggle, 1936–86); it differed from the Hundred Years' War, Louis XIV's wars of dynastic aggrandisement, the series of colonial-commercial conflicts of the eighteenth century, or the campaigns of Bismarck's Prussia in the nineteenth.

Most relevant authorities would now accept – at least as a basis for discussion – that the Spanish monarchy was driven by a species of enlightened self-interest more powerfully connected to the rewards of the world to come than to those of our tangible, mundane existence. I have put things in these terms in order to emphasise that Philip IV's motivation for war was in no abstract sense morally more acceptable than that of Louis XIV or Bismarck. An earlier generation of Spanish historians deliberately stressed Spain's 'spiritual essence', her refusal to compete in the race for 'enlightened' modernization, as a kind of perverse virtue and a source of national pride - this constituted, as it were, Spain's 'special path'.[9] Spaniards have often assumed, and outsiders have sometimes accepted, that wars which are motivated by religion are somehow more justifiable and less reprehensible than others; and of course from the ethical

[9] See A. Feros Carrasco, 'Sobre la decadencia de la monarquía hispánica en el siglo XVII', in A. Domínguez Ortiz et al. (ed.), *Historia de España*, vi (Barcelona, 1988), esp. pp. 340–44.

standpoint of religion itself they are indeed regarded as 'just wars'. Yet it is important for us today to realise that, however authentic and sincere their proponents, such conflicts were no less inspired by the imperatives of the ethnocentric – selfish fear or crude ambition. Since the Habsburg kings played for a prize which was infinite, and staked their souls on the outcome, it could be argued that theirs were the more terrible fear and the worse ambition. What self-aggrandisement could be greater, what ice-cold logic more Machiavellian, than those sanctioned by the prospects of salvation and eternal life? Similarly, although the miseries imposed on the common people by religious conflicts were no less real than those of a war for gold, for land or for trade, they may (arguably) have been easier to bear.

The perception of a *Causa Universal* was by no means limited to Castile or even to metropolitan Spain. Indeed the concept was discrete from that of *reputación*, which was undeniably subordinate to the greater ideological imperatives. In the mid 1970s, J.H. Elliott drew attention to the increasing resort to the term '*reputación*' as a justification for war, or risk of war, by ministers.[10] This phenomenon was recorded in the state papers with special frequency from the outset of the 'Guzmán Era' – that is, with the arrival in government of Baltasar de Zúñiga and his allies in 1617–18. Under the count-duke of Olivares, Zúñiga's political heir, the term becomes well-nigh ubiquitous. Elliott defined it as an unique meld of ideals to do with prestige and honour; in political practice, as having both external (defence) and internal (domestic) dimensions focused upon the authority of the king; and, in terms of its *raison d'être*, as a reaction to the perceived desertion of these ideals by the previous regime presided over by the duke of Lerma. Elliott was careful to lay down in advance of his argument the ineluctable fact that 'for the count-duke, just as it had been for Philip II, the main objective of Spanish power remained the advancement of the Faith'.[11] Yet precisely because it is accurate as observation and powerful as formulation, Elliott's hypothesis has to some extent had the effect of obscuring the primary reality of the religious commitment which lay behind, and produced, *reputación*.

The concept of *reputación* also had little currency outside the central circles of Madrid government, being of distinctly limited importance even to the governing groups of its major satellite bases. In his contribution to the volume of essays deriving from the Toro Symposium (1987) which celebrated the Spain of Olivares, Felipe Ruíz Martín returned to contemplate the basic principles which informed the Spanish system, and went on to develop a focus on the context of the present essay:

> What received emphasis in the making of policy in the Spanish Monarchy was a
> matter for the king – above all the king, but a king in perfect unanimity with his

---

[10] J. H. Elliott, *El conde-duque de Olivares y la herencia de Felipe II* (Valladolid, 1977). See also idem, 'A Question of Reputation? Spanish Foreign Policy in the Seventeenth Century', *Journal of Modern History*, 55 (1983), pp. 475–83.

[11] Elliott, *El conde-duque*, p. 80.

ministers. This was to do with the geographical agglomeration of a multi-state and pluri-national community, along with the maintenance in paramountcy of its political and religious beliefs. The count-duke of Olivares unreservedly belonged to this tradition, a position dictated by fundamental loyalties. As the local urban leadership of Castile increasingly rejected the burden, he called upon the other Iberian dominions, and especially the dependencies in Italy and the Low Countries ... In 1626 he officially proclaimed the Union of Arms, but already some years earlier he began to implement the philosophy behind it, namely that all parts of the Monarchy must exert their resources together in order not to lose the fruits which union provided – the earthly protection which emanated from Spanish Kingship, and was sanctioned by the Pope as Vicar of Christ. This assertion was not simply rhetoric or propaganda.[12]

Others, however, are reluctant to concur in this account of things. The secular scepticism appropriate to scholars deriving from the liberal-agnostic traditions of northern Europe is still much in evidence. Writing in the same symposium, for example, I.A.A. Thompson is dubious about Ruíz Martín's assertions. He agrees that during the seventeenth-century struggle, the Hispanic monarchy became a truly cosmopolitan entity – giving his account an independent section under the portentous heading 'Internationalization'. Thompson agrees that 'Olivares's ideal of a multi-national Monarchy was never nearer to being a reality than in the middle decades of the seventeenth century'.[13] However, whereas Ruíz Martín sees the process as creative, for Thompson it had largely negative characteristics. It did not occur as result of Olivares' programme of reform, but was merely an incidental by-product of the increasing contribution of non-Spanish resources to the defence of the monarchy. He gives no hint that inter-communal collaboration was anything to do with commitment, or that it was rooted in a common ground of history, religion or cosmopolitan culture. To the contrary, he argues that resentment over the process of 'internationalization' fuelled the growth of Castilian chauvinism, fanning back into life those elemental sparks of xenophobia last openly ignited by the rebellion of townships (the 'Comuneros') a century before, a 'little Castilian' mentality which (*mutatis mutandis*) lay behind the eventual fall of Olivares in 1643. Many complaints were heard in the 1630s that foreigners dominated not only the rank-and-file of Spain's armed forces, but also its high command. Alien technical experts were imported to construct new blast-furnaces, to manufacture weaponry and to improve the design of warships. Worst of all, foreigners had established themselves at senior levels of government: they were appointed to governorships and viceroyalties, whilst even the royal councils

---

[12] F. Ruíz Martín, 'El conde-duque de Olivares y las finanzas de la monarquía hispánica', A. García Sanz and J. H. Elliott (ed.), *La España del conde duque de Olivares* (Valladolid, 1991), at p. 462.

[13] I. A. A. Thompson, 'Aspectos de la organización naval y militar durante el ministerio de Olivares', ibid., at p. 262. For the quotation, I have used the English translation, 'Aspects of Spanish Military and Naval Organization during the Ministry of Olivares', printed in Dr Thompson's *War and Society in Habsburg Spain* (Aldershot, 1992), at p. 14.

– those of the treasury and war, amongst others – had been infiltrated by non-Iberian elements which, to compound the offence, were often non-noble, or even Jewish.

Conversely, it may follow from this that pro-Spanish awareness – at times, dependence – present in Catholic Europeans, from Croatia to Ireland and from Poland to Naples, was a fraternal feeling not as perfectly reciprocated by Spaniards themselves as the ideals of a Universal Monarchy sometimes proclaimed. Of course, in the last analysis, there was an insufficient sense of irenicism amongst the Catholic nations, and a deficient sense of community even among subjects of Philip IV within the peninsula, for the Universal Cause ever to be properly encompassed, let alone for it to triumph over its Protestant adversaries.

In the last analysis, Spain had to trust to its own conscience and not rely on those of other nations and other magistrates. In 1625 some councillors suggested that, in the interests of constructing a strong network of allies in Europe and thus encompassing the final defeat of the Dutch, Philip IV should underplay the religious issues involved in the struggle. A senior minister, the marquis of Montesclaros – an ex-associate of Zúñiga – rebutted this, arguing that 'of all those who may enter this league, the pope is the most important, because he will carry with him many of the Italian princes'.[14] Yet not many years earlier, on the eve of the Thirty Years War, the duke of Osuna, viceroy of Naples, had warned that Spain could never rely on the papacy to defend the Faith. 'In his spiritual role, the Pope has a great concern for this cause, but because of reason of state, he is liable to act totally to the contrary.'[15]

An increasingly bitter awareness of being more-or-less pusillanimously deserted by other responsible authorities – the papacy, France, and the empire, in that order – sharpened Spain's sense of isolation. This had a resonance in the preoccupations of its policymakers: an increasingly exclusive national mission in the 1620s; a febrile susceptibility to fear of 'international conspiracy' in the 1630s; and finally a veritable siege mentality in the crisis-torn 1640s. Even today, the remorse of Catholic Germany for its abandonment of the Spanish Peace (*'Friedensordnung'*) is not wholly extinguished.[16] Whether such feelings were ever justified is another matter. As Tierno Galván showed many years ago, the indispensable hard-core composition of Spain's 'special path' was merely an ethnocentric version of 'reason of state'. Though Machiavelli was officially anathema, many pro-Spanish writers, from Justus Lipsius onwards, espoused the idea of a 'true reason of state': that Spain should help God to help Spain, by embracing the principle that the end justified the means.[17] Olivares' close adviser Virgilio Malvezzi stated (almost in so many words) that when

---

[14] *Voto* of Montesclaros, 29 May 1625, PRO transcripts 31/12/32.

[15] Osuna to Philip III, 7 April 1617, BL, Add. 21004, f. 379v.

[16] See E. Straub, *Pax et Imperium: Spaniens Kampf und seine Friedensordnung in Europa zwischen 1617 und 1635* (Paderborn-Munich, 1980).

[17] Tierno Galván is cited in Tomás y Valiente, *Historia de España*, xxv, p. 25.

reason of state was exercised by Spain's enemies it was the devil's work, but when by Spain it was moved by the hand of God.[18] Even some Spanish experts are unable to regard this proposition as other than sheer hypocrisy. Where Viñas Mey, Jover Zamora and Fraga Iribarne (to name only three) sing in harmony on the objectives of Spanish policy – 'religion, peace, moderation, public faith, legitimacy, dynasty, respect for treaties' – others, such as Ródenas Vilar and Rodríguez-Moñino, discordantly identify a new Machiavel, a Spanish version of Richelieu, in the person of the count-duke of Olivares.[19]

At the very outset of Olivares' ministry, another of the count-duke's advisers wrote frankly about the objective of universal power, in phrases which would seem to bear out the wildest claims of many contemporary English propaganda flysheets about Spanish ambitions. As it happens, however, the writer was himself English. 'Every monarchy which has ever flourished for long upon the earth [asserted Antony Sherley] had the same ends – supreme dominion.' Sherley went so far as to advocate an alliance between Madrid and the Porte, in order to crush the Dutch nucleus of resistance, going on to propose that, once this was achieved, a Europe united under Habsburg leadership could launch a great crusade and finally wipe out the power of the Ottomans.[20] In the early years of Philip IV's reign, the Madrid party which recommended a sustained offensive against the infidel, and a commensurate (if temporary) retreat from northern European concerns, had by no means given up the struggle for influence, despite the disgrace of its leader, Philip III's confessor, Fray Luis de Aliaga.[21] This was a debate in which sympathisers like the Catholic Scot William Semple and the Arminian-Anglican, Anglo-Welshman Sir John Stradling had a vital interest. The former spent much of his life lobbying in Madrid for a Spanish invasion which would free Scotland of both the presbyter and the English. The latter was a sort of prototype All Souls appeaser who translated Lipsius and was attracted (if only up to a point) by the 'Universal Cause'.[22]

In discussion over the nature of the Spanish Monarchy and its policy, non-Spanish scholars have insisted on secularist interpretations ultimately

[18] V. Malvezzi, *Portraict of a Politicke Christian-Favourite, originally drawn from some of the actions of the Lord Duke of St Lucar . . .* (1647). p. 75.

[19] The textual quotation is from M. Fraga Iribarne, *Don Diego de Saavedra Fajardo y la diplomácia de su epoca* (Madrid, 1956), p. 97. See also, R. Rodríguez-Moñino Soriano, *Razón de estado y dogmatismo religioso en la España del XVII: negociaciones hispano-Inglesas de 1623* (Barcelona, 1976). For relevant citations of other scholars mentioned here, see Chapter 5, below.

[20] X. Flores (ed.), *Le 'Peso Político del Todo el Mundo' par Antony Sherley, ou un aventurier anglais au service de l'Espagne* (Paris, 1963), esp. p. 157ff.

[21] For Aliaga's influence, see P. Brightwell, 'Spain and the Origins of the Thirty Years War' (unpublished Ph.D. thesis, University of Cambridge, 1967), esp. p. 98ff.

[22] For Semple, see R. A. Stradling, *The Armada of Flanders: Spanish Maritime Policy and European War, 1568–1668* (Cambridge, 1992), pp. 25–32 and passim; for Stradling, G. Williams, 'Sir John Stradling of St Donat's', *Glamorgan Historian*, (1973), pp. 11–28.

derived from the age of scientific positivism. However, in the more pluralist intellectual world of the late twentieth century, it is no longer simply a question of scholarly skirmishing across well-defined cultural frontiers. Modern Spanish experts are less comfortable than were their forbears with patriotically-inspired tendencies to view their history as a spiritual mission, though they still wish to shuffle off the oppressive heritage of imperialist exploitation. Concerning the core-issue of the present volume, for example, a major Spanish authority argued in 1975 – the very year of the passing of the *antiguo régimen* of Church, Land and Army in Spain – that 'Spain's struggle from 1621 to 1639 was more a battle for economic survival, faced with the threat of intervention and suffocation by the Dutch, than the geographical expression of an expansionist or hegemonic programme'.[23] Alcalá Zamora went further:

> Explanations of Spain's foreign policy which concentrate on one element, whether ideological – the defence of Catholicism; or pragmatic – the pushing out of Spain's strategic frontier against the French; or, on the other hand, provide a compound of elements, ideas of *reputación*, dynasticism, inherited patrimonies, psychological factors, etc., all seem to me equally simplistic. Though these things had a role to play, what is important is that they tended to disguise the cruder and more prosaic realities of sheer materialism.[24]

J.I. Israel put a further gloss on this reading: with the death of Philip II, he asserts:

> there was an immediate and fundamental shift away from questions of sovereignty and religion . . . Under Lerma . . . Zúñiga . . . and Olivares . . . the central objective of Spain's war against the Dutch was to disband the Dutch East and West India Companies, force Dutch evacuation of the Indies east and west, break the Dutch stranglehold on the Scheldt and generally weaken if not destroy the Dutch mercantile system. [Moreover] the enforcement of [the anti-Dutch] embargoes was one of the central formative principles of Spanish policy and diplomacy for more than half a century.[25]

In reality the objectives placed in the forefront by Alcalá-Zamora and Israel were accidental, not essential. They were certainly of a different order of desirability (e.g. that between choosing a life-partner and eating an orange), and arguably even pertained to a different philosophical state of being. None of them came anywhere near fulfilling the role of a 'central formative principle'. The latter remained exactly the same as it had been under Philip II, that is to say, as J. H. Elliott succinctly describes it above. Yet Israel has announced that:

---

[23] J. Alcalá-Zamora y Queipo de Llano, *España, Flandes y el Mar del Norte: la última ofensiva europea de los Austrias madrileños (1618–1639)*, pp. 475–76.

[24] Idem, *Razón y crísis de la política exterior de España en el reinado de Felipe IV* (Madrid, 1977), p. 18. This contribution, given as a lecture in May 1976, seems to have been intended, in part, as a response to Elliott's interpretation discussed above.

[25] Israel, *Empires and Entrepots*, pp. xii–xiii.

There can no longer be any doubt that the Spanish Crown had come to accept the principle of Dutch political and religious independence by 1606 ... Prominent Spaniards at this time were deeply preoccupied with the fact of their country's economic and social decline and could not do otherwise than contemplate their relationship with the Dutch in the context of that process.[26]

The truth is that considerations of economic advantage never had a serious claim to attention on what might be termed the strategic level of policymaking, but occupied only a supporting, tactical (sometimes pragmatic) role in its execution. The sanctions of economics – which we see as profound and long-term - were for early-modern monarchies, to the contrary, superficial and ephemeral considerations. The claim that economic factors were emerging as the motor of decision-making under Philip II's successors is, quite simply, without foundation; it illustrates only an obstinate misunderstanding of baroque political culture. In their different ways, the policies of the Spanish monarchy and the Dutch Republic were both arrived at through consensus (and sometimes, confrontation). Unlike those of the latter, the politics of the former made no allowance for sectional (and little even for regional) interests; it refused to consider them as distinct or important enough to influence those of the community as a whole. Of course there were powerful individuals and groups associated with the Spanish System who wished to exploit the economic opportunities which both its quotidian functioning and its ultimate objectives could offer. Yet even in the field of relations with the United Provinces, the extent to which so-called 'mercantilist' projects were adopted in practice reveals (once again) the extent to which the crown was prepared to damage the material interests of its own subjects in the search for ideological victory. Olivares constantly rejected requests by the business interests of Spanish Flanders to ameliorate the effects of embargoes and prohibitions, and dismissed the suggestions of men like Albert Struzzi aimed at further integration of the Flemish and Spanish economies.[27]

In busy meetings of the council and juntas of state such matters rarely figured on the agenda, nor did they detain ministers for long in the delivery of their opinions. Methods of approach to history are changing swiftly these days – a process of which I strongly approve. Nonetheless, I find it very difficult to interpret the impressive absence of empirical evidence as proof that economic desiderata constituted a ghost in the machine of Spanish policy, a structured absence in its discourse. Of course there were occasional and partial exceptions to this rule, such as that which occurred in 1628, when Ambrogio Spínola came to Madrid to force the government to consider renewed negotiations with the Dutch. Olivares, temporarily outmanouevred in the council of state, played for time. He insisted on two linked preconditions for a new truce: that

---

[26] Idem, *The Dutch Republic and the Hispanic World, 1606–61* (Oxford, 1982), pp. xiv–xv.

[27] M. A. Echevarría Bacigalupe, 'Alberto Struzzi y el pensamiento antimercantilismo del Barocco' (unpublished typescript, Bilbao, 1991).

the rebel provinces should concede free exercise of Catholicism and that the Scheldt should be reopened for maritime traffic: 'In this way we will regain our lost reputation and put our [commercial] affairs in order without giving anything to the Dutch.' This was nothing less than a surrogate for victory. Even the royal confessor, Fray Antonio Sotomayor, felt able to vote with the majority in favour of such a proposal, but he and his colleagues were still far from 'accepting the principle of Dutch political and religious independence'. In any case, Olivares knew well enough that his negotiating position was inimical to the Dutch way of life and would never be accepted.[28] A year earlier, Philip himself had solemnly enunciated that:

> there is no political matter in which the smallest risk to religion can be adventured, and this principle must be maintained, against all other maxims of state and ephemeral pressures, if we wish Our Lord to assist us in our tasks.[29]

By the beginning of the next decade the short-term pressures for a deal with the United Provinces were more intense than ever. There were recurrent emergencies when the king was obliged to contemplate an armistice on the best terms he could get. The documents faithfully record these fluctuations. But by 1637 Olivares – though professing that 'he desired a truce with all his heart' – dismissed the latest clandestine initiative from the rebels as merely a Dutch ruse, inspired by fear that Spain would shortly overcome French military resistance, and thereafter turn upon the United Provinces with undistracted fury.[30]

In 1648 defeat was acknowledged and the independence of the United Provinces recognised. The motivation for this decision was the radically altered conditions of engagement since 1640. An unnerving chain-reaction of rebellions, revolts and conspiracies, inside and outside the peninsula, had faced the monarchy with the prospect of irreversible dissolution. In search of exactly this consummation France, first under Richelieu and then more intensely with the geopolitical schemes of Mazarin, had exploited opportunities to intervene in Catalonia and Italy. During seven years of desperate defence not only the Monarchy's armed forces but also the civilian populations of Castile and Naples had taken a dreadful buffeting. It was demonstrably God's will that one front - the most costly and most intractable – should be closed down, one mission abandoned, so as not to prejudice the whole of His work on earth.[31]

Spain also had the assurance that the Catholic faith would not be persecuted in the officially independent United Provinces. For a generation after Münster, some clerics continued to take this point to extreme lengths. 'Peace with any

---

[28] *Consulta* of council of state, 23 April 1628, AGS, E 2042. See also, Alcalá-Zamora, *España, Flandes*, pp. 302–6.

[29] Royal *apostilla* on *consulta* of council of state, 2 July 1627, AGS, E K1435, no. 1.

[30] Olivares' *voto* in *consulta* of council of state 24 May 1637, BL, Add. 36322, ff. 116–120. (This is a copy of the original in AGS, E 2052, misdated to 1631 by the copyist.)

[31] J. Castel, *España y el tratado de Munster, 1644–48* (Madrid, 1956), esp. pp. 9–11.

nation which actively oppresses Catholics would be a scandal for the whole Church', advised the cardinal of Toledo in 1667, when a treaty with England – persecutor of Irish Catholics – was being negotiated.[32] Meanwhile, Philip continued to defend Flanders doggedly from the French, 'since should those provinces be lost, it would be the end for the Catholic religion in them, and thus even Spain would face its ultimate ruin'.[33] Even in the reign of his son, Madrid continued to reward the loyalty of the Belgians by rejecting their demands for admission into the American trade system, a resistance to the requirements of political and economic 'progress', taken fundamentally on religious grounds.

[32] Quoted by G. de Gamazo, duque de Maura, *Carlos II y su corte* (2 vols Madrid, 1911) i, p. 99.
[33] Philip to Sor Maria, 17 Feb. 1656, C. Seco Serrano (ed.), *Cartas de Sor Maria de Agreda y del Señor Rey Don Felipe IV*, 2 vols, BAE 108, 109 (Madrid, 1958), ii, p. 10.

PART I

THE PROBLEM OF DECLINE

1

Seventeenth-Century Spain: Decline or Survival?

'¿Que dice Europa del Poder de España? Su valor ha faltado, ardid, y maña.'
(What says Europe of the power of Spain? That her courage, cunning, and skill
have all left her.)

Thus runs the opening couplet of a piece of political doggerel emanating from
Castile in or around the year 1670.[1] Most modern historians would agree with
its dictum. Many indeed may argue that the question itself is rhetorical, in
both contemporary and historical terms. Yet in reality European opinion
on the problem of Spanish power – even well into the second half of the
seventeenth century – was by no means as settled as these lines would suggest.
At about this time, for example, a diametrically opposed viewpoint to that of
the anonymous poet was forcibly expressed by the famous Moravian thinker,
Jan Comenius. The latter's treatise *Angel of Peace*, printed in 1667, once more
sounded the tocsin (by now, surely, a somewhat battered instrument) against
the universalist ambitions of the Habsburgs. Only the firm friendship of the
United Provinces and England, at that moment warring with each other, could,
Comenius thought, curb the designs of Spain and Austria, and unite European
resistance. This archaic alarum was, it is true, contradicted with equal force in
the same year by the publication of Franz-Paul Lisola's pamphlet *Le bouclier
d'état*, which descried the centre of plotting for European hegemony not in
Madrid but in Paris. However, an essential element in Lisola's programme of
'collective security' against France was the reactivation and mobilization of
the courage and resources of the Spanish monarchy. Indeed, this prospect was
precisely that which Louis XIV and his ministers most feared in their conduct
of foreign policy.[2]

English observers, only slightly less interested in what was a consuming
question of the 1660s, displayed an equal lack of consensus. 'Tis nature's
sweating-tub, a nest of wolves, the very seat of hunger and famine', was
one description of Spain in 1660.[3] Yet an English ambassador could write
in 1666 that

---

[1] BL, Eg. 327, f. 32. This otherwise unremarkable piece of satirical verse was evidently
popular, since another contemporary copy is in Madrid's BN. It may be noted that the failings
it identifies are not of a material, or even tangible, nature.

[2] For Comenius, J.V. Polisensky, *The Thirty Years' War* (1974), p. 9: for Lisola,
F.L. Nussbaum, *The Triumph of Science and Reason, 1660–1685* (New York, 1962), p. 150
and authorities there cited.

[3] Anon., *The Character of Spain, or an Epitome of their Virtues and Vices* (1660).

the monarchy, for all the clouds that hang over it from France, is not yet in so abject a condition but on the contrary has great and rich dominions, very little impaired ... and if they be so happy as to regulate the administration of the government, are a very puissant monarchy.[4]

Right through the spectrum of hypothesis, therefore, the terminal failure of Spanish power and ambition was far from being a fundamental maxim of international politics. Less speculative were the verdicts of the battlefield and the conference table. In 1667–68 these were duly delivered by the War of Devolution and the peace of Aix. The former had a dramatic effect on the maritime powers. They ceased their squabble and embraced, turning not (pace Comenius) to destroy the Spanish monarchy, but, in conformity with Lisola's wishes, to protect it from the threat of French arms.

This cautionary tale of confusion and uncertainty is accurately reflected in the state of current historical opinion on the phenomenon still represented by the vague and hackneyed phrase, 'the decline of Spain'. An undoubtedly significant theme in the general history of western Europe, the failure of the Spanish monarchy has traditionally (though again, nebulously) been allocated to the seventeenth century. Once the hulk of the great galleon had been found and identified, writers busied themselves like treasure-seekers, searching deep in the holds for 'origins', peering through the muddy waters for 'factors' of disaster to arrange into priorities and categories. Indeed, this process in the historiography of the peninsula began with the Castilian economists and political writers of the period itself, the *arbitristas* and *cronistas* whose views have continued to be so influential. Its two most recent phases have seen the nineteenth-century stress on religious obscurantism and illiberal politics (Ranke, Hume) give way to the essentially socio-economic diagnoses of pre-war specialists such as Hamilton and Trevor Davies.[5] In Spain itself whilst the first conclusion had always, quite naturally, been resisted, the second became accepted orthodoxy in the 1950s.[6]

By this time, however, Habsburg Spain was already being examined from new angles, and increasingly more subtle questions were being asked of various types of evidence. The apparently smooth confluence of economic failure, political decadence and military defeat was first challenged by Braudel at several points in his immense work on the Mediterranean. Braudel's comments, although of course arising from unsurpassed experience of the whole range of source material, had more the nature of intuitive assertions

---

[4] MS Journal of Edward, 1st earl of Sandwich (Mapperton, Dorset), ii, f. 470.

[5] L. von Ranke, *The Ottoman and the Spanish Empires in the Sixteenth and Seventeenth Centuries* (1843); M.A.S. Hume, *The Court of Philip IV: Spain in Decadence* (1907); E.J. Hamilton, *American Treasure and the Price Revolution in Spain, 1501–1650* (Cambridge, MA, 1934); R. Trevor Davies, *Spain in Decline, 1621–1700* (1957).

[6] See (e.g.), J. Vicens Vives (ed.), *Historia de España y América* (Barcelona, 1959).

than definitive or fully-developed arguments.[7] None the less, his powers of style and suggestion, and the epic context in which they were placed, inspired a growing awareness of the sheer scale of the problems which faced the Spanish monarchy, along with a gradual reappraisal of the relative efficiency with which they were normally tackled. The accumulation of new and intensive work on other areas of western Europe – especially perhaps the two other 'analogous' monarchies of France and England – in the century 1560–1660, confirmed the trend. Much of the literature associated with the 'General Crisis' controversy both symbolized and stimulated a shift away from economic, or purely economic, explanations of the stagnation/decline syndrome towards other fields of enquiry.

In the 1960s, accordingly, evaluation of comparative material and a renewed attention to non-economic factors produced seminal contributions which can now be seen as a distinct (though as yet incomplete) modification of the traditional picture of Spanish decline. A. Domínguez Ortiz's work on the relationship between government, policy and administrative structures culminated in 1960 in the publication of his *Política y hacienda de Felipe IV*, perhaps the most important Spanish monograph on Spain's seventeenth-century history. Domínguez Ortiz's book illustrated the dogged resilience and capacity of the monarchy in resisting disintegration and despair, evoking admiration at the continuity of policy and commitment despite economic failure and financial breakdown.[8] J.H. Elliott's early writings also implicitly questioned the dominance of the 'overwhelmingly economic interpretation'. They pointed up some incongruities in the generally accepted 'conjuncture' of factors; stressed the importance of a comparative (and therefore a relative) view placed in the European context; and finally hinted at the need for clarification on what he aptly termed 'the chronology of Castile's decline'.[9]

Professors Koenigsberger and Lynch also provided acute and stimulating general theories which, although not central to the present discussion, contributed to the atmosphere of revision and rethinking.[10] Consequently, a new 'school' of younger British and American specialists began work on various administrative, institutional and military problems faced byt the monarchy in the century of the 'General Crisis'. Broadly speaking, the articles and books which have resulted amount to a strong confirmation of Braudel's suspicions.[11]

---

[7] F. Braudel, *The Mediterranean and the Mediterranean World in the Age of Philip II* (trans. of 2nd edn, 2 vols, (1972–74), i, pp. 133–37, 355ff, 476ff; ii, passim.

[8] A. Domínguez Ortiz, *Política y hacienda de Felipe IV* (Madrid, 1960).

[9] J.H. Elliott, 'The Decline of Spain', *Past and Present*, 20 (1961), pp. 52–75, and often reprinted.

[10] H.G. Koenigsberger, 'Decadence or Shift? Changes in the Civilisation of Italy and Europe in the Sixteenth and Seventeenth Centuries', *Transactions of the Royal Historical Society*, 5th series, 10 (1960) and reprinted in his *Estates and Revolutions: Essays in Early Modern European History* (1971), pp. 278–97; J. Lynch, *Spain and America, 1598–1700*, vol. II of *Spain under the Habsburgs* (Oxford, 1969).

[11] Many of these are cited below.

In short, it can now be stated that the orthodox, economics-centred schema for 'the decline of Spain', though retaining much validity within its own terms of reference, is no longer sufficient and tends often to mislead on the general level. Indeed this message is positively anodyne compared with that which has recently floated across the Atlantic on a so called 'Trial Balloon', claiming that 'the "decline of Spain" in the early seventeenth century never happened'.[12]

The aim of the present essay is fourfold. In the first place it seeks to define the problem anew, partly by illustrating some current confusions, but also, more positively, by suggesting changes in our perception which might help to clear them up. The new framework will be larger, but also stronger, for (secondly and thirdly) I hope to support it by a juxtaposition of 'the decline of France' with that of Spain, and by an attempt to revalue those elements in the monarchy conducive to survival in the European struggle. Finally, it is intended that from these approaches can be developed a clearer understanding of the phenomenon in a chronological sense. On the other hand, I do not wish to deny that Spanish power declined during the reign of Philip IV, nor to question the fact that economic factors lay at the root of this decline. The argument is mainly intended to establish what might be termed 'differential chronologies' between these processes, and not to suggest a new interpretation which diminishes the role of economic forces.[13]

The current uncertain tone in general comment on the issue arises directly from the power of the economic explanation, based as it is on the massive documentary apparatus of E.J. Hamilton and his successors, the Chaunus.[14] This material provides us with a quasi-deterministic thesis, characterizing the 'decline' as both consistent and progressive. This resulted from the interaction of two kinds of elements – the dynamic one of economic decline (both absolute and relative), and the static (in modern parlance, structural) one of defects in political, social and religious institutions. In a comprehensive version which embraces the whole early modern period, and which in one form or another inhabits most textbooks, it suggests that the monarchy of the Spanish Habsburgs had a built-in propensity to decline, almost from the moment of its inception in the early 1520s. The kingdoms of the peninsula were materially unfitted to shoulder the responsibilities foisted on them by Charles V. Only the coincidental discovery of precious metals in America, leading to regular and mounting transatlantic shipments, permitted Spain to play a European role which was essentially artificial. Constant success in war and continuous injections of bullion brought with them addiction,

---

[12] M.D. Gordon, 'The Decline of Spain', *Journal of Modern History*, 47 (1975), pp. 98–100.

[13] Strong support for a greater sense of discrimination in this area is given in J. Alcalá Zamora y Queipo de Llano, *España, Flandes y el Mar del Norte, 1618–1639: la ultima ofensiva europea de los Austrias madrileños* (Barcelona, 1975), see esp. p. 152.

[14] Hamilton, *American Treasure*; H. and P. Chaunu, *Séville et l'Atlantique, 1504–1650* (8 vols, Paris, 1955–60).

both psychological and physical. American silver, originally the realization of some fantastic dream, the answer to every personal and national problem, quickly became a vital need. Repeated satisfaction of the craving had inevitable clinical consequences, and a poison spread gradually through the limbs of the body politic. Easy riches, bureaucratic growth and social conventions all combined to mock the virtues of investment and husbandry. The agricultural base was neglected or perverted; urban growth was parasitical, not productive; capitalist incentive vanished. Inflation and high wage rates priced Spain out of commercial markets, even those under her own political control, yet the search for more silver committed Spain to a virtually endless expansion of her overseas empire. The Atlantic eldorados constantly deprived Castile of a proportion of her population, often the most talented and ambitious.

By making possible continuous war in the prosecution of imperial policy, money also lay at the root of every other evil, especially since it necessitated, by a cruel paradox, supplementary revenue in the form of taxation. Defence commitments caused an excessive growth of impositions which fell mainly on the productive sectors of society, peasant and capitalist. The crown's vast income helped to preclude the development of representative institutions, thus denying political as well as economic influence to the indigenous business classes. On the other hand, the international bankers, creditors of the crown, were allowed to manipulate economic machinery for their own purposes. The gradual exhaustion of bullion supplies in the seventeenth century meant that material realities reasserted themselves, only now in terrifyingly exaggerated form. Spain was finished as a developing society and as a European power.[15]

The influence of the 'French school', with its priorities in demographic and other sociological areas, amplified this thesis, giving it particularly a more deterministic twist. The work of Lapeyre, Bennassar and their colleagues has pictured a society firmly anchored to primitive structures, prey to an inexorable cycle of debilitation, the Malthusian apocalypse writ large – war, taxation, famine, malnutrition, plague – in short, cumulative disaster, progressive weakness, final collapse.[16]

What, one may ask, is uncertain or confusing about this? The thesis seems, on the contrary, to be solid, logical and lucid. But these very characteristics of the socio-economic dialectic have tended, like any monopoly, to absorb and to distort. They constantly force other considerations to the sidelines, and sometimes swamp them completely. The exposition and interpretation of events by historians whose own interests lack genuine economic significance has often been pulled out of shape by the force of the statistical undertow.

---

[15] Two classic expositions are E.J. Hamilton, 'The Decline of Spain', *Economic History Review*, 1st series, 8, and reprinted; and J. Vicens Vives, 'The Decline of Spain in the Seventeenth Century', in C.M. Cipolla (ed.), *The Economic Decline of Empires* (1970), pp. 121–95.

[16] B. Bennassar, *Valladolid au siècle d'or* (Paris, 1967); H. Lapeyre, *Une famille des marchands: les Ruiz* (Paris, 1955).

Indeed, it seems to me that political, institutional and military material has been made to fit a kind of tailor's dummy, often with awkward results.

The outstanding anomaly arises from the uncomfortable fact that (as a glance at any chronological table will show) the process of Spain's external decline does not seem to synchronize with that of her internal decay. To put this another way, the failure of Spanish power in Europe, and those elements which directly supported it, seems a considerably later process than the socio-economic failure, and, more important still, a much less consistent one. They are, as it were, out of phase with each other. One would expect, of course, the latter to precede the former, and would not attempt to deny the causal relationship and chronological overlap between them. They are clearly not, however, physically or temporally identical, and are discrete features of a single phenomenon. This discreteness is sensible, and ought to be intelligible.

It is an underlying assumption of our own post-Keynesian era that the maintenance of power by any political entity for any length of time is not possible without a sound economy. It follows that economic stagnation impeded Habsburg imperialism and that economic breakdown brought about its quick collapse. Most experts agree that by the end of the reign of Philip III (1621) the decisive point of no return had been reached by the Iberian economy, after half a century of full decline. After Professor Elliott's twenty-year 'crisis of Castile', industrial output on any scale had ceased, exports had contracted to vanishing point, economic institutions were moribund, agriculture was permanently crippled and the population was steadily shrinking. The productive life of the Castilian economy was effectively over.[17] Yet the comprehensive military collapse one might expect did not occur – or rather it was remarkably delayed. Indeed, not until a decade of Philip IV's reign had elapsed did the Monarchy experience serious reverse (in Italy); it was a generation before the tide of Spanish power was decisively turned (in 1640) and another went by before the hegemony of the Spanish Habsburgs was finally dismantled (in the 1660s). Not until 1648 was Spain compelled to acknowledge loss of part of the patrimony of Charles V. Cession of territory to the major rival, France, took place only in 1659, and was even then relatively modest. An economically defunct Castile fought a fifty-year war of attrition in which every other western European power was at some time ranged against her, with the only intermittent (and always dubious) support of the Empire.[18] Major rebellions were suppressed in Catalonia and Italy; French invasions were successfully resisted in the 1640s and 1670s; Castile displayed astonishing military resilience during the War of Succession. The monarchy preserved most of its European empire until 1713 and its American empire until

---

[17] See (e.g.), Elliott, 'Decline of Spain', and J. Larraz, *La época del mercantilismo en Castilla, 1500–1700* (Madrid, 1963), pp. 43–44.

[18] 'All the kings of the world have made open or covert war against his majesty, except those of his own house': Olivares to the council of state, Sept. 1634: quoted in Domínguez Ortiz, *Política y hacienda*, p. 360.

a century later. Professor Elliott considers that 'the period between 1590 and 1620 . . . sees a rapid erosion of two of the principal foundations of Castile's sixteenth-century primacy (i.e. population and productivity) *and consequently of Spain's imperial power*'.[19] In fact, however, Imperial Spain survived for a further century,[20] and it was precisely the decade following 1620 in which its power reached a point of apogee. Elliott himself admits 'the early years of Philip IV come as something of an embarrassment, since the ailing patient not only refuses to die, but even shows vigorous and unexpected signs of life'.[21] Many of the available secondary sources reflect this embarrassment, consciously or otherwise. Let us take some examples.

Some years ago, in an important contribution, Dr Kamen explained that

> the vast Spanish empire had been built up almost entirely from Castilian resources, and by the beginning of the seventeenth century it was clear that Castile was no longer able to meet its commitments, principally because the economic basis of the old war machine was collapsing.

Cause and effect are clearly delineated here; the case is apparently closed. On the next page, however, we learn that 'the miracle is that the Spanish Crown [*sic*] continued to meet most of its foreign obligations throughout the seventeenth century'.[22] J.H. Elliott attempts to be more specific. 'In so far as the ending of Spain's hegemony can be dated to any particular moment, the great crisis of 1640–1 would seem to have been decisive.' Notwithstanding this death-certificate, Elliott goes on to admire 'the powers of survival of an empire whose . . . capacity for surmounting crises – *particularly that of the 1640s* – seems at times almost miraculous'.[23] For Spanish experts, too, Spain's malaise was fatal but not serious, though they (paradoxically) refrain from invoking the supernatural. For Professor Domínguez Ortiz, 'the conclusion to emerge . . . is a decisive one: Castile was weakened by the ruthless exploitation to which the global policy of the Habsburgs gave rise. *This policy in turn failed once the resources of Castile began to falter.*' (Or, in other words, at the end of the sixteenth century.) Later in his book, however, Domínguez Ortiz can write that 'even after 1640 the Spanish Monarchy was able to mobilize its huge resources in order to stave off defeat and . . . in the end obtain an honourable peace'.[24] Pierre Vilar, far from offering enlightenment, is most radically off-beam of all, not least in his curiously whiggish notion that English power was responsible for Spain's demise.

[19] Elliott, 'Decline of Spain' p. 187 (my emphasis).

[20] Idem, *Imperial Spain, 1469–1716* (1963).

[21] Idem, 'Decline of Spain', p. 168.

[22] H. Kamen, 'The Decline of Castile: The Last Crisis', *Economic History Review*, 2nd series, 17 (1964–65), pp. 63–76. (Emphases throughout this paragraph are mine.)

[23] J.H. Elliott, *The Revolt of the Catalans: A Study in the Decline of Spain, 1598–1640* (Cambridge, 1963), pp. 543, 542.

[24] A. Domínguez Ortiz, *The Golden Age of Spain, 1516–1659* (1971), pp. 29, 98.

> Rivalry [between England and Spain] lasted two decades, during which time Spain was stripped shred by shred. The Invincible Armada symbolised the Spanish desire to have done once and for all with this threat, and its failure in 1588 . . . was a double-triumph for Protestantism and capitalism, after which the world-wide structure of Spanish power could not last much longer.

Last, nevertheless, it apparently did, since 'the critical date [of Imperial decadence is] 1640', and 'the date 1713 lies at the lowest point of the curve'.[25]

One cause of the confusion manifested in the cited texts is (as we have seen) the strength of the economic argument and an exaggerated caution in appearing to contradict its prescriptions. The traditional military historian has no such compunction. The most recent of them, Martínez Campos y Serrano, can write forthrightly of

> the fact that, in spite of its tremendous decadence Spain sustained its apogee. Each time that all seemed lost, there rose up an innate force, or an illustrious personality who pointed the way to safety. At times, Spain pulled herself up by her own bootstraps . . . . In brief, the seventeenth century was in contrast to the sixteenth. In the latter, tactical victories with no strategic result. In the former, successive defeats, which the enemy could not turn to advantage. Is this decline?[26]

The monarchy which faced so many European rivals may have been an empty shell by economic criteria, but the shell itself was so tough as to be almost impenetrable. Like Mr Wopsle's *Hamlet*, Spain 'died by inches, from the ankles upward'.[27] Or better, since she indeed revealed over and again a capacity for recovery from military disaster, like the hero of some grand opera, swooning from death pangs one moment but in the next bellowing like a bull. In the middle decades of the century especially, Spain's fortunes fluctuated violently between extremes, a predicament aptly symbolized in the figure of the manic-depressive conde-duque de Olivares. To a much greater degree than subsequent, more objectived, commentators, Olivares was prepared to bury the empire at the first signs of failure. In the spring of 1637 he organized a whole series of fiestas in Madrid to celebrate the successes obtained by Spanish arms since Nördlingen (1634).[28] But by October failure in a relatively minor engagement caused him to write 'as to the condition of our affairs this year, it could not possibly be more miserable. We have lost our reputation with the loss of land.'[29] On the other hand, Olivares' own powers of recuperation and inspiration had already been demonstrated. Nor did this spirit lapse with

25 P. Vilar, *Spain: A Brief History* (1967), pp. 31, 45.

26 C. Martínez de Campos, *España bélica: el siglo XVII* (Madrid, 1968), p. 14.

27 As witnessed by Pip and Herbert Pocket in Dickens' *Great Expectations*.

28 G. Marañón, *El conde duque de Olivares* (abridged edn, Madrid, 1969), p. 71.

29 Olivares to the cardinal-infante, 28 Oct. 1637, BL, Add. 14007, f. 87. An even more dramatic example is cited in J. Deleito y Piñuela, *El declinar de la monarquía española* (4th edn, Madrid, 1966), p. 140.

his fall from power. In the autumn of 1643, with the monarchy on the brink of ruin, and Castile under threat of invasion, the cabal of ministers who had ousted the conde-duque committed themselves to final victory against France, and severely reprimanded a Councillor of State for spreading alarm and despondency in the provinces.[30]

To avoid wearying the reader with the recapitulation of the familiar details of *l'histoire événementielle*, the cyclical phenomenon of Spanish failure and recovery might be illustrated by the following summary table – admittedly more impressionistic than scientific.

Phase	Character
1588–1604	First general failure
1604–9	Partial recovery
1609–20	Equilibrium
1620–28	Strong recovery
1628–32	Second general failure
1632–37	Recovery
1637–40	Equilibrium (with tendency to failure)
1640–46	Third general failure
1646–56	Equilibrium (with tendency to recovery)
1656–	Fourth general failure, merging into progressive failure for the rest of the century

The outstanding feature of this sequence is its randomness, so that any graph-line (hypothetically) plotted from it would stand in an essentially discordant relationship with the slow and consistent declension charted by the monarchy's economic resources. Equally interesting, though of secondary importance, is the fact that although the 'conjunctures' of disaster (1588, 1628, 1640, 1656) have important socio-economic and financial elements in common, these tend more to intensify than to trigger the phase of crisis. They have the same role, therefore, as features of a distinctly non-economic nature – for example the fact that each period of general failure is associated with the death of an outstanding figure, each recovery with the arrival of another.[31]

Be this as it may, the reality of Spanish power remained of central concern to European statesmen for some time after 1640. Cardinal Mazarin, Oliver Cromwell and William II of Orange shared the conviction that the Spanish monarchy constituted the greatest single danger to national security and progress. Later still, Louis XIV's policies were dominated by his fear (amounting in Pierre Goubert's eyes to an obsession) that Spain's depression was only temporary and could well be succeeded by yet another upturn in the wheel of fortune.[32]

[30] *Consulta* of a *Junta Particular*, Sept. 1643, BL, Eg. 2081, ff. 166–168. The culprit was the marquis of Villafranca, eldest son of the duke of Alba.

[31] The great duke of Parma died in 1592; Ambrogio Spínola 'arrived' in 1604; Olivares 'arrived' in 1621; Spínola died in 1630; the cardinal-infante 'arrived' in 1634 and died in 1641.

[32] P. Goubert, *Louis XIV and Twenty Million Frenchmen* (1970), pp. 72–73.

What is also conducive to anomaly, however, is the fact that we are dealing here with the work of specialists – or, in the ugly term that is unfortunately gaining currency, 'hispanicists'. Such scholars are historians of Spain first, and of Europe second (if at all), but the majority of readers has the reverse priority. These latter are reading or teaching European history and their understanding derives essentially from a continental context. The facts and figures of the 'decline of Spain' – or rather 'the failure of the Spanish Monarchy' – are more or less meaningless if not translated into European terms, as any information is bound to be unless we are aware of the relative norms. Looked at from a European viewpoint, the reality of Spain's survival, her continuing ability to defend the empire from attack, is one of the outstanding features of the century.

The 'miracle' of Spain's survival as a positive factor in international affairs can, in my view, be explained, and not only by the modification of the mono-causal implications of economic criteria. As J.H. Elliott points out

> The decline of Spain is not just a Spanish phenomenon; it describes the end of the period of Spanish hegemony, and the relegation of Spain to the rank of the second-rate powers. This implies a deterioration in Spain's military and naval strength *at least in relation to that of other states* .... The first task must be to *compare*.[33]

Here we have a vital guideline, often missing from the topic, which is treated in a vacuum even in general textbooks. What was the relative extent of Spanish weakness in the first half of the seventeenth century? Even a limited pursuit of this line of enquiry produces an obvious answer. Quite simply, no enemy, or combination of enemies, was sufficiently strong and organized to administer a comprehensive and decisive defeat – in other words the death-blow – to the Spanish Monarchy. Because of this, Spanish preponderance was not effectively challenged until mid century, nor actually destroyed until still later.

Of Spain's major adversaries in this period, France provided by far the most important challenge and was to be the outstanding beneficiary (in European terms) of Habsburg failure. For the most part the maritime powers, England and the Dutch, were more concerned with sniping at the overseas empire, and its trade, than with frontal assault upon Spanish power in Europe. Though intimately affected by Spanish fortunes, neither was a serious competitor for political hegemony – nor indeed was either strategically placed to be more than a nuisance (albeit at times a serious one) to Spain's imperial defences. (The same considerations apply *mutatis mutandis* to Sweden.) On the other hand, despite tremendous financial difficulties, France was able to supply crucial subsidies to the Dutch (after 1625), to Sweden (1631–33 and 1637–48), and England (1656–58), not to mention many other associates and captains. It is appropriate, therefore, to concentrate attention on Spain's great neighbour.

---

[33] Elliott, 'Decline of Spain', p. 172 (my emphasis).

Detailed quantitative comparisons are unnecessary even where possible. There can be no doubt that the kingdom of France possessed considerably greater inherent economic and demographic resources, sufficient to overwhelm the harassed and preoccupied Spanish Monarchy in the 1630s. The point is that France's material advantages were not mobilized to a telling level of efficiency until the third quarter of the century. Research has long since exposed the myth of *le grand siècle*, the traditional view that from the moment of the Bourbon succession the kingdom was set on the highroad to inevitable greatness. The preparation for absolutism and ascendancy was nothing like as smooth and consistent a process as was previously supposed; indeed it has similar characteristics – in reverse, as it were – to the failure of Spain. For France's war-making potential was paralysed by deeply-rooted structural defects in government and society, the number and intractability of which are further revealed by almost every new monograph on the period.[34]

The relative position of Spain improves as we examine her competitor. To begin with, the French state was making no great economic or financial progress in the first half of the century. The industrial activities of Henry IV were small-scale, marginal and above all ephemeral; whilst in his fiscal reforms Sully 'n'avait fait qu'y introduire un peu d'ordre et pallier les maux extrêmes'.[35] A recent specialist study refers to 'the undoubted decline of the French economy' after 1610, whilst overseas trade contracted dramatically in the second quarter of the century.[36] In the same period according to R. Mousnier, 'bad harvests, subsistence crises, famines, plague [and] *cumulative economic crisis*' were the main features of French history. From the great plague of 1630 until the end of the Fronde, 'two-thirds of the kingdom was in a state of endemic economic and social distress'.[37] As in the case of Spain, I believe that we must avoid placing too much emphasis upon economic criteria when discussing relative military performance, especially in the short to medium term. France certainly emerged as the real contender for mastery in Europe under Richelieu and Mazarin. But the signs are that this happened in spite of economic stagnation, not because of economic progress.[38] Other factors, however, were of great significance in delaying French political maturity. For example, French politics was dominated by unfavourable conditions and traditions. For over half the period 1610–60 the kingdom was crippled by two prolonged phases of royal minority and its attendant disputes. 'Periods

---

[34] For a critical summary, see J.H.M. Salmon, 'Venal Office and Popular Sedition in Seventeenth-Century France: A Review of a Controversy', *Past and Present*, 37 (1967). See also, R. Mousnier, *La plume, la faucille, et le marteau* (Paris, 1970).

[35] V.L. Tapié, *La France de Louis XIII et de Richelieu* (Paris, 1967), p. 61.

[36] A.D. Lublinskaya, *French Absolutism: The Crucial Phase, 1610–1629* (Cambridge, 1968), p. 108.

[37] R. Mousnier, in his contribution to the *Past and Present*, 'General Crisis' symposium, reprinted in T. Aston (ed.), *Crisis in Europe, 1560–1660* (1970), p. 103 (my emphasis).

[38] See Goubert, *Louis XIV*, chap. 2.

of regency', comments Mousnier, 'were always difficult for France and seemed to threaten the dissolution of the kingdom.'[39] The civil war of 1615–20 merged into the war of attrition against the Huguenots (1620–29), which in turn was succeeded by a further decade of widespread tension and rebellion. Professor Lublinskaya has shown that the Huguenots – a genuine state within a state in the south and west – enjoyed the sometimes active sympathy of many Catholic nobles.[40] Furthermore, the eventual production of an heir to the throne in 1638 failed to guarantee the loyalty of even the royal family itself, which continued to indulge its traditional *amour propre* by opposition to the king's government. So far from rendering the outstanding service to the state so notable in the Habsburg dynasty, the cadet Bourbons ceaselessly intrigued, rebelled and sold themselves to the enemy.[41] Such matters were always of more pressing concern to the cardinals than problems of economic or foreign policy. Dynastic disloyalty was a canker at the heart of French government which often worked in conjunction with other disorders; the faction-fights of the aristocracy in the capital, the resistance of the parlements, and the disaffection of provincial magnates. R. Mandrou summarizes thus:

La revendication nobiliaire qui ne cesse guère depuis les États de 1614 jusqu'à l'installation à Versailles de la noblesse présentée entre 1670 et 1680, ne peut être considérée sous le seul aspect des mouvements d'humeur de Marie de Médicis ou de Gaston d'Orléans . . . . Au coeur de la crise du XVIIe siècle, pendant la Fronde mal nommée, le tragique marque la société française tout entière. Ces années 1648–1653 – elles mêmes précédées d'agitations multiformes depuis 1643 au moins – résument assez bien toutes des tensions; en quelques mois d'anarchie, elles ont vu . . . les parlementaires se rendre maîtres de la capitale . . . et s'allier ensuite aux princes.[42]

Further counterpointing these troubles were still others, associated with the perennial discontents of the French bureaucracy. The era preceding the personal rule of Louis XIV was one of intermittent conflict, often openly violent, between the crown and its own officers. The numerous class of *robins* was the major obstacle to political and fiscal reform, and its members were frequently to be found ranged against the king in outbreaks of rebellion.[43] Set alongside this, the nobility and officialdom of the Spanish monarchy appear servile and efficient.

Progressing down the scale, regionalist and even separatist elements can be

[39] R. Mousnier, 'French Institutions and Society, 1610–61', in J.P. Cooper (ed.), *The Decline of Spain and the Thirty Years' War, 1609–59* (vol. IV of *The New Cambridge Modern History*), p. 474.

[40] Lublinskaya, *French Absolutism*, p. 146ff.

[41] See R. Mousnier's catalogue in 'The Fronde', R. Forster and J.P. Greene (ed.), *Preconditions of Revolt in Early Modern Europe* (1970), pp. 137–38.

[42] R. Mandrou, *La France au XVIIe et XVIIIe siècles* (Paris, 1970), pp. 128–30.

[43] A.L. Moote, 'The French Crown *versus* its Judicial and Financial Officials, 1615–83', *Journal of Modern History*, 34 (1962), pp. 146–60.

found in many of the popular risings of the period, usually caused by the combination of fiscal pressure and economic distress. Hardly a year of Louis XIII's reign passed without some such outbreak: Pierre Chaunu estimates that 'aucune des vingt-cinq années qui précèdent la grande explosion généralisée de la Fronde, n'est une année de calme complet'.[44] After the French entry into the Thirty Years' War (1635), increasingly oppressive taxation, billeting of troops and the multiple local horrors of seventeenth-century warfare greatly augmented the incidence and scale of these rebellions. During 1635–39 alone, over half the kingdom was affected – Normandy, Bordeaux, Provence and Languedoc. Even in 1643 – the year of Rocroi – a third of France was seething with revolt in the rear of the royal armies.[45] Ultimately all the anarchic tendencies of French society boiled together to the surface in the complex civil wars of the Fronde, which threatened the complete overthrow of the rickety structure of French absolutism. Truly, as Professor Elliott suggested some years ago, 'if Spain may still be regarded as a giant with feet of clay, France itself is coming to seem none too steady on the ground'.[46] Moreover, this rapid sketch of French disunity has hardly touched upon the profound religious divisions of the kingdom, which were by no means confined to the Huguenot problem, nor ceased to have serious political implications after 1629.[47] It creates an overall impression in comparison with which Castile, for all its desperation, seems almost a haven of good government and public order.

Despite many attempted reforms and projects, the fiscal system of the cardinals' government remained archaic, confused and inadequate until the 1650s. Though figures are scarce and unreliable, it seems likely that the liquid revenue at Louis XIII's disposal was consistently less than that available to Philip IV. The concern to balance the budget, coupled with a reluctance to increase indirect taxation (ordained respectively by political and social conditions) severely restricted military strength and diplomatic flexibility.[48]

> The result of this was that the king was unable to maintain a permanent army. He had only a few regiments of regulars, of which foreign troops formed the backbone. In war time the situation quickly became critical. The budget estimates never took account of warfare and made no provision for it. Troops had to be raised hastily, and they were clothed, armed, paid and fed without any funds earmarked for the purpose.[49]

A glimpse of the chaos to which state finances were reduced by full-scale war is provided by the story that Richelieu, soon after the military debacle of 1636, brought to court an alchemist skilled at the transmutation of base

---

[44] P. Chaunu, *La civilisation de l'Europe classique* (Paris, 1966), p. 106.

[45] Mandrou, *La France*, p. 127.

[46] Elliott, 'Decline of Spain', p. 168.

[47] See (e.g.), the comments in R. Mousnier, *Peasant Uprisings in Seventeenth-Century France, Russia, and China* (1971), pp. 32–33, 55.

[48] Lublinskaya, *French Absolutism*, chap. 5.

[49] G. Pagès, *The Thirty Years' War* (1939; trans. 1970), p. 176.

metals to gold.[50] So far as we know, Olivares – despite his enemies' accusations of sorcery – never resorted to such methods. Moreover, with France in turmoil, his great rival soon took refuge in the shady fiscal expedients that are usually associated peculiarly with Spain, in desperate attempts to oil the creaking military machine.[51] For years, successive finance ministers had been frustrated in attempts to rationalize and streamline by circumstances similar to those which constantly tormented Olivares. The oft-quoted outburst by the beautifully-named Bullion in 1639, is as hysterical and fatalistic as any of the conde-duque's black forebodings from the same period.[52] The former was not alone in his despair. 'In 1642, Louis XIII expressed his fears that if war did not shortly cease there would be no French infantry willing to continue fighting.'[53]

By 1640 the demands of war had cruelly exposed the many and profound failings of French government. The fact of the kingdom's vast potential was offset, or sterilized, by retarded techniques of administration, by inadequacy and inexperience in nearly all the problems of large-scale conflict – in short, drastic deficiencies in areas where her adversary excelled.[54] All Richelieu's domestic and diplomatic preparations, which have for so long supported his reputation, had not been enough to render France suitable for the prosecution of the kind of war to which the Spanish monarchy had been accustomed for over a century.[55] In the first year of the struggle, far from remorselessly crushing an exhausted enemy, France came close to total defeat. Although it is true that the immediate crisis of 'l'année de Corbie' was slowly surmounted, it seems that only the unexpected windfall of Catalonia saved Richelieu from

---

[50] W.E. Brown, *The First Bourbon Century in France* (1971), p. 70.

[51] Tapiè, *La France*, p. 320ff.

[52] See O. Ranum, *Richelieu and the Councillors of Louis XIII* (Oxford, 1963), p. 145. Normandy, which was at this moment in rebellion for the third time in the century, bore a burden of taxation roughly comparable (in proportional terms) to that of Castile in the Spanish context. M. de Bullion estimated that it paid one-quarter of total royal revenue from direct taxation, Mousnier, *Peasant Uprisings*, p. 88. In 1620 Normandy yielded over 2,250,000 *livres* in direct taxation, compared to the 170,000 paid by Provence in all taxes, Lublinskaya, *French Absolutism*, p. 226.

[53] J.H. Shennan, *Government and Society in France, 1461–1661* (1969), p. 37.

[54] Cf. the rather uncertain judgement in a recent textbook: 'Gradually the slightly greater efficiency of Richelieu's France in the organisation of war had its effect'; D.H. Pennington, *Seventeenth-Century Europe* (1970), p. 325.

[55] In 1632 a French diplomat boasted that the forces of Spain 'disseminées dans ses nombreuses possessions fort eloignées les unes des autres, n'auraient été nulle part en état de résister a une puissance unie et compacte comme l'était la France'; quoted in A. van der Essen, *Le cardenal-enfant et la politique européenne de l'Espagne du XVIIe siècle* (Brussels, 1944), p. 7. The Spanish council of state proved more prescient – around the same time – when it expressed fears that all-out conflict between France and Spain would develop into a long and bitter war of attrition: A. Cànovas del Castillo, *Estudios sobre el reinado de Felipe IV* (2 vols, Madrid, 1888–89), ii, p. 336.

humiliation. In Professor Cooper's appropriate metaphor, 1640 meant simply that one gambler had hit the jackpot.[56]

Like the Swedish Empire before the emergence of the crucial Russian challenge, the survival of Spanish power and power-systems into the 1660s was therefore dependent on the inability of a much stronger neighbour to solve internal problems and to mobilize and direct resources.[57] In the wider sphere, the overall European pause in industrial, technological and even commercial progress, which historians have long referred to as 'the General Crisis of the seventeenth century', meant that all Spain's rivals were to some extent impeded by contraction of resources, or restriction of opportunities. In France and England, as in Castile, the vocation of 'projector' flourished in the first quarter of the century. They both showed to some degree symptoms of an economic malaise similar to that of Castile.[58] Other states too were severely hit by harvest failure and periodic pestilence. Above all, perhaps, they shared the susceptibility of France to open, factional conflict within their ruling elites. These frequently crippling struggles, to which Castile was much less prone, were often compounded by intense confessional strife. Passing reference to the domestic history of what have recently been called 'the disUnited Provinces', and to early Stuart England, should be sufficient to illustrate this point.

In tackling the problem with which this essay deals, it is not sufficient to refer merely to negative evidence. Crude comparisons of the type indulged above may highlight Spanish resilience, and I believe that we should attempt to emphasize the qualities of survival alongside those of decline. We must also endeavour to understand the nature of these qualities, which can, for the sake of argument, be divided into two categories, tending to shade into one another: the tangible and the intangible. Even the former type are not always capable of statistical analysis or quantitative 'weighting'; the latter are purely a matter for subjective evaluation. The clearest and most important of the 'tangible' factors is the financial situation of the monarchy in the seventeenth century.

An essential corollary of the economic argument for 'the decline of Spain' (one which usually remains unstated) is that for nearly a century Spain was by far the wealthiest European power. Her ability to command liquid fiscal resources, which could be quickly and efficiently converted to military strength, outstripped that of her enemies well into the period under review.[59]

---

[56] In his introduction to *The New Cambridge Modern History*, iv, p. 39. The metaphor is particularly apt in respect of Mazarin, who in his private life was an inveterate gambler.

[57] There are a number of interesting analogies to be made between the dilemmas of the Swedish and Spanish empires in this period. See the essays by Sven Lundkvist and Sven-Erik Astrom in M. Roberts (ed.), *Sweden's Age of Greatness, 1632–1718* (1973), pp. 20–101.

[58] As J.H. Elliott puts it, it is no longer possible 'to explain the economic decadence of Spain by basing it on the existence of a peculiarly Spanish version of Original Sin', 'América y el problema de la decadencia española', *Anuario de estudios americanos*, 28 (1971).

[59] See the remarks in P. Brightwell, 'The Spanish System and the Twelve Years' Truce', *English Historical Review*, 89 (1974), pp. 270–92 (at pp. 271–72).

The sensational evils which resulted from the imports of bullion divert attention from the fact that Spanish power – from the 1540s on – was built, not on 'normal' economic reserves, *but on a peculiar revenue attribute*. Though her growing population was important in the initial stages, Castile did not rely on an expanding economy when, under Charles V and Philip II, she constructed a world empire and achieved hegemony in Europe. American treasure may have asphyxiated the Spanish economy, but it also emancipated the Habsburgs from that economy. Despite the serious decline in transatlantic silver shipments after 1610, and in spite also of the clutch of disasters which befell the silver fleet in the 1620s, the crown continued throughout the Thirty Years' War to arrange its *asientos* with the Genoese and Portuguese bankers mainly on its American 'securities'.[60] Like Great Britain in the closing stages of its imperial history, Castile lived on its dwindling transatlantic investment and on what was effectively American credit.

Consequently, on the one hand, the monarchy maintained its territorial integrity, absorbing occasional defeats in detail, and at the cost of continuous war. On the other – and this was of growing importance in the reign of Philip IV – bullion gave the crown the political muscle and determination to seek other sources with which to supply the demands of imperial defence. In the 1620s there began the imposition of massive new taxation, especially in Castile and the Italian dependencies. The scale of the strategic undertakings of the 1620s – Olivares' plans for the *Almirantazgo* and the *Armada del Mar Oceano* to be built virtually from scratch – led not only to the famous project for the 'Union of Arms' but to a series of more improvised expedients no less doom-laden in the long run.[61] As early as the first year of the reign, privately owned bullion was impounded at Seville.[62] Two years later, in 1623, the council of Italy was brusquely informed of the need to exploit more thoroughly the resources of Naples and Sicily.[63] The tempo increased inexorably. As war continued, as reform failed, as Olivares' dictatorship grew more onerous, so the number and incidence of more or less arbitrary revenue devices multiplied. Forced loans (*donativos*), moratoria of interest on state bonds (the *media anata de juros*), increases of *millones* and other *servicios*, manipulation of the coinage and many other ingenious *impuestos* trod on each other's heels.[64] The new salt-tax provoked a rare rebellion in the Basque country even before the

[60] A. Domínguez Ortiz, 'Los caudales de Indias y la política exterior de Felipe IV', *Anuario de estudios americanos*, 13 (1956) pp. 311–83.

[61] Idem, 'Guerra económica y comercio extranjero en el reinado de Felipe IV', *Hispania*, 23 (1963), pp. 71–110; R. Ródenas Vilar, 'Un gran proyecto anti-Holandés en tiempo de Felipe IV', ibid., 22 (1962), pp. 542–58.

[62] Domínguez Ortiz, *Política y hacienda*, p. 286.

[63] Philip IV to count of Monterrey, 19 May 1623, BL, Eg. 335, ff. 394v–395. The extraction of large-scale *asistencias* from Italy had begun not many years before, during preparations for the suppression of the Bohemian revolt. It represented a major breakthrough in financing the wars in northern Europe. See Aston to Carleton, May 1620, PRO, SP 94/24, f. 338.

[64] Domínguez Ortiz, *Política y hacienda*, pp. 334–41, 386–87.

French declaration of war, whilst in the year following this event (1636), the infamous stamped-paper tax (*papel sellado*) was imposed throughout the monarchy.[65] At the same time the screw was tightened on Italy. Demands for conscripts and material supplies were accompanied by a whole programme of fresh taxation.[66] In 1637 the new viceroy of Naples, Medina de las Torres, protested, pointing out that the *Regno* alone was already supplying the royal coffers with more than the silver of the Indies.[67] But this,

> the difficult objective, and Neapolitan resistance ... did not prevent Medina from realising almost completely the list of *asistencias* imposed by the Spanish court. In the first eighteen months of his government, he provided for the war about seven million ducats, exceeding what his predecessor, Monterrey, who had inaugurated the new phase of Spanish policy, had achieved.[68]

All this meant that Spanish armies in the Low Countries were more regularly paid in the seventeenth century than they had been before, despite the fact that (until the 1640s) they were no smaller than those of Alba or Parma. The Thirty Years' War witnessed no great mutinies of the *tercios*, such as had often vitiated Spanish strategy in previous campaigns, and the outbreaks of 1606–7 proved to be the last.[69] It would be foolish to deny that the cost of staving off collapse abroad was to intensify depression and to accelerate debilitation at home. The mounting extortions from the Castilian and Italian milch-cows mortgaged the economies of these countries for centuries and caused endemic human misery on an almost unimaginable scale. Whilst the crown's commitment to its defence responsibilities remained intact, however, few of its ministers attached much importance to these facts. For the time being, their primary duty was being fulfilled.[70]

In common with other early modern states, and like the majority of its population, the Spanish monarchy lived a hand-to-mouth existence, a concept perhaps difficult to grasp in our age of long-term planning in every area of public and private life. War – the immediate issue – was the natural condition and overwhelming priority of governments, and other considerations followed at a respectful distance. Even fiscal realities could often be submerged by the exigencies of defence. Taking issue with P. Chaunu in a recent paper,

[65] Ibid., p. 229.

[66] R. Villari, *La rivolta antispagnola a Napoli, 1585–1647* (Bari, 1967), p. 146.

[67] Ibid., p. 131.

[68] Ibid., p. 138.

[69] G. Parker, *The Army of Flanders and the Spanish Road, 1567–1659: The Logistics of Spanish Victory and Defeat in the Low Countries' Wars* (Cambridge, 1972), pp. 185, 205. In 1634 Olivares claimed at a *Junta de Medios* that 'his majesty has maintained greater armies than any previous king, without ... a single mutiny in any place where they have been stationed'; quoted in Domínguez Ortiz, *Política y hacienda*, p. 360.

[70] 'We must live and fight to maintain things until the last drop of blood of your majesty's subjects is shed; and once this is gone – as it now nearly has – we may expect everything to come to an end, for there is no further remedy within human power.' Olivares to Philip IV, Dec. 1630, quoted in Alcalá-Zamora, *España, Flandes*, p. 119.

Dr Geoffrey Parker claims, 'It would not seem that the level of [Spanish] expenditure was in any way determined by the available revenues or the state of the economy . . . . Government policy in early modern Europe was seldom governed by economic desiderata.'[71] For example, even if Chaunu is right to suggest that the Spanish decision to intervene in Germany in 1618 was influenced by a (temporary) improvement in American trade, the idea does not take much account of the fact that in the decade 1610–20 the crown's revenues from bullion slumped dramatically by 50 per cent.[72] Furthermore, the renewed war in Flanders was later added to the German commitments (1621), after Chaunu's 'boom' had ceased, and in the teeth of the evidence – known to most councillors at least in general terms – that treasure resources were shrinking.[73]

As Professor Domínguez Ortiz's study repeatedly illustrates, Philip IV and Olivares rarely consulted their treasury officials in the formulation of policy. Such bodies as the *Consejo de Hacienda* and the various *juntas* of the reign, existed not (like their modern government counterparts) to provide an essential advisory and braking mechanism, but merely in order to find and administer the necessary funds.[74] *Hacienda* was, of course, a completely subservient and dependent body, both institutionally and personally. The attitude of the king and his *valido* towards it (reflecting a straightforward master-servant relationship) partly arose from the fact that they in no sense regarded it as the repository of public monies, for which they could be held to account.[75] Where and how the money (or rather, credit) was raised was of secondary importance; the vital thing was that it was raised, and no excuses

[71] G. Parker, 'Spain, her Enemies, and the Revolt of the Netherlands. 1559–1648', *Past and Present*, 49 (1970), pp. 72–95 (at pp. 93–94).

[72] P. Chaunu, *L'Europe classique*, pp. 94–95. Cf. J.H. Elliott, *The Old World and the New, 1492–1650* (Cambridge, 1970) and the table of bullion imports printed in idem, *Imperial Spain*, p. 175.

[73] Some weeks before his death, Philip III had called a special *Junta de la Plata* to examine the problem of falling returns. Its members included Don Baltasar de Zúñiga and the presidents of the councils of Castile, Indies and Hacienda (Treasury): see *consulta* of 20 Feb. 1621, BL, Add. 14017, ff. 8–13v. Upon his accession, Philip IV was informed by a senior treasury official that his assets would not fetch 100,000 ducats if auctioned in the public market: Domínguez Ortiz, 'Los caudales', p. 313. This did not prevent serious consideration of projects for a major *empresa* against the Ottoman Empire in July 1623: BL, Eg. 318, f. 10. Plans to counter the depredations of the North African pirates were being subsumed in the huge new expenditure on maritime strategy. Regular subsidies were being sent not only to Vienna but also to potential leaders of Huguenot rebellion in France, R. Ródenas Vilar, '¿Ayudó Felipe IV a los Hugonotes?', *Arbor*, 217 (1964), pp. 59–66. Not surprisingly, the 1620s broke all records of government borrowing, Braudel *The Mediterranean*, ii, p. 694.

[74] This is a paraphrase of the king's explicit statement of June 1646: 'The responsibilities of the treasury are to efficiently distribute the resources which are available and to bring forward methods which may suggest themselves for supplying those which are lacking'. Philip IV's holograph on a *consulta* of Hacienda, BL, MS Eg. 340, f. 82.

[75] Domínguez Ortiz, *Política y hacienda*, pp. 168–71.

were tolerated. In 1623, for example, the king wrote to the president of the council of finance in peremptory terms:

> The other day you were ordered to begin immediately to arrange a new contract in order to make up the Flanders subsidies to 300,000 ducats per month. And since it is important not to lose a moment in this matter it would be well if the members of the Council and the financiers with whom they are negotiating would meet every day, *even though it might be the holidays*, and arrive at a suitable conclusion . . . . Meanwhile, report to me on what is being done.[76]

On another occasion, Philip explicitly required *Hacienda* 'not to spend all its time pointing out difficulties but to attempt to resolve them'.[77] More than fifty years later Colbert complained to his master: 'I only beg your majesty to allow me to tell you that in war and peace you have never consulted your finances to decide your outgoings.'[78] To Olivares, as to Louis XIV, power was related to duty, glory and prestige in the first place, and to policy and strategy in the second.[79] The vulgar subjects of money and economics were merely handservants to these lordly considerations. Even to the student of our present century – especially those familiar with the operations of the European dictatorships – these circumstances should not really be surprising.[80]

The arguments above are not meant to suggest that the monarchy of Philip IV always met its financial commitments more fully and with greater ease than heretofore had been the case.[81] An atmosphere close to panic is not unusually conveyed by the documents, even in periods not to be regarded as genuine crises; hasty improvisation was the general rule, especially in the second half

---

[76] Philip IV to President of *Hacienda*, 15 April 1623, BL, Eg. 335, f. 361 (see also ff. 397v, 407, 448–449v).

[77] Quoted in Lynch, *Spain and America*, p. 83. Cf. Olivares, 'your highness cannot possibly imagine [the effort] which each maravedi costs, and the obstructions caused by the treasury' to the Cardinal-Infante, 27 Sept. 1632, BL, Add. 14007, f. 46v.

[78] Quoted in Brown, *First Bourbon Century*. p. 143.

[79] To Philip and his ministers, 'prestige was not a question of protocol but the reason for existence', Alcalá-Zamora, *España, Flandes*, p. 171.

[80] See (e.g.), W. Carr's admirable study of Hitler's methods (or lack of them) in *Arms, Autarky and Aggression: A Study in German Foreign Policy, 1933–39* (1972).

[81] It becomes immensely difficult to make relative judgements once it is realized that desperation in financial matters was not the exception, but the rule, in the government of Spain from the very beginning of its involvement in a pan-European strategy. After only two years of war in the Netherlands – in 1569 – the king's main financial adviser, Cardinal Espinosa, was begging the duke of Alba to reach an accommodation with the rebels, as 'I believe it is impossible for us to hold out further'; quoted in A.W. Lovett, *Philip II and Mateo Vázquez de Leca: The Government of Spain, 1572–92* (Geneva, 1977), p. 40. Even forty years later, when accommodation was achieved, there was little slackening of pressure. In the opinion of one authority, 'there were no more tragic years for the royal treasury and the troops that depended on it than the years of peace after 1609', I.A.A. Thompson, *War and Government in Habsburg Spain, 1560–1620* (1976), p. 97. It has never been convincingly demonstrated that lack of financial resources was ever an argument sufficient – at least on its own – to determine major decisions of peace and war.

of the reign, when bankruptcies became more frequent and less effective.[82] As the English resident Arthur Hopton succinctly expressed it in 1634, 'it is no wonder that many of their designs fail in the execution, for though this great vessel contain much water, yet it hath so many leaks as it is always dry'.[83] The colander, however, was so huge that the odd lake could sometimes be found at its bottom. Take two contrasting examples. In 1600, after the unexpected and serious defeat of the Archduke Albert at Nieuwpoort, an emergency operation was launched to stem the tide of Prince Maurice's advance. The councils and the secretariat worked at full steam, collecting lists of available levies, creating a command staff, finding means of transport by land and sea, arranging for supply of weapons, clothing and, of course, the necessary *asientos*. The whole business, it was estimated, called for the immediate provision of 600,000 ducats.[84] Now this was done at the very summit-point of royal revenue from American treasure, when more than four times that amount of finest silver had recently arrived for Philip III at Seville.[85] Fifty-seven years later the long-awaited birth of a male heir to the Monarchy (the ill-named Infante Felipe Próspero) was greeted with prolonged celebrations, reputed to have cost the king 600,000 ducats. In that year no silver arrived from the Indies at all.[86]

The actual financial circumstances of the crown were not, therefore, all-important; bluntly, it is not possible to translate in any meaningful way the formulation or the success of policy to the language of the slide-rule. It is not just that 'no one in the royal administration had an exact idea of income or expenditure. Financially speaking, the crown worked in almost complete darkness'.[87] For, in addition, as one of the monarchy's most numerate and perceptive servants, Virgilio Malvezzi, remarked, 'the varied and uncertain fortunes of armies cannot be discussed in terms of cut and dried figures and accounts'.[88] Expenditure on scale did not guarantee success, nor did lack of it bring inevitable failure. The gods of war smiled or scowled according to the patterns of a constantly changing kaleidoscope of factors, in which gold

---

[82] See (e.g.), Philip IV's notes of March 1650, on reports from Brussels, BL, Eg. 340, ff. 97–98v.

[83] Hopton to Coke, March 1634, BL, Eg. 1820, f. 340.

[84] See the *consultas*, letters and memos printed (from AGS, E 793) in CODOIN, new series, 3, (Madrid, 1930), pp. 39–53.

[85] This is a crude average calculated from the quinquennial total of 1596–1600, which – at 13,169,182 ducats – represented a record which was to stand for seventy years: Elliott, *Imperial Spain*, p. 175.

[86] A. Paz y Melia (ed.), *Avisos de Jerónimo de Barrionuevo* BAE 220–21, (Madrid, 1968–69), i, p. 130. See also, Domínguez Ortiz, 'Los caudales', p. 317. The prince died in November 1661, but only a week later the future Carlos II began his precarious existence. The second event necessitated another, equally expensive, round of fiestas: G. Maura y Gamazo, *Carlos II y su corte* (2 vols, Madrid, 1911), i, pp. 44–45.

[87] A.W. Lovett, in a *Past and Present* 'Debate', 55 (1972), pp. 156–57.

[88] Quoted in Brightwell, 'Spanish System', p. 286 and no. 3. Dr Brightwell's own wise remarks at this point are also apposite.

was only one – if sometimes a dominant – colour. Examples have been cited of victorious campaigns achieved when the *tercios* were badly paid, and of failure when remuneration was full and prompt.[89] To take the point a stage further, a general question may be asked of those who believe that 'cliometry' has the essential key to historical processes. The Spanish monarchy, in the period 1568–98, spent more than five times as much a year in the northern wars as the rebel Provinces, France and England together.[90] Why was it, therefore, that Spain did not win the struggle hands down – and thus (perhaps) avoid decline completely?

The answer is fairly obvious. If economic (and even fiscal) matters did not occupy the forefront of the political stage, it was because they were not as important to the exercise of power as they were to become in later centuries. In the modern world (that is to say since the industrial and technological revolutions) material resources comprise almost the only element of success for a great power. In the seventeenth century, however, the relationship was not so direct or intimate and was often complicated by other even more pressing realities. To the grand strategist of pre-industrial Europe, problems of distance, topography, climate were not always obviated by a ready supply of cash; a fact which the great Spínola quickly recognized upon his transference from the world of finance-capitalism to that of applied politics.[91] Such more or less intractable physical impediments often frustrated Spain's designs, but they also worked the other way in our period, protecting the monarchy from crushing and decisive reverses. But it was not simply that absolute victory (in the modern sense) was beyond the capacity of political entities. Spain was cushioned against the effects of economic decadence by a whole range of other factors, from the tangible to the quasi-spiritual. The monarchy enjoyed the accumulated experience of power, smoothly applied on a geopolitical scale, and thus moved in this hostile atmosphere with greater ease than its competitors.[92] Sound, and often inspired, administration at key strategic points; expertly organized transport and supply systems; wide European contacts in all kinds of services; inventive diplomacy; such attributes and many more oiled and supported the vast military machine which was itself so well-disciplined and commanded. The manifold skills at Philip IV's disposal, tempered and developed over a century of large-scale European conflict, were superior in quality to those of his enemies.

> Historians have paid too little attention to the gigantic tasks demanded of the Spanish administrative machine ... the Spanish empire ... expended the better part of its energy in these struggles. And yet it was better adapted than any other

[89] Parker, 'Spain, her Enemies and the Revolt', p. 75.
[90] Ibid., p. 90.
[91] Lynch, *Spain and America*, pp. 41–42.
[92] 'Concerning Spain's administrative apparatus. Slow? Antiquated? In any case, one thing must be admitted: it worked. The same was not always the case with England, Poland, Austria, or even France', Alcalá-Zamora, *España, Flandes*, p. 134.

to these necessary tasks and better organized to deal with them. Although much criticised, the Spanish empire was equal or indeed superior to other leading states for transport, transfer and communications.[93]

From the 1560s at least Spain had built up this expertise in the practicalities of power. The numbers and talents of the professional personnel who serviced the great machine were incomparable; together they made up 'the Spanish system' which dominated European politics until the 1630s. For the first third of the century, indeed, its predominance was if anything increased by the phase of economic and technological stagnation in western Europe, which meant that the apparatus of the monarchy did not become obsolete or insufficient. These minutiae, the details of applied political influence, gave Spain her tough exterior shell. It was a legacy to which Richelieu's France could never aspire and which continually compensated for the quantitative, material imbalance between the contestants.

Only in recent years have these matters been accorded sufficient study and recognition by historians. Following the path explored by Garrett Mattingly, Professors Loomie and Carter have extended our knowledge of the strength and brilliance of the Spanish diplomatic network, its fertile techniques of persuasion and immense reserves of influence.[94] It was this which underpinned the so-called *Pax Hispanica* of Philip III, and prepared the ground for the *época de triunfo* in the 1620s. Following Braudel's lead, Drs Parker and Taylor have further illuminated the monarchy's war and communications systems in northern Europe.[95] Their researches have illustrated, among other things, the methods by which the Spaniards kept open land and sea routes to the Low Countries into the middle years of the century, despite the tremendous strain placed upon them. Besides Professor Domínguez Ortiz's many contributions, other native historians have studied the operation of the Spanish politico-military establishment during the period of the many-fronted war.[96] Few of the resources they reveal are supported by evidence which lends itself easily to quantification or tabulation. They are, nevertheless, solidly real and not 'impressionistic', and cannot be ignored.

The survival of the Spanish Monarchy was encouraged too by 'intangible' factors – advantages of the less material kind – often not fully capable of exposition and analysis. Some of these have already been touched upon by inference. The unity of the dynasty, though not perfect, was always axiomatic;

[93] Braudel, *The Mediterranean*, i, p. 372.

[94] A.J. Loomie, *Spanish Elizabethans: The English Exiles at the Court of Philip II* (1963), and several articles on the general theme of Spain's technique of international politics; C.H. Carter, *The Secret Diplomacy of the Habsburgs, 1598–1625* (1964). See also, B. Chudoba, *Spain and the Empire, 1519–1643* (Chicago, 1952), p. 174ff.

[95] Parker, *Army of Flanders and Spain and the Netherlands*; H. Taylor, 'Trade, Neutrality and the "English Road", 1630–48', *Economic History Review*, 2nd series, 25 (1972), pp. 236–60.

[96] See (e.g.), P. Marrades, *El camino del imperio: notas para el estudio de la cuestión de la Valtelina* (Madrid, 1943); and R. Ródenas Vilar, *La Política europea de España durante la Guerra de los Treinta Años, 1624–1630* (Madrid, 1967); Alcalá-Zamora, *España, Flandes*.

it is illustrated by the careers of the Flanders archdukes and the cardinal-infante (to name only three). Though perturbed at times, the passive loyalty of all and the active service of many of the nobility (often at great personal cost) was a consistent feature of government.[97] Attention has recently been drawn to the higher education system in Castile, which provided candidates of great quality for the extended imperial bureaucracy.[98] Above all, Spain's involvement in a spiritual mission, however inchoate, and however compromised, guaranteed (far beyond the borders of Castile) cooperation which arose as often from conviction as expediency.[99] This identity of interest among the privileged was supported by the complaisance of the unprivileged. The relative absence of social disorder and rebellion amongst a working population which carried the burdens of empire on its shoulders is quite remarkable. In the heartland of the monarchy, the two Castiles themselves, the record of silent suffering since the great Comuneros revolt of the early sixteenth century was punctured only by a handful of local disturbances in the middle decades of the seventeenth. Even during the contemporary insurrections in the king's other dependencies, the extent of genuine loyalty to the monarchy amongst the rebels – except of course in Portugal – is as notable as the fact of protest.[100] Indeed it could be argued that the social norm of the Spanish empire in the Habsburg period as a whole was stability, in clear contrast to that of France.[101] The elements of conformity and homogeneity so crucial to Spain's survival were cemented by religious uniformity – especially important in the Iberian peninsula itself. Without doubt, the monolithic religious basis of Spanish life was of incalculable benefit to the affairs of government. It had finally been achieved by the expulsion of the Moriscos in 1609–14, a vast and efficient administrative operation, undertaken for politico-strategic purposes, and in wanton disregard of economic consequences.[102]

---

[97] For the military side, Parker, *Army of Flanders*, pp. 118–19; on the diplomatic aspect, A. Domínguez Ortiz, *La sociedad española en el siglo XVII* (2 vols, Madrid, 1963).

[98] R.L. Kagan, *Students and Society in Early Modern Spain* (Baltimore, MD, 1974).

[99] An important corollary to this topic, which has not yet received sufficient attention, is the artistic and intellectual influence of the monarchy in the first third of the century, diffused from northern Italy and Brussels: Braudel, *The Mediterranean*, ii, pp. 753, 833–35. A great age in French literature was prepared by long apprenticeship to Spanish examples, see M. Deforneaux, *Daily Life in Spain in the Golden Age* (1970), p. 7. M. Tapié asks about 1636 (with reference to Corneille) 'l'anneé de Corbie ou celle du Cid?', *La France*, p. 328. This particular 'conjuncture' aptly illustrates the continuing predominance of Spain.

[100] See (e.g.), H.G. Koenigsberger, 'The Revolt of Palermo in 1647', reprinted in *Estates and Revolutions*, pp. 253–77.

[101] Perhaps the most remarkable case is that of the Spanish Netherlands, the constant theatre of seventeenth-century wars. A minor aristocratic conspiracy in 1632 was the unique example of disloyalty in the whole period. No wonder that one Belgian historian writes of 'le loyalisme profond de nos ancêtres vis-à-vis du roi d'Espagne', Van der Essen, *Le cardinal-infant*, pp. 20–26.

[102] Braudel, *The Mediterranean*, ii, p. 798.

All these considerations, negative and positive, tangible and intangible, played some part in ensuring that Spanish hegemony in Europe did not vanish overnight subsequent to the massive calamity of 1640–41. The residual might of the monarchy remained, along with its total commitment to the traditional international policy of resistance to pressure and attack. Both had to be worn down gradually by the consistent and determined efforts of its adversaries. For some fifteen years the initiative switched giddily back and forth across the Pyrenees, never resting with one side long enough to produce a final verdict.[103] Ultimately – or so it seems to the present writer – the active involvement of Spain in the affairs of Europe ceased during the twenty years 1658–78, a phase which opens with the battle of the Dunes, and closes with the loss of Franche Comté. The central year of this span, 1668, appears as a kind of watershed, ritually celebrating the regression of Spain from world power to the more modest stature of the fifteenth century.

'The most glorious age of Spain', comments Braudel, 'lasted undimmed until Rocroi (1643) or even 1650.'[104] As the characteristic rider suggests, Rocroi should be seen (like the failure of the Great Armada) as the beginning of a chapter. The defeat, heavy as it was, was in any case more the result of human misjudgement than of the exhaustion of Spanish military and material resources.[105] It was succeeded not by the disintegration of the front lines and great losses of territory but by prolonged stalemate. Although the revolts of Catalonia and Portugal sandwiched Castile between theatres of war, more than four times as many troops were maintained outside the peninsula. The despatch to Brussels of a regular subsidy of 3,000,000 ducats per annum, though lower than the rate of the 1630s, was continued without serious interruption until the mid 1650s.[106] In the same period, by way of contrast, the French were completely unable to provide proper payment and supply for the army defending Catalonia.[107] During the Fronde, Spain recovered much of the ground lost in the previous quinquennium, including the harbours of Mardyck and Dunkirk (the latter of great strategic importance). As late as 1656, a major victory was gained by the Flanders army at Valenciennes, while even a year later Spanish cavalry units were able to cross the Somme barrier and forage as far as the region of Beauvais.[108] Mazarin's attempts to gain a compromise peace did not cease with his victory in the internal struggles, but culminated in the extremely reasonable overture of 1656, rejected by Philip IV purely on

---

[103] This period receives effective treatment in J. Stoye, *Europe Unfolding, 1648–1688* (1969) chaps. 3, 4; and in A. Domínguez Ortiz, 'España ante la paz de los Pirineos', *Hispania*, 19 (1959), pp. 545–72.

[104] Braudel, *The Mediterranean*, ii, p. 825.

[105] Parker, *Army of Flanders*, pp. 260–61.

[106] Ibid, p. 264; Cánovas, *Estudios*, ii, pp. 297–302.

[107] J. Sanabre, *La acción de Francia en Cataluña en la pugna por la hegemonía de Europa, 1640–1659* (Barcelona, 1956), pp. 246–48.

[108] Domínguez Ortiz, 'España ante la paz', pp. 546–48; Cooper, *New Cambridge Modern History*, p. 480. The town of Rocroi itself was taken in 1654.

grounds of prestige.[109] During the same period Madrid succeeded in reducing Catalonia and the rebellious Italian provinces once more to obedience.

In this context, the English alliance negotiated by Mazarin in 1656–57 was of decisive significance. On the one hand, this fortunate marriage of convenience indicated that the power of France was insufficient, even on land, to reduce Spain to seek terms. On the other, the introduction of a fresh and vigorous partner into the campaigns of 1657–58 was enough to turn the scales at last. The English navy prevented the arrival of the silver fleet in successive summers and, in an unprecedented operation, blockaded the Spanish coast for a whole winter. Cromwell's army made certain of Spain's defeat at the battle of the Dunes, which opened the whole of the Spanish Netherlands to conquest. The subsequent negotiations, however, resulted in a peace settlement in which both sides made concessions; the treaty of the Pyrenees was far from being the Diktat commonly implied in the textbooks.[110] Philip IV was brought to the conference table, moreover, not by military failure alone but by yet more profound concerns. The existence of a son and heir allowed him to agree to the infanta's betrothal to Louis XIV, an arrangement now free of the immediate dynastic threat which had previously been involved. Furthermore, the king had become convinced that the reconquest of Portugal – an aspiration which was becoming an obsession – was impossible without the retrenchment of commitments elsewhere.[111]

In many ways, Portugal is the key to the rapid debilitation of the monarchy's affairs which followed. No sooner had Philip freed his hands in the north than all available troops were transferred to the western frontiers of Castile. Immense efforts were made to garner and concentrate resources, both military and naval, on the reduction of Castile's small rebellious neighbour. Despite the closing of the Catalan and Flanders fronts, therefore, the 1660s saw if anything an intensification of the demands of war on Castile.[112] The result was the most prolonged and complete humiliation that Spain had yet suffered. Kept afloat partly by English and clandestine French aid, Portugal was equal to the challenge. Major attempts at invasion were repel;led in 1659 (at Elvas) and 1663 (at Ameixial). Undeterred by these disasters, and with astonishing determination, the Spaniards scraped together yet another pathetic force which met with annihilation at Villaviciosa in 1665. In the next year 4,000,000 ducats were spent on the war but failed even to produce an army able to take the offensive.[113] In the midst of the chaos Philip IV died, obstinate to his final breath. Domínguez Ortiz's tribute applies equally to the spirit of Castile itself: 'a monarch who to foreign ambassadors gave the impression of an inert

---

[109] L. Pfandl, *Carlos II* (1940; trans. Madrid, 1947), pp. 57–58.

[110] 'It is certain that if in 1659 France had not moderated its demands the contest would have been continued interminably', Domínguez Ortiz, *Política y hacienda*, p. 64.

[111] For the above paragraph, see sources cited in n. 103, above; and Marqués de Saltillo, 'Don Antonio Pimentel y la paz de los Pirineos', *Hispania*, 7 (1947), pp. 24–124.

[112] Domínguez Ortiz, *Política y hacienda*, pp. 79–86.

[113] Pfandl, *Carlos II*, pp. 141–42.

sphinx, but who at base showed an extraordinary tenacity in the prosecution of a struggle against innumerable enemies.'[114]

That spirit, however, was soon after to be broken. In 1667, Louis XIV attacked the Spanish Netherlands in the War of Devolution, fitting symbol of the devolution of supremacy. The French encountered little resistance; Spain, despite ample warning of the invasion, had nothing left to offer. Only the diplomatic intervention of the maritime powers, fearful of French expansion in a sensitive area, prevented the total loss of 'the Obedient Provinces'. At the conference of Aix-la-Chapelle, the powers hardly bothered to consult Madrid when deciding which gains the Most Christian King should retain, and the Spanish plenipotentiaries were merely summoned to ratify their losses. In order to meet the conditions of the guarantee drawn up by the Triple Alliance, Spain was compelled to send subsidies for the payment of the Swedish army. In this way a force of Protestant mercenaries was hired to defend the Spanish Netherlands, erstwhile home of the renowned Walloon infantry, against future French aggression.[115] In the same momentous year of 1668 a nadir of humiliation was reached with the formal concession of Portuguese independence. The world empire of Philip II thus ceased to exist.

'The weakness of the monarchy which but a short time before had held Europe in awe now lay exposed', comments Domínguez Ortiz on the 1660s.[116] The lines on the graph-paper had at last coincided, and Spain had sunk to the political level suggested by her economic condition. Again, several factors were at work in this ultimate 'conjuncture'. The economic scene itself had worsened considerably since 1640. Trade with America had not recovered from the disastrous slump of the early 1640s. Following a succession of complete or partial harvest failures in the same decade, plague ravaged the peninsula, causing mortality on a scale equal to that of the terrible outbreak fifty years earlier. Pestilence remained endemic in the Mediterranean provinces until the mid 1650s, so that in these years the demographic density of the monarchy probably reached its lowest point.[117] Just as half a century earlier, in the last phase of a general European war, Castilian manufacture and banking had virtually ceased, so now (except for the supply of the big cities), trade and exchange had almost died out and a money economy was at its last gasp. Spanish society was entering a kind of dark age. Four years of bad harvests in 1665–68 were accompanied by price stagnation and the worst monetary chaos of the century.[118] The commercial domination of Spain by foreigners

---

[114] Domínguez Ortiz, *Política y hacienda*, p. 79.

[115] The relations between Spain and the maritime powers during these negotiations are discussed in my 'Anglo-Spanish Relations, 1660–68' (unpublished Ph.D. thesis, University of Wales, 1968), pp. 272–87, 310–12.

[116] Domínguez Ortiz, *Golden Age of Spain*, pp. 110–11.

[117] Stoye, *Europe Unfolding*, pp. 102, 115.

[118] E.J. Hamilton, *War and Prices in Spain, 1651–1800* (Cambridge, MA, 1947), pp. 17–20, 123–25.

(especially the Dutch) had reached the stage where the monarchy no longer fully controlled its own affairs, much less those of all Europe.[119]

Nevertheless, it is still not clear that this economic Armageddon completely drained the crown of a capacity for political initiative. It is true that, after maintaining themselves on a plateau for a quarter of a century, bullion imports began to fall again around 1646, and this time the trend persisted. By 1655 silver engrossments were less than half of what they had been only ten years earlier, and for a period at the end of the decade they tapered away almost to nothing. Despite the 'final orgy of taxation' referred to by Professor Lynch,[120] the patience and reserves of the bankers were becoming exhausted.[121] The 'bankruptcy' of 1647 forced out the Portuguese houses. Those of 1652, 1662 and 1666 (plus a partial suspension of payments in 1660) caused the collapse or withdrawal of nearly all the Italian *asentistas*.[122] Yet the fiscal machinery did not cease to function. Amazingly, perhaps, the monarchy was still able to finance the war in Portugal, partly by what amounted to monetary prestidigitation, partly by the continued support of the remaining Genoese financiers.[123] Even the lack of resistance to France in the Flanders campaign of 1667 can be seen as more a reflection on the total breakdown of the old communications system than on the crown's ability to raise necessary funds.

Indeed, it seems at least arguable that the monarchy's qualitative resources – the politico-military establishment referred to earlier – gave out before the capacity to pay for them. There was, of course, a mounting level of actual losses on the war fronts. The haemorrhage which began in the 1630s and had never been stemmed meant that the traditional sources of cannon-fodder in Flanders and Italy were by now dried up.[124] 'Yesterday,' reported the letter-writer Barrionuevo in 1655, 'they proclaimed that whoever wished to enlist would be given six *reals* daily for sustenance, a payment in advance, and a full uniform. Such is the present necessity for men that a recruit cannot be found [in exchange] for an eye from one's head.'[125] Since 1640, the provinces

---

[119] Viçens Vives, 'Decline of Spain', pp. 130–33.

[120] In *Spain and America*, pp. 233–34.

[121] Cánovas, *Estudios*, ii, p. 302. Relations between Madrid and Genoa were strained enough to occasion rumours of war in 1654, Paz y Melia, *Avisos*, i, pp. 61, 73–75.

[122] Domínguez Ortiz, *Política y hacienda*, pp. 110–15, 126–37.

[123] Ibid., pp. 115–17. The crown's ability to raise the huge *asientos de dinero* of the Portuguese war in the 1660s would be more understandable if Michel Morineau's revision of bullion import figures proves valid. This claim runs counter to a basic implication in the work of Hamilton and the Chaunus, and suggests that a boom in receipts began in the 1660s, and had exceeded all previous levels – even those of the 1590s – by 1671–75: 'D'Amsterdam Sèville: de quelle réalité de l'histoire des prix est-elle le miroir?', *Annales: economies, sociétés, civilisations*, 23 (1968), pp. 178–205.

[124] Lynch, *Spain and America*, pp. 129–30; G. Parker, 'War and Economic Change: The Economic Costs of the Dutch Revolt', in J.M. Winter (ed.), *War and Economic Development: Essays in Memory of David Joslin* (Cambridge, 1975), pp. 49–71 (at p. 55).

[125] Paz y Melia, *Avisos*, i, p. 219.

of western Spain, Galicia, Old Castile and Extremadura, had been continually devastated and depopulated by the effects of the Portuguese war. In the early 1660s these areas were still being scoured for levies, even the sick and elderly being forcibly conscripted.[126] The now undivided military resources of the crown, concentrated on the reduction of Portugal, produced a grand total of only 20,000 men in 1665. Their miserable quality, and the concomitant decay of morale, can be gauged from the fact that the defeats of Ameixial and Villaviciosa were the bloodiest ever suffered in Philip IV's wars.[127] 'No man in the ranks performed his duty properly', complained Don Juan José of Austria after his defeat in 1663; 'our infantry have set a new example in history, for never before have they been beaten without offering resistance.'[128]

Don Juan himself, however, provided a typical example of falling standards of responsibility higher up the chain of command, both civil and military. In 1667 he was ordered to take up the defence of the Low Countries but refused to accept the appointment. Philip's bastard cited the exhaustion of resources, the perennial *falta de medios*, as the reason for his action. In reality he was motivated by political ambition and by fear of absence from the centre of power in Madrid.[129] Similar concerns were evident among many of the higher nobility in this decade, which saw the last, sick years of 'Felipe el Grande' and the opening period of Mariana's regency. Few heads of great families could afford to be in virtual exile whilst influence and patronage were shared out at court. In his declining years the king attempted to stamp out plurality of office-holding in order to discourage this feeling, but nothing could reverse the trend which saw once-envied posts in the diplomatic service and provincial government going to the lower *títulos* and younger sons. Even the golden throne of peculation in Naples no longer exerted the attraction it had in previous years.[130] As the conde-duque had stated in a famous memorandum, 'God has taken away all our military and political chiefs . . . . When God wishes to destroy a kingdom, don't say that He will deprive it of money, of men, or of fortresses, but of the good counsel and service of its leaders.'[131]

---

[126] J.O. Galindo, *España en Europa al advenimiento de Carlos II* (Bilbao, 1948), pp. 161–62.

[127] Pfandl, *Carlos II*, pp. 97–101. The most eminent names met with disaster in Portugal: the marquis of Los Balbases (son of the great Spínola), the duke of Osuna, Luis de Haro and Don Juan José.

[128] Quoted ibid., pp. 43–44. See also, Cánovas, *Estudios*, i, 207ff. During these campaigns, whole *tercios* were mustered at only single figures, Deleito y Piñuela, *El declinar*, pp. 189–200. The deplorable state of the army was considered at a special meeting of the council of state after Ameixial, *consulta* of 17 July 1663, BL, Eg. 347, f. 188.

[129] Lynch, *Spain and America*, pp. 238–39.

[130] Instances in Barrionuevo's epistles are legion and grow in frequency after 1660. In 1670, the English ambassador referred to the nobles fear that 'employment keeping them abroad in foreign countries gives opportunity to their enemies at home', Godolphin to Arlington, Oct. 1671, PRO, 94/59, ff. 8–9.

[131] March 1640: see Cánovas, *Estudios*, i, p. 415.

There was, then a *falta de obediencia* to add to all the other failings, which, though certainly present before the 1660s, now became acute. The nobility stuck like leeches to the febrile bodies of Philip and his pathetic successor, and the affairs of the whole monarchy suffered accordingly. Right through the hierarchy of the Spanish system the quality of talent and service was eroded. Olivares was again more prophetic than accurate when he claimed in 1632 that 'the greatest enemies of the king and of his monarchy, and those who are most at fault for everything, are we ministers and councillors'.[132] The accusation seems, however, to be perfect;y valid when applied to the Spain of a generation later. Although the numbers of the aristocracy had consistently increased under Philip IV, the Venetian ambassador in 1659 estimated a drastic decline in those who accepted military service.[133] In the previous year, the veteran captain Dávila Orejón bemoaned the fact that fewer than twenty gentlemen of the court responded to Don Luis de Haro's attempt to raise a company for the Portuguese war. 'They thought more of the pleasures of Madrid than of the prestige of his majesty's arms or of the honour of their nation', he commented caustically.[134] Shortly after, it was argued in a popular broadsheet that 'the grandees of Spain are of great assistance to the king of France, and unwittingly obtain his advancement, since they enrich themselves from the household of their master and leave him without the means of maintaining armies'.[135]

The decay of ancient values among the nobility also tended to support an element of deliberate withdrawal from the idea of empire, which can be detected in this period. An essential event in this process (if such it was) was the death of Philip IV, which removed the uniquely personal, dynastic and spiritual motivation which was the *fons et origo* of Spain's European policy.[136] Philip's attitude, perhaps in the last analysis the root cause of Spain's survival, had always been that which was summed up in her sentimental fashion by his so-called 'spiritual adviser' (in fact a veritable grey eminence), Sor María de Agreda: 'this little boat of Spain will never sink, however much the water laps across the decks'.[137] At his departure buoyancy, too, vanished. The monarchy

---

[132] Olivares to the cardinal-infante, 27 Sept. 1632, BL, MS Add. 14007, f. 46.

[133] Domínguez Ortiz, *Sociedad española*, i, pp. 273–74.

[134] Quoted in Deleito y Piñuela, *El declinar*, p. 199. F. Soldevila maintains that the loss of Portugal was not an inevitable consequence of Spain's economic exhaustion, but primarily a result of the growing spiritlessness and ineptitude of the governing classes: *Historia de España* (2nd edn, Barcelona, 1963), iv, pp. 364–66. It is likely that the quality of the bureaucracy was falling in these years with the atrophy of the universities, R.L. Kagan, 'Universities in Castile, 1500–1700', *Past and Present*, 49 (1970), pp. 44–71. See also the comments in Elliott, *Imperial Spain*, pp. 377–78.

[135] *El espíritu de Francia y máximas de Luis XIV* (Madrid, n.d.): quoted in Viçens Vives, *Historia*, iii, p. 293.

[136] See below, Chapter 7.

[137] Quoted in C. Seco Serrano (ed.), *Cartas de la Venerable Sor María de Agreda y del Señor Rey D. Felipe IV*, BAE, 108–9 (Madrid, 1958), i, p. viii.

was now saddled with a combined minority and succession problem; for the rest of the century, Spain was the land where the king was a child. Furthermore, Philip's death signalled the end of effective royal absolutism in Castile, which had always been the hub of imperial commitment. These, it seems to me, were the final stages necessary to complete 'the failure of the Monarchy'. The aristocracy succeeded to power and, with the triumph of faction over regency and of the regions over the centre, Castile's imperialism received its quietus. With increasing control of government, dominance in the Cortes, the towns and the church, the Castilian nobility diverted to its own pockets the money formerly earmarked for defence of the empire. The allocation of *mercedes* reached 3,000,000 ducats a year in the 1660s (exactly the amount annually despatched to Flanders during the Thirty Years' War), and 'the treasury virtually ran a welfare service for the aristocracy'.[138] In the next decade, the traditional dominance in government of the council of state, with its devotion to foreign policy, was overthrown by the emergence of the domestically orientated council of Castile. This long overdue shift of priorities recognized economic realities, it is true, but was not entirely dictated by them.

These events occurred simultaneously with the emergence of French absolutism from its chrysalis in the opening period of Louis XIV's personal rule, and the successful struggle to mobilize his kingdom's resources for diplomacy and war. To some extent, Spain and France had now exchanged intrinsic natures as well as international roles. The former was now encumbered with all the problems of minority, disloyalty, faction and inefficiency, whilst the latter confidently assumed the mantle of imperial greatness. Spain's relegation to the ranks of the minor powers did not, of course, mean that she escaped foreign embroilments altogether, nor did it ensure that internal decay would be halted. With the coming of the 'Spanish Succession' question, the concerns of the monarchy remained (in a negative sense) central to European affairs. In 1675–85 Castile endured an economic depression which represents the lowest point of all. After these convulsions, since things could hardly get worse, they slowly got better. However, it is worth remarking in the context of this essay, that commercial improvements in Catalonia and demographic recovery in Castile did not effect any repair in Spain's political position. The year 1668 had seen the surrender of a European influence which was never regained. Ten years later the crown conceded the territory of Franche Comté to Louis XIV, which he had acquired by the simple act of military occupation. In this feeble way the cradle of the Habsburgs, 'the oldest possession of my dynasty' as Charles V himself had called it, passed permanently under the sway of France. This event was surely an apt obituary on Spain as a European power.

---

[138] Lynch, *Spain and America*, pp. 233–34.

2

Domination and Dependence:
Castile, Spain and the Spanish Monarchy*

When Leopold von Ranke surveyed the history of the Spanish monarchy in its golden age, he naturally assumed himself to be dealing with a political community which, if not fully integrated, was united enough to support a prolonged era of European hegemony. For the German writer of the 1830s it was axiomatic that Spain's success in the sixteenth century arose from her ability to impose a common, more-or-less centralized political and economic regime upon her subject provinces; her failure, in the seventeenth, from the extent that this organization broke down under sustained pressure. 'In the Spanish Monarchy', he stated, 'government is unitary, it pursues always the same ends and applies the same methods, although with different results in different territories.'[1] Metropolitan Spain supervised a vital two-way process of personal and material exchange, sending out its administrators, armies and raw materials, receiving from Germany, Italy and Flanders colonies of merchants and artisans along with manufactured goods. True, some provinces (like Naples) suffered from Spanish rule, whilst others (like Milan) benefited. Catalan independence was sacrificed on the altar of unification. Yet this proto-autarky, if not as dynamic as a *Zollverein* nor as monolithic as a *Reich*, was a sufficiently viable system.

Historical orthodoxy on this subject as on every other has travelled far since its inception in the Rankean *écriture*. Indeed, well within his own lifetime, another German historian almost directly contradicted Ranke's conclusion:

> Spain, like Turkey, remained an agglomeration of mismanaged republics with a nominal sovereign at their head. Despotism changed character in the different

---

*Review article, reviewing the following books: M. Fernández Alvarez, *España y los Españoles en los tiempos modernos* (Salamanca, 1979); J.H. Elliott and J.F. de la Peña (ed.), *Memoriales y cartas del conde duque de Olivares*, i, *Política interior, 1621 a 1627*, ii, *Política interior, 1628 a 1645* (Madrid, 1978 and 1981); C. Rahn Phillips, *Ciudad Real, 1500–1750: Growth, Crisis and Readjustment in the Spanish Economy* (London and Cambridge, MA, 1979); J. Casey, *Crisis and Continuity: The Economy of Spanish Lombardy in the Seventeenth Century* (Cambridge, 1979); J.V. Serrão, *História de Portugal*, iv, *Governo dos Reis Espanhóis, 1580–1640*, v, *A restauraçao e a monarquia absoluta, 1640–1750* (Lisbon, 1979 and 1980).

[1] From a Spanish-language version, *La monarquía española en los siglos VXI y XVII* (Buenos Aires, 1946) of the relevant sections of Ranke's *Die Osmänen und die spanische Monarchie im 16. und 17. Jahrhundert*.

provinces with the arbitrary interpretation of the general laws by viceroys and governors: but despotic as was the government it did not prevent the provinces from subsisting with different laws and customs, different coins ... and with their respective system of taxation.[2]

Karl Marx, whose opinion this was, seems (*prima facie* at least) to have divined things as they really were in the Spanish monarchy rather more accurately than the master. The great count-duke of Olivares, whose whole political life was a struggle against them, stands as a testament to these realities. In the *Nicandro* (1643), his ultimate defence of his policies which takes its place as the final document in Elliott and de la Peña's collection, Olivares returned to his favourite theme.

> Foreign observers, whose fear makes them examine our deficiencies profoundly, have decided that all its provinces are of little use to the Spanish Monarchy, because of the fundamental weakness of its forces. They say it is but a fantastic body, defended by words and not by substance: because, sir, what good to your Majesty are kingdoms which are not obliged to assist when Your Majesty's realms are invaded?

Thus it is that an almost diametrically opposed thesis to that of Ranke is presently established, which argues that the Spanish monarchy was never anything more than a loose and accidental dynastic collection of disparate medieval jurisdictions. It was intractably divided, not only by sheer geographical distance, but by indigenous laws and social customs, economic barriers, linguistic frontiers and political aspirations. It was unable to evolve a sense of corporate identity, and had no common institutions rooted in ideas of a federal *res publica* as distinct from those of mere dynastic exploitation. Productive interchange of any kind was unimportant. The 'unitary' policy was entirely that of the Castilian oligarchs gathered around the seat of the monarchy in Madrid, and was sustained almost exclusively by the resources of Castile, its political and demographic heartland. The failure of Castile in the seventeenth century inevitably brought about the collapse of the system.

Both theories contain information essential to the understanding of the complex structure of the monarchy. Ranke's conclusions seem mostly (if not uniquely) relevant to the period of government of the conde-duque de Olivares, or at any rate to what might be termed 'the age of Olivares', embracing the half-decades before and after his actual tenure of power (1618–48). Paradoxically coterminous with the general European war which undermined its supremacy, this period was virtually the only one in which a consciousness of a cooperative monarchy can be detected. But this *was* brought into play largely by the warning signals of Castilian insufficiency, and its expression was never completely free of the language of a Castile-based dynastic policy. We should be unwise to call in question, moreover, the

---

[2] The quotation is from one of Marx's articles on Spain for the *New York Daily Tribune* ('Revolutionary Spain', 1854), K. Marx and F. Engels, *Complete Works*, xiii (1980), p. 396.

importance of the enormous obstacles which lay in the path of even the slightest progress towards integration. Nor can we doubt the extent of the monarchy's dependence upon Castile for long after such progress was determined upon, and (for that matter) once it had failed. Modern scepticism on the theme, deriving as it does from the early work of J.H. Elliott, is therefore more convincing in terms of structural history. Nevertheless, confronted with the now-established fact of the monarchy's effective survival, both in a socio-economic and a political sense, beyond the apocalyptic years of its great crisis (roughly, 1630–50), it may be timely to re-examine Ranke's assumptions concerning its positive characteristics in terms of *l'histoire de moyenne durée*. To what extent, then, was there a Spanish monarchy at all, as distinct from a mere Habsburg-Castilian polity? How far did a *realized* interdependence assist its response to the midcentury challenge? However elusive committed answers to these questions may prove, it can be stated at once that the relationship between Castile/Madrid and Catalonia/Barcelona was *not* the paradigm, and that the utter failure of policy and reciprocity charted in Elliott's seminal study was *not* typical of the general response within the Monarchy to the manifold needs of its common defence.[3]

Some grist for this mill may be gleaned from the rich harvest of studies of Spanish Europe – mostly pertaining to the parts rather than the whole – which has been gathered in during recent years. The present crop is of course selective, and hardly covers what might be regarded as a representative sample, except (to change the metaphor) in so far as the tip of the iceberg is composed of the same elements as the rest.[4] None of the authors was primarily concerned in composing the history of the Spanish monarchy. The animal did not graze at the forefront of their minds. None the less we are able to learn from their collective efforts something new about the nature and physiognomy of the dinosaur at a time when its rule of the earth was yielding place, amidst much blood and tumult, to a new age.

In his amply-proportioned textbook – as indeed its title unambiguously proclaims – Professor Fernández Alvarez is rarely conscious of any dimension to the daily life of the monarchy existing beyond the borders of peninsular Spain. Though the whole pre-modern period is covered, the sections on the external role of Spain consists for the most part of routine narrative. The author points out that the only Spain experienced by the rest of Europe was the Spain of war and war-administration, literally (if you like) the sharp end of the Spanish system. To compensate for this, he has produced a book which addresses the history of the first global power from a vantage point deep in the *meseta* of Old Castile. Professor Fernández Alvarez occupies the chair of history at the university of Salamanca, which recently celebrated its

[3] J.H. Elliott, *The Revolt of the Catalans* (Cambridge, 1963).

[4] For another selection from recent work, largely concentrated on the socio-economic history of the peninsula, see A.W. Lovett's review article, 'The Golden Age of Spain: New Work on an Old Theme', *Historical Journal*, 24 (1981), pp. 739–49.

seventh centenary, and which during the Habsburg period was paramount in the training of a universal bureaucratic elite.[5] His book is subsidized for publication by the local building society, and much of it is appropriately parochial in return. For example, the treatment of 'Urban Transformations' in the sixteenth century is dominated by a discussion (informative enough in itself) of the evolution of the Plaza Mayor as a centre of public life. The architecture, audience capacity, and use of this artefact in Salamanca, Valladolid and (a concession, this) Madrid are expertly examined. No opinion will be found here on Braudel's famous apostrophe to the towns as 'witnesses to the century', and no reference is made (except in the bibliography) to the work of Bennassar on Valladolid, progenitor of the many urban studies now greeting the light.[6] Another section, this time on 'The economic conjuncture of the sixteenth century', is largely devoted to the ideas (important enough in themselves) of the Castilian economist Luis de Ortiz. No mention, after all, appears of Chaunu's thesis on the macroeconomic cycles of the Atlantic world. Much about the book smacks of the lecture hall, and long stretches of it indicate that the author no more wishes to waste various contributions to tourist-guides than he does the course-notes of a long teaching career. Coverage of the Olivares period is characteristic. Don Gaspar de Guzmán, 'full of euphoria', comes to power in 1621 and renews the war with the Dutch. He leads Spain by the nose towards the disaster of Rocroi, 'the first open defeat of the *tercios viejos*', which launches the ascendancy of France. On the way he consistently attempts to 'Castilianize the customs of the peninsula, not so much out of love for Castile, but because the laws of Castile were less of an obstacle to absolutism'. Few of the facts in this dialectic are correct: to the interpretation I shall return anon.

By no means all of Fernández Alvarez's reflections are of this rather dismal order. His comments on the Renaissance in Spain are stimulating, even provocative, since he argues that it made little real impact upon the ruling classes, whether clerical or lay. During the sixteenth century only 400 books were published in Valladolid, where for many years the court was fixed, and none was printed in Oviedo until 1652. The aristocracy remained illiterate, representatives of 'a society which valued culture very little'. The universities were humanist institutions only to a limited extent. Indeed it might be felt (*pace* Bataillon) that 'Renaissance' had meaning in the peninsula mainly in the strictly literal sense – the major recovery from the late-medieval demographic depression, which coincided with the European intellectual phenomenon. Spain's true artistic rebirth came with the Baroque, the era of a cosmopolitan monarchy in which the pursuit of culture became almost universal.[7] On the other hand, even during the reign of Philip II,

[5] Including, in the opening years of the seventeenth century, the future count-duke himself.

[6] See, B. Bennassar, *Valladolid au siècle d'or* (Paris, 1967).

[7] For the relationship between Baroque culture and the nature of the monarchy, see J.A. Maravall, *La cultura del Barroco: análisis de una estructura histórica* (Madrid, 1975).

when the country was conventualized, several prominent intellectuals – not just the exiled Vives – kept up with scientific speculation north of the Pyrenees, successfully risking the attention of the Holy Office.

Fernández Alvarez's attention to such matters suggests that in many respects he has brought his lecture-notes up to date and spiced them with a personal flavour. He describes the development of the Spanish infantry and its tactics (for example) in terms not of the famous pike but of the despised arquebus, which is revealed as the key weapon of victory on the battlefields of Europe.[8] Yet he also takes care to point out that

> An existing machinery of war could give one prince dominion over another country which enjoyed a higher level of civilization [viz. Italy], and this may serve as a point of departure. Neither industry nor science yet conditioned war. During the Renaissance great surprises could still occur. For example, that European supremacy was entrusted to the Spaniards, a people well below the demographic and economic level of the rest of western Europe.

By the time of Philip II, indeed, Italians had largely reconciled themselves to this seeming contradiction. Though he commented specifically on their population weakness, the agglomeration of territories which comprised the monarchy seemed much less odd to the writer Giovanni Botero than perhaps it does from more modern perspectives. In his *Ragion di stato*, published in 1589, Botero saw little reason why Spain should not continue to dominate over more compact and populous states such as France. This hegemony, however, depended upon the efficient articulation of its separate parts, mainly by a resilient system of transference. In other words (Botero himself noted) the empire must be orchestrated by a polity which was essentially maritime. But even as he wrote the Spanish monarchy was suffering one of its most damaging conjunctures. The appalling losses of the *gran empresa de Inglaterra* inaugurated a period when, faced by a continental alliance of enemies, Spain's maritime supremacy – both in naval and commercial terms – was rapidly eroded. A coincidental sequence of harvest failures in Castile heralded a half-century of rampant demographic decline. Before the seventeenth century was many years old Botero's preconditions for the survival of the Spanish system had, apparently, ceased to obtain. Yet Botero was no more the last of his compatriots than he had been the first to acknowledge the enormous potential of the monarchy. From Mercurino Gattinara, Charles V's chancellor and main architect of an imperial administration, via Tommaso Campanella, its Neapolitan critic, to Virgilio Malvezzi, close adviser to Olivares, the belief persisted that its pretensions to the leadership of Europe were no more chimerical than illegitimate.

---

[8] It is characteristic, however, that there is no equivalent section devoted to the navy, despite its equal importance in the scheme of things. J. Alcalá-Zamora's *España, Flandes y el Mar del Norte, 1618–1639* (Barcelona 1975), is revelatory here, but we still lack modern, comprehensive treatment.

Botero's treatise was, almost certainly, amongst those read and noted by the conde-duque de Olivares as he prepared his programme for the recovery of the monarchy. How far his influence (or that of any other thinker) extended in this regard is more difficult to ascertain. In their magnificent edition of Don Gaspar's major extant writings upon the 'domestic affairs' of the kingdoms of Philip IV, J.H. Elliott and J.F. de la Peña show that, despite his acquaintance with a wealth of relevant literature, he never adopted any one prescription as it stood, even when dealing with the solution to a particular problem. Thus, despite the discernible influence of Alamos de Barrientos upon his economic thought – or (it might be added) that of Antony Sherley on his strategic plans – ideas were usually reshaped beyond any recognition of an individual hand. Olivares was a disciple, like Alamos himself, of the stoic pragmatism of Justus Lipsius. This Flemish philosopher (d. 1606) was very fashionable in the intellectual life of Spain – and particularly of Don Gaspar's own Seville – during the first quarter of the century. So far from being a dogmatist who was never prepared to reconsider or amend his policies, Olivares was actively suspicious of ministers who interpreted too rigidly 'the lessons of History' (in the sense of recent comments by Michael Howard),[9] or whose recommendations came supported by 'authority', whether ancient or modern.

The so-called 'Great Memorial' of 1624, then, was the work of a man at the height of his mental and physical powers, and one moreover who may be seen as the ideal product of his own imagined New Monarchy – born in Rome; growing up in Naples, Sicily and Salamanca; spending his early manhood in Seville. His concept begins at the level of *mentalités*. Communal feeling must result from the sharing of functional responsibilities, and more of the king's non-Castilian subjects should be involved in the day-to-day administration of his monarchy.

> This particularly goes for embassies and vice-royalties, presidencies [of the councils] at court, and to some degree in the posts of your royal household. Thus will be assured the security, establishment, perpetuity and growth of this monarchy in general; and the sole means of uniting it [is] the mixing together of such vassals, who presently regard themselves as foreigners, admitting them to all the said offices.

Unfortunately, no serious attempt to carry out these precepts was ever made. Some may regard them, in any case, as a disguised, insidious way of 'Castilianizing' rather than encouraging mutual tolerance and understanding. But other documents in this collection – presented by the editors with full contextual commentaries and exemplary scholarly apparatus – make clear that this interpretation is mistaken. Olivares' aim was to maximize the power of the monarchy *by and for* the power of his king; that is to say, he realized that

---

[9] I refer to Michael Howard's inaugural lecture (as Regius Professor of Modern History at Oxford), 'The Lessons of History', printed in *The Listener*, 12 March 1981.

only the will of Philip IV could release the latent promise of his patrimony, and that only its release would establish the will of Philip IV. But neither was desirable merely for their own sakes, but above all for the divine purpose, which was victory in the deadly struggle which rebels and enemies had forced upon the monarchy, a crusade which it was unable to forswear. Certainly, the conde-duque's ideals were 'absolutist', but to view his tactics as an attempt to impose Castilian political *mores*, seen as somehow conductive to this absolutism, is simplistic. Olivares spent far more energy in negotiating, subverting, and (ultimately) destroying *Castilian* impediments to his rule than ever he devoted to combating the *fueros* of the provinces. Opposition, usually passive, but none the less weighty for that, was entrenched at every level of government and society within Castile. It was this, along with the material exhaustion of the kingdom (which, however imperfectly, it reflected) that led him to insist that the provinces set aside their liberties in the common cause. It was this, given the opportunity provided by the rebellions his desperation had provoked, which eventually overthrew him.

Nevertheless, even under Olivares, there was no 'great rebellion' of Castile. Its absence was the crowning mercy of Habsburg Spain, and precluded an essential condition of the outright collapse of the Spanish system. We have learned from Professor Domínguez Ortiz how near to the surface a general explosion smouldered, and from Dr Jago one reason why it was, if narrowly, avoided.[10] As Carla Rahn Phillips reminds us, opposition forced the abandonment of Olivares' constructive plans for fiscal and commercial reform, forcing him to seek a series of improvised alternatives which 'drove the aristocracy close to rebellion'. However, little overt discontent, far less violent protest, is to be observed in the royal city of New Castile which is the subject of her book. Like all other Castilian towns, Ciudad Real declined. From a thriving market centre with an embryonic woollen industry, it became a sleepy backwater in the course of the century 1580–1680. Royal taxation policy played the main role in this, and in the closing period of Olivares' government (1637–42) was especially damaging. But the prosperity of the town and its *partido* had been ended long before, as a result of a more covert indirect tax. In the sixteenth century, the crown's protection of the *Mesta*, of the northern Castilian fairs, and of trade links with Flanders, meant that all the best wools of New Castile and La Mancha were earmarked for export, and most of the residue also went abroad at higher prices than local capitalists could afford. Despite a generation of greater potential investment during the fiscally undemanding Lerma government, the nascent textile industry of Ciudad Real was suffocated by 1621, sacrificed to the interests of Genoese financiers and Antwerp merchants. In the same period generally, the crown's imperial policy

---

[10] A. Domínguez Ortiz, *Alteraciones andaluzas* (Madrid, 1973): C.J. Jago, 'Habsburg Absolutism and the Cortes of Castile', *American Historical Review*, 86 (1981), pp. 307–26.

meant that 'the traditional cities of Castile lost importance to the cities of the expanded Habsburg monarchy – Naples, Milan [and] Antwerp'. At the same time wealth and political influence shifted away from the two Castiles towards the great cities of the periphery, Seville-Cadiz on the one hand, Bilbao-San Sebastian on the other.

Rahn Phillips's book is a slim volume as it stands. It contains many paragraphs of background in which the material is familiar and is further padded out with capitular overlap which some might regard as plain repetition. In essence, therefore, it is more of a long article than a short book. Its style can be irritating, particularly in the use of the new-minted jargon of demographic history. Constant recurrence of the phrase 'vital events' takes some getting used to; but 'vital statistics', and even (*mirabile dictu*) 'vital curves', stretch the reader's equanimity a little too far. (In this connection, the reference to '*Nuestra Señora del Prado's* conceptions' is perhaps careless rather than blasphemous). Caution must be to the fore in deriving conclusions from the book's population analyses, since they concern only two (admittedly large) parishes. All the same, they seem to open the door to two areas of inquiry.

First, it is evident that Ciudad Real suffered to a serious degree neither from the great plague of 1596–1602 nor from the further outbreak of 1647–49. The latter escape was probably due to geographical reasons, since the town was not far enough south east to pick up the so-called 'Levantine Plague'. It is possible to argue the same factor for the apparent immunity of Cáceres and Murcia from the earlier epidemic, but certainly not for that of Ciudad Real nor (more surprisingly) Medina del Campo, which lay in the main communications routes of their respective *mesetas* south and north of Madrid, and thus directly athwart the deadly path of the 'Atlantic Plague'.[11] By far the worst trial by disease undergone by Ciudad Real came in 1664–69, at a time when – it has recently been argued – Castilian urban demography had begun an upsurge.[12] Could it be that too much significance has been accorded the first epidemic in comparison with later outbreaks, like those of the 1630s and 1670s, which have attracted comparatively little attention? Or should we alter the emphases currently placed *within* discussions of Spain's population history in view of indications that the fundamental disease problem may have been endemic rather than epidemic, with an exceedingly complex local and chronological pattern? Such an exercise should help us (*inter alia*) to a greater understanding of the relationship between food shortages and disease, a problem of some importance which (as Dr Rahn Phillips points out) remains basically unsolved.

Second, it is notable that Ciudad Real's only important population reverse (before 1664) came as a result of the expulsion of the *moriscos* in 1610–11, when between two and three thousand were deported. This may have represented as much as 25 per cent of its citizens. Here we are dealing with a peculiar

---

[11] For the studies of Cáceres, Murcia and Medina del Campo, see Lovett, 'Golden Age'.

[12] H. Kamen, *Spain in the Later Seventeenth Century, 1665–1700* (1980).

feature of this bizarre monarchy which contemporaries themselves regarded (and *a fortiori*) as paradoxical. The Iberian Moors were in fact Spaniards but were looked upon not merely as foreigners but as alien enemies, because infidel. Yet, as Professor Fernández Alvarez remarks, hardly any Castilian town of note, following the dispersal of the Andalusian *moriscos* in 1570, was without its Moorish ghetto, usually situated outside the medieval walls, for reasons of security. According to the recent examination of the expulsion[13] some 300,000 were actually transported from or otherwise left Spain; another 10–12,000 died in acts of resistance or through the concomitant privation of the operation; leaving only 10,000 to eke out a clandestine existence. Yet as the authors admit, figures for Castile-Extremadura and Andalusia-Murcia are still by no means definitive. The proportion of the total represented by *moriscos* in Ciudad Real may have been abnormally large; certainly those of Toledo and Valladolid were much smaller. The possibility remains that the effect of the decree of 1610 upon 'greater' Castile has been underestimated. May one of the reasons for the puzzling slow repopulation of Valencia, by far the most seriously-hit province, be sought in the fact that before emigration to the Levant was considered, the easier option of evacuated houses, jobs and (to a lesser extent) land nearer home first offered itself?

The kingdom of Valencia had achieved little recovery from the depopulation caused by the expulsion (which removed one in three of its denizens) by the time of the second holocaust – of the plague of 1647 (one in six). James Casey's monograph examines the consequences of these events for the 'long depopulation' of his region. Yet he considers that another contribution to this process was structural, not conjunctural. Sancho de Moncada's contemporary identification of a reluctance to marry as the root cause of Spain's lack of people seems to be borne out in the case of the Valencian communities whose demographic history Dr Casey has investigated.[14] The 'flight from marriage' was of course a symptom of long-term poverty, a poverty so marked and universal that even the younger (and/or female) children of the local nobility could rarely afford the charms of wedlock. And in a society as obsessed with the abundance of violence as it was by the absence of sex, one of its most prominent members, the count of Real, was unable to meet the cost of constructing a common gallows.

If Valencia as a whole bore important socio-economic resemblances to other Mediterranean provinces of the Monarchy – Sicily and Naples as well as Catalonia – it also mirrored Castile in those key respects which conditioned its political relationship with the Madrid government. The indigence of the

---

[13] A. Domínguez Ortiz and B. Vincent, *Historia de los Moriscos: vida y tragedia de una minoría* (Madrid, 1978).

[14] This is especially interesting in view of the conclusion recently reached that the increased incidence of marriage was the main 'input factor' to the English population explosion of the eighteenth century; see E.A. Wrigley and R.S. Schofield, *The Population History of England, 1541–1871: A Reconstruction* (1981).

nobility allowed the crown to manipulate internal power-sources to its own advantage. In a manner similar to that discovered by Dr Jago for Castile,[15] the great families of Valencia were bound to the royal stirrup by the king's ability to protect them from the legal and economic consequences of bankruptcy, a prerogative systematically exploited under Olivares. Above all, the expulsion of 1609, by depriving the *senyors* of *morisco* rents and lumbering them with huge mortgages (*censales*), created at a stroke a complaisant province, pliable to the iron will of the conde-duque at a point when it was most useful to Madrid's policy. This factor was supported by others of a less ephemeral nature. The Valencian *Corts* was divided against itself, and its *diputació* (or standing committee) was constitutionally powerless compared to that of Catalonia. When difficulties arose, the personal appearance of the king before the estates in the capital never failed to work the oracle. Philip himself was the main Valencian landowner, where, in contrast to the crippling lack of patrimonial influence in Catalonia, his lands were more valuable than those of either of its premier dukes. This helped to assure his control of patronage, which remained virtually unchallenged both in the localities and in the central agencies of government (the viceregal administration and the *audiencia*). In the 1620s Olivares rendered this definitive by wresting influence over official appointments from the hands of the councillors of Aragon, in a move described in its general context by the editors of his *Memoriales y cartas*.

During this period, Valencia regularly provided a small fiduciary surplus which was used to defray administrative costs in the other two provinces of the crown of Aragon, and even to subsidize the war-effort. The concession, by the *Corts* of 1626 of a *servicio* of over one million *Lliures* (= *escudos*) with which a Valencian regiment of 1,000 men could be supported for fifteen years, was a considerable one in view of the kingdom's limited manpower. In addition, over 12,000 soldiers were levied by 'private' recruitment to the royal armies in the years 1626–37 alone. Little wonder that Casey, in some salutary sentences, states that 'the Union of Arms appears to have triumphed in Valencia'; and that 'Olivares scored a permanent triumph with his policy of making Valencia bear a little more of the expenses of the Monarchy'.

Nevertheless, there came a moment when the kingdom 'seemed poised to go the way of Catalonia'. This crisis arose (in 1646) entirely from the political inexperience of the viceroy, a nominee of the *antiolivarista* cabal which had ousted the great minister in Madrid. The trouble was quickly smoothed over by a tactful withdrawal. Unfortunately, the reader of Casey's book is referred for details of this important episode to the author's article, buried in a scholarly *Valenciano* journal. In a work of such modest physical proportions, this seems an unnecessary economy. It is a pity, too, that at no one point is the whole of local and regional administration fully and clearly explained. With such minor reservations, one can only admire this elegantly-written book, equally

---

[15] C.J. Jago, 'The Influence of Debt on the Relations between Crown and Aristocracy in Seventeenth-Century Castile', *Economic History Review*, 2nd series, 26 (1973), pp. 216–36.

informative and stylish over a comprehensively wide range of subjects, as a fundamental contribution to our knowledge of the Spanish monarchy. That nearly all the major signposts uncovered by his researches tend to confirm the directions pointed by existing regional studies of south-western Europe in no way diminishes Dr Casey's achievement. Moreover, in the area of this essay's primary focus, his arguments support the affirmation that stability, loyalty, and even – to a surprising degree – co-operation, were the norm in the relationship between the crown and its dependencies inside and outside the peninsula:

Political Behaviour in the Regions of the Spanish Monarchy, 1600–1700

Totally Loyal	Mainly Loyal	Minor Revolt	Major Revolt
Castile[a]	Andalusia	Vizcaya 1631	Catalonia 1640–52
Aragon	Basque Provinces	Naples[c]1647	Portugal 1640–68
Galicia	Valencia	Palermo 1647	
Canary Islands	Naples[b]	Messina 1675	
Balearic Islands	Sicily	Valencia 1693	
Sardinia			
Milan			
Flanders			
Franche Comté			

[a]Includes Extremadura, Asturias and Murcia
[b]Province
[c]City
N.B. The revolt of Portugal was unique in achieving secession.

If (in Dr Casey's words) 'Valencia had signally failed to develop a strong sense of its own identity'; and *thus*, like Galicia or Extremadura, remained contentedly a part of a larger community, 'what [in Botero's question] shall we say of Milan?' Botero continued, rhetorically:

> Is there a duchy more abundant in victuals, grain, rice, livestock, cheese, wines and flax, more replete with artifices and traffic, more densely populated, or more conveniently located? [It is] the richest and most civil part of Italy.

Whereas administration in Valencia appears to be automatic, Milan was a splendid example of true autonomy. Though the governor was always a Spaniard – his responsibilities as commander of the army of Lombardy, second in size and importance only to that of Flanders, made this essential – his powers were limited compared to those of the southern viceroys.[16] The

---

[16] Ambrogio Spínola's short tenure of the post (1630) was an exception, at least before the last quarter of the century, when several scions of the Austrian Habsburgs were appointed. A study of the army of Lombardy, along the lines of Parker's *Army of Flanders*, is much to be desired.

ducal senate, which had only three Spaniards in its total fifteen membership, possessed supervisory control of legislation, justice, religion and land tenure. Most of the specialist tribunals, including that of finance, were staffed by native Milanese. In this most traditionally urban of territories, the towns enjoyed firm legal and fiscal privileges. Even under Olivares the crown made little attempt to interfere with these arrangements. Doubtless at bottom its caution was due to Lombardy's crucial strategic role in the Spanish system; in this sense, at least, it was 'conveniently located'. It may also be true that the consequent presence of a field army, along with several large garrisons, had its influence upon the unambiguous conformity of the duchy to the norm of political behaviour outlined above. But even when Madrid did flex its muscles, as in the extension of billeting liabilities around 1600, and the widespread practice of this onerous imposition in the years 1630–60, resistance was never more than vocal and litigious.

As its title indicates, Domenico Sella's fine study of the Milanese is mainly an economic survey, touching only incidentally upon political matters. His general argument is, however, sufficiently central to our theme, since it consists of a convincing demonstration that the economic decline of Lombardy was not primarily due to Spanish maladministration, nor (specifically) to fiscal pressure arising from the monarchy's Fifty Years War. Sella analyses the descent of the province from the idyllic state described by Botero to that presented by the Frenchman Charles Bourdin exactly a century later; viz. that Lombardy 'is unquestionably one of the finest countries one can behold ... yet in the countryside one sees nothing but poverty and misery, and these are caused by the harshness of Spanish rule'. The latter remark has remained the keynote of historians of Spanish Italy down to very recent times, but – in the case of its northern dimension at least – Professor Sella finds it to have little foundation. The extent and duration of absolute economic decline have themselves been exaggerated. Though the findings of Romano, Cipolla and others in respect of the dramatic failure of urban-based industries (especially textiles) are confirmed, after mid century a reorientation of capital and energy took place towards rural manufacture, a feature of the Alpine foothills, which partially compensated. Moreover, following about 1660, a steady agrarian improvement can be traced. These trends went along with – and in part account for – a reduction in the power of the *città* over the *contado*, making for a better economic and social equilibrium. This was the *balanza* so admired in eighteenth-century Lombardy, under the rule of the enlightened Austrians, but which Sella finds to be considerably anticipated in the later Spanish period. At times, to be sure, the duchy suffered terribly, never more than during the tragic triennium of 1628–30, when dearth was followed by war and plague; an outbreak of mortality of an intensity perhaps unparalleled in any other European region in this century, which reduced its population by 33 per cent (from 1,200,000 to 800,000). Madrid, and Olivares himself, cannot avoid responsibility for this searing disaster.

In other ways, however, Philip IV's wars were not so pernicious, and indeed may have had a medium-tern effect which was positively benign. Cash and credit flowed – nay, at times, veritably poured – into the province. In the 1640s and 1650s, military subsidies from Castile, Naples and Sicily equalled its own revenue. Naples alone contributed an average of over a million *escudos* a year. Apart from balancing the budget, these huge sums buoyed the economy not only of Milan itself but of the smaller towns, especially those of military significance, where the construction of new fortifications was ubiquitous. The deficit-spending inspired by war actually helped Lombardy to arise from the depths of the financial-industrial crisis of 1618–24. In any case, this crisis came rather in the middle than at the beginning of a depression which was under way (both in the agrarian and manufacturing sectors) even before Botero penned his encomium; and was (moreover) a phenomenon which affected the whole of northern Italy, not just its Spanish-dominated regions. Sella states:

> The conclusion seems inescapable that the war was visited on an economy that ran well below full-employment levels for reasons that had little to do with wartime taxation ... a corollary to this is that general economic conditions would have been even more depressed than they actually were had it not been for the additional employment and the fresh rounds of income generated by deficit spending.[17]

Billeting of troops, becoming in this period part of the seasonal rhythm of life not only in Lombardy but in many other regions of war-torn Europe, was the trigger of violent protest and at length of general uprising not only in Catalonia but in Portugal also. In 1628, after he had stumbled stupidly into war with France in north Italy, Olivares began the imposition of his Union of Arms on Portugal. Within the year, the new levels of taxation involved caused riots in Lisbon and Santarém. In the salt-exporting town of Setúbal, they came on top of an existing depression, brought about by Madrid's prohibition of trade with the monarchy's Dutch and English enemies. When, in addition, a company of troops was quartered on the citizens in July 1630, it sparked off disturbances so serious as to be regarded as an insurrection rather than a riot. The incident began the gradual escalation of crisis in 'Philippine' Portugal which culminated in the *coup d'état* of a decade later. Professor J.V. Serrão traces the developments with the aid of a mass of new information. Indeed his masterly volumes, given the analytical detail of their content and the lack of modern secondary works in the field, will perform the function of a ground-breaking monograph more than that of a text-book.

During the 1630s the Lusitanian kingdom felt itself, not without reason, to be peculiarly vulnerable to the demands of Madrid's war policy. It was already being asked to make sacrifices, not only in respect of its commerce but also in the cripplingly expensive defence of Brazil. Then, following the appointment of Margaret of Savoy to the viceroyalty in 1634,

---

[17] The latter is also evident from the history of post-independence Portugal, examined in C.A. Hanson, *Economy and Society in Baroque Portugal, 1668–1703* (1981).

Olivares rapidly stepped up his demands. Technically, the infanta's posting was a concession to long-standing Portuguese appeals for a governor of royal blood. That of Miguel de Vasconcelos as secretary of state was also in line with the constitutional bases of the Union of the Crowns, which required the appointment of native Portuguese to major offices. In fact, however, Vasconcelos was a more dedicated creature of the conde-duque than any Castilian; and Margaret, in any case 'surrounded from the outset by Castilians', was in practice a cypher. Whilst the latter attended to her devotions, the former directed the execution of policy, beginning in a manner which outdid his master in tactlessness, a diminution of the *tratamento* (forms of address) accorded by the viceroy to the aristocracy.

Until mid decade, increases in indirect taxation (*sisas* on salt, oil, etc.) fell almost solely upon artisans and merchants – *o povo* as the Third Estate was called. In 1633, however, the Portuguese church suffered Don Gaspar's vampire embrace and, the following year, the *media anata* was imposed upon office holders. Soon the noble houses were being browbeaten for direct contributions to the war effort. When Olivares set up a new handpicked *Junta de Portugal* in Madrid (1638) the suspicion grew that he was about to drain off the resources of Brazil – in which thousands, at all but the lowest levels of society, had an interest – 'as a way of paying for the disastrous policy of the Thirty Years' War'. In the wake of further disturbances in Lisbon came the violent upheaval at Evora in 1637. Here, and at several other centres, the assault upon authority took the interesting form of the invasion of official buildings and the burning of tax-registers. Madrid's reaction was the dispatch of an army to the (temporary) occupation of the Alentejo region, which succeeded only in exacerbating resentment. The revolt of Catalonia in the summer of 1640 encouraged the ripening of conspiracy, plans which drew in almost the whole of the Portugese ruling class; and Olivares' concentration of all his reserves upon the punishment of the Catalans presented the perfect opportunity. The Spanish administration was overthrown in a few days of breathtaking action, virtually the only victim of which was the horribly mutilated secretary of state. This even proved to be the inauguration of a newly independent Portugal.

Professor Serrão's treatment finally lays to rest the myth of the 'Babylonian Captivity' of 1580–1640, which has enjoyed a depressing longevity amongst earlier schools of Portugese history, epitomized by the work of Rebelo da Silva. No more was the sixty-year union a 'long night' of subjection to a foreign power than the first of December, 1640, was a 'clear dawn' of a new age of self-fulfilment[19]. The very fact that the association lasted so long, indeed for fifty years without serious strain, is eloquent testimony to its mutual convenience. The balance of benefit was, if anything, in Portugal's favour. Although other subjects of the monarchy were rigorously excluded from Brazil, the Portugese themselves managed to penetrate the trade of the Castilian Indies on a considerable scale. Portugal's population increased by a remarkable factor of 10 per cent in exactly the period that Castile's fell by a similar figure. Its very populousness and prosperity encouraged Olivares in a course of action which caused an absolute degeneration of the arrangement, and in which the *suddenness* as well as the *completeness* deserved emphasis. This, in turn, was caused by the massive external challenge to the monarchy which began in the late 1620s, and not by any intrinsic 'decadence'.

Nevertheless, Serrão does not entirely throw over a case in justification of his country's glorious 'restoration'. Olivares, he states 'planned to ignore, insofar as it was not possible to suppress, the ancient privileges (*foros*) of the nation, and to reduce Portugal to a province of Spain'. It does appear that unlike Philip IV's other subjects, with the possible exception of the Neapolitans, the Portuguese were subjected to all the arbitrary fundraising measures which the conde-duque utilized in Castile. The ultimate effect of this may have been 'Castilianization', even in the pejorative meaning of the word. But, despite his cryptic reference to the existence of abundant documentation at Simancas, Professor Serrão makes no use of Spanish sources, even in his long chapter on 'Administration and Society'. (In contrast, Elliott and de la Peña, in lamenting the lack of of a study of Olivares' Portuguese policy, point out the shortage of known sources on the subject). It is true that, in common with his fellow-ministers and advisers, Don Gaspar regarded the Portuguese as part of Spain – like the Galicians or the Catalans – and as distinct from the extra-peninsular subjects of the monarchy, who were generally accorded the implicitly inferior status of *naciones*. Even in 1624, perhaps, it was not utterly chimerical to expect that this eirenic spirit would be reciprocated: 'the heart of the Portuguese [he opined] is essentially faithful, and the discontent that they display is out of pure love of their kings'.

By the 1630s, at any rate, what Dr Casey calls 'the heroic days of Olivares [when] something approaching a general policy for the Monarchy as a whole began to be elaborated', were already over. Though the Union of Arms was by no means the barren tree usually depicted, it never bore fruit sufficient to feed the ravenous appetite of the Spanish system, which consequently died the slow death of starvation. After the Mantuan war, and particularly following the outbreak of open war with France in 1635, planning was replaced by the improvisation more familar to historians of the period, as exemplified in Olivares's orders for the general 'defence of the Monarchy' (1634) printed in volume two of the *Memoriales y cartas*. It is unlikely, therefore, that any plan ever existed for the *anschluss* of Castile and Portugal, any more than for that between Castile and Catalonia.

Although historians are therefore making frontal advances in their knowledge of the Spanish monarchy, a satisfactory overall explanation of the relationship of the parts to each other, to the whole and to the head, is still lacking. It may be that we are heading back towards Ranke's view of a strong but flexible structure, like a great cedar which sways in a storm and survives despite the constant loss of branches. But explanation will become feasible only after careful examination of the histories of the northern regions of Spain, and of Spanish Flanders and Burgundy, not only along the lines of the project which Domínguez Ortiz is currently supervising on Andalusia, but also in the directions earlier pointed by Koenigsberger, Elliott and Villari.[18] We also need a Namier-type attention to the biographies of the monarchy's ruling class and its major professional functionaries whose beliefs and attitudes – especially about the nature of their political environment – should be explored. It is task enough to daunt ten Fernand Braudels, especially at a time when the wings of historical research are being busily clipped. But only thus will we be able to perceive why the Spanish system maintained its hegemony for so long, and why the Spanish monarchy survived until deliberately broken up by the European powers in the eighteenth century.

---

[18] H.G. Koenigsberger, *The Government of Sicily under Philip II of Spain* (1951); Elliott, *Revolt of the Catalans*; R. Villari, *La rivolta antispagnola a Napoli, 1585–1647* (Bari, 1967).

PART II

THE MAKING OF POLICY

A rather unconvincing study of Philip IV, slightly unusual amongst the genre, including props of sovereignty, such as the crown and sceptre (fictional representations, since neither existed in reality), as well as ermined cape and chain with the pendant lamb, symbol of the Order of the Golden Fleece. *(Biblioteca National, Madrid)*

3

Prelude to Disaster: The Precipitation of the War of the Mantuan Succession, 1627–29

Cardinal Richelieu's spectacular military intervention in Italy in 1629 plunged his ministry into a desperate crisis from which it only narrowly emerged intact. It marked the definitive departure of France upon the difficult road of outright opposition to the Habsburg hegemony in Europe. This policy – as the cardinal well knew – was in many ways potentially counter-productive, with a risk factor so high that failure might well have entailed the end not only of his personal career but, with it, the adolescent Bourbon state. Indeed, his initiative had the almost immediate consequence of a rebellious challenge from a prince of the blood and his domestic allies, amounting to a prototype *fronde des princes*. For decades to come, French society was to be impoverished by the manifold negative impact of war, while political stability was persistently affected by the unrelenting material and ideological pressures of continuous hostilities.[1]

In Madrid, the government of Philip IV and the count-duke of Olivares experienced a similar and almost simultaneous series of events. The Italian war of 1628–31 was at the centre of a congruent sequence of disasters affecting every aspect of life and government in the Spanish Monarchy, and aggregating to what one Spanish historian has recently called *el gran viraje* – the great turning point, or (more idiomatically) u-turn of its history. Philip IV's chief minister encountered a serious – if temporary – weakening of his influence; these years witnessed his desperate struggle against critics inside and outside Spanish government. Moreover, only a few years after the events, Philip IV himself characterized 1629 as 'the year in which by common consent my Monarchy began visibly to decline'.[2]

---

[1] G. Pagès, 'Autour de "grand orage": Richelieu et Marillac, deux politiques', *Revue Historique*, 179 (1937), pp. 63–97 is the classic study of the central political crisis. J. Humbert, *Une grande enterprise oubliée: les Français en Savoie sous Louis XIII* (Paris, 1960) deals with the French aspect of the war itself. More general treatment of French politics in these years is available in V.L. Tapié, *La France de Louis XIII et de Richelieu* (Paris, 1967), pp. 133–209. The evolution of Richelieu's policy towards the Habsburgs – with special reference to Italy - is studied in two useful articles by R. Pithon, 'Les débuts dificiles de ministère de Richelieu et la crise de Valteline (1621–1627)', *Revue de l'histoire diplomatique*, 74 (1960), pp. 297–322, and 'La Suisse, theâtre de la guerre froide entre la France et l'Espagne pendant la crise de Valteline 1621–1626, *Schweizerische Zeitschrift für Geschichte* 12 (1963), pp. 33–53.

[2] A. García Sanz, 'Coyuntura económica y proyectos de reforma: el gran viraje de 1628'. This contribution to the Toro symposium on the age of Olivares (held in September 1987)
continued

In the long series of Franco-Spanish wars, which provides a kind of *basso ostinato* to early-modern history, disputes over Italy were the fulcrum of policy-making experience for both sides. In a structural or geopolitical sense, the conflict over the Mantuan Succession therefore fits into a familiar pattern of national-dynastic competition. By the mid seventeenth century however, far from becoming mere routine, mutual suspicion was taking on a more intense character, moving into a dimension which was recognizably chauvinistic and even ideological. For many writers the Mantuan War neatly encapsulates all the spiritual and strategic questions at issue between Madrid and Paris. For several scholars, the causal connections between the Mantuan war and the main phase of general Franco-Spanish conflict, the twenty-five year war of attrition which began in 1635, are clear to see. Indeed, such is the number of crucial issues which hinge upon it, the Mantuan crisis appears like some vast sluice, a turbulent point of nature, which many tributaries empty into, flowing out again as a single mighty river of total war.[3]

More than a decade ago these considerations moved J.H. Elliott, the count-duke of Olivares' celebrated modern advocate, to suggest that the origins of the Mantuan crisis were exceptionally worthy of detailed attention.[4] For all the recognition of its importance, however, several key circumstances remain obscure and even perplexing, resistant to wholly satisfactory rational explication. Perhaps the most fascinating enigma resides in the actual decision of Philip IV's government to manufacture a succession issue in the first place, a decision expressed in the unprovoked invasion of a state hitherto not unfriendly to Spain. It may be asserted with emphasis at the outset that, in the context of the traditional behaviour of Spanish policy, it had the characteristics of a sudden, unprecedented and momentous departure – adjectives which do not normally spring to mind in discussion of Spanish

---

continued

appeared in revised form and title in the published proceedings; J.H. Elliott and A. García Sanz (ed.), *La España del conde-duque de Olivares* (Valladolid, 1990).

  Philip IV is quoted in J.H. Elliott, *The Count Duke of Olivares: The Statesman in an Age of Decline* (New Haven and London, 1986), pp. 347–48. Elliott's book presents a broad but typically lucid treatment of the Spanish crisis pp. 323–456, passim. My *Philip IV and the Government of Spain, 1621–65* (Cambridge, 1988), pp. 69–76, 89–102, concentrates on its political dimension. For treatment of the international context, see my *Europe and the Decline of Spain: A Study of the Spanish System, 1580–1720* (1981) pp. 88–114; Ródenas Vilar, *La política española*, pp. 151–93; and E. Straub, *Pax et Imperium: Spaniens Kampf um seine Friedensordnung in Europa zwischen 1617 und 1635* (Paderborn 1980), pp. 327–69. The most detailed diplomatic history of the Mantuan War, set firmly into the Italian context, is R. Quazza's *La guerra per succesione di Mantova e del Monferrato* (Mantua, 1926).

  [3] See below, Chap. 5 and authorities there cited. A subsequent view, however, is more sceptical of the causal connections between the Mantuan War and the general conflict: see D. Parrott, 'The Causes of the Franco-Spanish War of 1635–59', in J. Black (ed.), *The Origins of War in Early-Modern Europe* (Edinburgh, 1987), pp. 72–111.

  [4] J.H. Elliott, *El conde-duque y la herencia de Felipe II* (Valladolid, 1977), p. 94.

Habsburg policy. How was such a radical – and, as it proved, egregious – course of action arrived at?

If less surprising, France's reaction was by no means as predictable as the textbooks suggest – even those more recent surveys, generally less uncritical than their predecessors of Richelieu's projection of himself as the single-minded designer of Habsburg overthrow. The whole Mantuan operation, after all, was an amazingly daring plan, logistically problematic and fraught with imponderables potentially fatal to Richelieu's hopes, from the precarious health of Louis XIII to the dubious military potential – certainly in the international arena – of the royal army. An earlier intervention in Italian affairs (1625) had led to military humiliation and serious setback for Richelieu's political and diplomatic schemes. If this attempt proved painfully premature, the situation four years later seemed even less propitious.[5] What made Richelieu, whose whole position was inherently weak and exposed at this juncture, choose to launch a military challenge to Spain on terrain and in circumstances apparently so favourable to his enemy?

The death of Duke Vincenzo of Mantua took place on St Stephen's Day 1627. A week earlier Don Gonzalo Fernández de Córdoba, governor of Spanish Lombardy, had advised Madrid that this event was imminent. He took the opportunity to remind the king of his warning, issued the previous April, that the duke's asthmatic condition was worsening from the chronic to the acute, and that the doctors believed him unable to survive for long. Don Gonzalo also drew renewed attention to the potentially damaging consequences of this event for Spain's position in Italy, in view of the succession to Mantua of a French nobleman, Charles de Gonzague, duc de Nevers. On the latter question, he expressed a desire to take some form of prophylactic action, reported his request for the emperor's full political support and expressed concern at his own lack of resources for a possible military initiative. This despatch was received in Madrid on 3 January 1628 and discussed two days later by the council of state.[6]

Meanwhile, on 27 December 1627, Don Gonzalo reported the death of Duke Vincenzo and gave details of a provisional agreement, with the representative of the duke of Savoy in Milan, for joint military action. Once this treaty was ratified by Carlo Emanuele, he added: 'I intend immediately to enter with your majesty's arms into Monferrat, and to send a part [of the

---

[5] For France's multiple difficulties – political, military, logistical and financial – before and during the Mantuan War, see (variously) R.J. Bonney, *The King's Debts: Finance and Politics in France, 1589–1661* (Oxford, 1981), pp. 145–48, 162ff; Humbert, *Les Français*, pp. 24–26; Straub, *Pax et Imperium*, pp. 402–7; Parrott 'The Origins', pp. 93–94; Pithon, 'Les débuts difficiles', pp. 315–16.

[6] Fernández de Córdoba to Philip IV, 20 Dec. 1627, AGS, E 3437, no. 1 (here, Don Gonzalo correctly predicted that Duke Vincenzo would die before his letter reached Madrid). See also, draft *consulta* of council of state, 5 Jan. 1628, ibid., K 1445, no. 10.

army of Lombardy] to Mantua [proper] . . . in the name of the emperor.' In asking for urgent clearance for his proposals, Don Gonzalo explicitly assumed – in a crucial remark – that 'should your majesty take some other resolution, *it will be easy to restore* to the duke of Nevers any land which may have been occupied'. Writing to Turin two days earlier, he gave assurances that he was authorized *in advance* by Madrid to prevent any succession to Mantua which had not obtained the emperor's explicit approval, including (if necessary) armed intervention, particularly with regard to Monferrat. Although this authority was not referred to in his home despatches, we may conclude that this was nothing more sinister than a tactical ploy intended to encourage Turin's rapid adhesion to his side, and thus to gain precious time.[7]

On the morning of 11 January a further session of the Spanish council of state was held to discuss the Mantua problem.[8] At the time, the king was staying not in the old Alcázar of Madrid, but in the Pardo, a royal hunting-lodge some fifteen kilometres to the north west of the city. With him was a sufficient group of ministers to permit meetings of *estado*. It was decided that there was no viable alternative to formal acceptance of Nevers' succession to all the lands and rights of the dukedom of Mantua. After attending the meeting, and probably discussing its conclusions privately with Olivares, the king went off to enjoy his afternoon at the chase. Later that day, however, new information arrived from Italy. This comprised Don Gonzalo's letter of 27 December (already described) along with another, providing details of the legally dubious proceedings of Nevers and his family in securing their claim. The same package, doubtless made up in Genoa, contained the duke of Savoy's ratification of the treaty with Milan, direct from Turin.

The count-duke had apparently been satisfied with the conclusions of *Estado* earlier that day, but this news changed his attitude. It now appeared to him that the several infringements of feudal procedures and political protocol by Nevers, committed in attempting to strengthen and secure his claim, were serious enough to justify the emperor in withholding recognition. Until due satisfaction was received for these, and guarantees given for political good behaviour, Philip, acting as imperial executive, could rightfully occupy any part of the fief. Indeed, Olivares reckoned that the king had almost as much cause for wrath over Nevers' actions as had the actual overlord in Vienna. He convinced himself that the rapid deployment of Spanish troops was a valid response to the flagrant discourtesy of Nevers, and that given the support of Savoy for their flank – an exciting piece of opportunism on Don Gonzalo's

[7] Fernández de Córdoba to Philip IV, 27 Dec. 1627, ibid., 3437 no. 1 (my emphasis); same to Duke Carlo Emanuele, 25 Dec. 1627, ibid., K 1436, *carpeta* 1–4.

[8] Unless otherwise noted, information in this and the following two paragraphs is derived or deduced from 'Copia de voto del conde duque [. . .] en la ocasion de la muerte del de Mantua hecho a 12 de Henero 1628', BL Eg. 2053, ff. 232–238v. I have been unable to find any independent record of the council meeting of 11 January. Its absence tends to confirm the actual presence of the king.

part – they could not fail to carry out the exercise.[9] Before Philip retired for the night, Olivares sought another private consultation and placed before him the reasons for his change of mind.

Somewhat – perhaps entirely – to Don Gaspar's surprise, the king proved difficult to persuade. Despite his acute personal respect for proper procedure, Philip perhaps regarded Nevers' sins as too venial to justify an 'overkill' response. At any rate, he failed to react with outraged indignation and remained doubtful that the new information altered the position to the extent that his *valido* argued. Evidently accompanied by an unaccustomed sense of frustration, Olivares went back to his quarters and drafted a memorandum intended for Philip's eyes only. A long and rambling disquisition, it betrays many signs of the cumulative weariness of a long day's hard work. Sitting at his desk probably throughout the night, the count-duke attempted to survey all the complex contingencies of the Italian situation, but sheer mental fatigue precluded any cogency of expression, and at times even obscured the clarity of his conclusions. Even as an example of its author's 'thinking aloud' – a habit increasingly imposed by force of circumstances in the coming years – the document is particularly opaque and resistant to interpretation.

Understandably, but mistakenly, Olivares had inferred from Don Gonzalo's letter of 27 December that he was already in the saddle, despite his lack of orders. Equally erroneously, he seems to have construed his later remarks as an offer to be disavowed in the event of mishap. Olivares, desperate to win his point, in a move which he surely realized was spurious, presented the latter to the king as a cheap insurance against any serious loss of *reputación*. In every other respect the memorandum seems inherently unlikely to have affected Philip's resolve to the extent necessary to produce *outright conviction*, especially on such a complex, delicate and above all momentous matter.

Be this as it may, the king agreed to his chief minister's proposal that an opinion on the ethical justification for action be sought immediately from a *junta de teólogos*. There followed a delay of four days. This represents perhaps the king's own internal tussle after being presented with Olivares' memorandum on the morning of 12 January; or simply the logistical difficulties of assembling a hastily-convened group of clerical advisers of ministerial status to form a *junta de teólogos*. In either case, on or before 15 January the latter gave the Don Gonzalo-Olivares policy a clean bill of ethical health, support which was undoubtedly instrumental in gaining it the king's assent.[10]

To all intents and purposes the decision had now been taken. On 15 January Philip ordered that a *Junta Particular de Estado* should meet on the following

---

[9] Only a few weeks earlier, Olivares had heavily stressed the importance of gaining Savoy's friendship in the struggle to improve the monarchy's overall strategic position; see 'Parezer del conde duque de San Lucar sobre el estado de las cosas en todas partes. En Madrid a cinco de Diziembre de 1627', AGS, E K1435, no. 45.

[10] Letter of Olivares [? n.d.), AGS, E 2331, f. 48, cited by Elliott, *The Count-Duke*, p. 341 and n. 72.

day to review 'the principles which have obliged me to take this resolution'. He nominated the marquises of Montesclaros and La Hinojosa, the counts of Lemos and Monterrey, the duke of Feria, and Alonso Guillén de la Carrera. All these ministers had been broadly supportive of Olivares in previous years, whilst at least three (La Hinojosa, Monterrey and Guillén) might reasonably be described as *olivaristas*. Philip further instructed the secretary of the council of state, Juan de Villela, to make over all the relevant papers to his junior colleague, Gerónimo de la Torre, who was to act as secretary to the new junta. In a remarkable attempt to maintain security, the king added that Villela himself was not to inspect this material, emphasising with unusual force that the junta's proceedings were highly classified. 'Since it is convenient that its business should not be understood, it will proceed with the greatest secrecy and caution . . . doing nothing which may betray its purpose'. The implication of these remarks is that the *Consejo de Estado* itself was not to be informed of proceedings, at least for the time being.[11]

Olivares himself was confident of a favourable reception by the regular junta. A new envoy to France, Lorenzo Ramírez de Prado, had already been nominated, and was standing by for final instructions. These were drafted by a clerk on 15 January. To the list, in the different hand of Olivares's secretary, Antonio Carnero, and initialled by Don Gaspar, was appended an extra instruction: that the envoy should liaise with Guillén de la Carrera, in order to become fully informed of the latest developments over Mantua, prior to his departure.[12] The special 'Mantua' Junta was duly convened by Montesclaros, senior *consejero de estado*, on 16 January. Neither *minutas* nor *consulta* are apparently extant; indeed, although the Junta was still in existence a month later, and certainly met on several further occasions, none of its papers has come down to us. Nonetheless, its inaugural meeting evidently endorsed Philip's decision, for that same day Montesclaros himself drafted the terms of the letter to be sent to Milan.[13] This despatch approved Don Gonzalo's initiative, ordering him to broadcast that Spain was acting purely on behalf of the emperor. He was congratulated on his alliance with Savoy, which – however – it was imperative to keep secret. The crucial importance of the rapid capture of the citadel of Casale was emphasised. All the other states of Italy were to be assured that Spain had no plans for aggression or aggrandisement.

[11] Royal order to Juan de Villela, 15 Jan. 1628, AGS, E K1436, no. 6. For Villela's specific exclusion, see also Olivares's note to him, 13 Feb. 1628, ibid., 3437, no. 28.

[12] 'Lo que vos Don Ramírez de Prado . . .'; and note monogrammed by Olivares, (both) 15 Jan. 1628, AGS, E K1436, nos 8 & 10.

[13] 'Hizola [i.e. the draft order to Milan] el marq[ue]s de Montesclaros', 16 Jan. 1628, AGS, E E3437, no. 8. The missing records of the Mantua Junta were probably among the papers confiscated from the home of Olivares's main administrative functionary, Jerónimo de Villanueva, at the time of his arrest by the Inquisition in 1644: see Elliott, *The Count-Duke* pp. 668–69 and n. 116.

A final version, presumably approved by Olivares, was signed by Philip and despatched to Milan the same day.[14]

Despite careful precautions, within two days the decision was known to a wider circle of ministers than the *Junta de Mantua*. Olivares did not see fit to include the matter on the agenda of the full council of state. But in a discussion held on 18 January by the regular *Junta de Estado*, which reviewed the necessity of sending Ramírez de Prado, it emerged that Agustín Mexía and Fernando Girón (not intimates of the *valido*) were apprised of the details, and that the latter was extremely anxious about them. He opposed the new envoy's departure, arguing that Paris might reject him; 'since we see that things have reached the point that his majesty has been obliged to approve the treaty made between the duke of Savoy and Don Gonzalo, something which – to Don Fernando's understanding – France can only oppose with all its power.'

For different reasons, a majority of the junta, including Montesclaros and Feria, agreed that Don Lorenzo's journey should be delayed. In Olivares' absence, his obviously well-briefed associate, La Hinojosa, interposed to insist that things should go ahead as if nothing was amiss. His *voto* was endorsed by the king's *apostilla*. However, when the envoy finally left nine days later, the king suggested that he proceed slowly, so that messengers from Madrid could ride after and keep him abreast of developments in Italy.[15]

Two more weeks elapsed before the date of our next official information. The *Junta de Estado* met on 12 February; Olivares and six other ministers attended, in what amounted to a full review of the situation.[16] Two members who had not previously registered an opinion, the marquis of Floresdávila and the duke of Alcalá, agreed with Olivares' determination to press ahead. However, Mexía and Girón – who missed the meeting, submitting instead written *votos* from their Madrid homes – displayed powerful reservations. Both these veterans were clearly disturbed over this sudden and risky departure from conventional behaviour and policy norms. Mexía expressed his fear that Don Gonzalo's action would merely provide the French with an unprecedented pretext for armed intervention in Italy, and ruin the possibility of reaching a firm peace. Girón pointed out that international support for Spain was ominously unforthcoming. Even Vienna was taken aback by Madrid's sudden requisitions, whilst Venice and the papacy were already showing signs of rallying to the French. What worried him most of all was that Spain simply did not have the resources for a gratuitous war in Italy. In Don Fernando's view, the king should withdraw gracefully, before his commitment became

[14] Philip IV to Fernández de Córdoba, 16 Jan. 1628 (copy), BN, 2360, ff. 99–100v. See also, note of the same date, AGS, E 3437, no. 6. Don Gonzalo later confirmed the former document as the source of his instructions to go ahead; see his statement of 24 Feb. 1628, AGS, E K1436, no. 15.

[15] *Consulta* of junta of state, 18 Jan. 1628, and royal *apostilla* on *consulta* of junta of state, 27 Jan. 1628, AGS, E K1436, nos 7 and 9.

[16] *Consulta* of junta of state, 12 Feb. 1628, AGS, E 3437, no. 32.

too concrete, and his designs a matter of public knowledge in the courts of Europe.

Philip ignored this counsel, except for a remark that all the Spanish-aligned Italian states should be asked to discharge their duty, and assist Don Gonzalo both materially and morally, on pain of his severe displeasure.[17] The same day he wrote to Milan, confirming Don Gonzalo's orders and looking forward to news of his rapid execution of them. The king's subsequent correspondence assumed – not unreasonably – that the army of Lombardy had already made considerable progress in the occupation of Monferrat. In fact, Fernández de Córdoba's forces were not even to be set in motion for another six weeks.[18]

This was how things stood when, towards the end of February, Ambrogio Spínola, marquis of Los Balbases, arrived in Madrid. In company with his prospective son-in-law (and Olivares' cousin) the marquis of Leganés, Spínola had travelled from the Spanish Netherlands via France, where they had paid a courtesy call upon Louis XIII and Richelieu in their camp at the siege of La Rochelle. Richelieu seized the opportunity to warn his guests that France would not tolerate any meddling in the Mantuan succession, and would support Nevers' claim *à l'outrance*. According to an account later given by Spínola, he passed this message on to king and *valido* as soon as he arrived in Madrid. He urged them, accordingly, to pull back from the brink and rescind the orders sent to Fernández de Córdoba.[19]

Spínola's outright opposition to the Mantuan initiative was of a piece with his determination to press for a negotiated peace in the Low Countries. His main objective was to gain a majority in the *estado* committees on the Flanders issue – despite the clear disfavour of Olivares – but the major ministerial divisions which his activities inspired were adumbrated in the Italian arena. Several councillors, when informed that Don Gonzalo was now actually on the march, accepted that unilateral withdrawal was impossible on the grounds of preserving *reputación*, and recommended waiting on events in Monferrat. But when this information proved premature, the king suddenly appointed Spínola as head of a delegation of ministers to meet the French ambassador, du Fargis.[20]

Somewhat surprisingly, Olivares' anxiety to hush up the whole affair had so far been successful in its main objective. The French ambassador had still not discovered the true state of play. He wrote to Louis XIII on 8 March 'au sujet des mescontentements que les espagnols ont eu a publié d'avoir de M.

[17] Royal *apostilla* on *consulta* of 12 Feb. ibid.

[18] Philip IV to Fernández de Córdoba, 12 Feb. 1628, AGS, E 3437, no. 27. See also Elliott, *The Count-Duke*, p. 343.

[19] A. Rodríguez Villa, *Ambrosio Spínola, primer marques de Los Balbases* (Madrid, 1908), pp. 477–78. Spínola's claim was made over a year later in conversation with the papal nuncio: Elliott, *The Count-Duke*, p. 346–47.

[20] *Consulta* of junta of state, 23 April 1628, AGS, E 2042; royal order of 11 March (dated in error 11 Feb.) 1628, AGS, E K1445, no. 14/15.

de Mantoue, je semble assuré qu'ils ne produiron aucun effect contraire aux intentions de Votre Majesté.'[21]

The period of Spanish initiative was to persist for some time. Nevertheless, the affair was quickly developing into a battle of what today would be called 'intelligence'. At the end of March, exactly at the time that the army of Lombardy at last lurched into motion, Du Fargis became aware that something nasty was afoot. On the 30th, the *Junta de Estado* in Madrid considered Du Fargis' demand for talks on Mantua to defuse what was becoming a dangerous situation. Although this body met in Olivares' *aposento* in the Alcázar, Spínola, as the senior councillor of state present, spoke first. He argued that, without the loss of face involved in actually revoking Don Gonzalo's orders, an agreement with Du Fargis could and should still be reached quickly. Montesclaros and Feria, without explicitly supporting the marquis, evinced extreme nervousness about Don Gonzalo's failure to get on with his operation. Olivares, faced with lukewarm support, and the barely concealed sympathy for Spínola's position present in the *votos* of Lemos and Villela, played for time.[22]

Richelieu was apprised of the movement of Savoyard and (shortly afterwards) of Spanish troops against Monferrat in late March. Yet so preoccupied was the cardinal with the siege of La Rochelle – which he had promised his master would be over by the end of April – that he seems to have had no time for mature consideration of the matter until several weeks later. The overall weakness of the French strategic position obliged him to insist, both before and after this date, that no servant of Louis XIII should react in any way which might offer further provocation or justification to the Spaniards.[23] On 19 April he asked Du Fargis to take up Olivares' offer to discuss the case with a view to a compromise. The ambassador was to point out that the existing Franco-Spanish treaty (of Monzón, 1626) enjoined such a procedure; the Cardinal added, 'je vous prie encore un fois, dire à M. le conte d'Olivarez, de mon part, qu'il y a plus à gaigner avec nous que la despouille de M. de Mantoue'.[24]

---

[21] Du Fargis to Louis XIII, 8 March 1628, AAE, CE 15, f. 168v. The former's complaisance was doubtless due to the fact that he had been accredited to Madrid continuously since 1620. He was a follower of the pro-Spanish *dévot* line of Cardinal Bérulle, and had been deeply involved in the negotiations of 1626–27, with their strongly fraternal overtones, about which Richelieu was so equivocal, Pithon, 'Les débuts difficiles', pp. 317–21.

[22] *Consulta* of junta of state, 30 March 1628, AGS, E K1436, no. 25.

[23] Longueville to Richelieu, 26 March 1628, P. Grillon (ed.), *Les papiers de Richelieu: section politique intérieure* (6 vols, Paris, 1975–85), iii, p. 141 (see also, pp. 209–10); M. Avenel (ed.), *Lettres, instructions diplomatiques et papiers d'état du Cardinal Richelieu*, iii (Paris, 1858), pp. 33–34.

[24] Richelieu to du Fargis, 19 Apr. 1628, Avenel, *Lettres*, iii, p. 74; a Spanish copy of this despatch is at AGS, E K1436, no. 26 ('yo os suplico hablar desto libremente y francamente de mi parte al Snr Conde de Olivares y dezirle que ay mas ganancia en la unión de las dos coronas que en la empresa de desposseer Mons. de Mantua'). The contents of this interception can only have encouraged Olivares's belief in the paralysis of Paris.

Despite this publicly cautious – almost suppliant – demeanour, Richelieu's relevant memorandum of advice to the king, compiled (according to expert opinion) 'around 20 April', makes clear his strong inclination to oppose Madrid by force unless an honourable compromise, based on the military withdrawal of the invaders, could be arranged. He opined that the Spaniards had no intention of maintaining the negotiations for a new treaty of alliance except as a diversionary tactic. He assured the king that the fortress of Casale would be able to hold out for a considerable time, and estimated the size and nature of the force that Louis would need for intervention. By the end of April fresh troops, intended as the core of a relieving expedition to Italy, were already being raised in eastern France.[25]

Once taken, the cardinal's decisions bore out his warning to Spínola in January that France would support Nevers come what may. All the same, and even in the circumstances of his profound preoccupation with La Rochelle, his long official silence on the point – some three weeks of apparent meditation – is intriguing. Herr Straub has argued that the cardinal, painfully conscious of France's weakness and the difficulties involved in action, was inclined to overlook the events in Monferrat so long as the dukedom of Mantua *proper* was left unimpeded to Nevers' succession.[26] M. Grillon seems to imply that Richelieu's resolution was stiffened by the emotional appeal made, towards the end of this hiatus, by Nevers' sister, the duchess of Longueville, addressing him in terms ('unique et miraculeux cardinal') which closely anticipate the hero-worship of later French historians.[27] But it seems likely that the flinty sanctions of internal politics were rather more efficacious in sharpening Richelieu's determination.

Duke Charles of Nevers was already one of the most powerful of the great French landed magnates.[28] For nearly forty years he had been governor of the rich and strategically vital frontier province of Champagne. Consequently, by a long process of accretion, an area which – as Richelieu did not neglect to point out to Louis – afforded a primary route for any Habsburg invasion had become in many respects his political fiefdom. To add to these qualities, Nevers enjoyed an unique dynastic distinction which quite overshadowed his Mantuan pretensions. Descended on his father's side form the Palaeologi, he nurtured a claim to the empire of the East which was officially recognized by the Christian authorities of Greece. A decade before the events which form the subject of the present essay, he had revived this claim in response to the

---

[25] Richelieu to Louis XIII, 'vers le 20 avril', Avenel, *Lettres*, iii, pp. 78–85; see also Grillon, *Les papiers*, iii, p. 236.

[26] Straub, *Pax et imperium*, p. 348.

[27] Grillon, *Les papiers*, iii, p. 189.

[28] J. Bergin, *Cardinal Richelieu: Power and the Pursuit of Wealth* (New Haven and London, 1985), p. 68, refers to Nevers as a member of one of the 'leading aristocratic families', on par with the Guises. O. Lublinskaya, *French Absolutism*, calls him 'one of the most important of the grandees' (p. 244). See also Bonney, *King's Debts*, p. 76.

visit of a delegation from the Morea which had promised a full-scale Christian rebellion in his favour, if only he could mount a sufficiently powerful crusade. In close association with Richelieu's future adviser, Père Joseph du Tremblay, Duke Charles had made impressive efforts in this direction. Although failing to elicit formal commitment from any of the great courts, and receiving only a rather non-commital blessing from Rome, he had attracted a good deal of private support from individual would-be Rolands, and many joined his new order of Paladins, the Christian militia. In the period before the outbreak of general European war in 1618–21, his material preparations for a crusading expedition attracted considerable European attention. It was in this cause that du Tremblay made a celebrated pilgrimage to Madrid and held discussions with the duke of Lerma.[29]

Nevers' ambitions had been betrayed in several earlier adventures. As recently as 1626 he had become involved in the intrigues over the marriage of Gaston d'Orléans, the king's brother and heir. Though apparently unsympathetic to the more unruly pretensions of Gaston, like all his peers, he placed a high priority on preserving a residual freedom of political action, the sanctions of family honour and the order-code forbidding any clear subordination to the king's (lower-caste) minister. Duke Charles would certainly have been an extremely useful recruit to the noble faction which, within a year or so, was to begin forming in opposition to Richelieu, around the axis of Gaston and the queen mother, Marie de Médicis. It was said that the latter nurtured a strong distaste for Nevers arising from an ancient insult. More recently, however, Gaston had begun to make seductive overtures to the Gonzague connection – quite literally so, for (following the sudden death of his first wife) he had clandestinely proposed to Nevers' daughter, a development which held out a dazzling prospect in the constantly impending event of Louis XIII's death.[30]

Despite the disapproval of Louis XIII and Richelieu of this match, Nevers was attracted and flattered by the attention of the heir to the throne. Some evidence exists that, in the weeks immediately preceding the demise of Duke Vincenzo of Mantua, he had privately responded in a manner which was not unpromising from Gaston's viewpoint.[31] It complicated matters considerably that at this very time (winter 1627–28) Nevers was raising fresh

[29] G. Dethan, 'Nationalisme et idée de croisade au XVIIe siècle', *Revue d'histoire diplomatique*, 124 (1960), pp. 289–97; A. Huxley, *Grey Eminence* (1930), pp. 104–18.

[30] Bonney, *King's Debts*, pp. 148–50; Tapié, *La France*, p. 197.

[31] Nevers (Charleville) to Marie des Médicis, 6 Nov., and to Gaston d'Orléans, 8, 19 and 20 Dec. 1627, AN, SHE KK 1358 (*registre* on microfilm), ff. 295–302. These letters are incorrectly ascribed in the temporary catalogue available in the Salle Clisson, and seem to have been overlooked by historians of French politics in this period. The letter to the queen mother (in her capacity as regent of northern France during her son's absence at La Rochelle) warns about the dangers of denuding Champagne of men when hostile military activity has already been reported on its frontiers. The letters to Gaston largely concern mutual clients and appointments to commands in the Champagne regiments. But they also indicate an increasing degree of reciprocity in favours asked and granted, and (especially notable) an eagerness on Nevers' part to end his estrangement from Marie de Médicis.

troops, ostensibly for the reinforcement of the royal army at La Rochelle.[32] Concurrently with these events, he was activating a rapid sequence of moves in Mantua to safeguard his inheritance – including marrying his son, the duke of Retel, with unlawful haste to the only surviving princess of the Italian Gonzagas. It was possible, especially when looked at from the cardinal's viewpoint, that Nevers was quietly preparing the ground for a shift of alliance towards Gaston, and even towards the overall protection of the Habsburgs, a move which (in any case) he might have construed as indispensable for his peaceful succession in Mantua. If all went well – and especially were Louis to die childless – the dynastic network of estates, offices and connections built up by Nevers might provide the basis for his even greater aspirations, thus reviving a movement which still had substantial (if later) support from various elements all over Counter-Reformation Europe, and indeed beyond. As things actually worked out during the early months of 1628 Nevers' tactical errors, and the precipitate Spanish reaction, afforded Richelieu an opportunity to abort such unwelcome developments.

Even if Nevers had no serious intentions along the lines indicated above, the refusal of Louis to support his cause would surely have encouraged them. If nothing else, abandoning Nevers to his fate might have offered an ominous precedent to the other magnates, who might consequently have felt obliged to review their existing support of the Richelieu ministry. In all the circumstances, the pressure to extend unconditional and unlimited support to Nevers over Mantua could hardly have been more intense. To act otherwise would have constituted an appalling gamble with the patience of the noble grandees, and therefore a more immediate threat to the security of government and kingdom than anything represented by action in Italy. In early May, possibly before the date of his keynote memorandum to the king, Marie de Médicis – Nevers' alleged mortal enemy – wrote to Richelieu supporting his request for aid 'le plus prompte qu'il se pourra'; informing the cardinal that 'le roi ait agréable de recevoir sa démission du gouvernement de Champagne et le donner a mon nepveu le duc de Maine, son fils'. A three-way deal, the details and significance of which are at present elusive, had obviously been struck. Accordingly, Richelieu informed Louis that the Spanish action constituted open war against one of his subjects and therefore, unequivocally, against the king himself.[33]

By now, in a Madrid atmosphere of mounting tension, Olivares and Spínola had openly adopted adversarial positions. As the army of Lombardy finally

[32] Grillon, *Les papiers*, iii, pp. 209–10; Avenel, *Lettres*, iii, p. 127. It was appropriate that the men raised by Nevers took part in the invasion of Savoy a year later: ibid., p. 312.

[33] Marie des Médicis to Richelieu, 4 May 1628, Grillon, *Les papiers*, iii, p. 263 (see also, pp. 209–10). Until now puzzlement has centred on the reason for Marie's support of the second, follow-up campaign in Italy in 1630; see (e.g.) Tapié, *La France de Louis XIII*, p. 209. She is held to have been resolutely opposed to the initial intervention; see (e.g.) Bonney, *King's Debts*, pp. 148–50.

settled down to besiege Casale, and Olivares opened negotiations with du Fargis, at least four members of the regular *Junta de Estado* broadly supported Spínola on the Italian issue. The king followed the argument very closely, on one occasion placing hatch marks in the margin of a *consulta* alongside the combative contributions of the two main protagonists.[34] In June it emerged that Olivares had offered Du Fargis a compromise, based on major concessions by Nevers, guaranteeing Spain's strategic position in Lombardy, providing formal satisfaction for his *faltas de etiqueta* to Ferdinand II, and for Carlo Emanuele a satisfactory dividend on his risky investment. Feria and Montesclaros opposed this from a 'hawkish' position, believing that any terms could only be discussed with honour once Spain was actually in possession of Casale. Spínola and his allies also opposed it, on the more sensitive grounds that any agreement made between the powers in Madrid might be rejected by (the unconsulted) Nevers himself. Only Leganés, a young minister with painfully divided loyalties, stood firmly at his cousin's side. An even younger but longer-serving *olivarista* found this impossible. For the first time Philip's *apostilla* failed to support Olivares. Instead he expressed sympathy for the views of Girón, who along with Villela and the marquis of Santa Cruz had backed Spínola's position.[35]

In their details, at least, these debates were only of academic interest to Richelieu. Full of outrage at Olivares' audacity, he ordered Du Fargis on no account to sign anything put before him by the *valido*. The Spanish offer had been discussed by Louis XIII's *counseil privé* on 21 May, at which it was pointed out that it represented a demand 'que le Roy abandonne la protection ou la assistance de M. de Mantoue pour le Montferrat et le laisse prendre par l'empereur'; and would oblige Nevers – after all a subject of the king of France – 'a faire hommage au Roy d'Espagne'. Richelieu's attitude was in effect the same as that of Spínola, for he insisted that the new duke be consulted over negotiations, and informed Du Fargis that discussion in Paris, in which he was engaged personally with a Spanish team consisting of the marquis of Mirabel (resident ambassador) and Ramírez de Prado, and which might produce more reasonable terms, were to take priority. He added that an army of 20,000 men would be ready to advance into Italy as soon as La Rochelle surrendered; until then the situation demanded 'un grand finesse'.[36]

Perhaps as a result of their personal meeting, and doubtless having been the recipient of some useful advice on the conduct of sieges from the greatest living expert, Richelieu had taken a close interest in Spínola's fortunes in Madrid. Around this time he was apprised of the *disgusto* between Spínola and Olivares,

---

[34] *Consulta* of junta of state, 22 April 1628, AGS, E K1436, no. 27 (see also nos 28 and 37, which illustrate Olivares's increasing isolation, despite the fact that meetings were held in his own chambers in the palace).

[35] *Consulta* of junta of state and royal *apostilla*, 5 July 1628, ibid., no. 53.

[36] Draft notes for *conseil* discussions of 21 May 1628, AAE, CE 15, ff. 172–73, 202–8; Richelieu to Du Fargis, 4 June 1628, and Louis XIII to same, 27 July 1628, ibid., ff. 179–180v, 195.

and of the emergence of factional divisions amongst Philip's councillors. The latter information shortly assumed such a detailed aspect that it could only have come from an informed source within the Madrid government. In July, when making marginal notes upon a further set of proposals emanating from the Spanish side, Richelieu was able to identify specific points upon which 'messrs. du Conseil Despagne' had disagreed, which he could consequently exploit in negotiation. Moreover, news had reached him, via an intercepted letter of Spínola's intimate assistant, Carlo Strata, of the former's close political alliance with Girón and other ministers in opposition to Olivares. Little wonder that the 1630s were to see Olivares at times reaching his wits' end at the continuous and apparently irremediable breaches of security in the Spanish system. From this point onwards, the cardinal held the initiative in the 'intelligence war'.[37]

This advantage encouraged Richelieu's tactic of playing for time. The failure of his predictions over the fall of La Rochelle were partly compensated by his prescience about the survival of Casale. On the other hand, whilst La Rochelle held out, and England continued to assemble a new relieving expedition, his position remained essentially weak. That of Olivares was conversely still dominant: at any time in the summer the count-duke could have decided to cut his losses and pull out of Monferrat, using any number of more-or-less convincing pretexts, and with an apology from Nevers sufficient to preclude serious loss of *reputación*. By midsummer, indeed, Philip himself – never a convinced backer of the Mantuan venture – had understandably lost patience and was pressing for an expedient exercise in damage-limitation. On 8 July, after reading the record of another squabble in the junta, he demanded that 'if the ambassador can be brought to sign [the compromise], well and good; if not, it should be sent to Mirabel so that he can press the terms as they stand with full powers to sign; and it would be well for the marquis [Mirabel] to speak a little frankly in persuading the French to agree'.[38]

Two weeks later Philip penned an angry note on another *consulta* in which Olivares confronted criticism concerning discussions with Du Fargis:

> The dilatoriness of this junta has brought about the waste of an opportunity to reach the best agreement discussed so far. Many times I have told it to deliberate well, but to aim at taking a concrete resolution on this issue. [But now] the ambassador does not wish to sign this paper, and thus there is nothing left to say.[39]

---

[37] Paulo de Fiesci to M. de Hesbaules, Madrid 6 March 1628, ff. 150–51; Carlo Strata to Filippo Spínola, 12 June 1628, ff. 181–82v. (interception); Richelieu's marginal notes on copies of Olivares's proposals (? July 1628), f. 203: all AAE, CE 15. The English state papers for the 1620s contain several such 'leaks' from the headquarters of the Spanish system, PRO, SP 94/24–33 passim. Strata's letter also allowed Paris an insight into the nature of Spínola's quarrel with Olivares, which had ominous financial implications; see my *Philip IV*, pp. 71–72.

[38] Royal *apostilla* on *consulta* of the junta of state, 8 July 1628, AGS, E K1436, no. 57.

[39] Royal *apostilla* on *consulta* of junta of state, 23 July 1628, AGS, E K1436, no. 68.

It is not clear whether the king's anger was directed at all his junta ministers, including its convener, Olivares; or whether, alternatively, it resulted from an attempt by the latter to convince Philip that it was the junta's recalcitrant majority which had vitiated agreement, despite his own honest efforts. If the latter, reality was certainly otherwise, for – as we have seen – Du Fargis was firmly instructed to sign nothing put to him in Madrid. Richelieu may not have fooled Olivares; it is more than possible that the *valido* guessed at Du Fargis' instructions. In any case, it is evident that throughout the early summer he confidently expected news of the fall of Casale to arrive at any moment. The net result was seen in early August, when *for the first time* the whole matter was aired in the full council of state, and Philip noted that in the circumstances it was necessary to provide as much assistance as possible for the army of Lombardy in its siege of Casale.[40]

The collapse of talks with Du Fargis worried Philip all the more since on the same day information reached Madrid of the existence of a French army apparently preparing to march against Savoy. Du Fargis meanwhile reported that an English fleet had been sighted heading for La Rochelle. Olivares seized the opportunity for a deal. He offered the French twenty Spanish warships, to use as they wished, if Louis would explicitly renounce the idea of military intervention in Italy. The alarm concerning an English expedition proved false, but the offer would certainly have been rejected anyway. It was now autumn and the Italian rains had set in, with Casale still in Nevers' hands. Perhaps for the first time glimpsing the horrific prospect of failure, Olivares sent a highly choleric letter to Du Fargis. He complained that 'France's behaviour in this whole affair represents something to which she has never stooped before'. He added that the army of Lombardy's campaign in Monferrat was a kind of police operation, 'non contre un enemie comun et etrangère, mais contre un particuliér et domestique comme l'affaire de La Rochelle'.[41]

On 28 October Richelieu solved *his* private and domestic affair with the capitulation of La Rochelle. Not long afterwards, and several weeks ahead of Madrid, Paris learned (via its Dutch ally) of the entire capture of the Spanish treasure fleet at Matanzas Bay on 8 September. Instructions for a new envoy (M. de Bautru) which had been undergoing constant amendment, could now be finalized. In the circumstances, the terms brought to Madrid

---

[40] *Consulta* of council of state, 3 Aug. 1628, AGS, E K1436, no. 81.

[41] Note of Olivares to Villela, 22 July 1628, AGS, E K1436, no. 66; Du Fargis to Richelieu enclosing Olivares's note of 20 Sept. 1628, AAE, CE 15, ff. 251–53v. Upon the original of Du Fargis's memo, a nineteenth-century patriotic pencil has ringed the word *domestique*. It seems that Olivares did not share the information about the French preparations with the junta of state until nearly six months later. This subterfuge was certainly inspired by the urgent need not to further damage confidence in his Italian policy among ministers, *consulta* of 7 Jan. 1629, AGS, E K1437, no. 9, cited by Elliott, *The Count-Duke*, p. 365.

on 26 November were remarkably reasonable.[42] Though he was still not satisfied with them, Olivares was now in more accommodating mood. He even managed some of his own brand of *galanterie de gauche*. In Bautru's words, 'il s'estonnoit que Monsieur le Cardinal ne devenoit fol des Joyes de voir son maistre dans La Rochelle ayant la part qu'il a l'honneur d'avoir dans la confieures et dans ses Conseilles. Il repette par trois fois "yo me espanto que no se aya vuelto loco"'.[43]

The cardinal, resistant to flattery from such a direction, found Olivares' reservations about his scheme unacceptable. He told Bautru in early December that 'Sa M[ajes]tie n'a point changé les resolutions qu'elle a prise lors de vostre parlement'; adding, ominously, that 'le Roy fait estat d'avoir dans 15 jours vingt mille hommes de pied, et deux mil chevaux, sur la frontière d'Italie pour secourir Casal'.[44]

Olivares' technique of negotiation had been as clumsy and as self-revealing as his attempt at badinage, and the last of many chances, with the last weeks of a year of missed opportunities, slipped away. As its fateful successor supervened, the emphasis and dynamic of negotiations altered sharply. In a complete reversal of roles, now the Spaniards pressed – with mounting panic – for an agreement aimed at deflecting the forthcoming French blow, while Paris procrastinated. Just as so many other aspects of the case had earlier been mismanaged, Madrid now miscalculated the scheduling and extent of French intervention. Before the end of February, breaking all the unwritten rules of combat, whilst the snows were yet unmelted and to the astonishment of their enemies, Louis and Richelieu crossed the Alps and proceeded to wreak almost unprecedented damage upon *reputación*.[45]

Philip IV was furious, reproachful and remorseful. The humiliating loss of the silver-fleet was still a fresh wound, when the salt of the Susa armistice

---

[42] The crux was that Spain would choose from a number of suggested neutral authorities to occupy Casale, while Nevers made the requisite apologies, and gave Madrid undertakings as to his future conduct as duke of Mantua. From Richelieu's point of view, the offer 'semble très quitable et très avantaguese pour les Espagnols, puisque en effet Monsieur de Montuoe se despouille de son propre', AAE, CE 15, ff. 193–194. But Spain's *reputación* did not permit acceptance of this compromise; the French proposals meant that Philip still would have had to retire his army – in humiliation, if not unambiguous defeat – from the walls of Casale.

[43] Bautru to Louis XIII, 27 Nov. 1628, AAE, CE 15, ff. 285–85v. Bautru was Richelieu's replacement for the unreliable Du Fargis. For the evolution of his instructions, and drafts of other French versions of a compromise to be discussed in Paris and/or Madrid, see ibid., ff. 153–56, 163–64, 172, 193–94, 267. Bautru's mission was described as 'de faire un sorte avec le Sr D'Olivares que le differend de Casal et troubles d'Italie se terminant à l'amiable par l'entremise des deux Roys'.

[44] Richelieu to Bautru, 7 Dec. 1628, AAE, CE 15, f. 323. (N.b. The last three words of this quotation are crossed out in this draft copy.)

[45] See Bautru's reports of his audiences with Olivares of 1, 8 and 10 Dec. 1628, and the 'Projet d'accomodement sur les affaires d'Italie dressé par les Espagnols', 30 Jan. 1629, AAE, CE 15, ff. 294, 298, 304, 365.

and of Don Gonzalo's withdrawal from Monferrat was rubbed into it. Like the commander Benavides who had lost his ships at Matanzas, and whom the king was subsequently, and with marked personal determination, to bring to the scaffold for cowardice, Philip was trapped between powerfully conflicting emotions. Now he really wished to fight, yet the enemy held the advantage on the field and no reinforcements were immediately available.[46] Defeat in Italy would represent an appalling reverse for his monarchy. Yet merely one cost of resistance was a morally sordid agreement of his government to provide aid for the French Protestant rebels, which profoundly disturbed the king, despite his theologians' tactical reassurances. In the circumstances, perhaps it would be better to offer an honest concession, an admission of error, in order to avoid the greater calamity of outright conflict with his cousin, king of a Catholic state whose interests might yet be reconciled with those of Spain. Philip and Juan de Villela, possibly with the connivance of Spínola, drew up a document which, given all the events which had developed from the first decision to attack Mantua, amounted to little less than a surrender.

> In the interests of Christendom and for the peace and tranquillity of Italy, which I have always desired and worked for, I declare that neither now nor in the future will I do anything to impede the duke of Nevers' possession of the dukedoms of Mantua and Monferrat, nor will I threaten in any way the territories of the Christian King or those of his princes and confederates. The said king will [in return] make a similar declaration and will retire his army from Monferrat, Susa, Piamonte and Italy. I promise and swear on my faith and royal word, to observe this and maintain it firmly and truthfully for ever.[47]

Louis XIII appears to have rejected this overture. One of the longest and most geographically extensive wars ever waged in Europe between two of its major

---

[46] The council of state at first advised Philip not to ratify the truce made at Susa by Don Gonzalo; and the king entered an unusually vitriolic and belligerent *apostilla*. Nevertheless he also accepted that circumstances forbade the corollary of open war with France, *consulta* of 28 April 1629, AGS, E 3436, printed in M. Fernández Alvarez, *Don Gonzalo Fernández de Córdoba y la guerra de sucesión de Mantua y del Monferrato, 1627–1629* (Madrid, 1955), pp. 168–98.

[47] I have seen no fewer than four copies of this document, but have been unable to locate one at Simancas among the official files: (1) in Spanish, but with the endorsement 'Ratification du Roy d'Esp. de l'accord fait entre le roy [Louis XIII] et Don Gonzales, 1629', PRO, SP 94/34 f. 83; (2) 'Declaración que ha hecho S[u] M[agestad] sobre las cosas de Mantua y Monferrato', BN, 2361, f. 213; (3) untitled, in Spanish, AAE, CE 15, f. 462; and (4) a copy in Italian immediately consecutive to (3). The first two are dated 3 May 1629, and the latter two have a day later. Yet another copy exists in the Vatican Library (MS Barberini 3558, f. 61), suggesting some kind of papal mediation of this *démarche*. Technically, the offer represented a return to the *status quo ante bellum* and the secret arrangements of the treaty of Monzón. But it could only have been perceived in international terms as a Spanish climb-down of proportions approaching outright capitulation.

Copies of Spain's treaty with the Huguenot duke of Rohan (3 March 1629) are also apparently missing from the official files at Simancas but can be found in Paris and London, in the two volumes already cited here: PRO, SP 93/94, ff. 55–58; AAE, CE 15, ff. 452–461.

powers duly began, a conflict which was to be unmistakably of formative importance in the evolution of the secular state system. Though hopes of a crusade against the Ottoman were never wholly extinguished, even in the darkest days, it was somehow ironically appropriate for the future of Europe that the heir to Christian Byzantium, a plausible figurehead for a revived and united Christendom in arms, had been the inadvertent cause of its definitive frustration.

4

Mantua Preserv'd
or
The Tragicall Historie of
Count Olivarez,
Great Favorite of Spayne

This play is the image of a murder done in Vienna: Gonzago is the duke's name . . . the story is extant and writ in very choice Italian.

(*Hamlet*, III, 2)

Prologue

In some aspect, direct or otherwise, the 'Thirty Years' War' between France and Spain influenced the lives of most western Europeans in the middle decades of the seventeenth century (1629–59). It is no accident that these years witnessed a wave of European disturbances, an arguably unitary phenomenon which has been the terrain of one of the most frustrating and fertile of all historiographical debates. Less contentiously, the Franco-Spanish War is seen as forming the core of the Spanish monarchy's struggle to maintain its hegemonic position, and of the French campaign to undermine it, events which themselves evolved in a continuum of no less than half a century (1618–68). The universal significance of the issues at stake was as assiduously discussed by contemporaries as the war's consequences have been by historians. The geo-political circumstances of its origins, its ideological resonances and its economic and military ramifications are thus the subjects of repeated study.[1]

The Bourbon and Habsburg courts, where the relevant decisions were taken, were institutions which had developed an intense collective self-awareness. The transcendent importance of kings and favourites, and of their immediate social context, was celebrated and renewed, not only by increasingly elaborate household rituals, but by the artefacts which littered its environment. A uniquely vibrant political meaning was conveyed by ubiquitous public

---

[1] J.H. Elliott, *The Count-Duke of Olivares* (1986), pp. 278–386, provides the most detailed treatment of the historical background. A stimulating intellectual context is to be found in Maravall, *La cultura del barroco* (2nd edn, Madrid, 1980), esp. pp. 131–306, 453.

reference to the mythic-heroic narratives of polite post-Renaissance culture. All the Baroque arts of emphasis – hyperbole, metaphor, allegory and a hundred other devices – were continuously at work in the double function of massaging the sensibility of the political centre and reflecting it to the outside world. Louis XIII and Richelieu, Philip IV and Olivares – not to mention lesser functionaries through whom the cultural/structural protagonism of France and Spain was articulated – frequently expressed personal appreciation of the momentousness of things, their intimate and at times overwhelming sense of the epic reality of their own actions.[2]

In what follows, the context of *l'histoire événementielle* is provided by the so-called War of the Mantuan Succession, now seen more as the opening phase of the greater conflict than as an autonomous event. An attempt is made – partial in nature and avowedly experimental in tone – to shift the ground of analysis away from the strictly empirical towards the discrete area of textual comment, and the literary presentation of these events to history. From the distinct yet irremediable interaction of these discourses, it is clear that the reportage of events, often virtually simultaneous – even in this period – with the events themselves, conditioned perception, because a premediated historical meaning was inscribed in them. Above all, the contemporary discourse of mediation was an inherently *dramatic* one, arising inevitably from the consciously theatrical self-perception of the Baroque political mentality.

Act One: Behind the Scenes

During the course of 1628 it became clear that Madrid's attempt to challenge the claim of the French nobleman, Charles de Gonzague, duke of Nevers, to the succession of Mantua and Monferrat, had gone badly awry. As a result, the count-duke of Olivares's nightmare had been realized. Spain's allies in Vienna, fundamental to his strategic vision, had failed to cooperate in any effective manner. Louis XIII and Richelieu were preparing for military intervention in northern Italy, a venture in which they enjoyed at least the moral support of all the other interested states, including the Vatican. This obdurate miscalculation in policy, provoking a range of negative reactions within the Castilian ruling class, from dismay to outright opposition, coincided with the emergence at court of a tangible threat to Olivares' ministerial primacy. Other unresolved intra-administrative disputes over 'domestic' policy were reaching their points of maximum tension in the corridors of power. Meanwhile, as it were in the background, outside the walls of the palace, pressure on Olivares' government

[2] J. Brown and J.H. Elliott, *A Palace for a King* (New Haven, 1980); H. R. Trevor-Roper, *Princes and Artists* (1970); G. Davies, *A Poet at Court: Antonio Hurtado de Mendoza, 1586–1644* (London, 1976); R.G. Trewinnard 'The Household of the Spanish Monarchs' (unpublished Ph.D. University of Wales, 1991). For the sociology of the so-called 'Baroque' court, N. Elias, *The Court Society* (Oxford, 1983).

was increased by a sudden deterioration in the social and economic conditions of Castile.[3]

In precisely the same period, King Philip IV emerged from behind the conciliar arras – literally and metaphorically – to take a more active role. In the late summer of 1627 he had suffered a near-fatal bout of illness. Olivares expected at any moment to be called on to make obeisance to a new monarch, Don Carlos, the king's brother. He felt the cold wind of conspiracy blowing through the Alcázar, and was able to identify the leaders of a court faction intent on removing him from office. Meanwhile, the king's character had been rapidly matured. Shortly after his recovery, he began to draft memoranda on policy, which were independent of his *valido* in both creation and content. By the end of 1628 it seems that Philip was regularly taking the chair at *Consejo de Estado* meetings in his chambers. His discharge of this function was, indeed, described at this time by the dramatist-courtier, Hurtado de Mendoza.[4]

The king's new political profile was to receive its essential expression in an active military career. Before the end of 1628 Philip was demanding the fulfilment of his role as commander, specifically in the campaign theatre of Lombardy, familiar terrain in so much Ancient and Renaissance history – not least in the pages of Francesco Guicciardini, the historian whose work Philip was currently translating into Castilian. As Olivares' ill-luck would have it, Ambrogio Spínola, marquis of Los Balbases, the most celebrated soldier in Christendom, and an experienced administrator at the highest level, arrived at court in the immediate wake of these developments (February 1628). Before long, Olivares was able to convince himself that most of Spain's current military disasters were the result of the latter's influence with the king.[5]

Spínola had come primarily to effect a radical change in policy, by persuading Philip and his government to make a compromise peace with the United Provinces. The issue was fundamental to Olivares' whole conception of his political mission. The signs are that he was prepared to make it an issue of loyalty in his fellow-ministers and of confidence in the king. Despite this, in the course of that spring and summer, a majority of councillors deserted him on the Low Countries' question and were ultimately joined by Philip himself. Moreover. the king had never been convinced of the moral legitimacy of military action in Italy, and here too Spínola's criticism elicited considerable support.[6] Without question, the marquis was a minister capable

---

[3] J.H. Elliott and F. de la Peña, *Memoriales y cortes del conde-duque de Olivares* (2 vols, Madrid, 1978–81), i, pp. 211–28; V. Pérez Moreda, *Las crisis de mortalidad en la España interior, siglos XVI–XIX* (Madrid, 1980), pp. 109, 121, 299–300; A.V. Ebersole, *Dos documentos de 1627 sobre la economía de España* (Valencia, 1986).

[4] J.H. Elliott, *Richelieu and Olivares* (Cambridge, 1984), pp. 100–4; Davies, *A Poet at Court*, p. 38.

[5] See Chap. 12 below. On Philip's studies of Guicciardini, see my *Philip IV*, esp. pp. 307–13. For Olivares' most unrestrained attack on Spínola, see 'El conde duque de San Lúcar, voto en las cosas de Italia' (? Aug. 1630), BN, 988, ff. 262–77.

[6] See Chap. 3 above.

of designing policy in the round, on financial and fiscal issues as well as those of imperial defence. Philip was listening to an alternative voice. No evidence exists that the latter aspired to the *valimiento* itself, and in any case his origins as a Genoese banker rendered him quite unacceptable in such a role to the political society of Castile. Nevertheless, at least during Spínola's stay in Madrid (March 1628–July 1629) the monopolistic circumstances of Olivares' personal ministry were effectively suspended. Indeed, the hiatus almost certainly persisted as far as the resolution of the king-*valido* relationship in early 1630. *In relative terms* – that is in comparison with the chronological phases located before and after this crisis – the extent of the power Olivares wielded was limited.[7]

The count-duke reached his most vulnerable point in the months following March 1629, when the French, led in person by Louis XIII, and to Philip's extreme perturbation, achieved their military breakthrough in Italy. Olivares cast about desperately for the means to defend himself. As was to become his usual practice, he looked for a convenient scapegoat, and decided on the initial projector of military action, Gonzalo Fernández de Córdoba, who was accordingly relieved of his post as governor and commander in Lombardy. Olivares claimed that Don Gonzalo had acted in excess of his instructions, not only in reaching an offensive alliance with Savoy for the partition of Monferrat – the strategic objective of the whole exercise – but in setting his troops in motion at all. The commander in the field it was (as so often in Olivares' judgement) whose insubordination and military ineptitude represented a fatal combination.

Olivares' indictment was answered by his intended victim's formal *reacusación*. The dispute, involving as it did a direct collision between two of its members, obliged the council of state to a rare exercise of its judicial capacity – to act, in effect, as an *audiencia* of the plaintiff's peers. On this occasion, the *valido's* proceedings, even including his failure to consult the council itself (as such) over the original decision, were retrospectively approved. With only one dissenting voice, *Estado* found his conduct to have been above reproach. Philip himself concurred with this judgement, ordering the secretary of the council to convey his personal assurance of confidence to Olivares. On the other hand, the king may have been conscious of the evil necessity of this 'whitewash'; for it is notable that, within a respectable period, Olivares' case against Don Gonzalo was quietly dropped.[8]

Despite *Estado's* exoneration, evidence of Olivares' complicity in the Mantua decision, and of his administrative shortcomings in coping with its consequences – provided by the bitter and vengeful Don Gonzalo – found its way into a document inspired (and possibly written) by his brother, the duke

---

[7] Stradling, *Philip IV*, pp. 70–75, 92–102.

[8] M. Fernandez Alvarez, *Gonzalo Fernández de Córdoba* (Madrid, 1955), pp. 110–11, 116. (It seems likely that the lone conciliar dissentient was Spínola himself.)

of Sessa.[9] This represented the first serious public attack upon the count-duke; it was well-informed on a broad range of government activities, and acute in some of its conclusions. In it the Mantuan episode was held up as a typical example of the *valido's* megalomania and myopia. It was characteristic of a mesmeric figure, who dominated the person of the monarch and reduced him to the role of a 'ceremonial king'. Moreover (it was argued) the favourite had replaced all the great ministers of the early part of the reign with his own dependants. The court was inhabited by men who were in the favourite's pocket; Olivares was the puppet-master who activated the whole charade of the palace.

Manuscript copies of this literary poignard were handed around clandestinely at court, to the intense discomfiture of its main target. The treatise reached the king's eyes by the surreptitious connivance of some household functionary – possibly Olivares' secret enemy amongst the king's apartment staff, Matías de Novoa. According to one report, Philip's response was less sympathetic than Olivares might have wished; for he laconically advised his *valido* 'my dear count, you must be more careful and protect your back'.[10]

Olivares was deeply scarred by the consequences of the Mantuan adventure and the penetrating criticism it evoked. Nearly a decade later the wound still rankled. Following a year which had witnessed the Catalan rebellion, and only days after news reached Madrid that Portugal too had thrown off its allegiance to Philip IV, Olivares, seeking as usual to deflect criticism in committee, cited Mantua as a salutory case in which policy had been distorted by the carping (*murmuración*) of his enemies. He claimed that although twelve other ministers had voted in favour of the Mantuan enterprise, he himself held aloof from the decision.[11]

By this time it is not unlikely that Olivares had made away with the most damaging written evidence. Moreover, there was virtually no one left in government to contradict him from experience. Of the *consejeros* involved in the discussions over the Mantua War in the early months of 1628, few survived when the monarchy emerged from the immediate crisis it had precipitated. Only one from six members of the special 'Mantua Junta' (the beautifully named Guillén de la Carrera) still held office in Madrid by the time of the peace

[9] 'Memorial dado por el Duque de Cesa al rey Don Philippe 4 y su Magestad le leyó', BN, 18175, ff. 342–3v. The noise made by this attack had a truly international resonance. Several other contemporary ms copies are extant in Spanish and other European archives. These are the survivors of over 200 originals, one of which reached an obscure Irish Franciscan house in Antwerp by the summer of 1629, B. Jennings, *The Wadding Papers* (Dublin, 1961), p. 298. Another was in Novoa's possession long enough to be transcribed verbatim into his secret journal, CODOIN, 69 (Madrid, 1880), pp. 74–76. Though the role of Sessa is not definitively established, his rivalry with Olivares was of long standing, and on earlier occasions had assumed a specifically literary character.

[10] 'Papel que se dió a Su Magestad sobre la Privanza del Conde Duque . . .', BL, Add. 25689, ff. 166–70.

[11] Elliott, *The Count-Duke*, p. 599.

of Cherasco (May 1631). The marquises of La Hinojosa and Montesclaros were dead; the count of Lemos, disillusioned by the moral compromises of politics, had retired to a monastery; the duke of Feria had become viceroy of Catalonia; the count of Monterrey was now ambassador in Rome.[12]

As for those who had criticized the Mantua policy within the *Junta de Estado*, Spínola, Villela and Antonio de Mexía all died in 1630, whilst Fernando de Girón retired in 1628 after refusing Olivares' offer of the viceroyalty of Navarre, a blatant attempt to kick him upstairs. This left only the marquis of Leganés and the king's confessor, Sotomayor, along with Guillén – all creatures of the count-duke. One of his main domestic opponents, Cardinal Trejo, president of Castile, was dismissed and died early in 1630. The high rate of ministerial wastage was partly due to the inordinately high pressures of work and stress which characterized the decision-making centre of a world empire in the throes of crisis. But even more crucial was the count-duke's determination to ride himself of the 'old guard', along with lukewarm supporters and potential opponents, a process as complete and ruthless, if not perhaps as vicious in its circumstances, as the parallel and almost simultaneous one going on in Paris in the wake of the so-called 'Day of Dupes' (November 1630). In both courts, we are witnessing the exceptional virulence of faction politics which accompanied the prolonged, intense and multifaceted 'crisis' of Mantua.[13]

Following his own eventual fall from power, stung by the swarm of critical hornets that event had stirred up, Olivares repeated his charges against Don Gonzalo in even cruder fashion.[14] But on this occasion his assertions received nobody's credence. Philip continued to protect Don Gaspar's person and fortune, respected his memory, and refrained from any public attack on his record; but at the time of Olivares' death in 1645 the king singled out the Mantuan affair for explicit private regret. Writing in a moral context in which conscious deception is quite inconceivable, Philip testified that his profound reservations about the war in Italy had been overcome by his ministers – by implication including Olivares, whose *valimiento* the king now recognized as having been a mistake.[15] Olivares' self-exculpation was lost in the chorus of contemporary condemnation and disappeared under the weight of historical criticism. Such are the vicissitudes of power that the count-duke himself became the scapegoat, not only for Mantua but for the subsequent military failure of Spain and the definitive loss of its greatness.

[12] For the role of the special *junta de Mantua* in the decision, see Chap. 3, above.

[13] Elliott, *The Count-Duke*, pp. 382–83.

[14] 'Nicandro o antidoto contra las calumnias . . .' (1643), Elliott and de la Peña, *Memoriales*, ii, pp. 250–54. This was a reply to charges against Olivares, circulated by Andrés de Mena, in which the criticisms of the *valido's* policy over Mantua were resuscitated; ibid., pp. 228, 235–36.

[15] Philip to Sor María, 20 July 1645 and 30 Jan. 1647, Seco Serrano, *Cartas de la Venerable Sor María*, i, pp. 28, 92.

Act Two: Characters and Chorus

French historians' treatment of the Mantuan War has always been fond of contrasting the passionate and capricious Olivares with the cool, rational statesmanship of Richelieu, considering that the weaknesses of the former played into the hands of the latter. In many accounts, the well-deserved humbling of Spain is thrown into satisfactory relief by the grossly overweening figure of the Spanish favourite. Whilst rejecting the corrollary claim that the cardinal's vocation was to save Christendom from the lawless ambitions of Spain – exemplified in Mantua – Spanish critics of the Olivares regime found themselves able to agree in principle concerning the man himself. To many Spaniards – contemporary and modern – Olivares was a tyrant, whose career was epitomized by the Italian misadventure.[16]

In the case under review, the imperatives of nationalist propaganda are illustrated by the form in which the central evidential texts are cast. The bulk of the documents necessary to the historian for any treatment of the Mantuan crisis form part of the 'K' series of Spanish State Paper files at Simancas. This series, covering the diplomatic relations of Spain with France in the Habsburg period, has had its own chequered history. In a *cause célèbre* of Bonapartist rule in Spain, hundreds of bundles (*legajos*) were systematically filched from the archive by a zealous diplomatic agent and remitted to Paris. They became part of the collection of the Archives Nationales – which still uses the 'K' denomination for diplomatic/political series – and were only returned as a gesture of goodwill to Franco's Spain by the German authorities occupying France during the Second World War.[17]

During the long interim, the French archivists had examined and organized the original, untidy bundles of papers (*legajos*), causing many to be sewn into ordered files (*carpetas*). When they came to bind the documents dealing with the origins of the Mantuan War (now K1436), they adopted a blatantly suggestive order of arrangement. The items may be described in strict order of appearance. The volume opens with printed copies of the treaty of Monzón, negotiated and ratified in the spring of 1626. It is followed by a separate manuscript version of an additional clause, by which Louis and Philip agreed to act openly towards each other in the ultra-sensitive arena of Italy, negotiating

---

[16] The adulatory attitudes of French hagiographers of Richelieu, based on his foreign policy, are still detectable even in the modern work of writers like Mousnier. The heyday of such patriotic championship extends from the mid nineteenth century, when Hanotaux and Zeller flourished, until the work of Hauser and Burckhard in the 1930s. The French case against Spain is specifically considered in A. Leman, *Urbain VIII*, and in more detached fashion by W.F. Church, *Richelieu and Reason of State* (Boston, 1972). The Spanish side is covered with great depth but little objectivity by Jover Zamora in *1635: historia de una polémica*. Sides and issues are brought together illuminatingly by Elliott in *Richelieu and Olivares*, p. 113 et seq.

[17] See J. Paz's introduction to his catalogue, *Archivo General de Simancas, Secretaría de Estado, capitulaciones con Francia* (Madrid, 1914), esp. pp. v–viii; and A. de la Plaza, *Archivo General de Simancas: guía del investigador* (Valladolid, 1962), pp. lxxxi–lxxxiii, 16.

any problems as soon as identified; a clause which 'although secret will have the same force as the treaty, and will demand ratification in the same manner'.

In this initial set of commitments, reference is repeatedly made to the need for honest collaboration of the two crowns, along with explicit renunciation and denunciation of underhand dealings with each other's enemies. Over and over again, the peace and commonweal of Christendom is piously evoked. At this point, evidence is deftly placed of Olivares' personal eagerness to go even further, pressing the French ambassador, Du Fargis, with even stricter mutual undertakings, which the latter was not empowered to deal with. In any case, a fraternal alliance has come into existence. The atmosphere of sweetness and light is suddenly poisoned by the insertion of some original papers of Fernández de Córdoba – *dating from over a year later* – in which he seeks to tempt Duke Carlo Emanuele of Savoy into a clandestine alliance against Monferrat, citing the advance connivance of Madrid in this conspiracy. In the next letter this Machiavellian bargain is sealed.[18]

The presentation of K1436 in one sense takes the form of a dossier of evidence for a legal indictment. Equally, however, it is analogous to a theatrical scene, with Don Gonzalo as the evil agent of Madrid, creeping on to the stage to murder the peace of Europe. It contains an implicit image which visualizes the point made by Richelieu's propagandists throughout the 1630s. The silent but nonetheless palpable impression created by the text, of Madrid's perfidy and cynical ambition, Spain's indifference to the sufferings of Christendom, and the malign role played by Olivares, could hardly be more deliberate or complete.

The dumb-show convention of Senecan tragedy was widely imitated in the contemporary theatre – perhaps the most celebrated example is the 'Mousetrap' scene, inserted in the court production of the players by Hamlet, prince of Denmark, in order to expose the truth of the king his father's assassination. In the case of K1436, the argument is all the more convincing because the actual words of the drama consist not of some playwright's mimetic dialogue but of the indubitably 'original' State Papers. Yet it is the selection and juxtaposition of the documents which constitute this text, rather than their content, which communicates the essential message of this *coup de théâtre*. It is a waxworks tableau of Spanish villainy, and one which directly reflects the version patented for public consumption by Cardinal Richelieu himself.

A 'heroic comedy' entitled *Europe*, devised and partly written by Richelieu, was performed shortly before his death to a large and appreciative court audience.[19] The play was nothing other than a staged allegorical appendix to his *Political Testament*. It portrayed the attempted rape of 'Europe' by the lustful 'Ibère', who has been denied her affections; the valiant 'Francion' intervenes

---

[18] AGS, E K1436, file 1–4. For more detailed treatment of these documents, see Chap. 3, above, pp. 56–57, 59, 63–65.

[19] L. Lacour, *Richelieu dramaturge et ses collaborateurs: les imbroglios romanesques, les pièces politiques* (Paris, 1925), esp. pp. 141–54.

to protect the hapless damsel. In the printed edition of 1643, the frontispiece displays Louis XIII, attired as a Roman hero, in the act of challenging a ridiculous and bombastic Philip IV to combat. The action begins with Ibère's plot, in league with 'The King of Hungary' (The Empire), to abduct Europe's handmaiden, 'Ausonia' (Italy) – a reference to the Mantuan crisis itself. Spain's successive frustrations culminate with the discovery of the Cinq-Mars conspiracy to overthrow the cardinal and make a compromise peace, scenes which Richelieu composed on his deathbed in the weeks following the actual events of Spring 1642. In this conjuncture, Art is indeed the ubiquitous nymph Echo, who so immediately and so faithfully repeats reality. Europe's rejection of Spain is couched in definitive terms:

Ibère	Europe, il faut choisir. Soyez, belle inhumaine,
	L'object de mon amour ou l'object de ma haine.
Europe	Le choix en est tout fait: je préfère sans peur
	Ta haine découverte à ton amour trompeur.
Ibère	Mon amour toutefois vous ferait moins de peine.
Europe	Ta haine est mon amour, et ton amour ma haine.
Ibère	Contre vos protecteurs j'armerai les enfers.
Europe	Et le ciel s'armera pour m'ôter de vos fers.[20]

The cardinal, like Hamlet, and like the scholar-patriots of a later age, sought to demonstrate truth-through-drama. Thus he proclaims – in respect of Philip IV, as of King Claudius – that

> . . . the play's the thing
> Wherein I'll catch the conscience of the king.
> (*Hamlet*, Act I)

Such appeals wrung the withers of the French historical school in the heyday of their great nationalist era. The message was almost irresistible. Richelieu's claim to be the saviour of Europe was worthy of every endorsement, emphasising the heroic righteousness of his triumphs. It followed, even if only subliminally, that this privileged meaning had somehow to be inscribed in the 'original documents'. Thus the K1436 of the French archivists is more than a simple nationally biased presentation of the evidence to the historian-juror. It is a species of literary creation, evocative of the dramatized medium in which – centuries after the documents originated in the 'theatrical' ambience of baroque Europe – historical truth was generally imagined.

Like his French rival, Olivares often collaborated with established writers in order to communicate a public defence of controversial policies. Hack teams of pamphleteers had the task of gaining the attention of a European *audience*, or the support of an international *tribunal* (the emphasised words having similar synonyms in French and Spanish) which governed the level of their kings' prestige. But in addition – like Richelieu's play – they sought to convince the domestic sceptics; above all, a potentially hostile nobility, who increasingly

---

[20] Quoted ibid., p. 152.

were required to sacrifice their wealth, and their traditional political influence, to the war-policy of an exclusive centralism.

King and favourite at court formed a focal point of power and patronage – 'the observed of all observers'. The theatre, with its immediate and tangible communication of meaning, was the most persuasive instrument to hand in that crucial arena.[21] Spanish playwrights regularly presented staged versions of the regime's military triumphs (for example, Calderón de la Barca's plays about Breda and Nördlingen). Kings and princes stepped – as it were – straight from the battlefield on to the stage. Philip IV and Louis XIII acted roles in court masques. Charles I of England played the lead in several presentations (opposite his queen, Louis's sister) and actively intervened with Inigo Jones and his writers in set design and plot. The result was an explicitly ideological genre, having support of royal autocracy as its main function. In Caroline court life the theatrical dimensions of king and queen, as Cupid and Psyche, and as the unisex supreme being 'Carlomaria', was a dominant image.

Even when not required to act (stricto sensu), the royal personages often sat upon the stage and were called upon to resolve dramatic conflicts as a sort of rex ex machina. Little wonder that Le Vau was to present Louis XIV to his court on a sculptured stage of oak from which carved cherubims held back the carved curtains.[22] In Madrid, great courtiers such as the young duke of Medina de las Torres, Olivares' son-in-law and an intimate privado of Philip IV's, involved themselves closely as patrons of the comediantes and in personal direction of their work.[23] In London, the costumes worn on the stage were the cast-off finery of the courtiers themselves. In both courts, actors from the favourite companies became members of the royal household or of that of some eminent noble. Thus they were thoroughly integrated into the world of power, patronage and faction. Madrid's palaces provided home and employment for an astonishing number of writers. We are told that 223 lived off Philip IV in the course of his reign, compared to a measly sixty-six during that of Philip II.[24] The list included the dramatists Ruíz de Alarcón, Hurtado de Mendoza and Gabriel Bocangel, as well as the more renowned figures mentioned elsewhere in this essay. The ministers who dictated written

[21] The following remarks are based on L. Tennenhouse, Power on Display: The Politics of Shakespeare's Genres (1986), pp. 72–101; G. Parry, The Golden Age Restor'd: The Culture of the Stuart Court, 1603–42 (Manchester, 1981), pp. 184–203; S. Orgel, The Illusion of Power: Political Theater in the English Renaissance (Berkely and Los Angeles, CA, 1975), pp. 10–11; and N.D. Shergold, History of the Spanish Stage from Medieval Times to the End of the Seventeenth Century (Oxford, 1967), pp. 264–97.

[22] Le Vau's stage – completed for Louis XIV's court debut in 1654 – is still (1987) to be found installed in one of the main salles of the Louvre.

[23] 'Relación de la famosa máscara que hizo el Señor Duque de Medina de las Torres . . . 1629', in J. Simón Díaz (ed.), Relaciones de actos públicos celebrados en Madrid de 1541 a 1650, pp. 432–35.

[24] J.H. Elliott, 'The Court of the Spanish Habsburgs: A Peculiar Institution?', in P. Mack and M.C. Jacob (ed.), Politics and Culture in Early Modern Europe: Essays in Honour of H.G. Koenigsberger (Cambridge, 1987), pp. 5–24.

opinions for the king's councils (*votos*); the secretaries who arranged *viva voce* discussions of committees into written reports (*consultas*), were often amateur dramatists, actors, or inveterate playgoers.

The narrative and ethical content of the court theatre was also intensely self-reflexive. In particular, plays about the bloody downfall of favourites, in every way the most appropriate subject of a genre based formally upon the model of Seneca – the earliest Spanish dramatist, and himself a bloodily fallen favourite – came to dominate tragedy in the generation before the Mantuan war. Spanish writers, like the prolific Lope de Vega Carpio, tended to locate such plots in the medieval past of the Spanish kingdoms. English dramatists also utilized 'history', but much more often set their stories in the *locus classicus* of 'Machiavellian' politics and the power-violence syndrome, Northern Italy. To the English imagination, exotically sinister courts not far from Mantua or Monferrat were the perfect settings for political drama. Of the hundreds of known English plays of the (loosely defined) category of 'Revenge Tragedy', often incorporating explicitly political argument, a very large number are given a contemporary location in the petty courts of Italy, including several which were premiered in Charles I's London during the period of the Mantua crisis. The genre provided, moreover, an opportunity for confessional patriotism, for scoring points off the Catholic world, which is regularly pictured as politically decadent and corrupt.[25]

Philip IV eventually achieved his ambition of going to the front in general's garb; but in addition he was traditionally accredited with direct participation in the parallel war of the theatre. The most celebrated of royal *aficionados del teatro* was widely believed to have composed a play about the rebellion and execution of the earl of Essex, favourite of Elizabeth I (1601). This particular hero had a special significance for Habsburg *reputación*. Essex was the commander who had humiliated Philip II by the sack of Cádiz in 1596. As it happens, Philip IV revered his grandfather above all his other ancestors. In the present context it seems irrelevant whether the story of Philip's authorship has any factual foundation; what is important is the theatrical ambience which nurtures such attributions. The ambiguously-titled play of *El conde de Sex* may thus be regarded as a special example of revenge tragedy. Set in the London of *Hamlet*'s composition, it was perhaps inspired by the ghost of Philip II walking the nocturnal ramparts of the Madrid Alcázar.[26]

---

[25] W.W. Greg, *A Bibliography of the English Printed Drama to the Restoration*, ii, *Plays, 1617–89*, (1951), esp. pp. 418–23. Any complete list would include plays by Shirley, Tourner, Middleton and Rowley, Webster, Ford, Massinger and Davenant, the last-named being the Poet Laureate of Charles I. For the Senecan influence in contemporary Spanish drama, see R.A. Lauer, 'The Killing of the Tyrannical King in the Spanish Theater of the Golden Age (1582–1671)' (unpublished Ph.D. thesis, University of Michighan, 1983), p. 147 et seq.

[26] 'Tragedia más lastimosa, el conde de Sex', printed in E. de Ochoa (ed.), *Colección de los mejores autores españoles*, xiv (Paris, 1838), pp. 98–127. (The 'Sex' of the title is nothing more titillating than a crude hispanification of 'Essex'). Premiered at court in 1633, the play

continued

Seventeenth-century society, therefore, did not regard the theatre from the perspective which later developed – that is, as something firmly divided from (if in some arcane way representative of) 'real life'. The Baroque court, as cultural historians have argued in a wave of recent scholarship, was so close in its conventions and physical proximity to the theatre that the one was more than a metaphor of the other; they were both part of the same rhetorical discourse.[27] Their elaborate rituals and ceremonial, such as the notorious *etiquetas* of the Spanish Habsburgs, allotted every one of a thousand servants a written 'part' in a performance acted according to various overlapping diurnal and seasonal rhythms. The self-regarding narcissism of court life is illustrated by other quasi-dramatic elements. The busy painters' studios were factories for the production of courtier-portraits; in which subjects frequently appear in symbolically representational robes. Velázquez and his contemporaries frequently utilized subtle theatrical elements in the representation of both the structures and events of political life. Little wonder that González de Avila, in the year of Prince Charles' extended visit, gave his description of the court the title *Teatro de las Grandezas de la Villa de Madrid*.[28]

The layout of the palaces themselves focused attention on the main performers, and reflected everybody to everyone, as in the passage through the Hall of Mirrors, a conceit culminating in Versailles' *galerie des glaces* but patented a century earlier in the Ducal Palace at Mantua. Never far behind the frontiers of taste, Philip IV had his own Hall of Mirrors constructed in the Alcázar by Juan Gómez de Mora in the mid 1620s. But it was the Gonzagas who nurtured the most sophisticated, expensive and political art form yet known – for Monteverdi's operas were performed in Mantua's Hall. At the same time they enjoyed a constant interaction with a more ephemeral but equally significant genre. Perhaps the ultimate expression of histrionic self-observation was the troupes of dwarfish performers who accompanied and entertained the prince and courtier of the early seventeenth century, and who lived in a little palace-within-the-palace, through whose windows their domestic rituals

continued

was evidently a success for it was repeated in 1637, a rare distinction for presentations of its type; see N.D. Shergold and J.E. Varey, 'Some Palace Performances of Seventeenth-Century Plays', *Bulletin of Hispanic Studies*, 40 (1963), pp. 212–44 (at pp. 231, 243).

[27] See (in addition to work cited elsewhere) several contributors to A.G. Dickens (ed.), *The Courts of Europe: Politics, Patronage and Loyalty, 1400–1800* (1977). More specifically, J.E. Varey, 'The Audience and the Play at Court Spectacles: The Role of the King', *Bulletin of Hispanic Studies*, 61 (1984), pp. 399–406. 'The whole of Madrid was a theatre' says the aptly-named José del Corral in his *El Madrid de los Austrias* (Madrid, 1983), p. 117; (a *corral* was a contemporary open-air arena).

[28] *Teatro de las grandezas de la villa de Madrid corte de los Reyes Católicos de España ... por el Maestro Gil González Davila su cronista* (Madrid, 1623); for the *etiquetas de la casa*, see Y. Bottineau, 'Aspects de la cour d'Espagne au XVIIe siècle: L'etiquette de la Chambre du Roi', *Bulletin hispanique*, 74 (1972), pp. 138–57. See also L. Diez del Corral, *Velázquez, la monarquía e Italia* (Madrid, 1978).

could be continuously observed. Both opera and soap-opera were centrally meaningful in Mantua.[29]

J.H. Elliott has touched on some cognate ideas about the court politics of Philip IV in several of his recent publications. As he postulates matters, 'in a sense the king and queen *were* the play'. Olivares, as befitted the mesmeric domination of the king which many historians perceive, was the impresario or dramaturge. The monarch was 'little more than a marionette . . . occasionally brought on stage to be put through a series of carefully modulated movements . . . Philip was intelligent enough to learn his lines, but also docile enough to take direction'. Thus Olivares' fundamental political task – 'with his superb sense of theatre' – lay in the 'grooming of Philip IV for his star role'.[30] This interpretation seems little altered from that put forward in the 'Sessa treatise' of 1629 where (as we have seen) the king appears as 'un rey por ceremonía', manipulated entirely by the politician. It is a theme which has passed through many variations, reaching a kind of psychological melodrama with the version presented by Gregorio Marañón in his 1936 biography of Olivares.[31] Indeed, the traditional historiographical trope of the Philip IV/Olivares relationship is an essentially and intrinsically theatrical one. From the impresario's point of view, however, the whole production started to go horribly wrong in 1628.

Act Three: Plot and Counter-Plot

All over early seventeenth-century Europe court favourites met with violent public demise. Rodrigo Calderón was executed in the Plaza Mayor of Madrid

---

[29] The *appartamento dei nani* was completed in 1627 by Duke Vincenzo, who was obsessed with dwarfs. In order to defray the costs of this pastime, he sold the fabulous art collection of his predecessors to Charles I. These expenses crippled Charles' attempts to succour La Rochelle: see H.R. Trevor-Roper, *The Plunder of the Arts in the Seventeenth Century* (1970), pp. 28–36. In its turn, the English failure helped to clear the way for Richelieu's victory over the Huguenots, and thus for his timely intervention in Italy. Conversely, with Mantua's full coffers, Striggio and other supporters of Nevers were the better able to raise credit for the defence of Mantua against the Habsburg armies. In this suitable way, Mantua – one of the greatest Renaissance states for patronage of the plastic arts – was preserved by Mantegna and Titian as much as by Richelieu and Louis XIII. For Philip IV's hall of mirrors, see S. Orso, *The Decoration of the Alcázar of Madrid* (Princeton, 1986), pp. 32–117. The dwarfs of his court are described in M.B. Mena Marqués, *Monstruos, enanos y bufones en la corte de los Austrias* (Madrid, 1986).

[30] The quotations are from 'The Court of the Spanish Habsburgs'; but see also, Elliott, *The Count-Duke*, esp. pp. 174–78, and Elliott and Brown, *A Palace for a King*, p. 31ff.

[31] G. Marañón, *El conde duque de Olivares: la pasión de mandar* (Madrid, 1936). There have been five full editions, while the abridged version of 1939 in the popular *Colección Austral* went to thirteen impressions by 1969.

shortly after Philip IV's accession in 1621.[32] At Louis XIII's orders, Concino Concini was murdered and his mutilated corpse displayed to the mob in 1617. Twenty years later, Richelieu directed the writing of a play about the killing of Clitus by Alexander, apparently in order to teach Louis that favourites should not be casually slaughtered.[33] The king took the point well enough to allow his new favourite, Richelieu's own placeman Cinq-Mars, to conspire against the cardinal's life. In 1642, as in the earlier 'Day of Dupes' (1630), Richelieu turned the tables on his adversaries, and Cinq-Mars, like his predecessors – all traitors in the pay of Spain – ended on the block.[34] In 1628 the duke of Buckingham was stabbed to death by a lone assassin. The following year, one Lodowick Carlell ('Groome of the King and Queen's Privy Chamber') presented his drama 'The Deserving Favourite' at Whitehall, for the approval of Charles I.[35] Charles took the point well enough to sacrifice his chief minister, the earl of Strafford, whose execution in 1641 was to inspire a fresh round of pseudo-theatrical obsequies. Even in the 'Republican' United Provinces, the veteran chief minister, Oldenbarnevelt, was overthrown and executed at the behest of a prince (1618).

Old Polonius, chief minister at the court of Denmark, recalls that he once 'did enact Julius Caesar; I was kill'd i' th' Capitol; Brutus kill'd me' (*Hamlet*, II, 2). He meets his 'real' death on the point of a sword later, when acting behind the arras as a clandestine 'audience' of the conference of Queen and Prince. In the year after *Hamlet*, Ben Jonson put on his *Sejanus his Fall*, in which Tiberius's favourite is torn to pieces by the mob upon the instant that imperial favour is withdrawn. His successor exults:

> Now great Sejanus, you that awed the State
> And sought to bring the nobles to your whip,
> That would be Caesar's tutor, and dispose
> Of dignities and offices!
>
>   . . . now you're as flat
> As was your pride advanced.[36]

The count-duke of Olivares was no playwright, but in 1628–29 he wished to limit the damage the Mantua crisis threatened to wreak upon his ministry,

---

[32] The execution took place on a stage erected 'before an enormous crowd'; Elliott, *The Count-Duke*, p. 108. The tragic hero's performance excited the poets to dramatic metaphors of stoic fortitude similar to those later coined in England for Strafford and Charles I. A more cynical observer noted that among the published lists of Don Rodrigo's ill-gotten gains were 'debenture' places in the theatres of Valladolid and Madrid; Maravall, *La cultura*, p. 471.

[33] This drama was by Desmarets de Saint-Sorin, Richelieu's most intimate literary assistant: Lacour, *Richelieu dramaturge*, pp. 90–91.

[34] For the Cinq-Mars conspiracy, see P. Erlanger, *Richelieu and the Affair of Cinq-Mars* (1971), esp. pp. 129–56.

[35] Greg, *Bibliography*, p. 422.

[36] W.F. Bolton (ed.), *Sejanus, his Fall* (1966), Act V, Scene 6.

his programme of government, and his hopes of posthumous prestige. His normal vein of paranoia became steadily more pronounced as he fancied himself surrounded by secret enemies at court. This larger-than-life but deeply insecure figure, living in a context which was a cliché of contemporary drama, needed to present as strong a case as possible on the stage.

During the course of 1628 Pedro Calderón (no relation to the executed favourite, nor to Iñes de Calderón, actress-mistress of Philip IV) produced a *comedia* about the struggle of a royal *valido* to maintain his position against the intrigues of jealous courtiers. The text of *Saber del Mal y el Bien* (Knowledge of Good and Evil) is voluble on the theme of the precarious tenure of royal favourites. Don Alvaro de Viseo, whose name contains an anagram of that of Olivares, muses that

> In the theatre of the world,
> We are all merely actors:
> Some play a sovereign king,
> Others a prince or grandee,
> Whom all are pleased to serve.
> And at that point, in that instant,
> While the part lasts, one man is master
> Of the destinies of the rest.
> But when the comedy is finished,
> The role also reaches its end,
> And the death of the dressing-room
> Returns us all to mere equality.[37]

Calderón's play ended with a tribute to the relationship between king and *valido*. Olivares – who was 'deeply conscious of playing a part in the "theatre of the world"' – may have derived comfort from this, and Calderón was awarded a new household office.[38] Nevertheless, Olivares must have felt at times perilously close to Don Alvaro's 'la muerte en el vestuario'.

A year later, in the summer of 1629, Olivares was busily orchestrating a journalistic campaign to defend his record in government. Part of this was a new play entitled *Como ha de ser el privado* (What is required in a Favourite), by Olivares' formidable literary champion, Francisco de Quevedo.[39] The production was designed as a kind of corselet to help protect Olivares'

---

[37] D.W. Cruikshank and J.E. Varey (ed.), *Saber del mal y el bien*, primera jornada, p. 155 (my translation).

[38] Elliott, *The Count-Duke*, p. 287; D. Fox, 'Kingship in the Drama of Don Pedro Calderón de la Barca' (unpublished Ph.D. thesis, Duke University, 1979), pp. 32–57.

[39] The political significance of this play has attracted notice: J.H. Elliott, 'Quevedo and the Count-Duke of Olivares', pp. 227–50; J. Urrieta, 'Quevedo en el teatro político', in V. Garán de la Concha (ed.), *Homenaje a Quevedo* (Salamanca, 1982), pp. 173–85. My extracts (Act I, lines (in order of quotation) 249–64, 269–72, 700–7, 114–17), are translated from the text printed in the edition of J. de Blecua, *Francisco de Quevedo: obra poética*, iv (Madrid, 1981), pp. 149–221.

back from the daggers of his enemies. Indeed there is some evidence to suggest that it was performed in the immediate wake of Sessa's rude intrusion and Philip's recommendation. There is no more transparent example of the staged presentation of political actuality in the history of the theatre. The setting is the court of Naples, but the disguise becomes so threadbare that the unmodulated events of the 1620s keep sticking awkwardly out of the text. The play was probably staged in the *Salón de Comedias* of the Alcázar during the summer of 1629. Certainly, the argument is so apposite to his situation that Olivares could almost have 'inserted' many of its speeches. The play's hero, another (more perfect) anagram of Olivares, the 'Marquis of Valisero', pronounces that

> A favourite is merely the tiniest atom
> By his king's side, and is not even master
> Of the light he derives from the Sun.
> He is a minister of the law, an arm,
> An instrument through which the king's breath,
> His will, passes and sounds . . .
> The world should know that the favourite,
> Although he may counsel, cannot himself decide.

This unsubtle message and others related to it, are thrust home in a series of very palpable hits. Quevedo thus attempted to provide a wider 'audience' which – like the behind-the-scenes conclave of the Council of State – would absolve Olivares of responsibility for the Italian fiasco. Himself a noted swordsman, he steps forward on cue to parry the rapier thrusts of the duke of Sessa. After his promotion to the *valimiento*, Valisero soliloquizes:

> Fortune has exposed me
> Alone in the theatre of the world,
> To be the only target
> Of all its envy and complaint.

When Prince Charles and Buckingham travelled incognito to Madrid in 1623, to apply personally for the hand of Philip IV's sister, María, James I referred to his 'sweet boys and dear venturous knights worthy to be put in a romance'.[40] Quevedo duly obliged by basing his action upon these events. Embarrassing and unwelcome as the visit was, Philip had been none the less obliged to lay on a veritable riot of ostentation – fiestas, dances, games and shows of all kinds – for the five months of his guests' sojourn in Madrid. This provides the setting within which 'Valisero's' counsel in favour of a true religious policy, spurning an alliance with heretics founded on *razón de estado*, can be shown off to advantage. The king's stage name ('Fernando') and that of the infanta ('Margarita') are unexceptional; but that given to Charles himself is of the greatest interest. The Prince of Wales becomes in Quevedo's

---

[40] Quoted in P.W. Thomas, 'Charles I of England: The Tragedy of Absolutism', in Dickens (ed.), *The Courts of Europe*, pp. 191–211.

text 'Carlos, príncipe de Dinamarca'. The royal lover, masker and impresario, who was to lose a war on the battlefield and die on his greatest stage, the scaffold placed in front of Inigo Jones' Banqueting Hall, was also – at least in one sense – a prince of Denmark, by virtue of being the son of Queen Anne, sister of King Christian IV.[41]

King 'Fernando' reacts in a similar way to King James at the news of the prince's journey:

> Only in the theatres, or in books of fables
> Can we encounter such events. A powerful prince
> Come to my court and palace like a pilgrim
> To declare his love and supplicate my debt.

At the end of Act II, the disappointed prince recites a poem of unrequited love to 'Margarita', and threatens a bloody revenge against her brother's kingdom. In Act III, the news of victory over the punitive 'Danish' fleet at 'our Cadiz in Italy', and against the king's rebels overseas at Bahía (both 1625), are relayed to the king by 'Valisero', who also (however) has the difficult and unpleasant task of describing the defeat of Matanzas (1628). Since he has refused all reward for the former (so that 'History ... will not relate that Valisero took the king's gold'), the king refuses to blame him for the latter. The play ends in the marriage of 'Margarita' to 'the prince of Transylvania' (i.e. the *actual* king of Hungary and future emperor); and the proclamation that only in the unity of the Catholic (Habsburg) dynasty – cornerstone of Olivares' policy – can defeat be transformed into triumph. It is notable that the setback to Philip's prestige in Italy is simply too sensitive for cosmetic treatment. Ambrogio Spínola, moreover, is dismissed by silence. He has no 'representative' in the play, and his resounding contribution to the *annus mirabilis* of 1625 – the capture of Breda – is pointedly ignored.

Despite its blatant propaganda content, other aspects of Quevedo's homily seem less satisfactory from the perspective of its putative hero. In the very act of choosing between Valisero and his two rivals, the admiral and the count of Castelomar, the king – in a clear reference to the fate of Rodrigo Calderón – sternly warns

> If any minister who holds my favour
> Is justly found to be of guilt and blame,
> We will cut off his head in the Plaza Mayor.

---

[41] The names of the two rivals of 'Valisero' are also chosen with care – not without an element of deliberate irony. 'The Admiral', full of extravagant praise of his colleague, was 'in real life' Alonso de Enríquez, a devout enemy of Olivares. 'Castelomar', a name with Portuguese overtones, suggests another prominent *antiolivarista* (of Portuguese origin), Manuel de Moura, marquis of Castel Rodrigo. The uncle to whom 'Valisero' at first defers is called 'the duke of Sartabal' – a representation of Olivares' own uncle *Baltasar* de Zúñiga, who had preceded his nephew as chief minister of the crown until his death in 1622.

Quevedo pointedly characterizes his hero as 'the new Spanish Seneca'. The comparison was doubtless meant to praise Olivares' wisdom and states-manship, along with the stoic fortitude with which he invested these qualities. But the reference may have inspired uncomfortably mixed feelings in Olivares; not only because of Seneca's ultimate fate, but also since one of the most telling weapons in his enemies' armoury was the story of his birth in Rome, whilst his father was ambassador to the Holy See, on the ancient site of the palace of Nero – presumably the very place where Seneca himself had written. This allegation was noised abroad with the clear imputation that he had inherited not the moderation of the philosopher but the caprice and cruelty of the archetypal tyrant.

Act Four: Scene of the Crime

According to a story circulated shortly after the crime took place, and which still claims credit amongst historians, the murder of the peace of Europe by the Machiavellian favourite Olivares took place in a quiet corner of the garden of the Royal Palace (Alcázar) in Madrid.

Given the importance to them of the Mantuan issue, the Italian *corps diplomatique* in Madrid was keenly interested in the details of decision-making in the close committees of the Alcázar. The Venetian resident, Mocenigo – whose family patronized Monteverdi – reported that Olivares, the instigator of aggression in Monferrat, 'was always opposed in principle by the majority of the council, and by those who preferred to satisfy their own consciences in the service of the king, rather than to obey [Olivares'] inclinations'. At first, claims Mocenigo, the *valido* seemed to accept this rebuff, but gradually persuaded the king to support him. Following his arrival in Madrid, however, Spínola had 'gently but firmly rejected the count's enthusiasm' for the Mantuan policy. He immediately claimed much of the royal attention, whilst the rest of the court clustered round him almost as a saviour.[42] Political events, then as now, were seen in terms of the binary opposition of powerful personalities. In the last phase of the court crisis, at Christmas 1629–30, Philip left Olivares in Madrid for three weeks and accompanied his sister on the opening stages of her journey to Vienna as queen of Hungary. To many observers, the moment of Olivares' overthrow seemed at hand. The Genoese envoy Saluzzo's account of what Elliott calls a 'little drama', suggested that the duke of Alba might be the agent of Philip's liberation from his incubus.[43]

One of the first writers to make a systematic comparison – or protagonization – of Richelieu and Olivares was Guillaume de Valdory, who published accounts

---

[42] N. Barozzi and G. Berchet (ed.), *Relazione degli stati europei: lette al senato dagli ambasciatori veneti nel secolo decimosettimo*, 1st series, Spagna, 2 vols (Venice, 1856), i, pp. 650–53.

[43] Elliott, *The Count-Duke*, pp. 394–97.

of both statesmen in early eighteenth-century Paris.[44] He portrayed Richelieu as the harbinger not only of French national glory but also of the age of political rationalism in which Valdory himself lived; Olivares was seen as a *mélange* of religious fanatic and robber baron. But these, recognizable now as expertly contrasted ethnocentric stereotypes, were presented only by way of introduction to Valdory's careful selections from the work of another Italian writer, Vittorio Siri. The latter's detailed contemporary chronicle of the Franco-Spanish wars was published in serial multi-volume form, with the characteristic general title of *Il Mercurio, overo historia de' correnti tempi.*[45]

Siri was a typical product of an anti-Spanish school of Italian polemics, with antecedents stretching back to Machiavelli. Although written in Italian, his account was blatantly francophile, only to be expected of a writer appointed by Cardinal Mazarin as 'Historiografo della Maestá Christianissima' (i.e. to Anne of Austria). The first volume, including a brief account of the origins of the Mantuan War, was published – presumably not by coincidence – in the town of Casale, focal point of the whole Mantuan dispute, only fifteen years after the events themselves, in 1644. According to Siri's chronicle, the war was precipitated by Spain to prevent the succession of a francophone prince to the vital Mantuan territories. Olivares cynically attempted to exploit the Italian situation and France's preoccupation with the siege of La Rochelle. The Spaniards plotted their moves with Milan and Savoy, in advance of Duke Vincenzo's death. But it proved to be 'an ill-fated decision which was the beginning of the end of their prosperity'.[46]

In a later volume, when assessing Olivares' career on the occasion of his fall from power, Siri returns to the Mantua incident *a fortiori*. In a more expansive treatment, he states that the war was planned and launched by Olivares as part of a deep-laid design to make his master universal monarch, truly the Planet King of Madrid's propaganda. His policy was gradually to seal off the autonomous states of Italy from all outside influence, preparatory to absorbing them fully into the Spanish system; and included a plot to subvert the independence of Mantua, just as Venice itself had been conspired against a decade earlier. These machinations were interrupted by the sudden death of Duke Vincenzo, which threatened the ruination of Olivares' whole scheme. His immediate reaction was the alliance with Duke Carlo Emanuele for the invasion and partition of the Mantua inheritances. The intervention of Louis XIII and Richelieu was a success which amply demonstrated divine approval of their cause.[47]

---

[44] G. de Valdory, *Anecdotes du ministère du Cardinal Richelieu et du règne de Louis XIII* (2 vols, n.d., n.p. but Amsterdam, 1717); and idem, *Anecdotes du ministère du comte duc d'Olivares, tirés et traduités de l'Italien de Mercurio [sic] Siry* (Paris, 1722).

[45] *Il Mercurio overo historia de' correnti tempi di Vittorio Siri, Consiglieri di Stato e Historiografo della Maestá Christianissima* (7 vols, Casale and Lyon, 1644–64).

[46] Ibid., i, p. 17 (cf. Valdory, *Anecdotes du Richelieu*, i, p. 190).

[47] Ibid., iii, pp. 264–65.

Siri adds dramatic verisimilitude to his account with an anecdote which was to be repeated many times in future treatment of the subject. The story is clearly intended to encapsulate in one convincing scene the negative image of Olivares and Spanish government disseminated by French propaganda. Possessing as it does the dramatic unities of time, place and action, it also seeks to gain plausibility through the provision of detail. For all these reasons, it merits attention.

Siri relates that when Olivares learned of the death of Duke Vincenzo, he entrusted the matter to an *ad hoc* Junta of ministers, 'which was held outside Madrid, in a little park under the Royal Palace and between the walls of Madrid and the River Manzanares'. This was the meeting which decided on 'the wretched war against the duke of Mantua [i.e. Nevers], whence all the misfortunes which befell the Crown of Spain derived their origin'. Three years later (Siri continues), Olivares was walking near this spot with the English envoy, Arthur Hopton, when he suddenly interrupted himself with the words: '"Do you see those trees by the ruined wall? Here was discussed, resolved and decided the war of Mantua and Casale."' Hopton was amazed that the count-duke should tell him this strange tale, which in effect was to boast of bringing about 'by his own sole authority, a war so damaging to the crown of Spain'.[48]

In his biography of Olivares, despite a generally consistent defence of the count-duke's career against generations of detractors, J.H. Elliott accepts that Siri's story 'has the ring of truth'.[49] So it does, in dramatic or metaphorical terms; but upon detailed examination, it appears full of inconsistencies. To begin with, it could only have originated with Hopton himself, since the context clearly indicates that the two men were walking alone and *al fresco*. The Englishman was well aware of Olivares' sensitivity over the results of the Mantuan war. During another private audience accorded to Hopton around this time, the count-duke broke down into apopleptic speechlessness over the treaty of Cherasco – by which Spain had agreed a concessionary peace – and the embarrassed Hopton was obliged to change the subject in order to bring his interlocutor back to sentience.[50] All other sources are unanimous in suggesting that Mantua was not a subject to which Olivares was likely to make gratuitous reference at this stage. It seems even less likely that he would seek to associate himself with these calamitous events in the casual and compromising manner described by Siri. Moreover, the story is not corroborated by Hopton's letter-book from the period, or by the extant official diplomatic correspondence.

Siri himself appears never to have visited in Madrid in these years. He got the story not from Hopton but from yet another Italian diplomat, Ippolito Guidi, who came to Madrid with the duke of Modena in 1638 and remained

---

[48] Ibid., p. 267.
[49] Elliott, *The Count-Duke*, p. 344.
[50] Hopton to Dorchester, 18 July 1631, BL, Eg. 1820, f. 50v.

behind as the duke's resident. Guidi – a priest – was thus a colleague of Hopton as a member of the diplomatic corps in the 1640s. His account of Olivares' fall from power in 1643 was to achieve wide currency. The original printed version of this chronicle is certainly hostile to Olivares, and may be regarded, like the work of Siri himself, as belonging to the French propaganda school. It includes a long and somewhat fanciful list of Spain's territorial losses brought about by the *valido*'s overweening ambition. To the tail of this list, well over a century later, a Spanish editor – spuriously and even more fancifully – attached the phrase 'with the loss of Mantua'. Yet no edition of Guidi's own text contains treatment of the Mantuan War, let alone a version of the Garden Junta story.[51]

Equally perplexing are Siri's topographical references. In the text of his edition, Valdory identified the *mise en scène* as the gardens of the Buen Retiro Palace, tampering with the text in order to make things fit this attribution. Into Olivares' mouth he put the spurious extra words 'cette longue allée couverte d'arbres, qui sont un si bel ombrage du côté du Manzanares'.[52] But the Retiro Palace did not exist at the time of the Mantuan crisis. Construction did not begin until several years later, of what was to be a summertime residence, situated on the opposite side of the city, well away from the river. From Siri's original description of the whereabouts of the 'little park', we may assume that the walled garden of the Alcázar of Madrid, on the same level as the main building (today roughly the area covered by the Plaza de Oriente and the Sabatini Gardens) is likewise *not* the area referred to. If anywhere, the open space below the promontory of the palace, and between these heights and the river (known today as the Campo de Moro), seems to be the place Siri intends.

A further puzzle resides in the season when this promenade took place. The initial decisions to attack Monferrat were taken in the latter half of January. Madrid in January is a very cold city. Siri asks us to believe that the venerable members of the junta chose to pursue their discussions in the biting winter wind sweeping down from the Sierra de Gredos, in preference to the heated (or at least insulated) council-chambers of the Alcázar. Moreover, to reach an actual spot which matches Siri's description, they would have had to descend a steep path and to walk a distance of almost a kilometre. In the light of these hard realities, the Garden Junta story seems almost nonsensical.

Almost, but not quite. For it is a bizarre fact that the documentation of the Mantua decision seems to provide some tenuous but intriguing circumstantial evidence in its favour. As we have seen, the king indeed entrusted discussion to a *Junta Particular de Estado* in circumstances which were clearly regarded

---

[51] [I. Guidi], *Caduta del conte d'Olivares* (Ivrea, 1644), pp. 4–5; idem, *Relation de ce qui s'est passé en Espagne a la disgrace du comte-duc d'Olivares, traduit d'Italien* (Paris, 1650), p. 8; A. Valladares (ed.), *Semanario erudito que comprende varias obras inéditas . . .* (3 vols, Madrid, 1787–88), iii, p. 8.

[52] Valdory, *Anecdotes du comte-duc*, pp. 250–51.

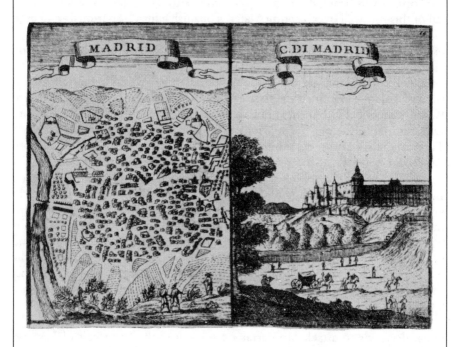

In these contemporary Italian engravings, the ground-plan of Madrid in the
left-hand panel shows the gardens of the old palace (Alcázar) on the banks of the
River Manzanares. The presumed scene of the Siri-Hopton anecedote lies
immediately to the north of the bridge. The right-hand panel gives a good
impression of the steep descent into this area from the palace buildings which
literally tower over them. A section of the medieval wall can be seen, marking
the southern perimeter of the park: it seems to fit Siri's description rather well
(see above, p. 88).

as top secret.[53] Around this time, the count-duke was becoming obsessed, and with good reason, about the confidentiality of government proceedings. The *consultas* of the special junta's meetings have not survived, and it seems possible that minutes were not taken. This would be consistent with conclaves being held in the open air, away from the prying ears of clerkish functionaries who may have had secret affiliations inimical to Olivares. Moreover, the crucial meeting of the regular *Junta de Estado* on 12 February 1628, which decided to confirm Don Gonzalo's orders, rather than to amend or withdraw them, appears to have been held in unusual circumstances.

The *consulta* of this meeting describes it (in a superscription) as being held 'Camino del Pardo' – [On] the Pardo Road'.[54] What can we deduce from this intriguing reference? The plan of the city made by De Wit, regarded as almost exactly contemporaneous with the happening described by Siri, shows that a section of the medieval city wall accompanied this road to the south, after it left the city at a gatehouse. When the road swings to the north, the wall continues to run due westward until it reaches the bank of the Manzanares, turning south at right angles to run along the river. This wall was indeed in a ruined state by the time of Philip IV's accession. Yet to fit Siri's description exactly, the Junta meeting must have taken place on the precarious lip of the river bank outside this wall, and far from any proper places of egress. Our sprightly councillors, after their descent into the *Campo de Moro*, and their kilometre walk, would then have had to climb over the wall – or at best negotiate the rubble of a fallen part of it – in order to assemble, somewhat like boyish trespassers in reverse, in the specified spot. This seems a rather excessive security precaution.[55]

If (therefore) we finally dismiss the idea of a location in Madrid itself, two alternatives remain. The first is that the crucial meeting was held in the gardens not of the Madrid but of the Pardo palace. It may be inferred from the endorsement of a document of 13 February that the king, with Olivares and several other ministers, had returned to the Pardo sometime before that date.[56] The second suggests a point of rest or refreshment (*merienda*) on the road to the Pardo from Madrid. Then as now, Spanish society was one lived, far more than we northerners normally realize, in the street and the open air. Impromptu juntas *were* occasionally held – for example, during a royal *jornada* to the provinces – in unusual circumstances, such as the king's coach. Olivares liked to discuss business *tête à tête*, in the garden or along the banks of the river, and often used his coach as a council-chamber.[57] Yet

[53] See Chap. 3, above.

[54] *Consulta* of junta of state, 12 Feb. 1628, AGS, E 3437, no. 32.

[55] For De Wit's map, see M. Molina Campuzano, *Planos de Madrid de los siglos XVII y XVIII* (Madrid, 1960). A generation later, Pedro Texeira's map shows similar details: C. Martínez Kleiser, *Guía de Madrid para el año 1656* (Madrid, 1926), see esp. pp. 7, 76–77, 85. Both originals are in the BN, Madrid.

[56] Olivares to Villela, 13 Feb. 1628, AGS, E 3437, no. 28.

[57] Elliott, *The Count-Duke*, p. 285.

surely neither of these options was utilized in the depths of winter; and to establish that an important committee met out of doors, even in August, would be unique in the present writer's experience of the Spanish State Papers. Despite Olivares' anxiety about intelligence failures in many central aspects of his governmental system, as a regular antidote such a stratagem would have been far too drastic and unmanageable.

The absence of the *Junta de Mantua*'s records means that the narrative can never be reconstructed. It may be speculated that they were among the sensitive material entrusted to the custody of Don Gaspar's most assiduous administrative functionary, the protonotario Jerónimo de Villanueva. Most of Villanueva's papers were confiscated by the Inquisition at the time of his arrest in 1644, including – according to a contemporary index made by a clerk of the Holy Office – a file concerning the Mantuan War. This file has subsequently disappeared. Possibly, however, Olivares himself carried the most sensitive material into retirement, to form part of the personal archive later destroyed by fire, in order to suppress evidence of his errors of judgment, and/or the better to prepare his own defence.[58]

Olivares' disclaimers of responsibility for Mantua did have some technical validity. The decision to invade Monferrat could only have been taken by the king, and was indeed regarded by him as resolved *before* he referred it to the junta. On the other hand, according to his later claim, and indeed given the principles of government to which he normally adhered, Philip would not have decided against the strong opposition of his councils.[59] The conversation described to Hopton may have been limited to favourite and king alone, held following the approval of the clerical junta for the decision. If so, the scene may have resembled the central confrontation of Monteverdi's political music-drama *The Coronation of Poppea*, reportedly derived from the personal experience of its composer in the amoral atmosphere of the Mantuan court.[60] The archetypal tyrant Nero, who despite being a composer of music and poetry is the very antithesis of a Christian Prince, rejects the advice of his minister, Seneca – Spaniard, Statesman, Stoic Philosopher and (not least) Playwright – and promotes his mistress to be imperial consort.

Nero	Leave off discussing. I shall have my own way.
Seneca	Do not anger the people and the Senate.
Nero	I do not care about the people or the Senate.
Seneca	Then at least care about yourself and your reputation.[61]

---

[58] Ibid., pp. x, 668–69.

[59] Above, n. 15; Stradling, *Philip IV*, esp. pp. 276–83.

[60] D. Arnold and N. Fortune, *The Monteverdi Companion* (New York, 1972), p. 129.

[61] From the translation of Busenello's text by R. Leppard (1964) in the booklet for the EMI LP recording, SAN 126–7. The Nero-Seneca relationship was the subject of Lope de Vega's play *Roma abrasada*, first printed in Madrid in 1625.

The opera was premiered in Venice in 1642, the year Philip IV left court for the military front in Aragon; an event which precipitated his loss of confidence in Olivares and the favourite's overthrow. Which character represents which in this dialogue depends on whom the reader perceives as culpable for the most disastrous decision of Spanish Habsburg history.

Epilogue

The origins of our fertile anecdote must therefore remain obscure to the empirical eye. Alternatively, they may be attributed to the pastoral imagination of the Italian Baroque, a scene from a drama or opera of political intrigue, set in a conventional backdrop landscape, with the painted towers of a palace in the distance. It could have been inserted in the great drama of history by Alessandro Striggio, chief minister of the duke of Mantua, who provided Monteverdi with the libretti for several operas, and who commanded the city of Mantua for Nevers against the Habsburgs during the siege of 1628. Whatever its origin, the story may be recognized as a metaphor – or metamorphosis – of something which actually happened; and its propaganda point fulfilled a role of obvious utility to centres of cultural and political power, both in Paris and Madrid.

Interpretation of the past by historians no longer invariably seeks to exclude the cognate discourses of 'fiction' and 'criticism'. The histrionics of history is a subject by no means restricted to the area of so-called 'High Politics', but currently informs investigation of worlds only tenuously in contact with the centres of Renaissance culture. Histories of events – whether town carnival, village personification, or the origins of wars in the corridors of power – are dramas being repeatedly played out with different emphases and in different costumes.[62] History itself, like *Hamlet*, is an arena of multiple and mutable auditions:

> *Hamlet* Do you see yonder cloud that's almost in the shape of a camel?
> *Polonius* By the mass, and 'tis like a camel indeed.
> *Hamlet* Methinks it is like a weasel.
> *Polonius* It is backed like a weasel.
> *Hamlet* Or like a whale?
> *Polonius* Very like a whale.
> *Hamlet* ... They fool me to the top of my bent.
>
> (*Hamlet*, III, 2)

[62] E. Le Roy Ladurie, *Carnival in Romans: A People's Uprising at Romans, 1579–80* (1980); N.Z. Davis, *The Return of Martin Guerre* (1985).

Gaspar de Guzman, count-duke of Olivares. This allegorical engraving, dense with scriptural references, celebrates Spain's victories in the 1620s. The count-duke of Olivares is depicted as a champion of the faith. He slays the many-headed dragon of heresy, who proclaims (from Micah) that 'all thine enemies shall be cut off'. The bird of faith sings 'my heart awakes' (from the Song of Solomon). Above, the escutcheon of Philip IV ('the munificent') promises that 'He that waiteth on the Master shall be honoured' (from Proverbs). (*Biblioteca National, Madrid*)

5

Olivares and the Origins of the Franco–Spanish War, 1627–35

> I have just heard with extreme sorrow of the death of His Highness Duke Vicenzo ... Deeply though I have respected all my patrons, I particularly had friendly feelings towards His Highness ... because I hoped that by his kindness I might have the capital that provides my pension ... but my fate, which has always been fickle rather than happy, has deigned to give me this great mortification.

With these highly disingenuous words, Claudio Monteverdi mourned the passing, late in 1627, of the last Gonzaga duke of Mantua.[1] We may hope that the 'extreme sorrow' of others was less inspired by anxious self-interest. What is certain is that, for many thousands of Monteverdi's contemporaries, the death of Duke Vicenzo was to bring in its train – quite literally – a 'great mortification'. In the three years following his letter, famine was succeeded by a war over the Mantuan Succession, and this in turn by the most appalling epidemic in the annals of this plague-ridden era. Together these phenomena reduced the population of northern Italy as a whole by about a quarter. Nor was this all. The significance of the duke's demise was more profound and far-reaching even than this collective tragedy – not to mention the definitive interruption to the artistic development of the Italian Renaissance entailed in the removal of Gonzaga patronage. His obsequies announced a momentous phase in the general history of Europe, a period which – it is no exaggeration to state – set a term to the dominance of the Catholic, Mediterranean civilization which for the past century or more had been presided over by the power of Spain.

Historians disagree over the significance of the so-called 'War of the Mantuan Succession', and its place in the sudden 'conjunctural crisis' which afflicted the Spanish monarchy in the late 1620s. Several writers certainly would not accept the broad assertions already made. It is true that we must be careful not to use the Chaunu model of *conjoncture* promiscuously and to curb a tendency to elevate any series of consistent or confluent data into a world-shattering 'turning-point'. Nevertheless, the more the crisis of Spanish power in 1627–31 is examined, the more difficult it becomes to resist such a conclusion in this instance. The war in Italy was, without doubt, the epicentre of disaster. Manuel Fernández Alvarez, whose monographic study of it was

---

[1] Monteverdi to Striggio, 9 Jan. 1628, in D. Arnold & N. Fortune (ed.), *The Monteverdi Companion* (New York, 1968), p. 79.

published thirty years ago, concluded that its consequence was to reduce the system of Spanish hegemony to a fundamentally defensive posture which was the prelude to its later collapse.[2] Since then, in several places, J.H. Elliott has thoroughly endorsed this view-point. In his most recent treatment, Elliott considers that the war was 'the most serious mistake' in the career of Philip IV's chief minister, the count-duke of Olivares, adding that 'for Spain, the results were an unrelieved disaster'.[3] Perhaps the most serious medium-term result of the limited war in Italy (1629–31) was to change the possibility of an unlimited military confrontation between Spain and France into a probability. The outbreak of a full-scale conflict thus became, as Elliott puts it, 'only a matter of time'.[4] Whilst the present writer regards these judgements as absolutely sound, it is surprising that few other scholars find themselves perfectly in accord with Elliott's *dicta* concerning the Mantuan War. H.G. Koenigsberger, for example, asserted some years ago that 'the evidence is all the other way'. Subsequently, Alcalá-Zamora supported this view, arguing that the Italian affair was a mere hiccough, a diversion from Madrid's main strategic objectives in Germany and (above all) in the Low Countries – to which, after the dust of Mantua had settled, Olivares duly turned his chief attention. These two authorities and (even more forthrightly) Geoffrey Parker maintain that Mantua was an incident without serious consequences: France gained little in terms of strategic advantage, Spain's setback was strictly limited, and her overall position in Italy undamaged.[5]

Some important *a priori* concessions must be made to the arguments of these sceptics. It can hardly be emphasised enough that they are correct in maintaining that the overriding priority of Spain's European policy under the count-duke was and remained the favourable settlement of the longstanding issue with the United Provinces. Of course, hope of an outright military solution to the Netherlands problem no longer survived amongst Philip IV's ministers. But Olivares still intended to extract from the Dutch rebels a new peace agreement which would restore *reputación*. This, indeed, was his *idée fixe*, since only such a success could provide the indispensable contrast between his government and that of his despised predecessor, the duke of Lerma, regarded as responsible for the shameful truce of Antwerp (1609–21). It may

---

[2] M. Fernández Alvarez, *Don Gonzalo Fernández de Córdoba*, (Madrid, 1955) esp. p. 122.

[3] J.H. Elliott, *Richelieu and Olivares* (Cambridge, 1984), pp. 95, 112.

[4] Idem, 'The Statecraft of Olivares', in J.H. Elliott & H.G. Koenigsberger (ed.), *The Diversity of History: Essays in Honour of Herbert Butterfield* (1970), p. 142.

[5] H.G. Koenigsberger, *The Habsburgs and Europe, 1516–1660* (1971), p. 243; J. Alcalá-Zamora, *España, Flandes y el Mar del Norte, 1618–1639* (Barcelona, 1975), pp. 125, 262; G. Parker, *Europe in Crisis, 1598–1648* (1979), pp. 201–5. Cf., however, two French authorities, J. Humbert, *Les Français en Savoie sous Louis XIII* (Paris, 1960), who sets out France's material gains from the treaty of Cherasco which ended the war (pp. 248–49); and M. Devèze, who notes that Richelieu himself considered that 'la guerre de 1635 est en germe dans l'échec des généraux espagnols devant Casal', *L'Espagne de Philippe IV: siècle d'or et de misère* (2 vols, Paris, 1970), i, p. 125.

be emphasised, furthermore, that this aspiration – the effective, if not actual, defeat of the Dutch – conditioned Olivares' attitude to France, both before and after the Italian war. A subordinate concession is that Koenigsberger and Alcalá-Zamora are also right to stress the dangers of detaching events in Italy from the coincidental pan-crisis of the monarchy.

The Spanish origins of the war of 1635 – surely the most momentous of all the conflicts of this war-dominated century – have never been properly studied.[6] This essay seeks to advance the argument that the war in Italy radically changed Olivares' perception of France, converting him from optimism, and even indulgence, to a pessimism coloured by his distaste for Cardinal Richelieu. This volte-face on the part of the minister was accompanied by a similar change in the attitude of his master Philip IV towards Louis XIII, a brother-in-law whom he had previously regarded with suitably fraternal feelings. As a result of Mantua, the count-duke recognized that the French government was irreversibly committed to frustrating the policy of Madrid by every available means, including (at the opportune moment) an offensive war. From this it followed that the ambitions of Olivares and Philip with regard to the Low Countries could not be realized until the removal of Richelieu brought with it a reversal of his policy. After 1631, accordingly, Olivares struggled obsessively to gather up and concentrate the resources of the Spanish system upon preparation for a war with France. Thus far, what has been said represents only a somewhat stronger version of what J.H. Elliott has written in all his publications on Olivares since 1963. But whereas Elliott believes that the count-duke's posture remained basically *defensive*, intended to equip the monarchy to repulse the inevitable French attack, and (at the most) to launch a decisive counter-attack when that unwanted moment arrived, a clean contrary conclusion can be derived from much of the available evidence. This suggests that Olivares' planning was rather more positive, and indeed that he came to favour a preventive attack upon France long before the latter declared war. By the early part of 1634 at the latest, his firm intention was – in a phrase borrowed from another discipline which is often useful in considering the origins of wars – 'to get his retaliation in first'.

Elliott's viewpoint, which has altered only slightly over the years, can be illustrated from his edition of Olivares' state papers:

> [After Mantua] the count-duke did not retain many illusions about the chances of avoiding open war with France, especially whilst Richelieu remained in

---

[6] None of J.H. Elliott's studies has been addressed directly to this issue, though several treat it fruitfully *en passant*. J.M. Jover Zamora's classic work *1635: Historia de una polémica y semblanza de una generación* (Madrid, 1949) outlines the strategic and 'ideological' causes of the war on both sides, but avoids any serious documentary analysis of its origins. Neither in his book nor in a later work, *Razón y crisis de la política exterior de España en el reinado de Felipe IV* (Madrid, 1977), does J. Alcalá-Zamora devote attention to the present theme. The narrative treatment in Devèze (*L'Espagne de Philippe IV*, i, p. 141 et seq.) is superficial, despite use of French and Spanish diplomatic sources.

power. But, conscious of Castile's weakness, he wished to avoid it for as long as possible in spite of pressure from other ministers for a preventive action ... In practice, a virtually open state of war ... already existed for some months before the formal French declaration ... [but nevertheless] all Spain's preparations were a political instrument in Olivares' hands with which to scare off his adversary.[7]

The intention of the great count-duke's historian is, therefore, to present a picture of his statesmanship as realistic, rational and, above all, responsible – in contrast to that of his fellow-ministers, on the one hand, and that of the king himself on the other. But in addition, Elliott's treatment has had the side-effect of establishing as valid and unassailable the contemporary claim made by Spain's team of literary apologists, that in 1635 the monarchy was the innocent victim of an unprovoked and gratuitous attack. The outraged polemic of writers like Quevedo and Pellicer has been all the more seductive because it was supported – indirectly and unintentionally – by the nineteenth-century school of French diplomatic historians who saw Richelieu as the original exponent of *Realpolitik* statesmanship. The cardinal's premeditated onslaught upon Spanish European hegemony was, in this classic thesis, the essential nucleus of his whole political programme in the creation of 'modern France'. Not surprisingly, therefore, down to the present day Spanish historians have uncritically supported their nation's case in interpretation of the events of 1635. In his recent examination of the issue, Fernández Alvarez asserts that 'many faults and errors may be levelled against Olivares ... but not that of seeking the war with France ... which was not Spain's fault, but that of France. Richelieu it was who launched a preventive war ...'[8] Since the circumstances of both historical event and historiographical phenomenon permit absolute security and satisfaction to both parties within their dialectics, this agreed thesis is firmly established in the history textbooks of all languages. After all, it has the further advantage of fitting with perfect neatness into the larger general explanation of Spanish 'decline' and French 'ascendancy'. Yet for all its inestimable value in providing us with an overall revaluation of a figure so long misunderstood, Elliott's defence of Olivares does not, in this instance, fully resist close examination. Moreover, the beliefs of Spanish historians are founded on little more than officially orchestrated propaganda.

Shortly before the death of Duke Vicenzo, Olivares drew up a memorandum in which he surveyed the European situation as a whole, but with special

---

[7] J.H. Elliott & J.L. de la Peña (ed.), *Memoriales y cartas del conde-duque de Olivares* (2 vols, Madrid, 1978–81), ii, pp. 108, 112. These points – all tending to the conclusion that Olivares's preparations and threats were essentially 'sabre-rattling', and that 'somehow he always managed to pull back from the brink of the abyss' – are further expounded in *Richelieu and Olivares*, pp. 114–17.

[8] M. Fernández Alvarez, 'El fracaso de la hegemonía española en Europe', in F. Tomás y Valiente (ed.), *La España de Felipe IV*, vol. xxv of the *Historia de España Menéndez Pidal* (Madrid, 1982), pp. 722–26.

attention to France.[9] He was fairly satisfied with things in general, and over Spain's great neighbour displayed a complacency verging on smugness. The comprehensive confidence of this document may have reflected a desire to impress the king, who had lately recovered from a serious illness, with his stewardship of affairs. Over France, however, there was much to justify the count-duke's analysis. Richelieu's position in government was at this stage highly ambivalent, and by no means supreme. The cardinal's earlier and precipitate essay in anti-Habsburg policy, the invasion of the Valtelline and Genoa in 1625, had resulted in his humiliation by the Spaniards.[10] Louis XIII was an unreliable master, who in the past had not spared the disgrace (and in one case the life) of ministers who displeased or failed him. Furthermore, Richelieu remained very dependent on the support of Marie de Médicis. The queen mother, along with her other son, Gaston of Orleans, and the aged but still powerful minister Marillac, formed a triumvirate which demanded a cautious attitude to the Habsburgs in order to concentrate on the reform of French government and the solution of the Huguenot problem. At the moment of Olivares' writing, this problem had developed into civil war in which Louis' army had been tied down for some months by the debilitating and unsuccessful siege of La Rochelle. As Olivares took pains to emphasise, the almost uninterrupted series of military and political successes achieved by the Habsburg alliance since the renewal of general war a decade earlier further reduced the possibility of any French adventure.[11] The war-effort against the Dutch was in a promising phase, a favourable strategic situation having been gained mainly by maritime and economic pressure. This had reduced not only the Dutch capacity to assist the other anti-Habsburg states, but even their own resolution concerning the continued resistance to Madrid. Wallenstein's huge army had imposed the emperor's writ across Germany, and he seemed on the point of effecting the juncture of imperial and Spanish forces in the Baltic – the very heart of Dutch economic power and the Protestant cause. Richelieu's persistence in subsidising the United Provinces and his impertinent dabbling in German affairs were, it is true, irritating. But on the whole it seemed to Olivares that France had very little room for manoeuvre in any potential attempt to harass the Spanish system.

Until this point, the count-duke had favoured a positive approach to France, one of refusing to exploit her internal weaknesses and generally assuaging her fears. Of course, he kept open the clandestine lines of communication with the Huguenots on the one side, and with the extreme Catholic party on the

9 'Parecer del Conde Duque de San Lúcar sobre el estado de las cosas en todas partes. En Madrid a cinco de diziembre de 1627', AGS, E K1435, no. 45. Statements of Olivares's views in this section are (unless otherwise noted) based upon this document.

10 R. Ródenas Vilar, *Política europea de España durante la Guerra de los Treinta Años* (Madrid, 1967) pp. 41ff.

11 Olivares made great play with these achievements in his submission to the council of Castile, drawn up a month or so earlier; see Elliott and de la Peña, *Memoriales*, i, pp. 235–50.

other – both of whom sought his support – but this was mainly a matter of sensible insurance. Several of his ministerial colleagues, amongst whom the marquis of Montesclaros and Don Pedro de Toledo were prominent, were by contrast highly apprehensive of French policy, and even demanded a pre-emptive war in order to bring Richelieu to heel, and to remind Louis of his proper religious responsibilities. The ambassador in Paris, who knew the Cardinal's mind, strongly supported this line of thought. Olivares, however, resisted these counsels. Eberhard Straub has recently – and rightly – corrected Ródenas Vilar's view that Olivares' friendship towards Paris was merely a smokescreen of deceit. On the contrary, it represented a feeling of *appaisement* in the old, non-pejorative meaning of the word. Olivares was convinced that Louis – if not the cardinal – could be brought to recognize that his safest and most conscientious course was to accept the hand of friendship sincerely proffered by Philip IV.[12] This attitude culminated in a major attempt at *rapprochement* during 1627. When the siege of La Rochelle was threatened by the duke of Buckingham's intervention, Olivares decided to honour an agreement with France (as yet unratified) by assisting Richelieu's campaign. This was not only a reasonably altruistic gesture, but one which was made in the face of voluble opposition in the Council of State. With considerable expense and effort, an expeditionary naval force was collected and despatched to intercept the English. In the event, it arrived too late, and Buckingham was repulsed without its help. This was a minor loss of face for Madrid, somewhat exacerbated by a rather ambiguous expression of Richelieu's gratitude which subsequently arrived. The count-duke was certainly a little piqued, remarking tartly that perhaps it would have been better to have aided the English instead. But his basic position was not disturbed, and he confidently assured the king that no serious danger was to be anticipated from France.[13] The one cloud on the horizon which Don Gaspar descried was the small but immensely troublesome state of Savoy. Duke Carlo Emanuele had for years been engaged on a career of opportunistic resistance to Spain's Italian interests. His orientation towards Paris had been demonstrated most recently in 1625, when he had supported Richelieu's abortive moves already mentioned. Savoy was a thorn in the side of Spanish Italy, and especially threatened Madrid's major *plaza de armas* in Lombardy. Olivares speculated that even if attempts to win Paris's confidence were ultimately hopeless, the collaboration of Turin would be exceedingly useful to the Spanish system. It would greatly reduce strategic and logistical problems in this nerve-centre as well as provide a

[12] Ródenas Vilar, *Politica Europea*, pp. 263–64; E. Straub, *Pax et imperium* (Paderborne, 1981) pp. 253ff; Elliott & de la Peña, *Memoriales*, i, p. 104.

[13] The abortive La Rochelle affair is documented in AGS, E K1435. See, in particular, the original decision in a *consulta* of the council of state, 2 July 1627 (no. 1); Richelieu's letter to Olivares, 21 Nov. (no. 124); and the latter's obvious irritation (nos 131–32). The official Spanish view, probably issued following the French invasion of Italy in 1629, can be found in 'Socorro que el Rey de españa embió al de Francia . . .', BN, 2359, ff. 1–3.

convenient barrier to French ambitions in the area. The count-duke evinced some enthusiasm on this point in his memorandum. Savoy was therefore on his mind at precisely the moment that it was flooded by the issue of the Mantuan succession.

Space does not permit a detailed account of the war of Mantua, but some attention must be paid to the extent of Olivares' personal commitment to it. Duke Vicenzo's rightful heir was a French nobleman, the duke of Nevers, and this seemed to pose its dangers to the security of Italy. Almost immediately (December 1627) Gonzalo Fernández de Córdoba, the governor of Milan, suggested that action was imperative. A limited but prompt military initiative, aimed at the occupation of Monferrat, the strategically crucial territory of the duchy of Mantua, would put Spain in a strong position to negotiate a satisfactory settlement of the whole issue. An important point in favour of Don Gonzalo's proposal was the fact that he had already secretly obtained the cooperation of Savoy in the plan he submitted to Madrid.[14] It is clear that the potential coup of detaching Savoy from its French connection strengthened Olivares' inclination to support Don Gonzalo. The former stressed this point in a long analysis of the situation which he gave the king just over a week after the latter's proposition arrived in Madrid. Evidently drawn up in haste, and with signs of emotional disturbance, this *voto* was a meandering document of the 'thinking aloud' variety.[15] Olivares admitted the various weaknesses in Spain's case for military action, and appeared highly conscious of the potential risks involved. He nevertheless struggled – with some desperation – to justify the move:

> The duke of Nevers is the legitimate heir to all the Mantuan estates, and simple justice is undoubtedly on his side ... [On the other hand] whilst Monferrat remains outside our control we can never close the door firmly upon those who seek to disturb the peace of Italy ... this is of the greatest value, and thus it follows that it is in the public interest for your majesty to hold Monferrat ... I desire more than anything else in the world to see your majesty master of Monferrat ...[16]

Olivares' dialectical difficulties here illustrated – and tackled with a tortuous casuistry of which his confessor would have been proud – were possibly caused by Philip IV's reservations. To soothe the king's conscience, the matter had already been referred to a *junta de teólogos*, which duly returned a favourable verdict.[17] Four days later, the king sent Don Gonzalo permission to move against Monferrat, in a letter full of cautions and instructions about the manner in which the act of aggression was to be presented to the world.[18]

[14] Fernández Alvarez, *Gonzalo Fernández de Córdoba*, pp. 57–59.

[15] 'Voto de Conde Duque sobre ... Saboya y Monferrato en la ocasion de la muerte del de Mantua, hecho a 12 de Henero 1628', BL, Eg. 2053, ff. 232–8v.

[16] BL, Eg. 2053, f. 237.

[17] Elliott, *Richelieu and Olivares*, p. 97.

[18] Philip to Fernández de Córdoba, 16 Jan. 1628, BN, 2360, f. 99.

In the wake of these delicate and awkward troubles there arrived in Madrid a servant of the king's who was widely regarded as the wisest and most experienced in the monarchy. Ambrogio Spínola, marquis of los Balbases, had come from Brussels in order to set before the Madrid government the need for a negotiated end to the war against the Dutch. Olivares was antipathetic to the man and to his ideas, yet such was Spínola's prestige as soldier and administrator that he soon assumed an important influence in policymaking. In the spring of 1628 a struggle was joined in the council of state which, whilst it involved genuine differences of principle, became steadily, and ever more nakedly, about power – nothing less than the survival of Olivares' *valimiento*. Almost from the beginning, a majority of councillors supported Spínola, whilst amongst the court aristocracy, opposition to the count-duke (derived from a variety of other causes) received a timely boost.[19] Whilst never transferring his sympathies *in toto* to the Spínola camp, Philip IV was evidently prepared to exploit the opportunity these events offered to clip the wings of his imperious chief minister. For nearly two years thereafter the king played a more overt and personal role in government than ever before, and in a manner which had serious implications for the count-duke's political future. Coincidentally with these difficulties at home, things began to go badly wrong with the campaign in Italy, and Olivares' embarrassment became increasingly acute. Having lost control of both king and council, week by week demonstrable evidence of his failure of judgement arrived on Philip's desk.

In later years Philip was to confess that Mantua represented the only unjust war of his reign, implying that the manifold misfortunes which stemmed from it were a clear sign of divine displeasure. Olivares also subsequently disclaimed responsibility for the war, going out of his way to announce in council that 'as for the Italian war, which has led to so many setbacks, there were twelve votes in favour and I alone, by the grace of Our Lord, did not vote'. Following his fall from power, he again returned to the issue; in the celebrated *Nicandro* (1643), he attributed the disaster of Mantua to the disobedience and incompetence of others, above all to Fernández de Córdoba.[20] However ultimately incompatible these divergences of memory, they were in harmony in one respect, in that they both identified the Italian war as the key event

[19] The clash over negotiations with the Dutch is fully documented in AGS, E 2042; see esp. *consulta* of council of state, 11 Aug. 1628. For the court and 'domestic' opposition to Olivares in 1627–28, see Elliott, *Richelieu and Olivares*, pp. 90–93.

[20] Philip to Sor María de Agreda, 20 July 1645, Seco Serrano, *Cartas de la Venerable Sor María*, i, p. 28, in which the king regrets following 'the counsels of my ministers' over Mantua. For Olivares's disclaimers, see J.H. Elliott, *The Revolt of the Catalans* (Cambridge, 1963) p. 518; and Elliott and de la Peña, *Memoriales*, ii, p. 250. However, the *valido* began to shuffle off responsibility as soon as it was clear that the Italian adventure was doomed to failure: see Q. Aldea Vaquero, 'La neutralidad de Urbano VIII en los años decisivos de la Guerra de los Treinta Años', *Hispania sacra*, 21 (1969), pp. 155–78 (at p. 171).

in the crisis of the Spanish monarchy.[21] Even at the time, the impression may be felt, Olivares was fully aware of the extent of his gamble not only with the whole basis of Spain's European influence, but also with his own future as its trustee. Nevertheless, the more complex his political difficulties became, the more his statesmanship faltered, and he drifted into a senseless obstinacy over the capture of Monferrat. As the wheel of fortune turned consistently against him – and not only in Italy – he insisted on throwing good money after bad. The three campaigns in northern Italy proved to be little more than prolonged agony for Spain, a series of frustrations instead of the stunning *coup de main*, the spectacular demonstration of vigilance and virility, that Olivares had envisaged. Everything hinged upon the resistance to Don Gonzalo's army put up by the great fortress of Monferrat, at Casale. While the Spaniards were stuck here without siege equipment and other reserve supplies, Richelieu proclaimed French support for Nevers' cause, and broadcast abroad a righteous condemnation of Philip IV's act of brigandage. The agrarian crisis of Castile hampered Madrid's ability to supply the army of Lombardy, a situation which was severely aggravated by the loss of the 1628 silver fleet to the Dutch. A chorus of European princes, loudest of all the pope, censured the Spanish action and took (what had quickly become) the French side. Indeed, Vatican support for Richelieu soon became tangible as well as moral, causing chagrin in Olivares and anxiety in Philip IV. In contrast, Spain's only legal supporter, the emperor, was tardy in providing military assistance.[22] By the end of 1628, the king felt himself, not without reason, to be universally discredited as well as defeated. And Olivares' position – 'partially excluded from the decision-making process' as he was – became extremely insecure.[23] In the full sense of the term, it is arguable that his *valimiento* – which implies a monopoly of influence with the monarch on major affairs of state – was in effect suspended.

In the winter of 1628–29 secret contact was made with Richelieu in an attempt to extricate Spain from its embarrassment on terms from which some prestige could be salvaged, and to stave off possible French military action.[24] In October, however, La Rochelle at last had fallen and the cardinal lost no time in preparing for direct intervention. When he and his master crossed the Alps into Savoy (March, 1629), the defeated Carlo Emanuele promptly deserted his new-found ally. By the terms of an armistice, the Spaniards were obliged to retire from Casale, and a military stalemate ensued. With the French invasion of Italy, however, the divided ranks of the monarchy's

21 It seems to have been widely identified as such at the outbreak of the war of 1635. See Gayangos, *Cartas*, i, p. 205: 'Dios se le perdone a quién fue la causa no se tomase Casal al tiempo del marqués Espinola cuando ya las cosas estaban a punto de acabarse . . .'

22 Philip to Aytona, 12 June 1628, BN, 2360, f. 119; Monterrey to Urban VIII (? May 1629), BN, 2361, f. 4.

23 Elliott, *Richelieu and Olivares*, p. 102.

24 Ródenas Vilar, *Política Europea*, pp. 173–82.

mandarins – at least on this issue – immediately reunited. A consensus arose that to acknowledge defeat in this hitherto impregnable but highly sensitive area would represent an unacceptable setback.[25] Precious human and material resources were therefore scraped up and shovelled into Lombardy during 1629–30. Fernández de Córdoba was replaced by Spínola, who ultimately sacrificed his own life upon the altar of Casale – the fall of which, Olivares stubbornly insisted, would restore everything that had gone awry with his programme.[26] During the 1630 campaign, imperial troops at last entered Italy in Spain's support. Despite a successful occupation of Mantua proper, they brought with them promiscuous destruction and the plague, which spread rapidly among a population already weakened by famine. In the autumn, moreover, the emperor withdrew following a unilateral agreement with France (treaty of Ratisbon), leaving Spain high and dry. The struggle for Casale had become hopeless, and in 1631 Madrid was obliged to negotiate from weakness, and under the unpropitious auspices of papal arbitration. The subsequent peace of Cherasco was a complete moral vindication of the French in that it unconditionally recognized Nevers' succession, and a pronounced political and strategic victory in its details and operation.

Spain had been forced to this miserable pass by the comprehensive collapse of her European strategy, for which the misconceived adventure in Mantua was mainly responsible. Whilst Madrid's attentions and energies were diverted, the Dutch had counter-attacked in Flanders. The army of Flanders was on the retreat, and both the security and loyalty of the Spanish Netherlands were suddenly in doubt. Across the Atlantic, the Dutch made a successful landing in Brazil and soon occupied the main Portuguese settlements centred on Pernambuco. Furthermore, in 1630 Gustavus Adolphus landed in Germany and proceeded to demolish the emperor's recently-imposed authority. Things were falling apart with an apocalyptic emphasis. Within little more than a year, the condition of Habsburg hegemony had been drastically impaired, and the dynastic alliance itself – corner-stone of Olivares' policy – was in a parlous state. Above all, the banner of *reputación*, hoisted so proudly by the count-duke on many previous occasions, was palpably tattered and besmirched. His fury was undisguised. He fulminated in council against emperor and pope, chief exhibits in a veritable gallery of scapegoats.[27] Having how emerged from his own political crisis and regained the king's support, he turned to attack his absent rival Spínola in the most forthright and damaging terms. The latter's misguided counsels, to which Philip had weakly given ear, were blamed by Olivares for many of the failures of Spanish arms in Flanders and

[25] See below, p. 113.

[26] Fernández Alvarez, *Gonzalo Fernández de Córdoba*, p. 72; Aldea Vaquero, 'La neutralidad', p. 170.

[27] See Ródenas Vilar, *Política Europea*, pp. 266–75 (*consulta* of the council of state, 10 Nov. 1630, from AGS, E 2331).

Italy.[28] Despite his anxiety to deflect criticism and his enormous capacity for self-delusion, it must have been cruelly obvious even to the *valido* himself that he had been mistaken in many of his sanguine predictions of 1627, and that all flowed from his fundamental misjudgement of French policy and capacity. Richelieu was, therefore, promoted to the status of *bête noire*, the cunning and determined architect of Spain's overthrow. If Olivares had been at fault, it was in neglecting earlier opportunities – which others had pointed out – to deal with the cardinal. His personal distaste for his French counterpart became steadily more intense, and his attachment to the idea of vendetta thus dominated the arena of European power-politics as notably as the theme of the noble revenger in the plots of a thousand contemporary dramas.

During the Mantuan War itself, Olivares had considered cutting the Gordian knot by a full-scale attack on France. Even before the French invaded Italy, he attempted to deter Louis and Richelieu by threatening 'a war in every theatre and by all the means at our disposal'.[29] When this failed in its purpose, information reached Madrid from more than one quarter that the French action was only a prelude to a confederated onslaught upon the monarchy, orchestrated by Richelieu in league with many, or all, of its potential enemies. A number of Philip's governors and envoys abroad – those in Italy almost unanimously – pressed for the ultimate reaction to the French outrage.[30] Moreover, this was the course now urged by no less a voice than that of Philip IV himself. The king's own desire for revenge on Louis XIII, which he articulated quite literally to Olivares, was inspired by his bitterness over a personal peace initiative which the French king had either ignored or rejected at the time of the armistice.[31] This was sharpened by a mixture of humiliation and jealousy that his brother-in-law had commanded an army on a daring and successful campaign. For much of 1629 (perhaps encouraged by Spínola), he put pressure on his ministers to agree to his leaving for Lombardy in order to lead the counter-attack on the French, projected for the campaign of 1630. In this context, Elliott is doubtless correct to stress Olivares' moderation when set beside the wounded pride of his master. If to others, for a variety of reasons, he sounded the alarm bells for a general war, to Philip he firmly maintained that Spain needed 'a few years of recuperation' before such a course could be seriously contemplated.[32] Yet his reaction was also tempered by the knowledge that war with France would increase – perhaps to an irresistible degree – the king's desire to take up a military career. This was a primordial consideration, since the political implications of Philip's leaving Spain would

---

[28] 'El Conde Duque de S. Lúcar, voto en las cosas de Italia . . .' (n.d. but from internal evidence, summer 1630), BN, 988, ff. 262–277.

[29] Philip to Aytona, 21 Jan. 1629, BN, 2361, f. 278.

[30] Alcalá to Olivares, 27 April 1629, BN, 10228, ff. 1–5; Fernández de Córdoba to Leganés, 3 March 1629, BPU, 56, ff. 302–303.

[31] See two documents apparently drafted by Philip on 3 May 1629 in an attempt to avoid overt hostilities with France: BN, MS 2361, f. 120; PRO, SP 94/34, f. 83.

[32] Elliott and de la Peña, *Memoriales*, ii, pp. 10, 22, 43.

inevitably lead to the reduction of the *valido*'s power, and very probably its definitive loss.[33] For Olivares, therefore, 'a few years of recuperation' had more than one motive, especially in view of the narrow escape from political eclipse he had recently experienced. For some three years following the peace of Cherasco, therefore, the thought of his king's martial aspirations provided a constant check on Olivares' policy – as indeed it did, for similar reasons, on that of Cardinal Richelieu. In addition, it is undeniable that given the weak physical condition in which the monarchy now found itself, a major war was hardly a serious option. To wage it with any prospect of success, and with any hope of an ultimate 'peace with honour' (*paz honesta*, the will o' the wisp of all Madrid's policies), it was first necessary not only to repair the damage to the Spanish system sustained since 1628, but even to improve upon the favourable balance which had previously prevailed. The count-duke determined to bring this about with all possible speed. The effort involved on the part of the subjects of Philip IV was, during the next decade, to represent a commitment unprecedented in European history, bearing comparison with the prolonged popular struggles of our own century.

A vital aspect of Spain's preparation for the supreme challenge was the diplomatic-strategic offensive of 1631–34. Occupying pride of place was the necessity to avoid a war on two fronts in Flanders by the negotiation of an armistice with the United Provinces. Olivares had consistently opposed the peace talks of 1629–30, which the king had sanctioned under the influence of the Spínola faction. Now, however, the (emphatically *pro tempore*) shelving of the Dutch problem appeared indispensable to its ultimate solution. In all the circumstances, the Spanish terms – which underwent almost continuous changes of emphasis and detail as events, and with them Olivares' calculations, developed in these years – were hardly likely to attract the Dutch, who now held the initiative on almost every point.[34] Whilst these talks chattered inconclusively on, however, a swarm of envoys and agents left Madrid and other centres of the Monarchy for the chancelleries of Europe, great and small. Dozens of emissaries were instructed to counter French initiatives and propaganda, to offer alliances and financial subsidies, to investigate the prospects of hiring mercenaries.[35] It was the time-honoured tactic of

[33] On the King's military aspirations, see Stradling, *Philip IV*, pp. 96ff. In June 1629, Olivares was obliged, against his better judgement, to give him an open-ended assurance of leading an army in a future campaign against France, Elliott and de la Peña, *Memoriales*, ii, pp. 10, 40.

[34] J.I. Israel, *The Dutch Republic and the Hispanic World, 1606–61* (Oxford, 1982), p. 226 et seq. (esp. pp. 244–45). It seems impossible to be certain of Olivares's sincerity in supporting even a *short* truce. If he was playing for time, then he achieved a measure of success in creating what was in effect a land-force armistice. Following the last major Dutch offensive in 1632 little active campaigning took place – a situation which suited both sides with the French entry into the war.

[35] Olivares despatched some of his closest supporters – many of them his personal *hechuras* (creatures) – to key administrative, military and diplomatic positions all over Europe in these years. One of the most talented, Francisco de Melo, was sent to Genoa to operate the communications centre of the network.

attempting to isolate an intended victim, similar to the effort made against the United Provinces in 1618–21, or – perhaps more strictly analogous – Louis XIV's moves against them in 1670–72. The Spanish motive for a suspension of the Dutch war was explicit; it was needed 'because of the likelihood of war with France on all our borders with that king'.[36] The phrase is almost an encapsulation of the agenda of Madrid's councils and juntas in these years. From 1631 onwards, Olivares began to broadcast a message which amounted to a state of emergency throughout the Monarchy, and by all the means available to him. The prospect of hostilities with Louis XIII was a ubiquitous warning, repeated endlessly in the government documentation of the period.[37] Just as no potential ally was left uncourted, no regional frontier was ignored in the drive to improve defences and to raise and station new armies. At home in Castile – and with hardly less thoroughness in Naples – the exploitation and mobilization of fiscal, material and human resources pressed ruthlessly ahead. It is clear that, with occasional differences of intensity, the count-duke was prepared to subordinate every other political consideration to the supremely reductive laws of defence and obedience.[38] In a short space of time, it produced a radically new phase of quasi-arbitrary government by one man and his party supporters – the Olivares dictatorship, which left no interest in the monarchy secure from its demands, and which eventually inspired the universal rebellion against him of 1640–43.

The failure to make headway in a truce with The Hague put a huge premium on successful negotiations with Vienna. It meant that the bulk of the army of Flanders could not be utilized against France, hence a military contribution by the emperor, and if possible his Catholic German allies, was essential to Spain's programme. 'The answer to everything must come from Germany', noted Olivares early in 1633,[39] but the task of eliciting the required response was fraught with difficulty. Throughout the 1620s the count-duke had continually pressed Vienna for a military commitment

---

[36] Olivares to Aytona ([? Sept.] 1630), BN, 2362, f. 11; see also Philip to Archduchess Isabel, 17 Jan. 1632, ARB, SEG 204, f. 236, which states that an armistice is needed 'in order to apply the army [of Flanders] to a more convenient task'. Isabel had orders to move the bulk of the army to the French frontier as soon as she had concluded a reliable agreement.

[37] For the regular 'is war in sight?' signals which invariably warned of sudden French attack, see (e.g.) Philip to Isabel 17 Jan. (above n. 36); same to Benavente, instruction no. 4, Nov. 1632, AGS, E K1424, no. 74; *consulta* of council of state, 8 Dec. 1632, K1424, no. 83; Philip to Carlos de Coloma, 2 March 1633, AGS, E K1425, no. 7 (see also nos 8, 9); *consulta* of council of state 6 Feb. 1624, BN 2365, ff. 66–67; 'Minuta de la Instrucción que llevó Don Esteban de Gamarra . . .', 13 July 1634. BN 2365, ff. 199–200v; and Olivares to the President of Castile, Jan. 1634, printed in Domínguez Ortiz, *Política y hacienda* (2nd edn, Madrid, 1983), p. 343.

[38] The most useful study of this process is still Domínguez Ortiz, *Política y hacienda*, esp. pp. 35–47, 332–48, 375–78. See also, however, J.H. Elliott, *Revolt of the Catalans*, p. 237 et seq.; idem, 'El Programa de Olivares y los movimientos de 1640', in Tomás y Valiente, *Historia*, pp. 407–25.

[39] Straub, *Pax et imperium*, p. 458.

against the Dutch, and his efforts had brought no reward. Now – and moreover at a time when the Madrid–Vienna 'axis' was more fragile than at any time since the Defenestration of Prague – Olivares was determined to gain the emperor's collaboration against an even more dangerous adversary. Yet Vienna was brought back within his grasp by the very factor which had caused Ferdinand II to wriggle free of it in 1630. By 1633 the threat from Sweden had developed to an extent which fulfilled all but his worst fears. The northern blizzard sweeping down upon the allodial lands of Habsburg and Wittelsbach made the refuge of Spanish steel and silver seem more attractive than ever before. Furthermore, whilst Ferdinand's great servant – or ally – Wallenstein appeared ever more unreliable, the ominous fact of Richelieu's assistance to the Swedes could hardly be gainsaid.[40] In these circumstances, Madrid could drive a hard bargain for its restoration of full support to Vienna. Olivares' team of diplomats working in Germany made some progress in 1632–33 in alerting the Catholic princes to the need for a showdown with France, but Ferdinand himself continued to procrastinate on such a fateful step.[41] Since bold military action against the Swedes seemed a necessary precondition for a diplomatic breakthrough, Olivares duly provided it. In 1633 the duke of Feria's small but highly-motivated army crossed the Alps, and for ten months conducted in south-western Germany one of the most brilliant campaigns of the Thirty Years War. Spanish land communications with Flanders were restored, and a Swedish attack upon Austria frustrated. Six months later (September 1634), the cardinal-infante's army followed suit. Together, Philip IV's brother and Ferdinand's son shattered the Swedish army at Nördlingen, to the extent that it was not able to operate as an integral force for nearly three years.[42] In between these two events, Olivares sent a new envoy to Vienna. By now a veteran statesman, the count of Oñate was well known to Ferdinand II, with whom he had initiated the original basis of the Habsburg alliance in 1617. A month after Nördlingen, the two men agreed the clauses of a contract for its full renovation.

Incontestable documentary evidence in support of the proposition that the treaty of 1634 was an unmitigated offensive alliance, intended for a 'first strike' against France, is at present not available.[43] It seems likely that the emperor's

---

[40] R. Birely, *Religion and Politics in the Age of the Counter-Reformation* (Chapel Hill, NC, 1981), esp. pp. 177–227, analyses the policy of Vienna in these years.

[41] H. Günter, *Die Habsburger-Liga 1625–1635: Briefe und Akten aus dem General-Archiv zu Simancas* (Berlin, 1908). See also, 'Lo que vos Antonio Sarmiento . . . haveis de hazer . . . a Lorena y a los electores y príncipes confinantes al Rhín', 28 Oct. 1633, AGS, E K1425, no. 67.

[42] For detailed treatment of these events, A. van der Essen, *Le cardinal-infant et la politique européenne de l'Espagne* (Brussels, 1944), pp. 120 et seq., 327–423.

[43] Neither of the two recent studies by Straub and Birely are forthcoming on the point, while the documents printed in Günter (*Die Habsburger-Liga*) from the specifically German *legajos* of the *Estado* series at Simancas are suggestive but ultimately inconclusive.

firm military commitment, linked to a suitable time-schedule, resided either in a secret article or in a 'gentleman's agreement' with Oñate. In any case, it may be argued that the weight of circumstantial evidence puts the existence of such an understanding beyond reasonable doubt. Shortly before his conclusion of the treaty, Olivares had warned Oñate that 'you *must insist* upon the emperor's concurrence over this war'; and Philip's unambiguous congratulations to the count when news of it reached Madrid indicate that this is precisely what was achieved.[44] An envoy assured the king of Hungary that Madrid would give Vienna full advance notice of any belligerence, but that 'any more delay [in attacking France] would cause great damage' to the Habsburg cause.[45] Early in March 1635, rumours reached Spain that the imperialists were having cold feet. Olivares told the council of state that 'we are still ignorant of the finer points of the German situation, whilst your majesty finds himself preparing at great expense to comply with the requirements of the alliance, in which it is expressly laid down, *if not in so many words*, that war will be declared against France'.[46]

Meanwhile, some progress had been made towards the raising of a new army on Germany's Rhineland frontier with France. This force was to be largely made up from imperialist and other German sources, but with a nucleus of *tercios veteranos* and generally subsidized by Spanish credit. It was projected as 40,000 men, more than twice the size of the average field army of the time, and decidedly *not* a force designed for defensive operations.[47] In the event, of course, no imperialist-backed army proved able to take the offensive in 1635. But only a month before the French declaration of war, Olivares repeated his point with even greater force: 'despite fears that the Imperialists view with disquiet the prospect of a joint war against France [he announced in council], our latest despatches from Germany take the fact of such a war *as already accomplished*'.[48] Though the point of his confidence in imperial commitment seems clear, it is possible that this was partly a bluff on his part to strengthen the nerves of his colleagues. It makes no difference, however; for the count-duke had by now completed his arrangements for a pre-emptive strike and orders for the movement of Spanish forces against France were already on their way.

After Cherasco, direct Franco-Spanish relations were shot through with a duplicity as palpable as it was mutual. By temperament, Olivares did not feel

[44] Günter, *Die Habsburger-Liga*, pp. 416–17, 429 (my emphasis). The alliance was set to come into force on 1 January 1635.

[45] Castañeda to Leganés, 2 Oct. 1634, BPU, 56, ff. 294–296.

[46] Olivares's *voto* in *consulta* of council of state, 3 March 1635, AGS, E 2050, no. 32 (my emphasis). The military clauses of the league, however, would seem to bear him out well enough; see 'Sumario de la liga entre el Emp. y su Mg. Cat.', BN, 11000, f. 188.

[47] Philip to Monterrey, 31 Oct. 1632, AGS, E 3860; Aytona to Philip, 12 May 1633, BRB, 16169, ff. 99v–100; Günter, *Die Habsburger-Liga*, pp. 427–34.

[48] Olivares's *voto* in *consulta* of council of state, 19 April 1635, AGS, E 2050, no. 43 (my emphasis).

comfortable on the shifty ground of diplomatic dissimulation. The 'cautious statesman, with a natural instinct to play for time' pictured by Elliott, seems to be little in evidence on close examination of the 1630s.[49] Olivares' patience was tried by Richelieu to breaking point and beyond. Indeed, in the aftermath of defeat in Italy (1632), he sent as envoy to Paris the most provocative choice possible, in the person of Fernández de Córdoba. The latter delivered to Richelieu a sermon ('it is a great mortal sin to aid the enemies of the church') and a warning that if he did not mend his ways, Spain would retaliate 'even though it might mean war'.[50] This was sabre-rattling indeed, and when the cardinal made a dusty response, Don Gonzalo was recalled. Later the same year, he and the francophobe marquis of Mirabel (resident ambassador) were replaced by Cristóbal de Benavente y Benavides. The ineluctable basis of Benavente's mission was made clear:

> The greater number of misfortunes which have occurred and continue to occur in my kingdoms and provinces can justly be attributed to the French . . . Their aim is well known; to procure the diminution of my greatness, discrediting my forces and objectives as they have always done.[51]

Benavente was instructed to speak sweetly in public, and Spain's need for a breathing-space was stressed. Nonetheless, like all other Spanish representatives, he was left in no doubt by Olivares that Richelieu was the 'natural enemy'.[52] The major task of Benavente's embassy was therefore to gather information and to improve Spain's standing with his diplomatic colleagues at the French court, rather than positively to seek a resolution of Franco-Spanish difficulties. Indeed, it is noteworthy that Benavente later compiled a celebrated manual of diplomatic ethics and tactics, in which he specifically discussed the problems of an envoy who knows that his master intends to declare war on the prince to whom he is accredited.[53]

During each year from 1632–34, the French army made small but threatening strategic moves in the Rhineland and Alpine *irredenta*, given out (not without

---

[49] Elliott, *Richelieu and Olivares*, p. 117. Here and elsewhere, Elliott suggests that in 1631–35, Olivares consistently resisted the pressure of other ministers to take the plunge. As we have seen, both before and during the Mantuan War, there were indeed groups of 'hawks' in the king's councils who pressed for a radical solution to the French problem. After 1631, however, I have found no serious indication of such pressure either inside or outside the council and juntas of state, except for Olivares's two Savoyard advisers, who certainly appear to have been influential in 1634–35 (see below, p. 112 & n. 59).

[50] 'Instrucción que se dió a Don Gonsalvo de Córdoba año de 1632 yendo a francia por embajador', BN, 10685, ff. 227–40.

[51] 'Instrucción a Don Xtobal de Benavente en cosas de la Reyna Madre y otros', 20 Nov. 1632, AGS, E K1424, no. 74.

[52] Elliott, *Richelieu and Olivares*, pp. 114–15.

[53] C. de Benavente, *Advertencias para reyes, príncipes y embaxadores* (Madrid, 1643), chap. 21 ('Si el Embaxador puede mentir para evitar graves daños . . .'), which actually gives the hypothetical example of an envoy whose king has prepared the appropriate forces *and issued orders for the attack* (pp. 478–79).

justification) as defensive responses to Spain's military build-up in Lombardy. Benavente protested loudly against this, claiming at the same time that 'my master does not wish to light the fires of conflict but to pour water on them', whilst Philip stressed that 'the world must see that on my part there has been the greatest demonstration of good faith'.[54] Benavente could be certain of a sympathetic response in Madrid when he reported, early in 1634, that

> Richelieu has offered nothing in satisfaction of our complaints, since his method of negotiation is constantly to lie and deceive. To my mind, whatever kind of agreement we may make with the French, whilst the Cardinal remains in their government it will never be observed.[55]

Olivares' constant assertion that France was on the point of general belligerence seemed about to be confirmed in the spring of 1633, when troop movements in Alsace coincided with an ominous rumour which reached Madrid. This apparently well-founded intelligence revealed that Louis XIII had decided to apply to Rome for a dissolution of his marriage with Philip IV's sister. It was an open secret that the pair were both personally and sexually incompatible, and since the pope (Urban VIII) was regarded as a client of France, the divorce was expected to meet few obstacles. The double Habsburg-Bourbon marriage treaty of 1612 had been expressly designed as a symbol of the 'perpetual peace and amity' between the crowns. The understandable fear in Madrid was that its threatened fracture contained an entirely contrary message.[56] In the event, the suit was never filed, and Spanish apprehension was exaggerated. Despite his king's impatience and martial proclivities, Richelieu had no intention of an open war with Spain, at least in the short term. His internal political difficulties were, at this stage, if anything more severe than those of his Spanish counterpart, and he was aware that war might fatally exacerbate them. On the other hand, his celebrated 'system' of war by proxy was running smoothly, and France's diplomatic influence was steadily on the increase. Even when his methods began to falter – following Nördlingen and the victorious march of the cardinal-infante to Brussels – the arguments for such a radical alteration of his stance were far from convincing.

In terms of documentary evidence, of course, the key decision-making processes of Bourbon government are considerably less accessible than those of the Spaniards. Nevertheless, it seems likely that the long-established textbook certitudes concerning the cardinal's reaction to Nördlingen, and his alleged advance decision to go to war in 1635, are founded on little more than conjecture allied to hindsight.

Both, moreover, rely on *a priori* and perhaps mistaken assumptions about

---

[54] Philip to Benavente, 5 March 1635, AGS, E K1425, no. 12.

[55] 'Copia de carta de D. Cristóbal Benavente . . . sobre la sesión que tuvo con el Cardinal Richelieu . . . a 5 de henero de 1634', BN, 18192, ff. 60–71v.

[56] Philip to Benavente, 31 May 1633, AGS, E K1425, no. 25.

Richelieu's own careful planning and his psychic vision into the future.[57] Unlike his successor, Richelieu was no gambler but a clinically rational statesman. It simply did not make sense to enter a war in which his most powerful ally, Sweden, had been perhaps definitively disabled, and its military confederation virtually dismantled, with the enemy holding the initiative in most of the vital theatres. Indeed – and on the contrary – in a passage of his *Political Testament* probably composed in early 1635, the cardinal strongly advised his master *against* another major war. He was profoundly concerned for the king's health which had collapsed to danger-point on each campaign in the past, though Louis invariably insisted upon active participation.[58] His only heir was his brother Gaston, Richelieu's inveterate enemy. In all the circumstances thus far adduced (and many perforce left aside here), to provoke a war *à l'outrance* with the Habsburgs would surely, in Richelieu's reckoning, involve an unacceptable level of risk to everything he had striven to encompass. The question thus arises: why *did* he nevertheless declare war in May 1635? His change of mind was inspired by exactly those circumstances which were later specified in the official justification of belligerence, but which both French and Spanish historians have (for different reasons) always discounted. In the winter/spring of 1635 the information reaching Paris from several different centres of Spanish activity convinced Richelieu that Olivares was preparing a mighty and imminent blow.[59] The conviction was perfectly correct, and France's taking the field first helped to throw the Spanish plans off balance. The conclusions of José Maria Jover, in a celebrated study of the propaganda

[57] The view that Richelieu deliberately prepared in 1634–35 for a war which he intended to launch, come what may, in the latter year has been restated *a fortiori* by Parker (*Europe in Crisis*, pp. 243–44). The evidence for the view that 'France had skilfully isolated her enemies before launching a simultaneous attack on several fronts' seems considerably more circumstantial than that for the converse hypothesis, relating to Spain, which is advanced here. (However, the two propositions are not incompatible.) For the evolution of what the cardinal himself referred to as the *'guerre couverte'*, see H. Weber, 'Richelieu et le Rhin', *Revue historique*, 239 (1968), pp. 265–80.

[58] H.B. Hill (ed.), *The Political Testament of Cardinal Richelieu* (Wisconsin, 1961), pp. 38–39.

[59] It seems possible that Spain's intentions were betrayed by two close confidants of Olivares, the Savoyards Prince Tommaso and Alessandro Scaglia. Both men played a leading role in the evolution of the former's plans for a preemptive strike; see M.A. Echevarría Bacigalupe, *La diplomacia secreta en Flandes, 1598–1643* (Leioa, 1984), pp. 208–11, and below, pp. 113, 116. Prince Tommaso was denounced as a double-agent by the Brussels authorities – the accusations reaching Madrid at the very moment that his plans for an attack were being (nevertheless) approved; see *consulta* of council of state, 14 Jan. 1635, AGS, E, 2050, no. 3. Richelieu's interception of Spanish diplomatic dispatches was cited as one of the justifications for the invasion of France in 1636; see *La disposición y forma que han tenido las armas de S.M. Cat. para entrar por la provincia de Guipúzcoa ... Año 1636*, APR, SH 37. Olivares had always been worried about leaks in security over high-level decisions (see Elliott, *Richelieu and Olivares*, p. 115), and so many were the centres of military preparation in 1634–35 that there seems no reason to doubt the honesty of Richelieu's claims to be forewarned. His information was indeed both accurate and complete.

issued by both sides in the wake of the fateful events of 1635, were suitably patriotic and have never been challenged. The French claim to be frustrating a 'grand attack' was merely a loincloth to cover naked and cynical aggression. According to Jover, not only were the Spanish polemicists justified in their righteous indignation over the *Dolchstoss* of a Catholic sister, but the event also marked a portentous stage in the moral metamorphosis of Christianity into the monstrous and nihilistic atavism of modern Europe.[60] These transcendental assertions are founded on a premise which is diametrically mistaken. It might be added that whereas Richelieu went to some lengths to observe the ancient protocol of princes – for example, the absurdly anachronistic gesture of Louis' herald before the gates of Brussels – Olivares, in contrast, had intended to invade without notice, in what was almost literally a piratical onslaught.

Some ten days after news of the French declaration of war reached Madrid, Olivares unveiled what Elliott refers to as his 'master-plan of campaign'.[61] The various elements and contingencies discussed in this document, however, already had a considerable history. Its origin and background may be compared to those of the notorious 'September Programme' of the German Chancellor Bethmann Hollweg, drawn up a month after the start of the First World War but incorporating ideas which had long been official and semi-official policy. As early as May 1625, during the French attack on Genoa, Don Pedro de Toledo had proposed a three-pronged offensive of reprisal, to be launched from Flanders, Navarre and Catalonia.[62] These ideas resurfaced during the 1629 emergency, along with the suggestion (proposed by Feria and Alcalá, amongst others) of a joint Habsburg invasion of France from the Rhineland redoubts.[63] In 1632 the disaffected Savoyard Prince Tommaso, who had taken Philip's service, assured Madrid that only decisive military action could prevent a league of predators, led by the French and the Dutch, from falling upon the Spanish monarchy.[64] From this source and many others proposals pullulated in 1632–34 for the support of malcontent movements within France, both real and imaginary. Several of these were taken up, but the schemes received a severe setback in 1632, when Gaston of Orleans attempted a major rebellion against the Richelieu regime. His precipitate action, uncoordinated with the policy of Madrid, was crushed;

[60] Jover Zamora, *1635: Historia de una polémica*, esp. pp. 145–49, 238–40, 474–77.

[61] Elliott, *Revolt of the Catalans*, pp. 309–19. The document in question is cited in full below, p. 118, n. 79. See also E. Zudaire Huarte, *El conde-duque y Cataluña* (Madrid, 1964), pp. 117–18.

[62] Elliott and de la Peña, *Memoriales*, i, pp. 138–39.

[63] See above, p. 105, n. 30. see also, 'Siete puntos sacados de los despachos y cartas de Su Magestad, y del Conde Duque, y de D. Gonsalvo de Córdoba de diferentes fechas', 25 April 1629, BN, 2361, f. 202.

[64] 'Memorial del Snr Príncipe Tomás para el Conde Duque', Aug. 1632, AGS, E K1424, no. 62; 'Discurso sobre la gerra [sic] de Italia', 23 May 1629, BL, Sloane 2545, ff. 1–19, sums up a widespread belief in these years that the monarchy was the object of a massive conspiracy organised by its actual and potential enemies.

and the consequent dissipation of actual and potential help for his strategy so annoyed Olivares that he declared any further subsidies would be 'no more than money cast out of the window'.[65] In practice the usefulness of Gaston, now thrown entirely into dependence on Spain, was too great to ignore. In 1634 detailed military agreements were signed, both with Orleans and the duke of Lorraine, whose territory had been usurped by the French. The former's army – to be commanded by Prince Tommaso – was to be in position on the French frontier with Flanders by September, whilst the latter was required to add his forces to the confederate army in the Rhineland.[66] Meanwhile, a new army raised in Spain and ostensibly to be commanded by Philip IV in person, was taking shape (if with difficulty) in the Catalan borderlands; yet another was slowly forming itself in Navarre.[67]

Although his preparations were still far from mature, the constant tension took its toll upon the overworked Olivares and, in the spring of 1634, his patience snapped. Incursions of French troops into Spanish spheres of interest, which followed Richelieu's renewal of the treaty of mutual assistance with the Dutch, apparently convinced him that action could be no longer delayed. At roughly this point he was the recipient of an opportune and convincing proposal for an amphibious attack upon the port of Marseilles. Olivares, and a *junta particular* to which he referred it, reacted enthusiastically to this project, which was accordingly scheduled for immediate implementation. It was described as a scheme 'to place a halter upon France . . . drawing her forces down to the areas where your majesty is superior', and away from the Flanders and Rhineland fronts.[68] A large naval flotilla would take Marseilles, providing the base of operations for a landing-force of about 8,000 men. This nucleus could hope to attract the aid of malcontent noble and urban elements in Provence. Alternatively or additionally, it might link up with the army of Catalonia, striking through Languedoc – a region equally fertile in disaffection to Paris. The marquis of Santa Cruz, son of Philip II's great admiral, was appointed to command of the operation in April.[69]

[65] Olivares' memorial of [? March] 1633, AGS, E K1424, no. 89.

[66] Philip to cardinal-infante, 9 June 1634, ARB, SEG 210, ff. 350–357.

[67] For the armies of Catalonia and Navarre, see memorials of A. de Rozas to J. de Villanueva, 3 March 1633, 29 July 1634, AGS, E K1425, nos 14, 119.

[68] Memorial by M. Pérez de Xea (n.d. ? Feb. 1634) and *consulta* of a special junta, 9 March 1634, AGS, E K1664, nos 3–4. This *legajo* is almost entirely devoted to the *empresa*. Nos 5–20 contain various estimates of the resources necessary, some bearing Olivares's holograph comments (e.g. no. 15). No. 21 orders Pérez de Xea to send men to reconnoitre the harbours of Marseille and Toulon, while nos 22–25 are the requirements sent to all parts for collaboration with Santa Cruz. Although Richelieu specified this project in 1635 as a major reason for his declaration of war (Jover Zamora, *1635: historia de una polémica*, pp. 474–75). Spain's pursuit of it for much of the previous year has not previously been noticed.

[69] 'Instrucción que vos el marqus de Santa Cruz . . .', April 1634, AGS, E K1664, no. 32. The marquis had been a member of the special junta which examined Pérez de Xea's proposal. His appointment was further recommended by the need for Genoese assistance, especially the plan to locate the base of operations Genoa itself. Santa Cruz was very popular with the Genoese since he had commanded the force which rescued them from the French in 1625.

Olivares gave this surprise attack the highest priority, and the Spanish system in the Mediterranean was suddenly galvanized by a stream of orders. Early in February the viceroy of Catalonia had been warned 'with all secrecy that he may be ordered to invade France at the beginning of April'.[70] Instructions were now despatched to the cardinal-infante in Milan to provide a *tercio* of Castilian troops for the *empresa secreta de Marsella*. Despite his crippling shortage of such regiments, Don Fernando immediately complied, and by April 1,500 infantrymen were on the march to Genoa.[71] Such were the unlooked-for extra demands upon the resources – especially maritime – of Sicily and Naples that their viceroys (in contrast to Philip's brother) persistently objected to the expedition.[72] Brushing aside these protests, Olivares hurried on with plans for an overhaul of the galley squadrons, which were to gather in Genoa as base of operations.[73] Orders were put out that excessive naval activity in the area was to be explained by the threat of an Ottoman attack upon Sicily, and the need for secrecy was repeatedly (if uselessly) stressed. Commanders and envoys in all parts were to await news of the progress of the expedition, and act accordingly.[74]

The Marseilles 'task force', in common with others which took shape upon Olivares' strategic maps during 1634, was to act ostensibly on behalf of an authority other than Philip IV. The sovereign rights of Gaston, Marie de Médicis, Lorraine, even the duke of Guise, were to be variously invoked, in tandem with specious proclamations about assisting the 'liberties' of French communities. But there could hardly have been serious expectation in Madrid that Richelieu and his king would react any differently to these flags of convenience than to that of 1628, when Philip had acted technically in the name of the emperor. Both the risks and the stakes involved in Olivares' new venture were dimensionally higher than they had been over Mantua, but it is difficult to see that his behaviour had been substantially altered by the earlier experience. Nobody, it has often been remarked, begins a war unless he is sure of winning it; the evidence suggests that Olivares is one of several outstanding exceptions to this rule. As in the case of Mantua, he pressed ahead with obsessive urgency. Insuperable supply and logistical

---

[70] Elliott and de la Peña, *Memoriales*, ii, p. 118.

[71] Cardinal-infante to Philip, 23 April 1634, ARB, SEG 210, f. 96.

[72] Santa Cruz to Olivares, 12 Aug. 1634, AGS, E K1664, no. 61.

[73] The *veedor general* of the Spanish galleys, Gerónimo de la Torre, was entrusted with the task of supervising repairs of the various units and their despatch to Santa Cruz; see his commission and correspondence for 1634 in AGS, CJH 722, passim.

[74] There had been a rumour earlier in the year that the French had invited a Turkish attack in support of their anti-Spanish schemes: Gayangos, *Cartas*, i, p. 22. Originally it was intended for security reasons that Santa Cruz's real purpose be kept secret even from senior proconsuls in the north, such as Aytona in Brussels (AGS, E K1664, no. 6). But Aytona certainly had wind of it by June (to Olivares, 1 July 1634, AGS, E 2049); and by August, Melo in Genoa was holding the lines of communication open to all parts of the Spanish System (Philip to Monterrey, 8 Sept., E 2049).

problems, exacerbated by poor weather conditions, prevented Santa Cruz and his subordinates from meeting the deadlines (in any case totally unrealistic) imposed by Madrid. Following a series of delays, the marquis added his plea to that of Monterrey, viceroy of Naples, that the expedition be postponed.[75] Not until late in September did Olivares yield to these representations, on condition that everything should be ready in the spring of 1635. The diverse elements of the expedition were therefore ordered to remain together in Genoa, but 'not to move unless either the French declare war, or Gaston and Prince Tommaso invade France'; it was to be timed to coincide with 'the conjuncture of future events'.[76] The winter saw frenetic activity both in strategic discussions and military preparations in every quarter. In December, Prince Tommaso sent Olivares a fully-fledged 'master plan' for the campaign of 1635, which the *valido* brought to the council of state for consideration. In the course of two long meetings, presided over by Philip IV in person, Olivares firmly endorsed this programme. No substantive objections were raised by the other councillors. Indeed, if anything, the king was more enthusiastic than his *valido*. Although he agreed that the main thrust of the attack on France was to come from the Rhineland (confederate) forces, he was less certain that the army of Flanders should be held back if a quick victory was to be sought. In Philip's prescient view – expressed in an eleven-page *apostilla* – 'nothing should be done to impede the possibility of this army giving support against France, either if the situation [on the Dutch front] permits it, or if it should be necessary in an emergency'.[77] For his part, Olivares expressed support for the operation in the following terms:

With three units prepared to act against her allies, and five against France herself . . . there is no possibility that the blow can misfire . . . but everything must begin at once, for unless they are attacked vigorously, nothing can prevent the French from becoming masters of the world, and without any risk to themselves.[78]

It is not inappropriate, therefore, to regard the 'master plan of campaign' as having origins and significance much deeper than those which Elliott assigns to it. Neither is it utterly fanciful to detect within it a certain degree of

[75] *Consulta* of council of state, 2 Sept. 1634, AGS, E K1664, no. 70. This seems to have been the first discussion of the *empresa* in the regular council, though it is interesting that in July, Olivares had broached the subject of provoking an open war with France – perhaps in order to test the atmosphere among *consejeros de estado*; see Elliott, *El conde-duque y la herencia*, pp. 96–97.

[76] *Consultas* of council of state, 27 Sept., and junta of state, 5 Nov. 1634, AGS, E K1664, nos 74, 102.

[77] *Consulta* of council of state, 14 Jan. 1635, AGS, E 2050, no. 3.

[78] Olivares's *voto* in *consulta* of council of state, 16 Jan. 1635, AGS, E 2049; this document encloses the oddly-titled 'Apostilla de Principe Tomas', dated December 1634. Between them they incorporate virtually all the suggestions made from various sources during the previous decade for attacks against France, and represent the most complete and ambitious statement of the 'master-plan'.

coherence, if more impressively so in design than in execution. Involving as it did the coordinated and (ideally) synchronized movement of two fleets and four armies – perhaps as many as 100,000 effectives – it was surely the most ambitious military conception of early-modern Europe. With hindsight, it is easy to dismiss it as unrealistic and grandiose, and it would be idle to deny that these elements are indeed present. On the other hand, we should do well to remember how close Olivares came to the outright defeat of France when – a year late and considerably reduced in scale – he actually launched his offensive. Given the material circumstances of the age, the narrowness of his failure seems as worthy of comment as the failure itself. In any case, it may be argued that Spain's political objectives vis-à-vis her neighbour kingdom were by no means chimerical. In many of the documents utilized for the present essay, the attack upon France is referred to as a 'diversion' rather than a full-scale war. Of course this reflects in part habits of self-delusion, and in part legal niceties or euphemisms for external consumption, of the kind of which history provides commonplace examples. But the term 'diversion' also demonstrates that Olivares and his associates never lost sight of the fact that the 'master plan', for all its size and importance, was still only a means to the end of negotiation from strength (and a consequent *paz honesta*) with the United Provinces, with whom Richelieu had again renewed his alliance in February 1635. It follows that, despite Richelieu's understandable claims to the contrary, the question of the political destruction and/or military occupation of the kingdom of France never arose. Olivares' aim was limited to the downfall of Richelieu, which would surely result from the overwhelming defeat of Louis XIII's army. Neither was it fanciful to believe that this would bring about a more accommodating attitude to Spain in Paris, perhaps restoring the more compliant policies of Marie de Médicis, to whose benign influence Louis would be returned. Intense opposition to Richelieu was known to exist at every level of French society and in almost every corner of the kingdom. It was not unreasonable for Olivares to count upon considerable indigenous armed support for his intervention in France. In many ways, therefore, the war of 1635 must be seen as similar in character and motivation to Spain's earlier invasions of France in the 1590s.

A further point is that Olivares was relying to a significant extent on a rapid removal of France from the list of his enemies. More than anyone else he realized that the monarchy simply did not possess the reserves of resources and manpower for a war of attrition. For this reason, amongst others, he was obliged to opt for military preparations in width rather than in depth, a method which anticipates the modern strategy of *Blitzkrieg*, both in its military and socio-economic dimensions. Like Hitler when launching his attack on the Soviet Union in 1941, Olivares hoped that 'we have only to kick in the door and the whole rotten structure will come tumbling down'. As he told the king in June 1635, his master-plan would either 'win and finish the war with supreme brevity, or else utterly finish with the monarchy. I regard the matter as settled, since if things are managed in this way, not only will it yield the fruit which I promise, but also great savings in expense and blood.' Having completed this exhausting survey of the readiness and resources of a monarchy now confronted with its supreme ordeal, Olivares took up his pen to add a postscript to the secretarial draft:

> Sir, this is my opinion; it would be idle to deceive myself, because I have the feeling that I am going to lose my life – not in the war itself (which would be a happy fate) but merely in the task of making all ready for the struggle. I am so unwell that my head cannot bear the flame of the candle or the light of a window, which seems as strong as the glare of the streets in the August sun. But God may not want my health to improve, nor anything of mine to flourish, except insofar as it represents the smallest hair in the balance of service to your majesty . . . To my present judgement it seems that this is either to lose everything irretrievably or enable us to save the ship. I would be a traitor not to put things as I find them . . . here go religion, king, queen, nation, and all besides with them. And if there is not enough strength, let us die in summoning it, for it is better to die than to fall under the sway of heretics, as I hold the French to be. Thus everything will come to an end, or Castile will be the leader of the world . . .[79]

It remains only to narrate the immediate events surrounding the outbreak of this epic struggle in the early summer of 1635. Following the *Estado* discussions of January, the cardinal-infante was ordered to be prepared for all-out war with France.[80] Whilst the main army of Flanders was not to be committed because of the continuing hostilities with the Dutch, the armada of Dunkirk – Spain's elite naval force – was to be made ready for the capture of a useful port on France's northern or western coast.[81] Matters were further advanced by a council meeting on 3 March. The marquis of Valparaiso in Navarre (who estimated his force at 15,000 men) was instructed to stand by to effect a juncture with the army of Catalonia, and to expect the arrival of Philip to take command.[82] A down-payment of half of a total subsidy of 320,000 escudos was despatched to the confederate Rhineland army for the coming

[79] 'El Conde Duque sobre lo que se deve disponer para executar la jornada de V. Mgd.', 14 June 1635, AGS, E 2656.

[80] Philip to cardinal-infante, 19 June 1635, AGS, E 2049.

[81] Cardinal-infante to Philip, 26 Jan. 1635, ARB, SEG 212, ff. 66–67. It was left open at this stage whether the armada of Flanders would support Prince Tomasso's army along the Channel coast or the joint force of the king and Valparaiso, striking up from Guipúzcoa. For the latter plans, see H. Courteault, 'L'invasion du Pays Basque par les Espagnols en 1636', *Revue de Béarn*, 2 (1905), pp. 319–22.

[82] *Consulta* of council of state, 3 March 1635, AGS, E 2050. This discussion took place with the aid of strategic maps of the French borderlands. The meeting probably also considered a 'Relación de lo que tiene ocupada el Rey de Francia desde que el Sueco entró en Alemania asta todo el año pasado de 1634', which listed over fifty places where French military action had been monitored, Oxford, Bod., Add. C. 126, f. 202. See also Valparaiso to Philip, 22 March 1635, AGS, E 2056, in which he suggests the capture of Bayonne as a base for further operations in south-west France.

campaign.[83] On 8 May frantic government efforts to raise cash concessions from the *Cortes* of Castile were reported:

> The king has sent them a decretal in which he expresses his regret for the weight of the burden upon the *Reino*, but pleads that the state of affairs is so urgent that he must be given one and a half million ducats – six hundred thousand within six or eight days, and the remainder after six months. It must be a great emergency which forces him to use such earnest language . . .[84]

In April, Benavente was told to pack his bags in Paris and to leave without offering any explanation to his hosts.[85] On 10 May, Santa Cruz's main squadron left Naples, with instructions to link up with forces waiting in Genoa and proceed with a landing at either Marseilles or Toulon. The enemy, however, struck the first blow. Before the end of the month, the council considered the cardinal-infante's news that the French had entered Luxembourg, and unhesitatingly recognized a state of war, noting Monterrey's report that Santa Cruz 'may now already be at work in France'.[86] The appearance of Louis XIII's champion at the walls of Brussels on 19 May was thus in every sense a formality. Nevertheless, the moral capital gained by technical French belligerence was welcome; and perhaps even more so the actual capital provided by the confiscation of one million ducats' worth of French goods in Spain which the same technicality justified. This week also witnessed a splendid omen in Madrid. The news reached court that the silver fleet had come in to Cadiz with nearly 2,500,000 ducats for the king, fully a million more than the average for the decade.[87] Early in July, an observer excitedly retailed a report 'that his majesty yesterday announced to the council that forces amounting to 80,000 men are poised to attack France, and this very day the Imperialists ought to be on French soil'.[88]

In fact, however, the 1635 campaign was a severe disappointment. On 21 May Santa Cruz lost eleven of his ships, wrecked by storms upon the Corsican coast. The *empresa* was once again postponed, and not until September did it sail from Genoa, only to capture the tiny Lerins islands off Cannes, its strength reduced and the element of surprise completely lost.[89] The invasion of France by Gaston and Prince Tommaso never took place, since their army was routed by the French on Flemish soil in the first major action of the war. As a result of these mishaps, no move could be made by the Rhineland army, the Pyrenees forces, or the armada of Dunkirk. Though the

[83] Philip to cardinal-infante, 15 March 1635, AGS, E 2050.

[84] Gayangos, *Cartas*, i, p. 186.

[85] *Consulta* of council of state, 19 April 1635, AGS, E 2050.

[86] *Consulta* of council of state, 29 May 1635, AGS, E 2050, enclosing Monterrey's report that Santa Cruz had sailed from Naples. See also *consulta* of council of state, 2 June 1635, AGS, E K1664.

[87] Gayangos, *Cartas*, i, p. 198; *Relación* of contents of 1635 *flota*, BN, 11137, f. 117.

[88] Gayangos, *Cartas*, i, p. 201.

[89] A detailed *relación* of this campaign is printed ibid., pp. 276–88.

cardinal-infante cleared the enemy from Flanders in the course of the summer, it was abundantly clear that the master-plan would have to wait until 1636, and would now require the full participation of the army of Flanders. But Olivares was not downhearted; indeed he felt relief at emerging from the forest of deceit and secrecy into the open field of simple struggle. In November, poised for the greatest military effort of Habsburg Spain, he exhorted his master:

> Neither your father nor your grandfather had the opportunity which your majesty is now vouchsafed to settle the affair of Holland with all advantage and prestige. For God has been pleased to place in your majesty's hands the master-key to everything.[90]

---

[90] Quoted in Elliott, *El conde duque y la herencia*, p. 97.

6

'The Two Great Luminaries of Our Planet': Spain and France in the Policy of Olivares

> 'All this is what moved the Spaniard of 1635 to the roots of his being, from the count-duke himself to the last soldier in Flanders.'
>
> (J.M. Jover)

Every year on 7 September the citizens of the Guipuzcoan town of Hondarribia celebrate the festival of the *Alarde de Armas*. It is a *feria* of the normal Spanish pattern, but with one striking difference. The twenty-one companies of the honorary citizen militia, discharging the function of the religious societies (*cofradías*) for the occasion, parade through the town to hear Mass at the church of the Virgin of Guadalupe. In this way Fuenterrabía – to revert to the Castilian version of the town's name – still gives thanks to God for its successful delivery from the hands of the French, following sixty-nine days of siege in 1638.[1] During this period of supreme danger, the first French incursion onto Spanish soil for well over a century, Juan de Legorra and five companions of the Vizcayan community (*anteiglesia*) of Mallavia (near Durango) voluntarily enlisted in the Basque regiments preparing for the relief expedition, 'without any pay and solely for the benefit of our fatherland'.[2] In August that year, hundreds of local mariners gave their lives in the attempt to succour Fuenterrabía, when the Cantabrian squadron was trapped and destroyed by the French fleet at Guetaría.[3]

These incidents took place after two decades of continuous war. The Madrid government increasingly had been obliged – especially once France became committed to open war against it – to resort to dubious methods of conscription in order to fill up the ranks depleted by the annual toll of war. Yet despite the widespread damage and resentment caused in many localities by this policy, not to mention a myriad other debilitating and ubiquitous war-related demands, thousands of other men from all over Spain also responded freely to the call to save Fuenterrabía. With the unique exception of Catalonia, all regions of the peninsula contributed to the campaign which led to the glorious repulse of the invader.

At the other end of the scale from our Vizcayan volunteer, the count-duke of Olivares was able to savour his ultimate public triumph. He was

---

[1] *El diario Vasco*, 8 Sept. 1986.

[2] *Pleito* of March 1639, ADV, Secretaría 32 leg. 1180, no. 8.

[3] For a description, see J. Alcalá-Zamora, *España, Flandes, y el Mar del Norte, 1618–1639*, pp. 392–400.

the recipient of the fulsome (if hardly spontaneous) gratitude of king and people.[4] The plenitude and ostentation of this flattery culminated in the celebrated equestrian portrait by Velázquez, which scholars now believe was commissioned to mark the event and actually pictures Olivares leading the royal army into battle against the French. Fanciful as this imposture may have been in literal terms, its metaphorical point is more difficult to dismiss.[5] For in many ways the count-duke was indeed the architect of victory, a triumph which (moreover) represented an extraordinary vindication of the most profoundly meaningful of his policies, the Union of Arms. A larger (if not greater) Fatherland than that referred to by Juan de Legorra was predicated on these events – the victory, the manner of the victory and the enthusiasm of its celebration. For it would be perverse not to recognize in them a spirit, however inchoate, of patriotic feeling, a suggestion of that sentiment which nowadays one almost dare not mention – I refer to *Hispanidad*, the currently unfashionable concept of 'Spanishness'.

It was something of a happy accident that Velázquez's portrait of Olivares was completed more-or-less alongside several others which were designed to be hung in the *Salón de Reinos* of the Buen Retiro palace – that tangible and magniloquent expression of the heroic unity of the monarchy. In form and content it has many points of resemblance to the painter's equestrian studies of the royal family, on the one hand, and the series of victorious battle scenes, on the other. Appropriately, therefore, in order to honour the count-duke, Velázquez produced a unique fusion of these two genres, recording in immortal fashion his qualities of both statesman and warrior. Olivares' leadership in the epic struggle with France had clearly brought about a kind of apotheosis, elevating him dimensionally above all other royal servants, be they heroes of the field or worthies of the council chamber.[6] 'Librador de la patria' was the title by which Philip IV decreed he should formally receive a toast at

---

[4] D.L. Shaw, 'Olivares y el Almirante de Castilla, 1638', *Hispania*, 27 (1967), pp. 342–53.

[5] J. Brown, *Velázquez: Painter and Courtier* (New York, 1986), pp. 136–38. Although this understandably upset not only Almirante Enríquez but also other captains who had actually been present at the battle, it may well have been Olivares's foresight which enabled the town to hold out for long enough for relief to arrive. That same spring, concerned at the possibility of a French initiative in the region, he had commissioned a special survey of Fuenterrabía's defences; see 'Relación de lo que ajustado Don Diego de Isasi Sarmiento . . . y parece conveniente hacerse para asegurar las Plazas de Fuenterrabía y Puerto del Pasaje y San Sebastian de una sorpresa', 16 April 1638, BN, 6734, ff. 175–177.

[6] L. del Corral revived the idea – first put forward by K. Justi in the classic *Diego Velázquez and his Times* (1889) – that the paintings of the *Salón de Reinos* represented a kind of Valhalla: *Valázquez, la monarquía e Italia* (Madrid, 1978), p. 49. The intended destination of the Olivares portrait is still unknown. Nevertheless, it seems interesting to speculate that the fusion of genres was deliberately made in order to emphasise the count-duke's status as lying somewhere between those of other great military heroes of the monarchy and the royal family. For an account of the paintings commissioned for the *Salón* and their political significance, see J. Brown and J.H. Elliott, *A Palace for a King: The Buen Retiro and the Court of Philip IV* (New Haven and London, 1980), p. 141ff.

the king's table, from a golden goblet, on every anniversary of the victory of Fuenterrabía.[7] Effectively he was already recognized as *alter nos* – in the phrase the king used to sum up his role when ordering the count-duke's final mundane transfiguration as *Teniente General* in 1642.[8] By then, the moment had arrived, so important in both their lives, when they rode together to fight the French in Catalonia.[9]

Leaving aside the significance examined above, the siege and relief of Fuenterrabía was only one incident in a war which lasted, for all intents and purposes, from 1629 until 1659; thus exactly fulfilling the prophecy of a Thirty Years' War uncannily ventured by Olivares at its inception.[10] If we take a further step backwards, we can see that this war itself, for all its unmatched duration, was only one episode in a series of conflicts – a new version of the Punic Wars, straddling the history of the early modern epoch – in which these two dynastic powers disputed the political supremacy of Western Europe. 'The antipathy of the French and the Spaniards' represented, according to one commentator, 'the opposition of the two great luminaries of our planet'.[11] In the emblematic language of the age, they contended for the places of sun and moon in the firmament, for the prizes of gold and silver (or lead) in the estimation of Europe. Indeed, their mutual antipathy was as central and fundamental to the history of that age as the misunderstandings of the Cold War and the suspicions of the Superpowers have been to our own.

By the mid seventeenth century, the apparently ceaseless confrontation of France and Spain, with its unparalleled level of organized destruction, had come to dominate the development of the whole of south-west Europe, directly or indirectly affecting the conditions of existence of most of its 40,000,000 inhabitants, and consuming a substantial proportion of their lives, labour and material production. Whatever the reservations about the methodology of international history, and the inevitable use of the (doubtless repetitive) political vocabulary through which the origins of wars are mediated, it seems to me obvious that we must seek to explain phenomena of this negative potency, if only for the same reason as the scientists continue to study the causes of earthquakes or hurricanes.

---

[7] J.H. Elliott, *The Count-Duke of Olivares* (New Haven and London, 1986), pp. 540–41. One wonders whether Olivares ever reflected on the fact that Philip himself was a total abstainer. Meanwhile, the Madrid populace were so carried away by the victory celebrations that a crowd of them broke into the wine-cellars of the palace and proceeded to toast Olivares – to considerable excess – at the king's expense; R.G. Trewinnard 'The Household of the Spanish Habsburgs, 1606–65: Structure, Finance and Personnel' (unpublished Ph.D., University of Wales, 1991).

[8] F. Tomás y Valiente, *Los validos en la monarquía española del siglo XVII* (2nd edn, Madrid, 1982), p. 101.

[9] For the significance of this event, see my *Philip IV and the Government of Spain* (Cambridge, 1988), esp. chaps 3 and 8.

[10] J.H. Elliott, *Richelieu and Olivares* (Cambridge, 1984), p. 96.

[11] See below, note 36.

As will already be appreciated, looked at in terms of *longue durée* Franco-Spanish competition had roots which considerably pre-dated the era of Olivares, and it continued to disturb the peace of Europe for many years after his death. None the less, it is the prolonged sequence of military exchanges set in motion under the guidance of Olivares and his French equivalent, Cardinal Richelieu, which is rightly seen as central and definitive. There is no denying that the powers emerged from this crucial phase of rivalry having more or less exchanged places in terms of their power positions. Even if (in 1660) France was not immediately able to pick up the sceptre of hegemony which had fallen at last from her enemy's nerveless fingers, she had decisively regained a superiority which Spain had possessed uninterruptedly since the battle of Pavia in 1525. My tasks in this essay are to sample the flavour of the historiographical debate over the causes of the Richelieu-Olivares war; briefly to elucidate the context of the count-duke's policy towards France, mostly in its ideological and strategic aspects; and finally to analyze the Count-Duke's personal attitudes and responses to this priority defence issue of his government.

Organized hostility between France and Spain is now thankfully a matter for historical discussion, commemorated otherwise only in harmless rituals like those of Fuenterrabía. But if discourse alone mediates experience, more than a passive analogy may be made between the world of the academic historian and that of popular chauvinism. Like it or not, a burdensome heritage of national sympathy is deposited on modern writers by their predecessors, and assiduously passed down through generations of the collective cultural conscious, as much a totem of our identity as a treasured family heirloom.

The most complete statement of the Spanish national case in modern interpretation of my theme is that made by José María Jover Zamora. Forty years ago Jover Zamora studied the contemporary propaganda of the Richelieu-Olivares war in terms which suggest that the embers of the old conflagration were not entirely cold.[12] He restricted himself to certain printed texts, and to Spanish secondary works, without reference to the unpublished state papers. He found the Spanish apologists' case – propounded by a formidable *oeuvre* including works by Quevedo and Saavedra – to be entirely convincing. All the more so since (as he took pains to emphasise) 'we are certainly not concerned here with a group of hired propagandists, obedient to government direction'.[13] Accordingly, in a celebrated meta-historical thesis, he maintained that the Spain of Olivares had no plans for universal domination, no intentions of extending its territorial size and, above all, no designs of any kind against France. Quite on the contrary, he argued, the Spanish Monarchy represented a mission for a reconstituted Christendom. If Spain wished to influence the other powers of Europe, it was only in order to shine a beacon

---

[12] J.M. Jover Zamora, *1635: historia de una polémica* (Madrid, 1949).
[13] Ibid., p. 448.

of love and peace into their darkness, and to lead them forward to the Promised Land – quite literally, for any *Pax Hispanica* would be the basis for a general crusade to reconquer Jerusalem.

Whilst the Spanish monarchy struggled to maintain (or revive) an Age of Gold, France promoted an Iron Age in its stead. France's determined selfishness led the atavistic nation-states of Europe forward – or rather backward – into the era of international anarchy. So far from being faithful to the legacy of St Louis, the Most Christian King was an inveterate ally of the Islamic powers. Most pernicious in resisting Spain's sublime message, inventing for use against it the evil doctrine of *raison d'état* she was, because nominally Catholic, more heretic than her allies the Protestants themselves, truly a Judas amongst nations. The France of Richelieu, which so persistently accused Spain of plotting for universal hegemony, was nothing other than *Francia Mala*, which had to be saved from itself.

Jover's own position differed little in substance from that of the self-righteous team of Spanish polemicists whose works he studied. He summarized it thus:

> The triumph of the French . . . would represent . . . the definitive renunciation of Europe's spiritual unity . . . the emphatic victory of the heretics. It would mean the triumph of the spiritually neutral, agnostic state over the political community which existed to serve a transcendental purpose; the subversion of a firmly sustained providential destiny; permanent injustice; the shattering of the Spanish Monarchy; and the triumph of the satanic schemes of one man. In sum, it would involve the overturning of a whole system of values.[14]

From our present vantage-point, Jover's empathy with his subjects reflects unerringly towards us some of the basic *mores* of Francoist historicism, which itself provided nothing less than the ideological and cultural basis of the Nationalist movement (*movimiento*) in its policy for postwar Spain. Spain's historic alienation from France had been bitterly revived in the 1930s and 40s, in ideological terms which were lineally descended from those of the Counter-Reformation world. In a context which, for their part, the French governments of the later period could hardly be expected to appreciate, a profound hostility towards the ideas of the modern *afrancesados* – secularism, agnosticism, freemasonry and the broad intellectual heritage of the French Revolution – existed among adherents of the Nationalist cause, which they did not hesitate to attribute and articulate. The Second Republic, which had incorporated persecution of the church into its constitution, had been morally and materially supported by France. Many Spaniards were inclined to blame France at least as much as the U.S.S.R. for the horrendous ordeals of their church both before and after 1936, and indeed for the basic causation of the Civil War by which, at a terrible cost, Catholic Spain – which again, as in the

---

[14] Ibid., pp. 445–46. (The latter page also contains the sentence quoted at the head of this chapter.)

seventeenth century, called itself *La Causa Universal* – was morally obliged to extirpate the forces of evil materialism.[15]

The post-Civil War atmosphere in which the young Jover wrote was, therefore, a xenophobic and in particular an anti-French one, which he could hardly help but breathe onto the page. Moreover, his pathway had been marked out for him a few years earlier by the well-established scholar Carmelo Viñas Mey. In what must have been a memorable lecture in 1946, the latter enunciated a passionate *credo*. The early-modern French state was stigmatised as the *locus classicus* of political error. Philip II was bitterly attacked for neglecting the opportunity to strangle the monstrous infant of Gallic nationalism, during the Wars of Religion. After the death of Henry IV, Spanish power was easily strong enough to conquer and permanently disassemble her neighbour; but, 'once more' – as the author ambivalently puts it – 'Spain sacrificed itself to the religious ideal'. France repaid Spain's fraternal forbearance by constant intrigues against her.

> The idea of politics as 'the existential struggle of friends and enemies' . . . is the authentic creation of seventeenth-century France, which it opposed to the idea of the united international community sustained by Spain.

In 1635 (concluded Viñas Mey) Richelieu, supported by a selfish and equally Machiavellian papacy, 'had done away for ever with the idea of Christendom'. If not quite the serpent in the Eden of Spain's *Siglo de Oro*, France was certainly the fratricidal Cain whose sins confirmed God's judgement enshrined in the Fall.[16]

Between them, these two writers sounded the keynote for subsequent Spanish historiography. During the 1950s a homogeneous school of historians of Spain's Counter-Reformation policy, including Manuel Fernández Alvarez, Manuel Fraga Iribarne and Eulogio Zudaire Huarte – to name only a few – eagerly subscribed to and expatiated upon this patriotic interpretation.[17] In 1950, after a careful study of the relevant documents in the K series of *Estado*, returned to Simancas by the Nazi regime in Paris, Luis Fernández Suárez concluded that:

> Cardinal Richelieu developed a new concept of politics. Until that time, the state was conceived as a lesser evil, necessary in order to permit individuals to live in society, but subordinate in everything to religion. This was the Tridentine

---

[15] See J.J. Ruíz Rico, *El papel político de la iglesia católica en la España de Franco, 1936–71* (Madrid, 1977); J.A. Tello Lázaro, *Ideología y política: la iglesia católica española, 1936–59* (Zaragoza, 1984).

[16] C. Viñas Mey, *Relaciones entre España y Francia de Felipe II a Felipe IV: conferencia pronunciada el día 20 de Diciembre de 1945* (Madrid, 1946), pp. 8–14, 24.

[17] M. Fernández Alvarez, 'El fracaso de la hegemonía española en Europa', in (ed. Tomas y Valiente) *Historia de España Menéndez Pidal*, xxv (Madrid, 1982), pp. 722–26; M. Fraga Iribarne, *Don Diego Saavedra y Fajardo y la diplomacía de su epoca* (Madrid, 1956), esp. pp. 71–76, 89–109; E. Zudaire Huarte, *El conde-duque y Cataluña* (Madrid, 1964), e.g. pp. 146–47.

doctrine, maintained by Spain . . . But with the start of the seventeenth century, the ideas of Machiavelli . . . arrived at their ultimate influence. Religion . . . was now looked upon as a relative and not an absolute value . . . Nevertheless, Spain's sacrifices were not destined to be entirely sterile.[18]

Only with the mid 1970s did an unsentimental and balanced assessment of the problem become available with the work of José Alcalá-Zamora.[19] In the interim, a maverick interpretation was put forward by Rafael Ródenas Vilar.[20] It was an example of thinking produced by the mixed feelings detectable on both sides of the discursive divide. Anxious to demonstrate that the Spain of Olivares was not a naive antediluvian polity easily outwitted by the intelligent, modern France of Richelieu, Ródenas adopted a position diametrically opposed to all his predecessors.

To take the most controversial particular example, Ródenas demonstrated beyond reasonable doubt that Philip IV's government provided financial aid for the Huguenots in 1629. For his part, Jover reported that one of his authors, the clerical *olivarista* minister Alonso Guillén de la Carrera, had admitted only that *talks* had been held with Huguenot envoys, denying that actual assistance had ever been sent. Jover accepted this apparent disclaimer, adding for good measure that 'the Spanish people would not be content with denying this accusation, but were going to reject it vehemently, unanimously and with good reason'.[21] It is true that both Olivares and Philip IV always publicly denied the *fact* of assistance; yet as they (and Guillén) well knew, a treaty with the French Protestant rebels had been signed, and subsidies were almost certainly despatched.[22]

Nevertheless, broadly speaking, Ródenas's interpretation must be regarded as somewhat bizarre. He attempted to portray an Olivares endowed with even more Machiavellian cunning than his French rival, weaving a skein of duplicity so elaborate and complex that neither the author nor the reader can adequately unravel it. The hypothesis is a bizarre relic of a decade when the notorious Spanish inferiority complex vis-à-vis France was perhaps at its height.[23]

---

[18] L. Suárez Fernández, 'Notas a la política anti-Española del Cardenal Richelieu', *Simancas*, 1 (1950), pp. 1–53.

[19] Alcalá-Zamora, *España, Flandes*; idem, *Razón y crisis*.

[20] R. Ródenas Vilar, *La política europea de España* (Madrid, 1967).

[21] Jover Zamora, *1635: historia de una polémica*, pp. 129, 155–60.

[22] Philip instructed an envoy to Paris to state that 'the idea of helping the heretic could never live for a moment in my breast' ('Instrucción que se dió a Don Gonzalo de Córdoba año de 1632 yendo a francia por embajador', BN, 10615, ff. 227–40). Ródenas devoted a separate article to proving the contrary; see, '¿Ayudó Felipe IV a los Hugonotes?' *Arbor*, 57 (1964), pp. 59–66.

[23] Ródenas Vilar, *La política europea*, esp. pp. 92–107, 149 et seq. It is easier to see how this book came to win the Luis Vives Prize than to understand how it achieved publication by the Consejo Superior de Investigaciones Científicas, in those days the academic organ of the Francoist state. However, it is important to note that despite its fundamental dissent from his own ideas, the postgraduate work of Ródenas Vilar was actually supervised by Jover. (For Professor Jover's later views on the general question, see the postscript to this chapter, p. 142).

For all this, it was a French scholar who first exhibited such tendencies, and who initiated the modern phase of historiographical debate in 1920. The Catholic pacifist writer Auguste Leman was profoundly disturbed by the negative moral implications in the interpretation of Richelieu's France so proudly promoted by his compatriots.[24] He rejected the thesis of the great pioneer of *raison d'état* – a view central to the prevailing orthodoxy of French history – arguing that the cardinal was motivated not by pragmatic ethnocentrism but by the cause of *defending European freedoms* against a ruthlessly expansionist Spain.

> Un ministre espagnol à repris au compte de son maître les ambitieux projects de Charles-Quint et de Philippe II. Le comte duc Olivares, qui conduit tout la politique du roi d'Espagne, Philippe IV, travaille à enfermer la France dans un formidable cercle qui, en se resserrant, doit la broyer si elle ne parvient pas à le rompre . . . En un mot, Philippe IV a tout agencé, tout disposé pour la bataille définitive, qu'il va livrer à la puissance français. Le signal de l'assaut serait déjà donné et la guerre d'Italie se fût transformée en une guerre générale . . .[25]

By implication at least, Leman suggested that Spain had no monopoly of idealism in its attitude to Christendom; indeed that her mission was fatally compromised by being only able to recognise a Christendom shaped in her own image. He supported this contention by reference to the policy of the Vatican, which never endorsed Spain's claims to be the instrument of God's providence amongst nations. Under the Barberini pope, on the contrary, Rome arbitrated in a rigorously proper and even-handed manner between its two eldest daughters, true to its solemn duty of preserving the tranquillity of Europe.[26]

Leman's argument seems positively irenic beside that of Roland Mousnier. As recently as 1964, Mousnier was capable of an outburst, not ostensibly intended as a riposte to Jover, but so uncharacteristically intemperate that it must have issued from the heart. It condemned the spiritual falseness of Habsburg Spain and the gullibility of its ultramontane French supporters, in terms directly reminiscent of Richelieu's propagandists and the choicest vituperation of the Black Legend.

> En apparence, les Habsbourg étaient les champions du Catholicisme. En réalité, leur victoire, leur hégémonie incontestée, auraient été un danger permanent pour le pape, pour l'Eglise, pour la religion, qu'ils auriaient opprimés . . . Beaucoup, même en France, confondaient catholicisme et Espagne, et, soucieux avant tout de la religion, suivaient aveuglément le Roi qui semblait en incarner les intérêts.

[24] A. Leman, *Urbain VIII et la rivalité de la France et de la maison d'Autriche de 1631 á 1636* (Lille-Paris, 1920), and its less interesting sequel, *Richelieu et Olivares* (Lille, 1938). Unlike his Spanish predecessors – with the distinguished exception of Cánovas – Leman made telling use of the *Estado* series at Simancas.

[25] Leman, *Urbain VIII* p. 5–6.

[26] Ibid., p. 107. Leman's defence of Urban VIII, however, has been thoroughly undermined by Q. Aldea Vaquero; see 'La Neutralidad', pp. 155–78.

La propagande religieuse espagnole couvrait les ambitions de l'Espagne. Le 'catholicon d'Espagne' troublait la vue de beaucoup de bons Français, leur faisait voir un beau toutes les manoeuvres de la politique espagnol, ou leur faisait excuser les déloyautés, les perfidies, les corruptions, les cruautés des Espagnols par cette croyance que ce qu'ils commetaient, ils l'accomplissaient 'pour le paix et pour nostre mère Saint-Eglise'.[27]

Mousnier's tirade may stand as the official view of French historiography, which fully reciprocates the *odium theologicum* of the Spaniards.

The factors which were brought to bear upon Spanish policy-makers in their address to the French problem comprised a volatile mixture of tangible and intangible materials, some of them centuries old, others of more recent or immediate origin. Despite its enormous complexity, it lacked one ingredient which for several generations of historians has almost automatically been regarded as essential – economic factors are, quite simply, absent from the formula. Contrary to some recent reassertions of an obsolete economic empiricism, no element of economic jealousy or competition over material resources was present – even subliminally – in the calculations of Madrid.

Of course this is not to say that individuals and groups of the business community of the Monarchy – *hombres de negocio* of a myriad undertakings – had no vested interests in Franco-Spanish relations. It was just that the influence of such interest-groups was severely limited. Olivares (as Viñas Mey indeed pointed out) certainly implemented *methods of economic warfare* just as he exploited many other tactics suggested by the *arbitristas* in his domestic reforms.[28] As it happened, none of them was appropriate in dealing with France. But even in supervising the *guerra económica* his inspiration and objectives had no economic content whatsoever. References to religious imperatives pullulate in all the public and private justifications of the king, the count-duke and every other counsellor of policy. This appears in the documents to such an extent, with such an emphasis, and in such a consistent disregard of any economic rationale, that to characterize it as dissimulation or self-delusion, illustrates in the historian little more than a wilful cynicism.

Of course I do not mean this to imply that the policy of Madrid was *in fact* somehow 'pure', representing a spiritual exercise which we irredeemably corrupt moderns may look back upon with remorseful nostalgia. Such an assertion is obviously beyond the realm of our discipline. But it seems necessary at least to insist that the political mentality of Philip IV and Olivares was fixed in a different dimension. Their discourse was Christianity. It was immanent truth to them, and therefore should be axiomatic in their explication by us, that the monarchy existed to execute the will of a providential God. To

---

[27] R. Mousnier, *L'assassinat d'Henri IV, 14 Mai 1610: le problème du tyrannicide et l'affermissement de la monarchie absolue* (Paris, 1964), pp. 102–3.

[28] Viñas Mey (*Relaciones*, pp. 24–33) thereby opened a new field of inquiry, followed up by Domínguez Ortiz, Ródenas Vilar and others.

paraphrase Mirabeau, Spain was a church with a country, not a country with a church. The fundamental *asiento* of the Spanish system was the provision of souls for a Catholic heaven. The state's only *raison d'être* was to fortify life and death by all the rites of Holy Mother Church. When Olivares wrote that 'salvation is all that counts', and that all else was 'vanity and madness', he expressed what was nothing other than the open secret of his universe.[29] Grace justified all, and the higher truth – what was coming to be called '*Authentic* Reason of State' (*Verdadera Razón de Estado*), to distinguish it from the pagan, Machiavellian kind utilized by the French – was Spain's unique commission.[30]

Olivares' admirer and close counsellor, the talented Virgilio Malvezzi, expressed this perfectly in a contemporary hagiography of his chief. Explicitly in the ethical context of policy towards France, 'it was thought that the duke erred in [resorting to] reason of state'. Not so, asserted Malvezzi, for

> he cannot err in the service of the Catholic King, that errs not in the service of God, [which] are so conjoyned in the concernings of this King that no distinction of any understanding can disjoyn them . . . Oh King! Oh Grandee! Oh Catholic! What thing think you can defend your Kingdoms, not your treasures, not the Armies, it is God defends them, because you have defended Him, and because you do defend Him, and that you may defend Him.[31]

It can hardly be emphasised enough that Spanish policy-makers and apologists believed unquestioningly that *raison d'état* as practised by their enemies, was the work of the Devil, but when enlisted for Spain, the will of God.

From this it more or less follows that in the seventeenth century peoples in conflict naturally believed each other to be guilty of confessional heterodoxy, for this both rationalized war and focused chauvinist hatred. During wars with France, therefore, the Inquisition was unusually active against the despised Provençale immigrants (*gavachos*), especially in areas where it (and the Madrid government) sought to make an impression, like Catalonia. In 1635, for example, they arrested one Pedro Ginesta, an immigrant more than eighty years old, for eating meat on a Friday. The indictment stated that 'being of a nation infected with heresy, it is presumed that he has on many other occasions eaten meat on forbidden days'.[32] When a well-wisher at the court of Charles I warned Madrid that Richelieu was secretly scheming to woo English Catholics away from their traditional affiliation to Spain, he claimed that this was tantamount to inciting them to embrace heresy, 'and with this to stir up

---

[29] Quoted by Elliott, *Richelieu and Olivares*, p. 23.

[30] On the development of this useful concept, see J.A. Fernández-Santamaría, *Reason of State and Statecraft in Spanish Political Thought, 1595–1640* (New York, 1983).

[31] V. Malvezzi, *The Portraict of the Politicke Christian-Favourite: Originally Drawn from some of the actions of the Lord Duke of St Lucar* (1647), pp. 74–76. The original is *Il ritratto del privato politico christiano* (Bologna, 1635).

[32] Quoted in H. Kamen, *Inquisition and Society in Spain* (1985), p. 163 (see also pp. 167–68).

the arms of England against Spain . . ., which is to use the cloak of religion in order to destroy religion itself'.[33]

An undeniably *national* character accompanied religious fervour like a kind of shadow which can be clearly perceived only in strong light, and is incapable of separation from its substance. Particularist ideas had evolved during the sixteenth century in both France and Spain, to the extent that recognizable patriotisms – the identification of distinct *patrias* – can be said to have taken cultural hold.[34] But such nascent feelings were not intense enough (I would argue with reference to my text) to move the seventeenth-century Spaniard 'to the roots of his being' (*ab radice*, to use Jover's phrase). Certainly they were far from acquiring the finished, steely qualities of modern nationalism, yet they undoubtedly contributed in some measure to mutual alienation and tension. They were the reason why Louis XIV, in declaring two centuries of conflict to be over, needed to claim that there were no Pyrenees.

At the same time, inside both communities there survived – perhaps at this stage quantitatively stronger – a traditional belief in a joint Franco-Spanish destiny, a fraternal idealism which dulled the edge of national rivalry. Indeed it was the latter groups which had experienced an intense strengthening of their convictions with the waxing of the Counter-Reformation. In the seventeenth century, they propagated this message at the very centres of their respective ruling cliques, and were in no sense marginalized. Apprehensions concerning a shared faith in danger, missionary zeal, religious institutions, in short a broad community of spirit and aspiration, was a profounder reality which in the eyes of many annihilated selfish jealousies and passing suspicions. For example, we cannot doubt that Philip IV nurtured such feelings, and looked upon the achievement of a new *Pax Romana* as the utopian objective of his monarchy's policy. Peter Paul Rubens, who was on close terms with the king during 1628–29, was among those who believed that war between France and Spain was internecine – even civil – in its essence. 'Surely it would be better [asked Rubens, rhetorically] if these two young men who govern the world were willing to maintain friendly relations with one another instead of throwing all Christendom into turmoil by their caprices?'[35]

Another influential advocate of this viewpoint was 'Doctor Carlos García', whose book provides part of this essay's title. First published in 1617 – that is to say, at the very beginning of the rise to power of the Zúñiga-Guzmán interest in Madrid – it was the work of a Spaniard domiciled in France,

33 [?] to Philip IV (?1636), NMM, PHB 1b, ff. 191–195.

34 Space forbids dalliance with this seductive but complex theme. Perceptive remarks are made on it, with relation to the Olivares period, by Alcalá-Zamora (*España, Flandes*, esp. p. 114); and generally for the epoch, by P. Chaunu, *La civilisation de l'Europe classique* (Paris, 1966), pp. 19–20. A more recent and specific examination is held by H.G. Koenigsberger, 'National Consciousness in Early Modern Spain', in his *Politicians and Virtuosi: Essays in Early Modern Europe* (London, 1986), pp. 121–48.

35 Quoted by H. Trevor-Roper, *Princes and Artists: Patronage and Ideology at Four Habsburg Courts, 1517–1633* (1976), p. 149.

concerned to build bridges between the congenitally suspicious crowns.[36] His motives were unambiguous:

> Who can doubt but that if they would live in agreement and peace, these two nations will be able to communicate the miraculous gifts of science, virtue and letters which God has given them to other less fortunate peoples, rescuing from the devil's grasp an infinite number of souls, who at present by their lack of enlightenment and good doctrine are entombed in the chaotic darkness of ignorance and error?[37]

García analysed the growth of mutual isolation and enmity in terms easily understandable today, describing anthropological details of divergences in custom, character, food and dress. Yet all these are wiles of the Devil in frustrating God's obvious design. They have become so entrenched, he bitterly admits, that antipathy is now imbibed 'by the babies sucking at their mother's breasts'.[38] More than any other observer (save perhaps Saavedra Fajardo) García painfully conveys his sense of tragedy at the situation.

No such reservations troubled the conscience of Juan Caramuel Lobkowitz, a Benedictine professor at Louvain, whose pro-Spanish rantings were so extreme that they seem almost a counter-productive caricature inspired by the enemy. Though a Madrileño by birth, like so many adherents of the monarchy whose perspective point was outside Spain (compare Semple, Sherley, Malvezzi, Campanella), Caramuel was hypnotized by the potent spell of Madrid's Catholic imperialism. During the first year of the great Franco-Spanish war he composed his *Declaración mística de las armas de España*, which argued that the very name *España* derived from the Greek *Pan*, and thus Spain was destined to embrace everything![39] Lobkowitz's arguments were founded in part on the interpretation of astrological signs, and he entertained no doubt as to which of the two powers was the greater luminary of the universe. France was merely a sterile moon which took its heat and light from the sun of Spain.

> This Serene Catholic monarchy embraces the whole world.
> All other monarchies which unite themselves with the Spanish
> will be made great and exalted; and all those who oppose
> it with war will be cast down.
> It is not possible that the invincible power of this monarchy
> can ever be diminished.

[36] C. García, *Oposición y conjunción de los dos grandes luminares de la tierra: la antipatía de los Franceses y Españoles* (Rouen, 1617). Printed with Castilian and French versions on recto and verso, the work was reissued at Cambrai in 1622 and again during the Mantuan War (1630), the latter bearing the interesting variation of its title to *Antipatía de los Franceses y Españoles: obra apacible y curiosa . . .*). It was published again in Ghent in 1645. English translations appeared in 1641, 1647 and 1704, and a German edition in 1676.

[37] García, *Oposición* (1622), pp. 385–87.

[38] Ibid., pp. 10–15, 241.

[39] C. Lobkowitz, *Declaración mística de las armas de España invictamente belicosas* (Brussels, 1636), pp. 5–12.

> No power on earth is great enough to overthrow the arms of
> Spain.

Ultimately, proclaims this treatise, in an assertion which would have delighted Jover 'the more men are raised from Spain's soil, the more her mundane character diminishes and her spiritual essence increases'. Spain alone (asserted Lobkowitz) had been vouchsafed the ultimate and inalienable virtue, which was to exist and to act only for God's purpose. It followed, therefore, that the true vocation of Europeans was merely to incline themselves heliotropically in the direction of the *Rey Planeta*, Philip IV of Spain.[40]

South of the Pyrenees, when contrary emotions about France were present in the same breast, there was little doubt which usually held the ascendancy. After all, the family unity of Christendom could only be achieved on Spanish (i.e. God's) terms; those that Philip and Olivares often referred to as the *paz honesta*, the honourable peace. Even Rubens was ultimately bound to admit this point – indeed, he was one of those who, following the Mantuan War, advised Olivares to make a preemptive military strike against France in order to remove Richelieu, the major obstacle.[41] Pro-Spanish commentators of all nations were unanimous in their judgement that Richelieu alone had perverted the true vocation of the French kingdom. Jerónimo de Barrionuevo summed up these feelings in a poetic obituary of the cardinal good enough to quote in full.

> Since we ourselves have let his will
> Get profit from our good and ill,
> Here lies the devilish cardinal,
> Half Christian, half heretical,
> And when before his marble stood
> One might never see, for blood,
> His purple cloth, his priestly hood.
> Product of barbarian brain,
> Reason of State may he carry again
> Back to the hell from whence it came.[42]

It is notable that not until Madrid's hegemony had approached much nearer its quietus was a strong recrudescence of irenic sentiment brought to bear on its policy, by advocates such as Saavedra Fajardo (who had earlier, more in sorrow than anger, defended the war policy) and Sor María de Agreda.[43]

---

[40] Ibid., pp. 44, 56, 112, 174, 182.

[41] Rubens to Olivares, 1 Aug. 1631, R.S. Magurn (ed.), *The Letters of Peter Paul Rubens* (Cambridge, MA, 1955), pp. 374–81.

[42] A. Paz y Melia (ed.), *Los avisos de Jerónimo de Barrionuevo*, BAE, 220–21 (Madrid, 1968–69), i, p. 32.

[43] For Saavedra, cf. the works written before 1640; e.g. his *Locuras de Europa*, J.M. Alejandro (ed.) Salamanca, 1973), pp. 18, 23, and the sentiments in the *Idea de un príncipe político-cristiano* BAE 25 (Madrid, 1949), *Empresa*, xxvi, pp. 70–71, with his letter to Philip IV of 4 April 1644, from the peace conference in Munster, CODOIN, 82 (Madrid,

continued

Until the passing of Richelieu and his master, and the succession of Philip's sister as regent – when for a time the king hoped that a family compact could be arranged[44] – no major Spanish voice seriously maintained that a Holy Catholic League with France should be pursued *as a priority*. Indeed, most of the Spanish political class of this period were convinced that French policy and society had been thoroughly and irremediably contaminated by Protestantism. More profoundly horrifying to their sensibilities than any plague, the prospect of such contagion made collaboration with France hardly a viable option. Eternal hostility towards her, though regrettable, was better than the risk of religious infection, so deadly to the whole communion of the monarchy. Writers of the new school of international politics, which emerged in response to the maturation of the Spanish system under Philip II, and as various in origin and inspiration as Giovanni Botero, Alamos de Barrientos, Juan de Mariana and Antony Sherley (all of whom were read by Olivares) evinced little sympathy for France. Although diseased by heresy and politics, and impoverished by civil war, France was yet revengeful, and had to be carefully watched. The eldest daughter of the church had fallen and was a lost soul; none of these observers, not even Padre Mariana, considered that France could be saved by Spain's paternal example and guidance.[45]

In contrast, it was precisely in the period *before* 1640 that collaborative convictions were strongest in France and struggled to dominate royal policy. A pro-Spanish party flourished inside both Louvre and Luxembourg palaces until the 1630s and, even after eradication from these strongpoints, continued to exert a strong gravitational pull on the loyalties of influential Frenchmen. This credo, which few had yet come to regard as treasonable, was subscribed to as widely as it was deeply in France – it had not one but several local habitations in the kingdom. In certain circumstances *les devots*, the zealot Catholic nobles, lay and ecclesiastical, spiritual heirs of the Lorrainers and the League, could call upon whole townships and regions to support this cause in arms.[46] No real equivalent existed on the other side. Indeed after 1614, and the expulsion of the last *Morisco* communities from Spain, Paris had no serious source of fifth column support anywhere inside the Spanish

continued

1886), p. 26. For Sor María, (e.g.) her letter to Philip of 14 August 1645, *Cartas de la Venerable Sor María de Agreda y del Señor Rey Don Felipe IV*, ed. C. Seco Serrano, BAE 108–9 (Madrid, 1958), i, p. 33; and T.D. Kendrick, *Mary of Agreda* (1967), pp. 130–36.

[44] Philip's *apostilla* on *consulta* of council of state, 28 May 1643, AGS, E K1420, no. 88.

[45] G. Botero, *The Reason of State*, ed. P.J. and D.P. Waley (1956), pp. 92, 103–4; B. Alamos de Barrientos, *L'art de gouverner*, ed. J.M. Guardia (Paris, 1867), pp. 99–108; X. Flores (ed.), '*El peso político de todo el mundo*' par Anthony Sherley (Paris, 1963), pp. 59–63; on Mariana, see A. Soons, *Juan de Mariana* (Boston, 1982).

[46] See (e.g.) the list provided by Rubens to Olivares in the letter cited above, n. 41. Such interests were regarded as 'a Spanish fifth column' which, during the first third of the century, constantly threatened a takeover of power within the French state: A. Eiras Roél, 'Desvio y "Mudanza" de Francia en 1616', *Hispania*, 25 (1965), pp. 521–60.

monarchy, whereas Madrid could stir in a stew of bitterly divided loyalties, which simmered even within the French royal family.

In strategic terms, a levelling factor did exist – the geographical separation of the major power-centres of the Spanish monarchy, which allowed France to probe its interstices in the Rhineland, the Swiss Alps and, above all, in Northern Italy. If Madrid held a spoon with which to stir up French internal strife – a phrase that was often used in council (*atizar a los Franceses*)[47] – France for its part was equipped with a crowbar which she could use to prise apart the smaller but tectonically vital stones of the Spanish fortress. In the Ligurian and Lombard plains, pockets of potential pro-French support discomfited Madrid. Not only Savoy and Venice but also several of the minor principalities were susceptible in this respect, as tentative moves by both Henry IV and the ministries of his son's minority had amply demonstrated.[48]

Thus we have a fascinating situation of all-round equipoise, a balance which is dialectically as elegant as it was actually delicate, and which may be held to characterize Franco-Spanish relations in this period. The Spanish Monarchy was *comparatively* united in politics and ideology, but rendered vulnerable by the geographical dispersion of its power. The geographically compact kingdom of France, on the other hand, was weakened by ideological and political division. Both governments were intent on eradicating these weaknesses, an ambition which almost sums up the careers of Richelieu and Olivares. Perhaps in the end the struggle was determined by the simple fact that Spain's weakness was structurally intractable. The supreme necessity for royal government to counter or compensate for the Spanish monarchy's geographical divisions had been outlined by Furió Ceriol at the time of its very creation, early in Philip II's reign, and before the outbreak of the Religious Wars which had eclipsed Spain's powerful neighbour.[49]

During the course of the year 1624, the two principals and one amateur observer returned a fortiori to this theme, and in a manner which had striking resemblances. The latter was the Welshman, James Howell, present on business at the Spanish court:

> The French in a slighting way compare his [Philip IV's] Monarchy to a beggar's cloak, made up of patches. They are patches indeed, but such as he [King Louis] hath not the like . . . and if these patches were in one piece, what would become of his cloak, embroidered with flower-de-luces?[50]

[47] See (e.g.) Philip's *apostilla* on *consulta* of council of state, 14 Jan. 1635, AGS, E 2050, no. 3.

[48] J.L. Cano de Gardoqui, *La cuestión de Saluzzo, 1588–1601* (Valladolid, 1962); A. Corral Castañedo, *España y Venecia, 1599–1604* (Valladolid, 1955); A. Bombín Pérez, *La cuestión de Monferrato, 1613–1618* (Valladolid, 1975).

[49] F. Furió Ceriol, *El concejo i consejeros del príncipe* (Antwerp, 1559); repr. BAE, 36 (Madrid, 1855), pp. 317–37.

[50] J. Howell, *Epistolae Ho-Elianae: Familiar Letters Domestic and Foreign* (10th edn, 1737), p. 164.

Richelieu himself – who came to power in this year – emphasised the point in one of his earliest analyses.

> On ne peut douter que les espagnols si aspirent à la domination universelle et que jusqu'à présent les seuls obstacles qu'ils ont rencontrés sont la séparation de leurs Etats et le manque d'hommes. Or, par l'acquisition de ces passages [the Valtelline] ils remédient a l'un et à l'autre.[51]

The cardinal's remarks could hardly have been better timed, for Olivares was just then urgently advising his master:

> Your majesty should hold as the most important business of his Monarchy that of making himself king of Spain. What I mean, sir, is that you should not rest content with being king of Portugal, of Aragon, of Valencia, count of Barcelona; but you should work and consider with mature and secret council in order to reduce these kingdoms so that they should comprise Spain . . . If Your Majesty could encompass this he would be the most powerful prince in the world.[52]

Much of the foregoing would seem to provide yet another illustration of the Marxian nostrum, that 'men make their own history, but not in circumstances chosen by themselves'. The introduction to this essay referred to the seventeenth-century phase of Franco-Spanish conflict as 'the Richelieu-Olivares War'. Is it valid, at least on the Spanish side, to make such an attribution? As we have seen, Olivares made the most of the credit which accrued to him from the victory of Fuenterrabía in 1638, just as on previous occasions he had never neglected to underline his indispensable role in the military successes of his master's monarchy. Yet he was not great enough (or should we say, by this time, *sane enough*?) to accept the personal consequences of failure. In the 1640s, having experienced the collapse of his war-plans and the overthrow of his power, the count-duke disclaimed any responsibility for initiating *either* of the two great conflicts associated with his ministry.[53] These pathetic attempts at exculpation are, in one sense, little more than the whinings of the favourite (*los balidos del valido*). But in the case of the Dutch War, the disclaimer has a certain technical validity; moreover, its renewal was founded on a wide consensus within the monarchy. Perhaps, also, he had some ethical point over the French case, for the policy of confrontation with France was one which for many years others advocated and he resisted.

The evidence of the count-duke's state papers, at least before 1627, suggests that at the outset he was not given to either school of thought, whether of hostility or fraternity. In this he was being faithful to his own conception of acquired political experience. He was an acutely self-aware thinker who – despite his fondness for history – pointed out that it was unwise to deduce rigid

---

[51] Quoted by L. van der Essen, 'Le rôle du cardinal-infant dans la politique espagnole du XVIIe siècle', *Revista de la universidad de Madrid*, new series (1954), p. 363.

[52] From the 'Gran Memorial' of 1624, Elliott and de la Peña, *Memoriales y cartas*, i, p. 96.

[53] In the 'Nicandro'; ibid., ii, pp. 249–50.

conclusions from the past. The 'science of contingencies' was meant to exercise a control over predisposition and even prejudice. Nearly all Don Gaspar's favourite authors had said as much; the statesman must never simply accept the plain lessons of the past unless he can be sure than they are adaptable to present circumstances.[54]

Perhaps this prescription really did operate in the case of France, because it was changing circumstances which changed Olivares' mind. For five years he refused to accept that even a serious – far less a mortal – threat to Spain existed from this direction. He consistently rejected proposals for a preventive attack on France, advocated (sometimes in detail) by a powerful lobby of fellow-ministers.[55] Only in the post-Mantua crisis – already, perhaps, too late – did he appreciate his error. Thereafter his mind was radically changed. He struggled to control his instinct to strike hard and quickly in order to rectify the mistake; he attempted patiently to await the right conjuncture of opportunity and preparation. Unfortunately, such forbearances – which he had always found difficult – had by now, through continuous overwork and anxiety, become intolerable to his temperament. The count-duke was ultimately unable to bear the mounting tension – he decided prematurely to launch an ambitious and overpowering offensive.

In the winter of 1622–23, during his debut appearances at the council of state, Olivares was understandably cautious. Even before the coming of Richelieu, he displayed only a lukewarm confidence in the 'eternal alliance' of the dynasties, declared and symbolized by the double royal marriage of 1612.[56] Concerned by the need to carry the war in Flanders to a successful conclusion (a priority which must always be seen as the *basso ostinato* of his policy) he agreed that eternal vigilance was necessary towards France; adding that, despite minor provocations, 'I do not consider it in Your Majesty's interests to break with France'.[57] Around this time, moreover, the new chief minister was busy in reading Sherley's treatise *El peso político* (*Political Power in the Whole World*) in which France was estimated as being *potentially* dangerous, but *actually* weak, especially in terms of political stability and the quality of its fighting men.[58] Perhaps this influenced Olivares to feel that any threat from France to the monarchy's frontiers in the Mediterranean regions could be countered by a sufficiently large reserve militia in process of training. It may be pointed out that in terms of practical contingency planning – a fact which no commentator to date seems to have focused upon – the French army was the only one which could be realistically expected to provide a major adversary for

---

[54] Ibid., i, p. xlix; J.A. Maravall, *La cultura del barroco* (Madrid, 1975), pp. 146–48. Richelieu's feelings on this point were identical: see H.B. Hill (ed.), *The Political Testament of Cardinal Richelieu* (Madison, WI, 1961), p. 58.

[55] Elliott and de la Peña, *Memoriales y cartas*, i, pp. 104, 138–39.

[56] See Olivares's *votos* in the council of state from 5 Nov. to 8 Dec. 1622, copied in BN, 5588, ff. 270–273.

[57] *Voto* of 26 Nov. 1623, BN, 5588, f. 307v.

[58] Flores, *El peso político*, pp. 59–63 (see also, pp. 37–38).

the forces of the Union of Arms. Sherley's dissection seemed to be borne out by the military lessons of the war of 1625, in which a thrust against Genoa by the Franco-Savoyard alliance was parried with relative ease. The other glorious events of that year, which gave rise to an overt triumphalism both inside and outside the council of state, and the unfavourable peace which Richelieu was obliged to accept in 1626, could only confirm such an outlook.[59]

Some eighteen months later, when the defenders of La Rochelle were holding out against Louis XIII's army – the latter assisted by the Dutch – it was understandable that the count-duke should cast a cold eye on French pretensions. As far as he could tell, France's current capacity to harrass the Spanish system was of little more than nuisance value. Observing that England seemed determined to prosecute its conflict with France, he recalled that not too long ago even the puny English had been able to invade, devastate and dictate terms to the larger kingdom. Though evincing a sensible desire to prolong its neighbour's internal divisions, he suggested that Spain had little to fear from her. Of course, he recognized that France's allies 'comprise virtually all the heretic powers that exist in Europe', and that only Richelieu's abandonment of the Dutch partnership could ever inspire any confidence in his government in Madrid. Nevertheless, at least on the surface, there was little substantial alteration from his *votos* of 1623.[60]

Here we must take pause; for this memorial was compiled only three weeks before the end of the Gonzaga dynasty precipitated the crisis of the Mantuan succession, and only a month before Olivares engineered a major strategic initiative which was clearly designed as a defensive insurance measure against France. Read carefully in context, it can be seen as a preparation for a diametrical change of policy, but one which he needed to introduce as it were *sotto voce*, both for the sake of his own image and for presentation to the king. Care was necessary on the latter point since Philip had been seriously ill during the very weeks that the policy of *rapprochement* with France had received a nasty setback. A little earlier Olivares, with the king's enthusiastic endorsement, had extended a costly olive branch in Richelieu's direction. This was no mere diplomatic gesture but took the concrete form of military assistance against the Huguenot rebels in La Rochelle, according to the terms of a treaty of friendship recently agreed upon. Unfortunately, the naval *empresa* despatched to confront Buckingham's fleet had been frustrated of its objective, and its usefulness was subsequently depreciated by the cardinal. Especially in view of the irritation Olivares exhibited at this unaccustomed and public failure of *reputación*, it seems probable that his overall attitudes were changing, perhaps rapidly. However, there were difficulties. On the one hand, the king, who as a result of his illness was likely to be behindhand with

[59] Alcalá-Zamora, *España, Flandes*, p. 216 et seq. Ródenas Vilar, *La política Europea*, pp. 58–70.

[60] 'Parecer del Conde Duque de San Lúcar sobre el estado de las cosas en todas partes', 5 Dec. 1627, AGS, E K1435, no. 141.

his work, with an uncertain grasp of events at this particular juncture, would experience difficulty in appreciating the reasons for an unwelcome volte-face. On the other, the La Rochelle expedition had been strongly opposed by a majority in council, whose members may not have been easily able to conceal their own vindication.[61]

The Mantuan initiative – early in 1628 – was, we must remember, the first Olivares had made which constituted an explicit move against Louis XIII. He must have felt that the death of Duke Vicenzo, at a uniquely favourable moment when France was entirely unable to intervene, was a providential sign – a feeling doubtless shared by the *junta de teólogos* who so promptly endorsed the Italian adventure. The decision taken by Don Gaspar and the king was further underwritten by a special subcommittee (*junta particular*) which included several of the ministers (Montesclaros, La Hinojosa, Feria) who had long been pressing for action against France.[62] In order to further disable the French, Olivares activated the scheme for massive financial subsidy of the Huguenot leaders Rohan and Soubise, which had been supported by a similarly constituted group earlier in the decade, and secretly sanctioned by the 'theologians'. Taken together, these events suggest that Olivares had moved firmly to the side of the hardliners even before the climacteric of 1629, when Louis XIII and Richelieu invaded Italy and issued their epoch-making challenge to *reputación*.[63]

Thereafter Olivares' attitudes hardened by the week. After 1630 his papers regularly brand the French as the ubiquitous instigators of evil. Increasingly facile resort is made to the clichés of anathema, until a climax is reached in 1634–35. In these years Olivares planned, with energy inspired by fear and ambition driven by loathing, to unleash upon France the dogs of war, a many-headed hydra comprising Spanish veterans, Flemish sailors, Italian conscripts and German mercenaries.[64] These avengers would be spearheaded by a fearsome horde of Cossacks, who – Don Gaspar eagerly anticipated – would bring devastation to the villages of France. Having attempted to arrange

[61] See, in AGS, E K1435, a *consulta* of the council of state, 2 July (no. 1), bearing the king's enthusiastic endorsement for the policy of aid to Louis XIII against the Huguenots and English; and Olivares's memos of 28 and 29 Nov. (nos 131–32). Only the day after the memorial cited above (n. 60), his determination to maintain a positive French policy was wavering: see *consulta* of (?) junta of state 6 Dec., printed (from the same *legajo*) in Ródenas Vilar, *La política europea*, pp. 263–64. (All dates refer to 1627.)

[62] Royal order of 15 Jan. 1628, AGS, E K1436, no. 6.

[63] Elliott, *Richelieu and Olivares*, pp. 126–27. Olivares had changed his mind rapidly over the Huguenot issue. In the summer of 1623 he roundly asserted that 'in no circumstances is it convenient or legitimate for Your Majesty to assist heretics against Catholics, and this would be the case were he to assist those of La Rochelle against their king': *consulta* of council of state, 3 July 1623, BN, 5588, f. 300. But little over a year later he secretly obtained the junta of theologians' clearance for precisely such a move; Ródenas Vilar, *La política europea*, pp. 32–36. It is notable that Richelieu and Louis XIII also frequently consulted a committee of 'several competent theologians' over ethically dubious issues: Hill, *Political Testament*, p. 35.

[64] See Chap. 5, above p. 95.

for the invasion of the enemy by no fewer than five geographically separate forces, he insisted that 'we must try to ensure that all these operations take place at the same time, for unless we attack them with great vigour, the French will neglect no opportunity to make themselves masters of the world'.[65] We are a far cry from the complacency of the 1620s.

In his first major policy note after the formal declaration of war, Olivares insisted that everything – 'religion, king, queen, nation and everything besides' – had to be committed to the cause of victory; 'It would be better to die than to fall under the dominion of others, and worse still of heretics – for this is what I take the French to be.' It was not enough to commission a team of gifted hacks to communicate condemnation of France to the literate leaders of opinion inside and outside the monarchy. He ordered that even the commissioning officers (*alfareces* and *maestros*) on recruiting drives in the Castilian countryside should deliberately inspire their men with hatred of the French.[66] In the same spirit, the local pulpit was to be commandeered for *la causa universal*, used regularly to broadcast francophobe messages to the population.[67] Even before Richelieu's announcement of the war, its first political victim was registered. The case of the duke of Aerschot, the distinguished envoy of the loyal Estates of Flanders, arrested in Madrid on skimpy charges of secret connections with Paris, was the harbinger of many.[68]

Given the escalating tensions of total war, the alarm of treason sounded everywhere, in pubs as much as in palaces. Amongst those who were added to the list of *desaparecidos* were protégés of the *valido*, like Don Francisco de Quevedo, now suspected of being a French agent; and the duke of Nochera, accused (*inter alia*) of the ultimate cultural crime of dressing himself and his retainers in the French fashion.[69] Spy-fever permeated the cities, for as Pellicer reported:

> The most dangerous war which the French wage against us is that of their spies, who with fanatic skill prepare as many evil schemes in our midst as can be imagined. The leader of this treason was Captain Francisco Pérez de San Juan, a Portuguese ... Many were the trails which led to him, and great was the torment to which he was subjected. But he revealed many crimes and accomplices, and in the end he paid for his plots, since in company with ten

[65] *Consulta* of council of state, 16 Jan. 1635, AGS, E 2049.

[66] 'El Conde Duque sobre lo que se deve disponer para executar la jornada de V. Mgd.', 14 June 1635, AGS, E 2656.

[67] See (e.g.) a batch of *Consejo Real* documents in BN, 7760, esp. ff. 158–171, exhorting the hierarchy to organise services and prayers for victory, providing them with detailed liturgical suggestions and appropriate propaganda material.

[68] Elliott, *The Count-Duke* pp. 469–71; the papers of the investigation are at AGS, E 2871.

[69] J.H. Elliott, 'Quevedo and the Count-Duke of Olivares', in J. Iffland (ed.), *Quevedo in Perspective* (Newark, NJ, 1982), pp. 227–50; and (for Nochera), idem, *Historia de España Menéndez Pidal*, p. 494.

others, they garrotted him secretly last Wednesday, and threw the bodies into the stream of Briñigal, a quarter of a league outside Madrid.[70]

Which such barbarities, so familiar to our own century, continued a war which had been from the beginning marked by an excess of cruelty we do not always find even in the period of the Thirty Years War. When the French army first entered Luxembourg and the Basse-Meuse in late April 1635 reports of terrible atrocities were received with anger in Madrid. Francisco de Quevedo and Cornelius Jansen were moved to excoriate in print the power which had permitted – or perhaps inspired – the murders of priests and the desecration of the eucharist in the horrors of Tillement.[71] (Again, 1635 reaches forward to 1936.) Though this is speculation, it seems possible that Richelieu decided upon the celebrated declaration of war by Louis XIII's herald at the gates of Brussels in order to smooth over this embarrassment and restore some 'traditional' respectability to the French cause. How otherwise can we explain the cardinal's apparently gratuitous resort to a ritual hardly less anachronistic and pointless than duelling by his usual standards of judgement?

Not until the failure of his offensive strategy was obvious, and outright disaster looming, did Olivares seriously consider peace negotiations. In the first autumn of the war he rejected a papal offer of mediation, inspired (it was said) by Richelieu.[72] A year later he advised the council that 'our rule is never to trust the French, nor to believe that from their hands we will ever receive anything other than insults and offences'.[73] Around the time of the executions noted above, he repeated that 'my principle is that the cardinal never tells the truth, and wishes always to deceive and confuse us'.[74] By the spring of 1640, however, he at last privately and grudgingly acknowledged God's decision for peace: 'God must want us to make peace, because he has deprived us visibly and absolutely of all the means whereby to wage war.' Yet he again rejected the intervention of Urban VIII, because 'the French fight everywhere in the cause of heresy, and without their aid, innumerable sufferings and losses of souls would never have been imposed upon the church'.[75] Not long afterwards Spain suffered the double rebellion of Catalonia and Portugal. Intestinal wars began, bringing French armies into the peninsula – a presence which was to

[70] J. Pellicer y Tovar, *Avisos históricos* (3 vols, Madrid, 1789–90), i, pp. 20–21 (May 1639).

[71] *Consulta* of council of state, 29 May 1635, AGS, E 2050, no. 4; Jover, *1635: historia de una polémica* pp. 253–54, 293–305.

[72] Gayangos, *Cartas*, i, pp. 332–38.

[73] *Consulta* of council of state, Aug. 1637, AGS, E 2052 (copy in BL, Add. 36322, ff. 137–147v.).

[74] Memo by Olivares, (? June 1639), printed (from AGS, E K1419) by Cánovas, *Estudios*, i, pp. 410–12. Don Gaspar's conclusion, therefore, was that 'we can do no other than pursue the war with a fury greater than ever before'.

[75] Olivares to Philip IV, March 1640, in Cánovas, *Estudios*, i, p. 415; to Urban VIII, April 1640, BL, Add. 25689, ff. 395–401v.

last for nearly thirty years. The Hydra had turned savagely upon its master, tearing at the entrails of the helpless Spanish Hercules.

Nevertheless, Olivares continued to vacillate, now physically weakening, beset by conflicting emotions and strains. Following the *Corpus de Sangre* in Barcelona, and the subsequent rebellion of the Catalans, he betrayed this loss of confidence in soliciting the opinion of the veteran Count of Oñate. When this retired statesman strongly confirmed his own feeling that peace was essential, the paranoid *valido* took it as a personal criticism, and – reversing his earlier conclusion – recommended an all-round revival of the war-effort.[76] It was only the death of his hated French rival which convinced Olivares that the *paz honesta* was a viable possibility:

> We could hardly have a greater blessing than to arrive at a peace, for the state of our affairs renders honest and almost necessary any settlement we can get; and if we could obtain it with despatch and security, and without indignity, it would be good in the present conjuncture.[77]

An observer hardly less hostile to Olivares than Richelieu, but lying so deep and silent within the body politic that not even the most zealous spy-hunter could hope to sniff him out, was the long-serving *ayuda de cámara* (assistant chamberlain in the king's apartments), Matías de Novoa. In his secret diary, Novoa also noted Richelieu's passing. He commented that the cardinal had been 'the mortal enemy of humanity's natural aspiration', that is, God's purpose to unite all men in the faith; but admitted – since no opponent of the tyrant Guzmán could be entirely without merit – that he had been 'the best servant whom the king of France has had, and the greatest subject of France herself'.[78] One great luminary had sunk beneath the horizon, and within a week the other was able to cease his dazzling journey across the political firmament.

Postscript

As I explained in defending the above essay during the Toro conference, my comments on what Spanish historians had written during the 1940s and 50s were not intended as strictures. I had no intention of negative – far less, bitter – criticism of my elders and betters; nor did I mean to imply any political judgement, either in general terms or upon private persuasions. My intention was merely to analyze their work in its historiographical context (a long-established technique) and with a little admixture of more up-to-date 'cultural history'. In point of fact, I am not personally opposed to everything

---

[76] 'Voto de Conde Duque . . .', 20 Aug. 1640, AHN, E 674, no. 5.

[77] *Consulta* of council of state, 10 Jan. 1643, AGS, E 3860.

[78] M. de Novoa, *Historia de Felipe IV, rey de España*, CODOIN, 86 (Madrid, 1886), pp. 74–75.

which the Franco regime represented in Spain, and I hope that these days it is possible to state this much without running the risk of exaggerated or unjust accusations.

My concern was not with the central thesis put forward by Jover Zamora, in his *1635: historia de una polémica*, that the writers of the generation of 1635 believed profoundly in the Spanish cause, and that their passionate advocacy derived from deeply-rooted conviction of its purity of inspiration. There is a difference between simply propounding this thesis – with which I find myself in agreement – and advancing it with the evident personal support of the historian for the cause itself. The latter impression is one I cannot avoid when reading Jover Zamora's book.

As it happens, Professor Jover has recently returned to this subject in a contribution (published in collaboration with M. López-Cordón) to the new edition of a well-known general history of Spain.[79] On this occasion, however, he puts forward opinions which are very different to those he held forty years ago. In the new pages we find (for example) a full and open recognition that the anti-French writers patronized by Olivares were in reality a team of official propagandists. Furthermore, Professor Jover now claims that the author and minister Guillén de la Carrera actually admitted at the time that Madrid was extending financial aid to the Huguenots.[80] In addition, his views on the writers whose work previously so impressed him has changed radically.

> What overweening pride lurked behind the passionate eulogies of the House of Habsburg, with their aspirations to universal empire, and depreciation of their enemies; and how confident they were in a Providence excessively compromised by purely Spanish interests.

But, above all, Jover and his collaborator have put forward a general hypothesis to which I would like to return later.

Oddly enough, not long before Jover had decided effectively to renounce his previous position as regards the authentic meaning of the Olivares phase of Spain's 'crusade', a new and even stronger version of exactly this idea was formulated by the German author Eberhard Straub.[81] In the essay itself I had no space to deal with contributions to the debate emanating from other countries apart from the two main protagonists of France and Spain. On this basis, I left aside other writers, old and new, like the Catholic Englishman Lord Acton or the Marxist Czech Polisensky, who have made interesting and relevant comments on the ethical role of the Spanish state in its imperialist phase.[82]

[79] J.M. Jover Zamora and M. López-Cordón, 'La imagen europea y el pensamiento político-internacional', *Historia de España Menéndez Pidal*, xxvi, *El siglo de Quijote, 1580–1680*, i (Madrid, 1986), pp. 335–449.

[80] Ibid., pp. 409, 442.

[81] Straub, *Pax et imperium*.

[82] Lord Acton, *Lectures on Modern History* (1906: Fontana edn, ed. H. R. Trevor-Roper, 1960), esp. pp. 59–60; J.V. Polisensky, *War and Society in Europe, 1618–48* (1978), pp. 34–35.

But it is impossible to overlook Straub, because he argues throughout his book that it would indeed have been better for the future of Europe and world history if Spain had triumphed, and if the Habsburgs of Vienna had stood consistently and loyally alongside their Spanish cousins during the wars of the seventeenth century. Straub insists that the religious motives of Philip IV's government were utterly sincere, and that virtually the whole of the blame for the ultimate failure of the Habsburg cause can be laid at Vienna's door. In this way the 'Peaceful European Order' (*Friedensordnung*) aimed at by Olivares was frustrated, above all by the events of the war in Mantua.

To my mind, the religious belief which consistently inspired the bellicose policies endorsed by Spain's ministers is fundamental to our understanding of that epoch. It is beyond any reasonable doubt that the personalities concerned were inspired, and even compelled, by spiritual demands intrinsic to their mental make-up. Clearly in one sense it is hardly important, before the bar of history, whether any concrete reality existed for such principles, or whether the Spaniards acted properly in pursuing them. But our inability fully to understand or sympathize with these beliefs should not prevent us from recognizing them for what they were. The metaphysical world may be a strange and uncomfortable one for historians, but it nonetheless exists. Also we should not forget the original meaning of the word 'propaganda', and the confidence (referred to in the body of essay) placed in the concept of 'Authentic Reason of State'.

It seems, therefore, that Professor Jover has moved from an extreme viewpoint to its opposite when he states that

> The decisions of the ministers ... rested almost always upon material factors [and] the Monarchy intervened in a devastating war because the economy of the Iberian peninsula demanded it ...

especially adding (as he does) that the ideology of the monarchy 'was nothing more than a ponderous doctrinal apparatus of politics'.[83] I am convinced that this opinion represents a major misjudgement. Many times during his career Antonio Domínguez Ortiz has reminded us about 'the criterion of the subordination of economics to politics' in the policymaking priorities of the Monarchy.[84] In his opening statement to the Toro conference itself he drew attention to the very exiguous presence of economic motives in Olivares' programme of reform, asserting at the same time that its inspiration was an ethical one, conceived in the service of God.

Earlier in this century other Spanish intellectuals reached similar conclusions. José Ortega y Gasset, in arguing 'Against the Economic Interpretation of History', cited no less an authority than Max Weber when insisting on the

---

[83] Jover Zamora and López-Cordón, 'La imagen', p. 410, citing as authoritative the views of J.I. Israel in *The Dutch Republic*.

[84] A. Domínguez Ortiz, 'Guerra económica y comercio extranjero en el reinado de Felipe IV', *Hispania*, 23 (1963), p. 89.

structural influence of religious attitudes in political and economic matters. Salvador de Madariaga placed the greatest possible emphasis upon the essentially religious character of the state created by the Catholic Kings.[85] Neither of these thinkers were men of the right, or connected in any way with the so-called 'Black Spain'. On the contrary, both were writers whose background lay in Spain's rich liberal and European tradition, and for this reason they respected the analytical value of an economic approach to history.

Finally, it is of little value for historians to cite the apparently evil and Machiavellian schemes of Madrid's international diplomacy as examples of an institutionalized hypocrisy; or – even worse – to regard an economic strategy, adopted in order to defeat economically powerful enemies, as an end in itself, not simply as a method towards obtaining the verdict ordained in heaven. These days we are firmly held in an intellectual climate which is almost entirely secular and not religious, material and not spiritual. But the centuries of faith were many in number and their massive presence is not located all that far behind us, at least for those who are inclined to turn and look.

[85] J. Ortega y Gasset, 'Against the Economic Interpretation of History' (first published 1925); English edition in *Invertebrate Spain and Other Essays* (1937), pp. 172–89; S. de Madariaga, *Spain* (1930), esp. pp. 40–47.

The duke of Medina de las Torres, Philip IV's most intimate *privado* and Olivares's son-in-law, is portrayed here as viceroy of Naples in 1639. From Parrino's *Teatro eroico . . . del regno di Napoli* (1694).

A Spanish Statesman of Appeasement: Medina de las Torres and Spanish Policy 1639–70

In spite of the current renaissance of interest and research in the history of Habsburg Spain, very little of significance has yet appeared in English on the post-Olivares period of Spanish government and policy – the period in which the Spanish monarchy declined from a position of European hegemony to that of a second-rate power, the virtually helpless prey of her continental maritime adversaries. The nineteenth-century histories of Dunlop and Hume, which interspersed sections of court diaries with superficial, descriptive chronicles of foreign and military affairs, were not substantially improved upon by R. Trevor Davies' (admittedly posthumous) study of *Spain in Decline*.[1] The more recent studies by Professors Elliott, Lynch and Domínguez Ortiz tend to be somewhat exiguous on the years following the great crisis of 1640 (albeit to differing extents) whilst displaying a common freshness of approach and presentation.[2] This is quite understandable, since the situation in Spanish historiography itself is not much better. The uniformly dismal, perhaps still humiliating, features of this period are a natural deterrent to study in contemporary Spain. Domínguez Ortiz and Valiente apart, researched monographs are non-existent, and it has been left to the Anglo-Saxons to venture, on a modest scale, into the uncharted territories of administrative and monetary history.[3]

Although there is little immediate prospect of this problem being adequately remedied, the present essay is intended to make a small contribution towards filling some gaps in our knowledge, at least in the field of the nature of Spanish government, and its attitudes to imperial defence, in a period of accelerating material debility. During the course of doctoral work on Anglo-Spanish relations in the 1660s, my attention was drawn to the career of a major Spanish statesman who has a claim to be considered one of the most unjustly neglected figures of his century, the duke of Medina de las Torres.

---

[1] J. Dunlop, *Memoirs of Spain in the Reigns of Philip IV and Charles II*, 2 vols (Edinburgh, 1834); M.A.S. Hume, *The Court of Philip IV: Spain in Decadence* (1907); R. Trevor Davies, *Spain in Decline, 1621–1700* (1957).

[2] J.H. Elliott, *Imperial Spain, 1469–1716* (1963); Lynch, *Spain and America, 1598–1700* (1969); Domínguez Ortiz, *The Golden Age of Spain, 1516–1659* (1971).

[3] A. Domínguez Ortiz, *Política y hacienda de Felipe IV* (Madrid, 1960); V. Tomás y Valiente, *Los validos en la monarquía Española* (Madrid, 1963); E.J. Hamilton, *War and Prices in Spain, 1651–1800*; (Cambridge, MA, 1947); H. Kamen, *The War of Succession in Spain, 1700–1715* (1969), esp. chap. 2.

Closer for longer periods to the 'sources of power in the monarchy than any of his contemporaries, Medina held high office for an uninterrupted span of forty years. For most of this period he was an intimate *privado* of Philip IV, and for a few years of it was only a short step away from the *valimiento* itself.[4]

These facts would in themselves merit deeper study of Medina's career than has hitherto been forthcoming, but his importance is considerably enhanced by the maintenance of a line of thought and policy consistently critical of the traditional assumptions on which Spanish foreign policy was based. Medina was one of the first to reach and express the conclusion that the exhaustion of Castile and her Italian dependencies demanded the conclusion of a secure peace settlement with Spain's major European rivals. For thirty years, he almost alone amongst Philip IV's close advisers consistently sought means of extricating the monarchy from the heavy and continuous burden of war which the Habsburg inheritance involved, and which was mutely and uncritically accepted as a condition of their being by so many Castilians, from the king downwards. For much of this period Medina, ultimately in as many words, urged Philip and his councillors to accept a diminution of the monarchy's role in European affairs; to adjust, however painfully, to the realities of Spain's condition; and to withdraw from the exposed and vulnerable trenches of European hegemony. By the end of his life he had reached a position of outright appeasement, the feeling that the preconceptions of honour and prestige, the categorical imperative of continuous struggle imposed by the glorious past of the monarchy, and so dear to many of its influential subjects, were as nothing compared to the human and material responsibilities of government. By then (the late 1660s) he was convinced of the need – in his own words – for 'peace at any price'.

Extravagant tributes have been paid to Medina's character and abilities, by Cánovas del Castillo in the last century, and by Gregorio Marañón and Ludwig Pfandl in more recent times.[5] Nevertheless, he has remained a relatively obscure figure in Spanish studies of the period and is virtually unknown to English scholars. References to him are frequently vague and confused, and abound with errors, probably caused by his immense accumulation of titles and offices.[6] Ignorance of Medina's career and significance has other origins, however. His notable sexual promiscuity, which obstructed his advance after the death of Don Luis de Haro to the office of *valido*, which he coveted intensely, perhaps also explains a certain distaste in examining

---

[4] I use these terms with a distinction first suggested to me by some sentences of Tomás y Valiente, see *Los validos* (1st edn, 1963), pp. 53–4, implying that the king could have several favourites (or *privados*) to whom he vouchsafed his company, but only one supreme political adviser (or *valido*).

[5] A. Cánovas del Castillo, *Estudios del reinado de Felipe IV* (2 vols, Madrid, 1888–89), ii, pp. 371–73; G. Marañón, *El conde-duque du Olivares* (3rd edn, Madrid, 1952), pp. 275–84; L. Pfandl, *Carlos II* (Madrid, 1947), pp. 137–48.

[6] Earlier scholars were careful to recommend caution in the treatment of Medina for the reason above stated. See Gayangos, *Cartas*, vii, p. 426, and Cánovas, *Estudios*, ii, p. 371.

his career among Spanish historians. (Maura, for example, refers primly to 'the licence of his private life, which increased with age, and exposed him to the vilification of the people'.)[7] The actual failure of his aspirations to supreme power has also, naturally, conduced to historical obscurity, although he possessed outstanding qualifications for the highest office.[8] What success Medina did obtain, moreover, came at a time when perception and statesmanship could never hope to correct the material losses of preceding generations, even when it prevailed against the opposition and mental paralysis of his contemporaries.[9] In any case, ignorance of Medina in all the secondary sources for the period demands at the outset the establishment of his 'pedigree'.

Don Ramiro Felípez Núñez de Guzmán – to reduce Medina to his mere family name, sonorous enough in all conscience – was the nearest thing to a life-long personal friend that King Philip IV possessed.[10] Born about 1600, he was Philip's constant companion for lengthy periods, stretching from the middle 1620s to the last hours of the king's life. Medina's rise to prominence was truly meteoric. Although a representative of one of the most ancient and noble families of Castile – the main line of Guzmán – he was living the quiet life of a country squire in 1624, when the count-duke of Olivares, a distant kinsman, sought him out, and, amidst considerable sensation, married him to his only child, Doña María. Besides intending to bolster and purify his own Guzmán lineage – which was that of a cadet branch – Olivares thus made a deliberate gesture of independence from the traditional connexions and interests of the inbred higher nobility of Castile. The establishment *grandeza* took this insult as deeply to heart as many others that the count-duke was to offer them during his rule. Especially in the ranks of the Haro family (whose young scion, Don Luis, was the foremost thwarted candidate for María's hand) hatred of the Olivares–Guzmán connexion, and opposition to the *valimiento* of the count-duke originated in this affair. Their feelings are understandable, since up to this point Don Ramiro's family itself had no record of service to the crown, and lived on extremely modest rents which only barely qualified them to claim a title of nobility. This title – that of marquis of Toral – had in fact been granted to Don Ramiro's father as recently as 1612.[11]

---

[7] G. Maura, *Carlos II y su corte* (2 vols, Madrid, 1911), i, pp. 54–55. See also (e.g.) P. Aguado Bleye, *Manual de la historia de España* (10th edn, Madrid, 1969), ii, p. 823; and Marques del Saltillo, 'Don Antonio Pimentel y la paz de los Pirineos', *Hispania*, 26 (1947), pp. 24–124 (at p. 40).

[8] A fact admitted even by Maura, *Carlos II y su corte*, i, p. 122.

[9] Cánovas, *Estudios*, ii, p. 371; Pfandl, *Carlos II*, p. 138.

[10] The following section relies on the work of Cánovas and Marañón already cited in this chapter, and the other biographical sources cited in notes 5–7, except where otherwise noted.

[11] J. de Atienza, *Nobiliario español: diccionario heráldico* ... (2nd edn, Madrid, 1954), p. 976; J. Wadsworth, *The Present Estate of Spayne* ... *with a catalogue of all the Nobility with their Revenues* (1630), p. 2. Wadsworth, an apostate Jesuit and anti-Spanish propagandist, also noted the family motto, haughty and dismissive even by Castilian standards, 'Reyes de nos y no nos de Reyes' – 'Kings derive from us, not we from kings'.

At the outset of his career, therefore, and in spite of his great personal charm, Don Ramiro was the object of the jealousy, resentment and class contempt always felt for the *arriviste* amongst the ruling class. From the beginning, Olivares warned his son-in-law of this hatred,[12] which close association with the growing dictatorship naturally intensified. Nevertheless, the young nobleman's rise was now assured. The dukedom of Medina de la Torres (by which he was usually known thereafter) was created for him by Philip IV, on Olivares' request, as part of his dowry settlement. The tragic death of María in childbirth at the age of seventeen failed to affect the count-duke's affection for, and promotion of, his young protégé.[13] By 1627 Medina was *consejero de estado* and a regular member of other committees and juntas, in some of which he even acted as Olivares' spokesman.[14] His friendship with the king stemmed from his tenure (lasting until Philip's death) of the post of *sumiller de corps*, in which Olivares placed him as a key figure in his elaborate system of 'protective supervision' of the king's activities.[15] So well did Medina fulfil the demands of this office that he was credited by many with the paternity of the *hijo de la tierra*, Don Juan José, son of the actress Calderona, and later acknowledged by Philip as his own bastard.[16] A short time later, Olivares also appointed him to the lucrative treasurership-general of Aragon, by which time he seems to have been second only in the count-duke's camarilla to the notorious Jerónimo de Villanueva.[17]

[12] 'Instrucción del Conde Duque de Olivares para su yerno', 9 Oct. 1624, cited by Elliott, 'The Statecraft of Olivares', p. 121.

[13] Marañón explicitly pointed this out in *El conde duque*, p. 283. See also J. Deleito y Piñuela, *El declinar de la monarquía Española* (3rd edn, Madrid, 1955), pp. 113–14. Doña María was marquesa de Heliche in her own right, but Don Ramiro does not seem to have used this title (nor his own original one of Toral) after her death. It later passed, probably as a result of the litigation over Olivares' legacy, to the eldest son of Luis de Haro.

[14] *Inventario general de manuscritos de la Biblioteca Nacional de Madrid*, ix, pp. 201–2.

[15] Feeling ran so high at court on this appointment that the admiral of Castile (Don Alonso de Enríquez) who had aspirations to this office, protested publicly to the king, who replied that 'he to whom I have given it is as good as you'; see Novoa's account in CODOIN, 69, pp. 39 et seq. Novoa was a keen opponent of Olivares and these pages illustrate his sympathy with the grandees in these disputes. On the vital importance of the post of *Sumiller de corps*, see below, pp. 167–69.

[16] This famous piece of scandal has survived through the writings of the gossip-mongering Mme d'Aulnoy, whom Marañón calls 'a picturesque imposter', adding that the whole story 'was, without doubt, invention'; *El conde duque*, p. 39. For editions of d'Aulnoy, see *Memoirs of the Court of Spain* ... (1692) and *The Letters of the Travels into Spain* (2nd edn, 1692). Though this version is certainly preposterous, its basic point was resilient and widely credited. The earl of Sandwich was apprised of it soon after his arrival in Madrid in 1666; MS Journal of Edward, 1st earl of Sandwich (Mapperton, Dorset), iii, p. 668. Philip later made Medina responsible for the upbringing and education of the child, and the duke was always consulted on his welfare; Marañón, *El conde-duque*, p. 279; Pfandl, *Carlos II*, pp. 98–99. The curious may compare the images of Philip, Medina, and Don Juan José reproduced in F. Soldevila, *Historia de España* (2nd edn, Barcelona, 1963), pp. 287, 356.

[17] J.H. Elliott, *The Revolt of the Catalans* (Cambridge, 1963), p. 256.

For the next twenty-five years, Medina continued to accumulate honours, titles and estates, partly by the joint patronage of Olivares and Philip, partly by reason of two further marriages, each as beneficial to his interests as the first. Indeed, the earlier of these alliances, to the Italian princess Anna di Carafa in 1637, represented a minor political triumph in addition to its financial advantages. The great Carafa dynasty, whose influence stretched into many parts of Italy and was particularly strong in Naples, was by tradition unsympathetic to Habsburg rule in the *Regno*, and had often obstructed Spanish policy. Medina's accession to a very high place in the Carafa interest now promised to bring it firmly within the orbit of Madrid at an important juncture in the monarchy's affairs.[18]

This development, however, was not entirely welcome to Medina's own overlord. Coming as it did during the period of mounting pressures and his growing sense of isolation, the count-duke felt slighted by his son-in-law's attitude. Ten years before, he had specifically counselled Don Ramiro 'establish your own reputation, and do not count on my remaining in a position so subject to sudden change'.[19] The Carafa marriage (and his now secure place in the king's affections) indicated that Medina had acted on this advice, to the extent that he no longer actually depended on Olivares's material patronage. Despite this evidence of successful tutorship in *el arte del privado*, Olivares complained bitterly to Philip of being kept in the dark about Medina's intentions – 'he has never spoken a word to me about it . . . nor has he written to the count of Monterrey, or anyone else'.[20] Though on the one hand Medina remained intellectually and emotionally attached to his benefactor, and on the other Olivares recognized the political convenience involved, the Carafa affair did cause a serious breach in their relationship. For his part, however, the king was delighted at the good fortune of his *compadre*. Approving the match, he bestowed upon Medina a whole package of *mercedes* to facilitate it, including the right of future succession to the viceroyalty of Naples itself, at that time one of the most sought-after posts in the king's bequest.[21] Furthermore, his new bride, heiress to a fortune reputedly the greatest in Italy, brought him huge estates and a princely title (that of Stigliano or Astillano). With these, Medina acquired a degree of

---

[18] Maura, *Carlos II y su corte*, i, 54. By this time, the fortunes of Olivares's young star were the subject of interest outside Spain. Charles I, questioning the Venetian envoy on the Carafa engagement in 1633, 'seemed to know about the duke of Medina Lastores', *CSPV, 1632–36*, p. 133.

[19] See note 12, above.

[20] Memorial by Olivares, 13 Aug. 1634, AGS, E 3332.

[21] List dated 20 Dec. 1634, AGS, E 3332. The Naples appointment unfortunately involved the displacement of the count of Monterrey, another kinsman and nominee of the count-duke, which put a strain on Guzmán family unity when Medina left to take up the post in 1637. By this time, on the other hand, the quarrel with Olivares himself had been patched up, and the two men parted – according to one observer – very amicably: Gayangos, *Cartas*, i, pp. 361, 382, 467.

economic independence unique among his contemporaries in the most exalted sphere of Spanish administration.

This happy entrance into the highest ranks of the Neapolitan aristocracy, combined with his authority as one of Olivares's most trusted lieutenants, was of great benefit to Medina in his years as ruler of the *Regno* (1638–43).[22] The viceroyalty, as fraught with difficulty as it was lined with gold, was handled by Medina with tact and understanding. He fought hard to alleviate the worst effects of Spanish taxation on the non-privileged classes during this, the worst-ever period of government rapacity, yet at the same time managed to retain the loyalty of the nobility and the confidence of Madrid – an achievement somewhat equivalent to squaring the circle. His popularity and authority were enhanced by personal courage during a French naval assault on Naples in 1638. When in the same year the *Regno* was shattered by an eruption of Vesuvius, and a subsequent series of earthquakes, he reacted with great humanity and compassion. Medina's experience of these disasters, bringing him fact to face with the common world of the monarchy, made him aware of the appalling consequences of endemic warfare, even on a province normally far removed from its actual location. Close observation of want, devastation and death on a massive scale, intensified intolerably by the exactions of war, left a permanent impression on his political thinking. Even so, without emulating the egregious record of his immediate predecessor as viceroy, the count of Monterrey, whose cupidity was already a byword, he returned from Italy a very wealthy man.[23] He was doubly fortunate, moreover, in leaving Naples before the outbreak of the savage popular reaction which the culmination of fiscal, economic and natural disasters finally unleashed in 1647.

Medina returned to Spain in October 1643, at the end of his second term of office (the normal maximum), and not, as is sometimes asserted,[24] as a result of the disgrace of Olivares the previous January. As might be expected, however, he subsequently shared to some extent in the oblivion of his mentor, and his influence in government was interrupted by the events of 1643, engineered as they were by the *grandeza* led by the Haro group of dissidents. Medina came

[22] Medina's viceroyalty forms the main background, and to some extent the subject, of R. Villari, *La rivolta antispagnola a Napoli, 1585–1647* esp. chaps 4–6. Harsh treatment of Medina and his spouse, based on a chronicle by one Capecelatro, a victim of the viceroy's displeasure, is A. de Reumont, *The Carafas of Maddaloni: Naples under Spanish Dominion* (1854), pp. 154 et seq. For more balanced accounts, see notices of Medina in *Diccionario de la historia de España* (2nd edn, Madrid, 1968), ii, pp. 297–98; and 'Los virreyes lugartenientes del reino de Nápoles' in CODOIN, 33, pp. 521–22.

[23] Deleito y Pisuela, *El declinar*, p. 115. Medina's riches were not all due to peculation, though his record as a raiser of funds was impressive. His Italian rents were vast; see the list of lordships in Villari, *La rivolta*, p. 271 – no fewer than thirteen titles. The legacy of resentment left behind by Monterrey created severe problems for Medina in his early administration of the *Regno*; ibid., pp. 273, 258–59.

[24] E.g. by Cánovas, in his *Bosquejo histórico de la casa de Austria* (2nd edn, Madrid, 1911), p. 270; and Pfandl, *Carlos II*, pp. 16–17. The fact that the post was obtained by the admiral of Castile, one of the chief *antiolivaristas*, does, it is true, conduce to the assumption.

back, then, to find his bitterest enemies firmly in control of affairs, and their chief, the count of Castrillo, completing the manoeuvres necessary to place his nephew, Don Luis, at the head of the new regime.

The king himself dearly hoped to protect Medina from the general proscription of Olivares' associates. Indeed, only a few days after Don Gaspar's dismissal, Philip assured his friend in Naples that, 'I remain here to favour and honour you as always, and to give you support whenever you may need it'.[25] In the circumstances it proved difficult to discharge this remarkable commitment. The collapse of the count-duke's system and the exigencies of war on the Aragonese frontier made Philip unusually dependent on the higher nobility, and in particular the Haro faction, at this juncture. Consequently, victimization proceeded at court. The humiliation of the main scapegoat, the protonotario Villanueva, is well known. At the same time, Monterrey and the marquis of Leganés, two other close kinsmen and lieutenants of Olivares (los dos ladrones – the two robbers, as they were called popularly)[26] suffered imprisonment and banishment respectively.[27] Likewise, Haro and Castrillo made strenuous attempts, after his return from Naples, to prevent Medina's return to court. Philip's disapproval created obvious incongruities in the plans of Medina's enemies, since on the one hand they were trying to accuse him of corruption (in Naples) and attempting to redistribute his offices, yet on the other hoped to solve their dilemma by naming him plenipotentiary in the important negotiations then beginning in Germany.[28] In the event neither the fears of the Haros, nor the advice of Philip's new and most intimate confidante, Sor María de Ágreda, prevented Medina from re-establishing his personal relationship with the king – an emotional tie which he was careful to support with material blandishments.[29] Though keeping his offices and escaping actual punishment,[30] Don Ramiro's political power was circumscribed for some time. Perhaps as many as five years elapsed before he returned to the Consejo de Estado, and in this period, apart from exercise of his less central duties, he presented a low profile to his adversaries.[31] The nature and extent

---

[25] Philip to Medina, 20 Jan. 1643, AHN, E 869, ff. 63–64. See also Marañón, El conde-duque, p. 358.

[26] E. Chamberlayne, The Rise and Fall of . . . the Count Olivares . . . (1652), p. 31.

[27] CODOIN, 86, pp. 290 et seq.; C.L. Penney (ed.), Printed Books of the Hispanic Society of America, 1468–1700 (New York, 1965), p. 250.

[28] J. Pellicer y Tovar, Avisos, iii, pp. 95, 100, 245; CODOIN, 82, pp. 117–19; ibid., 86, pp. 92, 156. Even this last witness – Novoa, who hated Medina – commented on the inconsistency of the government attitude; ibid., p. 465.

[29] Sor María to Philip, 13 Oct. 1643, F. Silvela, Cartas de la Venerable Sor María de Agreda y del Señor Rey Don Felipe IV, 2 vols (Madrid, 1885–86), i, pp. 5–6. For Medina's costly insurance with the king, see Domínguez, Sociedad española, i, pp. 248–49.

[30] Indeed he was actually appointed at this juncture to the presidency of the council of Italy, which since January had been critical of his Neapolitan administration; Cánovas, Estudios, ii, p. 373; Villari, La rivolta, p. 236.

[31] This conclusion is based on the negative evidence of council and junta attendance (1643–48) to be found in CODOIN, vols 82–84, 95, passim.

of his private influence on Philip can, of course, only be guessed at, but on at least one occasion he was consulted directly on a matter of high policy of which even Sor María was kept ignorant.[32]

Medina made no attempt to redeem himself by cutting his ties with the count-duke. During the years of Olivares' exile, madness and death – Marañón's famous 'twilight at Toro' – Don Ramiro consoled and defended him, and he was the chief mourner at Olivares' funeral.[33] Subsequent relations with the ruling clique were not improved by prolonged litigation over Olivares' testament, which once again brought Medina and Haro into direct competition. Indeed, despite the latter's assumption of many of the *valido*'s political functions, it was the former who emerged in the 1650s with the lion's share of his material legacy, including – contrary to many appearances in contemporary and modern literature – the title and lands of San Lúcar la Mayor, that is to say the 'duke' half of Olivares's famous denomination.[34]

After 1645 Monterrey and Leganés were pardoned and resumed their membership of the central organs of state, including the junta set up by Haro.[35] Evidently, despite his (limited) recognition of Don Luis's special position in 1647, the king hoped to lessen his dependence on the *antiolivaristas*. It seems, however, that not until early 1649 did Medina answer the call; from this point on his attendance at council was regular, and his influence therein was immediately felt. Supported by an important section of conciliar feeling, the duke's confidence grew steadily in the 1650s and by the later years of Haro's government amounted to a definite source of 'opposition'. Since this phase is analyzed at length below,[36] we may pass on at this point to a brief description of Medina's later career.

With Haro's unexpected death, in December 1661, Philip announced the end, so far as he was concerned, of rule by favourite, and this time stuck to his resolve. Though thereby balked of the ultimate prize, Medina de las Torres became, in effect, chief minister until Philip's own passing in September 1665. Officially recognized by the king only as one of a triumvirate, his 'colleagues' Castrillo and Sandoval were never prominent, the former by reason of

[32] Over the projected marriages of the *infante* Baltasar Carlos, and Philip himself in 1646; Philip to Medina, 17 Jan. and 24 Dec. 1646, BL, Eg. 339, ff. 30–45. Sor María was merely informed of the king's decision in the latter case; Silvela, *Cartas*, i, p. 180.

[33] Deleito y Piñuela, *El declinar*, p. 147; Marañón, *El conde-duque*, p. 365.

[34] Proceedings over the count-duke's legacy continued sporadically almost to the end of the century, involving at some stage all the various branches of the Guzmán clan; see Marañón, *El conde-duque*, pp. 477–81. For examples of error in ascription of the main honour, see Deleito y Piñuela, *El declinar*, p. 151; Bleye, *Manual*, p. 798; and the complete confusion in Tomás y Valiente, *Los validos* (1st edn), pp. 21–21, 100, 202–4. Since the title 'Conde-duque de Olivares' was often accorded to Don Luis by syncophants (and even, at times, the king) the mistaken assumption that Haro inherited the dukedom of Sanlúcar la Mayor is understandable, since he certainly held no other ducal title; CODOIN, 96, p. 471; J. Pellicer y Tovar, *Alma de la gloria de España* (Madrid, 1650), p. 37.

[35] CODOIN, 82, pp. 244, 373.

[36] See below, pp. 166ff.

constant illness. Significantly, Medina now took over the foreign affairs of the monarchy, whilst Castrillo was assigned the domestic role implied by his presidency of Castile.[37] In addition, other factors reduced the power of the Haro clan. In 1662 Haro's son, the marquis of Heliche, was involved in a sensational conspiracy directed at the lives of the royal family. Though spared the scaffold by Philip's clemency, this prominent enemy of Medina's, who had hoped to succeed to his father's influence, was removed from the scene, whilst the family shared, to some extent, in his disgrace. Another powerful adherent of the Haro faction, the count of Peñaranda, who had been Don Luis's chief lieutenant in external affairs was absent from Madrid as viceroy of Naples (until 1664).[38]

In the less than four years available to him in this strong position, Medina was able, though not without difficulty, to initiate the policy of retrenchment which is the main concern of this essay. Even after 1665, despite truly immense pressure, and although he was excluded both from the official *Junta de Gobierno* and from the intimate counsels of the queen-regent, Mariana, the duke managed to preserve the basic lines of this policy. He was instrumental eventually in the peace settlement involving treaties with England (1667) and Portugal (1668), and was the major voice urging the acceptance of the necessity to make concessions to France after defeat in the War of Devolution. At the same time, Medina alone was responsible for the renewal of strong links of understanding with the empire, a policy extremely unpopular with his enemies, which had withered away almost to nothing since the fall of Olivares. Of these achievements, only the peace of Aix with Louis XIV proved less than durable, whilst the Anglo-Portuguese settlement was a lasting tribute to his statesmanship. Still involved in the struggle to achieve secure peace for the monarchy, Medina died in December 1668.[39]

The context in which Medina's policies evolved (roughly the second half of Philip IV's reign) was one of unrelieved depression and crisis for the Spanish monarchy. Space does not permit particular elaboration of it here, and in any case the main features of Spanish decline (even this phase of it) are already well known.[40] Medina's own appreciation of them was surprisingly intense and exact and, as his policy-documents amply illustrate, no man had more absorbed the messages propounded by the *arbitristas* during his formative

[37] Soldevila, *Historia de España*, iv, p. 351.

[38] Trevor Davies, *Spain in Decline*, pp. 72–3; CODOIN, 23, p. 529.

[39] These events receive fuller treatment below, pp. 159ff. Pfandl regards Medina's death as one of Spain's major setbacks in this epoch, *Carlos II*, p. 152.

[40] The best summaries are those of J. Reglá, 'La epoca de los dos últimos Austrias' in J. Vicens Vives (ed.), *Historia de España y América* (2nd edn, Barcelona, 1971), iii, esp. 250–353; and Vicens Vives himself, 'The Decline of Spain in the Seventeenth Century', in C. Cipolla (ed.), *The Economic Decline of Empires* (1970), pp. 121–95. More closely relevant to themes dealt with here is A. Domínguez Ortiz, 'España ante la paz de los Pirineos', *Hispania*, 19 (1959), pp. 545–72.

years. Of more pressing concern still, however, was the international situation of the post-Olivares period. For Spain this situation meant, simply, continuous war, and by 1648, when the monarchy finally washed its hands of its *damnosa hereditas* in the Netherlands, most of its subjects could hardly remember any other condition of life. It should be emphasised that heavy military commitment did not cease with the independence of the Dutch. The struggle with France remained on a full footing until 1659, and broke out again in 1667. Taking full advantage of the respite provided by Mazarin's strategic and diplomatic successes, Louis XIV geared his early planning to the isolation of Spain in Europe, whilst steadily building up his own military resources. In the period in which she faced war with France, England and Portugal, Spain's only allies were the prince of Condé, Charles Stuart and the duke of Lorraine – respectively a rebel, an outcast and a soldier of fortune, and in sum more in the nature of a liability to her efforts.

As the Spaniards quickly realized after the final defeat of Charles I, England was in many ways the key to the problem. The failure of their efforts to turn this key in the early 1650s resulted in the coalition of three powers (associated by various military, financial, strategic and commercial agreements) which forced Spain to retire from the international contest in 1659. Again, this did not bring peace to the monarchy. The Pyrenees settlement did not include the English Republic and the policy of the Restoration government, enshrined in the Anglo-Portuguese Marriage Treaty (1661), not only implied but encouraged the unofficial continuation of Cromwell's war with Spain. Until at least 1663 units of Oliver's army continued to confront the Spanish *tercios*, or what was left of them, in the Low Countries (around Dunkirk) and in Portugal. Not without reason, Spain felt itself threatened by English moves at sea, in particular by the projected creation of a naval base at Tangier, ceded (in the Spanish view, illegally) by Portugal to Charles II. Across the Atlantic, Cromwell's 'western design' began a phase of piratical anarchy in the Caribbean, the classic period of anti-Spanish depredation in the area, emanating from Jamaica, covertly encouraged from London, and continuing until 1670. English assistance meanwhile kept Portuguese hopes of independence alive and decided the crucial 1663 campaign in their favour. Charles II's sale of Dunkirk to France (1662) further undermined the security of the Spanish Netherlands. Not surprisingly, in this period the Madrid government considered itself still openly at war with England as well as the Portuguese rebels.[41]

From 1648 until 1668, therefore, the monarchy was burdened with various war fronts – in Catalonia, Flanders and the Castilian borderland with Portugal; in Mediterranean, Atlantic and Caribbean waters. Isolation was completed by

[41] Chap. 8, below p. 177, provides the background to Anglo-Spanish diplomacy after the peace of the Pyrenees. Hamilton's claim that these years 'were characterised by peace and domestic tranquillity' in Spain is invalid, *War and Prices*, p. 124. Though mainly defensive in nature, military operations along the Portuguese front were continuous, and the negative effect of this war on resources and morale can hardly be overestimated; Domínguez, *Política y hacienda*, pp. 79–86.

the deterioration of relations with Vienna. The only element of promise lay in the results of the treaty of Münster, which during this period brought the Dutch Republic, for strategic as well as commercial reasons, more and more within the orbit of Madrid. This too, the consequence of an attitude of diplomatic realism, was a lesson not lost upon the subject of this essay.

The origins of Medina's attitude to the problems confronting the monarchy undoubtedly lie in his experience as viceroy of Naples. There he inherited a terrible fiscal, economic and political crisis brought on by the rapid escalation of Madrid's demands for *asistencias de guerra* from the *Regno*, and characterized by Philip's order (to Medina's predecessor, Monterrey, in 1636) 'to extort everything possible from the wealth of Naples'.[42] Despite his relative success in this invidious task and in dealing with the crisis generally, Medina quickly came to realize the disastrous implications of Olivares' commitment to war, and the limitations of the 'Union of Arms' devised to support it. By March of 1639 he could no longer restrain his feelings:

> The concern caused me by the fall of Breisach and its consequences; the entry of French arms into Piedmont; the disturbances and dangers to which I see His Majesty's kingdoms exposed and the problems which the multiplication of taxes pose to his service ... inspire me to write these lines ... despite the danger to which I may expose myself, the ignorance or licence of which I may be accused by speaking in this way ... The kingdoms and states of our master are exhausted in the highest degree, and those that do not suffer war themselves bear the burden of taxes, the raising of levies, the imposition of billeting, the depopulation of the countryside, and the general extinction of prosperity. This responsibility is not divided equally, as it is with our enemies, with the result that only the crown of Castile, and the kingdoms of Naples and Sicily are required to offset all the revenues of France and the Estates of Holland and their adherents ... The conclusion must be that His Majesty cannot maintain this war much longer in its present form, nor expose all his kingdoms to such manifest peril, and must therefore by necessity seek out those means by which it may be possible to progress towards peace.[43]

On at least one further occasion Medina renewed these representations directly to the king, still some time before the catastrophes of 1640 which so justified his viewpoint.[44] For some time, however, his correspondence with Olivares had been intermittent.[45] Their earlier quarrel had by no means been thoroughly settled, a circumstance which gives the ring of truth to the concern the viceroy expressed for his own position.[46] On the other hand, Medina's tactical

---

[42] Quoted by Villari, *La rivolta*, p. 124.

[43] Quoted ibid., pp. 129–30.

[44] Medina to Philip, 20 Feb. 1641, RAH, 1053, ff. 403v–405. As the reader may deduce from the textual content here, the actual date of this letter is a year later than I was led to believe by the published abstract in the *Indice de la colección de D. Luis de Salazar y Castro*, 39 (Madrid, 1970), p. 226.

[45] Marañón, *El conde-duque*, pp. 283–84.

[46] See above, pp. 151–52.

suggestions should not be taken as representing a reaction against Olivares's basic strategy. As will shortly become evident, Don Ramiro was an admiring pupil of the count-duke's statecraft and always supported its major principles. During the 1630s Olivares had encouraged Medina's intellectual development along lines similar to his own. As well as sharing the king's taste for the arts, especially the stage,[47] Medina read widely in the works of history and political economy favoured by the count-duke. In the middle decades of the century, his library, enriched by inheritance from his patron, acquired a reputation second to none in Castile.[48] Indeed, it seems reasonable to suppose that, to some extent at least, Medina was groomed by Olivares as his successor in a political sense.[49]

In much of his thinking about the European stance of the monarchy, Medina closely reflected Olivares's ideas. His viceroyalty had also made him conscious of the question of security for the Italian and Low Countries provinces, dependent as it was on the preservation of maritime communications. Both these strands of thought required Medina to insist on the maintenance of good relations with England and the empire, for which Olivares had consistently struggled. Like his master, he felt that strategic understanding with these powers would provide a long-term insurance of the monarchy. Unlike Olivares, however, Medina's calculations arose from an overwhelming sense of the need for a general peace in Europe. This conviction might be thought natural in a man whose every mature political experience – from 1627 on – had been gained in an age of almost consistent defeat and frustration of Spanish arms and aspirations; the wonder is that his fundamental commitment to it was shared by so few of his contemporaries. Medina took Olivares's famous cry of desperation, forced from his lips by the awful catastrophe of 1640, 'God must want us to make peace, since he is visibly depriving us of the means for war',[50] as a positive and optimistic keynote for the future. He felt, too, that the arts of diplomacy, embodying a Spanish genius rather overlooked by the count-duke in his personal craving for absolute monopoly of initiative, could now (i.e. after 1643) be called on to lead the monarchy out of the wilderness of endemic war. The vigorous and continuous pursuit of diplomatic means involved, however a sense of compromise and concession which did not come easily to Castilians, and least of all to their king. The duke of Medina's persistent advocacy of compromise – made possible in himself, as a good Castilian, by what can only have been a species of deep conversion – was something which did not endear him to his government colleagues and always vitiated his influence upon Philip IV.

[47] He is said to have directed two productions at court of plays by Lope de Vega in 1631; N.D. Shergold, *A History of the Spanish Stage* (Oxford, 1967), p. 278.

[48] Domínguez, *Socieded española*, i, p. 290. According to Reglá, Medina also had a reputation as a writer; 'La epoca', p. 302.

[49] Cf. (e.g.) Marañón, *El conde-duque* (1st edn, Madrid, 1936), p. 148, and Cánovas, *Estudios*, ii, p. 373.

[50] Quoted by Elliott, *Imperial Spain*, p. 338.

So far as the king himself was concerned, Medina's cause was not helped by the treaty of Münster, achieved after years of painful negotiation in 1648. Concessions to the Dutch had to be wrung from Philip by prolonged argument and pressure,[51] and his final capitulation on this front undoubtedly weakened the chances of the diplomatic offensive widening into a general settlement. The Münster compromise – a shameful one from Philip's point of view – increased the king's obstinacy on other issues. It was this, more than any failure on the part of Don Luis, which caused the successive breakdowns in negotiations with Cromwell (1654) and Mazarin (1656), leading in turn to the fatal Anglo-French alliance of 1657.[52] Medina's acute concern at the prospect of losing England's friendship can be seen in some *consultas* (of the *Consejo de Estado*) dating from the early 1650s. He displayed extreme reluctance for the monarchy to extend even the mildest recognition to Charles II after his father's execution, and urged Philip IV to arraign and execute those responsible for the murder, in Madrid, of Ascham, the envoy of the Commonwealth. The king's vacillation on both these issues caused great resentment in London and undoubtedly contributed to the subsequent failure of negotiations. Throughout the well-known Cromwell–Cárdenas discussions Medina was the main advocate of concession, insisting on the need for success 'even should it be necessary to attempt impossibilities'.[53] The failure to appease England led, of course, to war in 1655, but Medina roundly condemned the misguided attempt to compensate by the meaningless alliance with the exiled Stuarts which so ingenuously fulfilled one of Cromwell's main political objectives.[54] With the Protector's death, however, Medina changed horses decisively and, unlike Haro, did not lose confidence in a Stuart restoration because of the lack of immediate progress towards it.[55] The failure of Don Luis to respond unambiguously to Charles II's overtures in this period, an attitude criticized by Medina, had its consequences in the omission of England from the peace settlement of 1659–60 and the subsequently ungrateful policies of the Restoration government.

[51] See (e.g.), the barely concealed desperation of the junta of state in a *consulta* of Oct. 1647, after four years of inconclusive negotiations, CODOIN, 84, pp. 21–22.

[52] Domínguez, 'La paz de los Pirineos', pp. 549 et seq.

[53] *Consulta* of the council of state, 12 April 1654 (abstract); F.P. Guizot, *History of Oliver Cromwell and the English Commonwealth*, 2 vols (1854), ii, pp. 441–45; see also i, pp. 362–63. Philip's reaction to pressure in the Ascham case is a perfect illustration of his general attitude to political realities – 'there shall be no hurry, and no reason of state shall cause more to be done than is just and right. I would rather lose my dominions than fail in doing that which is my first duty, and my council of state will never advise me to do otherwise'; ibid., i, pp. 366–67.

[54] R.A. Stradling, 'Anglo-Spanish Relations from the Restoration to the Peace of Aix-la-Chapelle, 1660–68' (unpublished Ph.D. thesis, 2 vols, University of Wales, 1968), introduction. See also R. Crabtree, 'The Idea of a Protestant Foreign Policy', *Cromwell Association Handbook* (1968–69), pp. 2–19.

[55] F.J. Routledge, *England and the Treaty of the Pyrenees* (Liverpool, 1953), p. 72; idem (ed.), *Calendar of the Clarendon State Papers*, iv (Oxford, 1932), p. 91.

These events, involving as they did comprehensive military failure and (even more important) the final collapse of Spanish communications, amply confirmed the duke's worst fears. He firmly ascribed every setback to the breakdown of relations with England:

> Just as past experience has always taught us, the war with England is a pernicious one for Spain, closing our commerce with the Indies, and threatening supplies of treasure. This belligerence above all lies at the root of our great lack of resources, and the want of those vast sums which we have needed to prosecute war on so many fronts for so many years. If war should continue for even one more campaign, it will witness in my opinion the loss of Flanders and the opening of the Indies to conquest and heresy.[56]

After the conclusion of the peace of the Pyrenees, Medina exerted his influence (improved to the extent already noted by Haro's death) to keep open a line of contact with a bellicose English government. The need for such a policy was in his view increased by the Anglo-Portuguese alliance, an opinion which ran counter to that of most others in the Spanish policy-making apparatus. One of the king's main inducements for the peace with France had been the opportunity it gave him to concentrate all Castile's resources on the recovery of Portugal. The Braganza alliance with England frustrated this objective, and Philip's natural resentment (against his erstwhile pensioner Charles II) posed severe problems. Medina's persistence was nevertheless rewarded when, in early 1663, he was allowed to initiate a *rapprochement*, which survived even the humiliating defeat of Ameixial and developed soon afterwards into a mutual exchange of ambassadors between Madrid and London.[57]

This renewal of diplomatic links, a prospect inconceivable only a short time before, was immediately inspired on Medina's part by the belief that England could mediate an end to the Portuguese war – thus surmounting the problem, on which Philip and others were uncompromising, of direct negotiation with the rebel regime. It was made possible, moreover, by a change of attitude by the English (associated particularly with the rise of Henry Bennet, earl of Arlington, in Charles's counsels) who were becoming increasingly disillusioned with the rewards of the Braganza connexion, but wished to use it as a lever to prise from Spain the commercial and colonial concessions refused Cromwell a decade earlier.[58] The English price for the service of mediation was, in the eyes of most of Medina's colleagues, impossibly high. To obtain a negotiated settlement of the Portuguese war was in any case fraught with

[56] *Voto* of 10 July 1659, AGS, E K1618, printed in Saltillo, 'Don Antonio Pimentel', pp. 102–22. See also, Domínguez, 'La paz de los Pirineos', pp. 571–72.

[57] The appointment of the English ambassador, Sir Richard Fanshawe, dates from the autumn of 1663, PRO, SP 94/45, ff. 173–189. For Medina's nomination of the count of Molina to Whitehall, *consulta* of council of state, 31 July 1664, AGS, E 2532.

[58] Bennet met Medina in Madrid during his sojourn as Charles II's envoy before the Restoration. For their collaboration against severe opposition in both capitals at this juncture, see the exchange of letters in Sept. to Oct. 1663, PRO, SP 94/45, ff. 99, 113. The English motives for detente are examined in Stradling, 'Anglo-Spanish Relations', i, pp. 99–139.

difficulty. To exacerbate hurt Castilian pride by purchasing the good offices of England, when the latter was currently aiding *el tirano Braganza*, encouraging piracy and refusing to restore Cromwell's conquests, further increased the risks of the operation. Yet Medina, rightly convinced of the impossibility of reconquest in Portugal, was determined to perform it. In his view, English involvement had ensured Spain's defeat by Portugal, as earlier by France, and their demands could only be met by concession. Success in this area would, conversely, promote a secure understanding with Charles II and in turn provide a possible basis for a European confederation; thereby insulating the monarchy from the risk of further war or at least removing the main burden of such war from its shoulders. 'It is fundamental', he told Philip early in 1663, 'that your Majesty should be convinced of the benefits which will follow from English friendship', and continued, in a passage strongly reminiscent of Olivares,

> I have no doubt that England's strength lies at sea, and precisely for this reason your glorious ancestors always wooed her. They recognized that the monarchy, which comprises dominions divided most of all by the oceans, could by naval power be preserved, and by the same means made vulnerable. So they were obliged to seek as allies those nations who were strong in this respect, refusing it, with honour, only when our own strength justified the risk. And this maxim, valid for all time, is more than ever so at present.[59]

Five years of thorny diplomatic exchanges, and the life of a recalcitrant monarch, were to pass before the independence of Portugal ended this aspect of Medina's struggle. These facts alone indicate the enormous difficulties and resistance which he faced. What consistently encouraged him, however, was the precedent of successful negotiations with the United Provinces. Since 1648, relations with the erstwhile eighty-year enemy had been smooth, and compromise had brought general and specific benefits in its wake. Throughout the exchanges with English representatives in Madrid (1664–48) Medina used earlier agreements with the Dutch as a working model for a new tripartite settlement with England and Portugal.[60] When, after the Portuguese victory of Villaviçiosa (1665), these concessions were rejected as unsatisfactory by both London and Lisbon he went still further. Despite the increasing weakness of his health, and of his influence in government, Medina singlehandedly pressed for the recognition of Portuguese sovereignty and the improvement of commercial offers to England, making her the 'most favoured nation' in Spain's foreign trade.[61] Even after the achievement of his immediate aim of peace for the monarchy in Portugal (and Flanders) in 1668, he continued his efforts

[59] 'Voto del Señor Duque de San Lúcar en materias de Inglaterra', 23 Feb. 1663, AGS, E 2532.

[60] See (e.g.), 'Anotación de los capítulos de 12 de Septiembre', and *consulta* of the council of state, 7 Oct. 1665, AGS, E 2534, 2535.

[61] Mapperton, Sandwich MS Journal, ii, pp. 202–6 (June, 1666); *consultas* of council of state, 20, 30 July 1666, AGS, E 2538.

on the English front. He firmly believed that England, as Holland, could be brought into a commercial partnership which would be reciprocated, in its own interests, by political support. Foreseeing, too, that England's potential was far greater than that of the United Provinces, as a guarantor of the integrity of the Spanish Empire, he outlined to Charles's ambassador, Sandwich, in 1667–68, a programme of commercial and financial inducements, in return for strategic support, which in some respects went further even than the so-called Asiento Treaty of forty years later.[62] Rapid justification of Medina's beliefs (though admittedly somewhat ambiguous) was apparent in the reaction of the maritime powers to French aggression and the creation of the Triple Alliance; whilst shortly after his death the Anglo-Spanish Colonial Treaty brought peace to the Caribbean, partly through the final cession of Jamaica, the first clear legal recognition by Castile that her monopoly of political sovereignty in the new world was at an end.[63]

In his policy towards Austria, Medina displays even stronger links with the thinking of Olivares. As a convinced supporter of the traditional dynastic connexion, he incurred the deep distrust of those who hated the great man's memory. Most councillors of Medina's generation believed that Olivares's expensive attachment to the empire had been not merely profitless but seriously counter-productive. Nevertheless, in the Madrid of the 1660s, Medina's value to Vienna was recognized by the consistent support given him by the Emperor Leopold through his ambassador, von Pötting.[64] Indeed, it was solely due to Medina that family understanding, damaged by imperial 'desertion' in 1648, and further fractured by the surrender of the senior infanta to Louis XIV in 1660, was partly revived. Only thus, in the duke's view, could Spanish influence in Italy be preserved against French pressure. His general strategy ran closely parallel to that of Franz-Paul von Lisola, the most notable individual advocate of a system of 'collective security', arch-publicist and opponent of Louis XIV's designs for European hegemony.[65] In 1664 this itinerant (and often embarrassing) envoy of Leopold's travelled to Madrid in order to join forces with Medina. Between them they persuaded Philip to allow the betrothal of the infanta Margarita – that most delightful of all subjects of

---

[62] Sandwich to Arlington, 21 Sept. 1667, PRO, SP 94/53, ff. 55–58; Mapperton, Sandwich MS Journal, v, pp. 527–28; 'Discourse of What Advantages His Majesty may Further have from Spain by a Nearer League', *Hispania Illustrata, or the Maxims of the Spanish Court* . . . (1703), pp. 93–105.

[63] Commercial concessions by Spain are examined in Stradling, 'Anglo-Spanish Relations', esp. chaps 3, 7. See also J.O. McLachlan, *Trade and Peace with Old Spain, 1667–1740* (Cambridge, 1940). For the colonial issues, see A.P. Thornton, *West India Policy under the Restoration* (Oxford, 1956), esp. chap. 3.

[64] Pfandl, *Carlos II*, pp. 118–19.

[65] Lisola, born a Burgundian subject of the Spanish monarchy, published his famous pamphlet against Louis, *Le bouclier d'état*, in 1667. See his tribute to Medina, recorded by Sandwich in April, 1666: 'He is a man governed by true maxims for the good of Spain, and will always be persuaded when reason is shewed him'; Mapperton, Sandwich MS Journal, ii, p. 143.

Velázquez's brush – to the emperor, and stage-managed her proxy marriage and despatch to the childless Leopold in 1666.

As these events imply, the concession to Austria envisaged by Medina was more significant even than that to England, since it involved the ultimate fate of the monarchy itself. In the meantime he felt, like Olivares, that these alliances were the twin pillars on which Spanish policy must be based. Although it is true that he saw them, in the last resort, as providing a basis for continued resistance to France, his calculations started from the premise of peace. The equilibrium thus created could be enough to deter Louis from open renewal of continental war, providing the conditions of tranquillity so desperately needed by the monarchy; not – as with Olivares – conceived as mere respite and recuperation, but as the permanent environment for a concrete recovery of all aspects of life. To achieve this Medina realized that the innate preconceptions of Spanish government must change, that Castile had to retire from its high aspirations as the leader of Christendom, jealously and stubbornly reacting to the slightest imputation on its prestige or integrity. Spain, that is to say, now ought to resign, consciously and completely, from its traditional role as imperial monopolist in Europe and overseas, the role which had always excited resentment, fear and in the last analysis, war, amongst her European rivals.[66]

Medina's memoranda to Philip IV and his widow, along with his written opinions in the *consultas* of the period, refer constantly to the decadent condition of all aspects of administration and socio-economic conditions in the monarchy – a tendency which culminates in the detailed analysis contained in the *voto* of August 1666. This approach to policymaking, beginning from first material principles, has a distinctly modern ring even to a present-day student, and was certainly unique in his own time. Needless to say, the *mores* of Medina's policy were in complete contrast to those of his king, whose exclusive dedication to public and dynastic image was, if possible, increased during the period of his relationship with Sor María. Time and again, Medina attempted in vain to instil into Philip a sense of the reality of his affairs, to convince him of the priority of *raison d'état*, to convey to him that Spain's survival would not be governed by metaphysics – so often, characteristically, the subject of his correspondence with Sor María[67] – but the harsh dictates of power. Stoic acceptance of the transition of imperial influence is not,

---

[66] These attitudes are synthesised in Medina's great *voto* on the Portuguese War of Aug. 1666, the original of which is to be found in AGS, E 2538. This document, deeply admired by Cánovas, was reproduced almost verbatim in his *Estudios*, ii, pp. 513–45 (to which reference is made hereafter), and paraphrased by Pfandl, who says of it: 'one cannot encounter in the whole bibliography of sources for this period . . . any example in which a contemporary has given an account of the politics and society of his country with such clear vision, expressed with such sincerity', *Carlos II*, pp. 138–47.

[67] Their joint obsession with the doctrine of the Immaculate Conception dominates the exchanges of this period, during which only occasional and routine expressions of regret indicate the king's awareness of his subjects' sufferings; see Silvela, *Cartas*, passim.

however, a common feature of governments and ruling elites, no more in twentieth-century Britain than in seventeenth-century Spain, and Medina's advocacy of it brought upon him the enmity of many sections of Castilian opinion.

One of the most striking examples of Medina's technique can be found in a *voto* on the Pyrenees negotiations in 1659. Here he plainly told Philip that 'your divine duty is not to continue attempting to defend what is defenceless', but vigorously to pursue a lasting peace in Europe. He attacked in particular the king's personal commitment to the prince of Condé, and the demand that Mazarin restore Philip's ally to all his old honours and estates in France, which threatened once more to prevent agreement. This prestigious matter, much nearer the king's heart than the condition of his own subjects, was dismissed as irrelevant by Medina.

> The public good is the supreme law [he argued] and your Majesty cannot avoid on such trivial grounds the overriding responsibility to secure peace for Christendom, contentment for your people, and a healthy inheritance for your children ... the raising of new revenues, and the continuation of taxes already imposed, cannot be justified if they are to be consumed by an unnecessary and wilful war.[68]

This was a theme he developed strongly after Philip's death, when less inhibited from encroaching on the sacred ground of royal honour and prerogative:

> The true reputation of states does not consist of mere appearances, but in the constant security and conservation of their territories, in the protection of their subjects and the wellbeing thereof, in the respect which other princes have for their authority and military strength ... Glorious actions are not founded in the vulgar vanity of words, but in deeds of substance.[69]

Spain, he maintained, had none of these attributes left. The pretence of greatness did not disguise, but merely intensified, her widespread ruin; the disappearance of commerce, the omnipresence of disease, the collapse of communications, the extinction of reliable soldiery, the intolerable condition of the royal finances, all passed at some point under the detailed review of Medina's pen. In July 1664, for example, he outlined the need for reform of the monarchy in its head and members, beginning with the royal household: 'only from which can it flow outwards to the many concerns of your Majesty's kingdoms'. In conditions of peace, Philip could undertake the improvement of *Hacienda*, and 'take one example of what King Louis has done, since he adjusted the peace with Spain, improving the value of his own patrimony by 24,000,000 [escudos] annually whilst your Majesty's is mortgaged for five years hence'.[70] Medina's request that the monarchy, for the first time

---

[68] Saltillo, 'Don Antonio Pimentel', pp. 116–17. The king's conscience was, however, immovable on this point, which he actually succeeded in carrying at the peace conference.

[69] *Voto* of Aug. 1666, Cánovas, *Estudios*, ii, pp. 524–25.

[70] *Consulta* of council of state, BL, Eg. 347, ff. 188–194.

in a long reign (and in the modern phrase) 'give peace a chance' was inspired above all, however, by a deep appreciation of the human misery and material ruin of its lands.

> What is worst of all [he wrote in July 1659] is the condition of the countryside, the lack of cultivation of the fields, to such a degree that in Spain and Italy more than half the land is not farmed because of depopulation and deprivation. Unless we achieve peace we will find ourselves without people, without money, fleets, officers, without strongholds or munitions, in short without any means of defending ourselves.[71]

It was this rationale which led Medina in the 1660s to a position of outright appeasement of the European powers, an attitude which he adopted in spite of his own lingering resentment of the policy of France. His papers are studded with types of argument familiar to any student of the 1930s. The reaction to Condé's case, for example, however justified by other considerations, was, after all, the abandonment of a formal ally in order to assuage a powerful enemy. In the same way, it was French power and success alone which led Medina to argue that Louis XIV had a perfectly good and just legal case behind his claim to Rosellón and Cerdaña in 1659 ('and this, along with a few places in Flanders is not too high a price for peace').[72] He was even capable, as over England in 1663, of using the stock-in-trade argument of appeasers:

> It is true that we have many good reasons for war against the English, but your Majesty cannot react in this way until better occasions offer themselves. Our present weakness obliges us to suffer what England demands in the matter of concessions in trade – which, if granted, they will observe the peace more religiously.[73]

The French invasion of Flanders in the spring of 1667 greatly increased the urgency of Medina's plans, by setting an even higher premium on a settlement with Portugal and English support. It was at this point that he recommended surrender to the Braganzas on every point at issue, and 'at whatever price',[74] and promised whole eldorados to Charles II, including annual subsidies, freedom of trade with America, special trading privileges and monopoly interest in particularly lucrative goods.[75]

The ease with which Louis XIV's armies inflicted swift and comprehensive defeat on Spain in the Low Countries brought Medina's reasoning to perhaps its fullest expression in the winter of 1667–68. The time had now arrived, he believed, for the monarchy to consider seriously the shedding of territories

---

[71] Saltillo, 'Don Antonio Pimentel', pp. 105–6.

[72] Ibid., p. 111.

[73] *Voto* of Feb. 1663, AGS, E 2532. For examples of 'appeasement' in negotiations with Fanshawe, see *consulta* of council of state, 9 Oct. and Royal Order of 13 Oct., 1664, AGS, E 2533.

[74] Medina to Diego de Prado, 28 Nov. 1667, BL, Eg. 338, ff. 470–505.

[75] See above, n. 62.

it could no longer defend, both in Europe and America. His argument was cast in the vivid political metaphor of the diseased body, of which Olivares had once been especially fond. Spain's malaise, according to the duke, was now both acute and chronic, no longer to be cured by the application of purgatives or placebos. Bleeding must now give place to surgery, 'and, for the preservation of the whole, it is necessary to sacrifice a part'. Better, therefore, for the monarchy to restore bodily health by an amputation which might anticipate, or prevent, the wholesale dismemberment threatened by its enemies.[76] The completion of the various peace settlements of the end of this decade, and the extent of success which they had in realising Spain's major objectives, was the work of a man who inherited the ideas and talents of the count-duke of Olivares, reinterpreted and deployed according to the exigencies of the post-Olivares period of consistent and accelerating Spanish decline.

As the above might suggest, the progress of Medina's career aroused constant opposition, particularly from the Haro interest and its main champions, Don Luis himself, Castrillo and Peñaranda. The quarrel began with, and always fed upon, the squalid pattern of rival connexions, patronage and petty jealousies, which, despite their sterile fascination for an earlier school of writers, should never be dismissed as beneath the attention of the student of seventeenth-century politics, least of all in Castile. The Haro–Guzmán affair, originating in the mid 1620s, culminated in 1664 in the grand Romantic fashion of a fatal duel between one of Medina's sons and a grandson of Castrillo,[77] and faded out only with the deaths of these senior protagonists in 1668, when the struggle of Nithard with Don Juan of Austria supervened. The significance of this somewhat operatic scenario lies in its concern with the nature of government, and crucial issues of policy, reproducing as it does to some extent the outlines of earlier political struggles at the court of Spain.

With the death of Olivares, Medina became head of the house of Guzmán, the family which Cánovas del Castillo, over a century ago, characterized as a brood of vipers in Spanish history.[78] For the purpose of his resounding condemnation of the power-hungry and rebellious Guzmanes, Cánovas included the Haro family amongst them – a procedure which was strictly correct. In effect, however, the Haro failure to inherit the Guzmán interest turned them into advocates of a point of view not much different to that expressed by Cánovas. Medina's obvious qualifications – his loyalty to Olivares; his already sensational wealth, augmented by inheritance, and contrasting with the crippling bankruptcy of many notable contemporaries;

---

[76] *Consulta* of council of state, 21 Jan. 1668, AGS, E 2542. For the significance of this diagnostic technique, see Elliott, 'The Statecraft of Olivares', pp. 125–27.

[77] Paz y Melia *Avisos*, ii, p. 306.

[78] Cánovas, *Bosquejo*, p. 294.

above all his easy charm of manner as a *gran señor* and his relationship with the king – naturally intensified the resentment of his rivals.[79]

As we have seen, the passing of the initiative to the Haros in 1643, and the prolonged phase in which, in the person of Don Luis, their interest dominated government, was not sufficient to allay this antagonism. After 1649, at least, the conciliar independence of Medina grew steadily, and received support from other disaffected members, especially Alba, Oñate and Velada.[80] Indeed, Medina's activities in the *Consejo de Estado* can throw some light on the question – still by no means settled – of the nature of Don Luis de Haro's *valimiento*. Despite Professor Valiente's careful examination of the subject, the destruction by fire of most of Don Luis's personal papers renders any firm conclusion unlikely.[81] Certainly, however, he was never referred to in his own lifetime, by Philip or any other official source, as *valido*. Whether this arose from his own modest character and/or his awareness of the king's sensitivity on this point (both of which are suggested by Valiente); or, more intriguingly, from the opinions of the influential grandees who had shuffled him into power, and whose representative, to some extent, he remained, is at present impossible to say. At the end of his career he was accorded the title *primer ministro* (for a particular and unique purpose, the negotiation of the Pyrenees treaty) – clearly representing something rather less than *valido*, either in a 'constitutional' context, or in that of the history of the *valimiento*. At the same time (1659) Haro was made *consejero de estado* – a title Medina had enjoyed since the mid-1620s – though he rarely bothered to attend meetings.[82]

According to Valiente these facts have little significance, since Haro was able to control (or bypass) *Estado* from outside.[83] Though it is true that Philip made over to him the care of the 'cabinet papers', a clear instance

---

[79] Like other unofficial records of this period, Barrionuevo's newsletters contain several references to Medina's pretensions as the legal heir to Olivares, and to his flamboyant displays of wealth; Paz y Melia, *Avisos*, i, pp. 87, 93, 123, 201–2, 210, 214, 243. For the political dependence on the king caused by chronic insolvency among the nobility, see Jago, 'The Influence of Debt'.

[80] Paz y Melia, *Avisos*, i, p. 123 (which notes the bitter rivalry of Medina and Haro); ii, pp. 104, 308. See also Dunlop, *Memoirs of Spain*, i, p. 364. Other supporters included Don Ramiro's kinsmen, Monterrey and Ponce de León, and the marquis of los Balbases, son of the great Spínola; Saltillo, 'Don Antonio Pimentel', pp. 41–45. Most of these had been associated with the government of Olivares: Oñate and Velada had served the policy of friendship with England as envoys in the 1630s. Deleito y Piñuela's suggestion that Haro – essentially good-natured – was prepared to tolerate this opposition, may have some truth: but it appears that his patience, and that of Peñaranda, his main lieutenant, often wore thin; see Paz y Melia, *Avisos*, i, pp. 76, 307.

[81] Tomás y Valiente, *Los validos*, pp. 17–20, 97–101. Haro's house, the scene of many junta meetings and repository of many relevant documents, was twice seriously damaged by fire in the 1650s, and his collection subsequently suffered other ravages; Paz y Melia, *Avisos*, i, pp. 88, 220.

[82] Tomás y Valiente, *Los validos*, pp. 100, 185. I have found one instance of Haro's attendance (with Medina) dating from March, 1659: *Indice . . . Salazar*, 25, p. 359.

[83] Tomás y Valiente, *Los validos*, pp. 50, 99.

of his signal favour, it is also true that in the period after Olivares' fall, the king rarely refused to accept the advice of *Estado*.[84] As Valiente himself suggests, membership of this body was in Olivares's case a vital element of the *valimiento*, for lack of which the setting-up of *juntas* could not wholly compensate.[85] It seems to the present writer that Valiente's assertion that 'no one can doubt that Haro obtained all the power in government which the other two great *validos* (Lerma and Olivares) had enjoyed' is a little too confident.[86] The more tentative conclusion reached nearly a century ago by Cánovas, that Don Luis replaced Olivares only 'up to a certain point', seems still to be preferred, along with his famous view that 'the chief ministers, *validos* or *privados* of the epoch were, above all, councillors [of state] and with such character alone intervened in all matters not reserved for the king personally'.[87] Unlike Olivares' case, none of Don Luis's own political writings – testaments, memoranda or other documents – exist to give us an insight into his influence and policy. The existing official evidence can be construed as indicating that Don Luis was a kind of coordinator responsible in policy to the *Consejo de Estado*, through the king, a view as generally plausible as that held by Valiente.

One unofficial observer, the earl of Clarendon, who (as Sir Edward Hyde) was in Madrid in 1649 on a mission from the exiled Charles II, noted that Haro was 'as absolute a favourite . . . as any favourite of that age', but felt the need to qualify (even to contradict) this judgement: '[Yet] no man ever did so little alone . . . In the most ordinary occurrences, which for the difficulty required little deliberation . . . he would give no order without formal consultation with the rest of the council.'[88] Cánovas's view of Philip IV (after 1643) as *un rey papelista*, whose will alone inspired policy, tends it is true to underestimate Don Luis, and Professor Domínguez's reference to the latter as 'a kind of bashful *valido*' may be more just.[89] On the other hand, a picture of Haro as something more than just another adviser, but less than a *valido* in the Lerma-Olivares sense, seems to suit best, since it bears out the king's own obvious opinion and seems implicit in the description *primer y principal ministro*.

Whatever else might be said about the firmness or otherwise of Haro's grip on government, there existed a definite Achilles heel. His strenuous efforts to remove Medina de las Torres from the vitally important post of *sumiller de corps* and to substitute himself or a kinsman signally failed.[90] Both Lerma

---

[84] Cánovas, *Estudios*, i, pp. 267–68, 295; ii, 279 et seq.

[85] Tomás y Valiente, *Los validos*, p. 90.

[86] Ibid., p. 20.

[87] Cánovas, *Estudios*, i, pp. 295–97, 257–58.

[88] W.D. Macray (ed.), *Clarendon's History of the Rebellion*, 6 vols (Oxford, 1888), v, 92–93.

[89] Cánovas, *Estudios*, i, p. 297; Domínguez, *Política y hacienda*, p. 63 (see also pp. 167–69).

[90] CODOIN, 86, p. 92 et seq.; Pellicer, *Avisos*, iii, p. 238.

and Olivares had been careful to procure this office very early in their rules.[91] Although the latter had delegated it to Medina in 1626, a decade later, when his protégé went to Naples, he revived in his own person the antique and long-defunct office of *camarero mayor* (to which the *sumiller* was technically junior) in order to fill the vacuum.[92] At the fall of Olivares this senior post was again 'frozen' and, like that of *sumiller*, was never obtained by Haro. Medina therefore retained (*inter alia*) the right of constant and unimpeded access to the royal person, including (presumably at Philip's discretion) the duty of sleeping in the king's bedroom.[93]

In view of this and the increase in Philip's political initiative. Medina's position was clearly important, though its nature precludes any detailed exposition. When (probably in 1649) Don Ramiro re-entered direct politics, he took his place as one of *Estado's* most senior members, immediately assuming a prominent role in discussion.[94] Hyde, whilst deploring his 'addiction to all kinds of deboshry', regarded him as early as November 1649 as second only to Don Luis in influence. According to the English observer's somewhat inconsistent recollection, Medina

> neither depended upon nor loved Don Lewis . . . [but] had power enough with the king to do his own business, which was only to provide for his vast expenses [*sic*], being indeed the king's greatest confidant in his walks of liberty, and so never crossed Don Lewis in the general managery, and seldom came to Council except he was sent for . . . He was a man of parts and wanted nothing to be a very good statesman but application, and he was industriously without that.[95]

Notwithstanding Hyde's stricture, Medina's application and political interest increased steadily in the 1650s. By the end of the decade (at the latest) it was impossible for Haro to exclude him from the select *Junta de Estado*,[96] and in committee he argued his case with the force and freedom of a man assured of the personal indulgence of the chief executive.[97] On the other

---

[91] For Lerma, P. Williams, 'Philip III and the Restoration of Spanish Government, 1598–1603', *English Historical Review*, 88 (1973), pp. 751–69. Dr Williams considers that the appointment 'formally confirmed Denia's status' as *valido*.

[92] CODOIN, 77, p. 147. It is possible – as John Elliott pointed out to me – that this *effective* resumption of the *summiller*'s prerogatives by Olivares may have been as much a result of his quarrel with Don Ramiro.

[93] On the ritual importance of the sumiller, see Y. Bottineau, 'Aspects de la cour'. By 1623 this office and that of *camarero* were regarded as indistinguishable. M. Bottineau's article is based on a report commissioned from Medina by the king in August 1646, in which he attempted to redefine the situation after Olivares' intervention.

[94] Guizot, *History*, i, p. 385; Cánovas, *Estudios*, i, p. 265.

[95] Macray, *Clarendon*, v, pp. 93–94.

[96] Tomás y Valiente, *Los validos*, p. 99.

[97] Routledge, *Calendar*, iv, pp. 114, 117, 120; Saltillo 'Don Antonio Pimentel', pp. 41–45. A clear example of his freedom of action as early as June 1651 is noted in *CSPV, 1647–52*, p. 182. In 1659, he reacted strongly against an attempt by Philip to discipline the council of state; Tomás y Valiente, *Los validos*, pp. 202–3. It seems to me that Medina's friendship with the king

continued

hand, Don Luis de Haro failed to achieve that monopoly of intimacy, counsel and patronage which earlier incumbents had established as hallmarks of the *valimiento*. What he did attain in government, moreover, was partly vitiated by his being denied many of the public honours and much of the material legacy of the count-duke, an aspiration so important in the social milieu of the Habsburg court. The former frustration was partly, and the latter entirely, due to the ambitions of the duke of Medina.

When the positions of the warring factions were reversed after 1661, Medina's ascendancy was challenged more strenuously and effectively than that of Don Luis had ever been. Despite the poor health of Castrillo and the disgrace of Heliche; despite even the immense accretion of the duke's personal fortunes through his recent marriage to Doña Catalina de Guevara, countess of Oñate in her own right,[98] his hold on power remained insecure. Opposed and obstructed by important figures like the marquis of Caraçena and the duke of Medinaceli from the start, his position was even more tenuous after 1664, with the return from Naples of Peñaranda, the most active and influential adherent of the Haro connexion.[99] Medina's domination of *Estado* was never consistent. He was neither *valido* nor *primer ministro*; Philip had firmly suppressed both title and function. The king's mere survival at least meant that Medina could keep his policy alive; whilst, paradoxically, Philip's death, the removal of a kind of standing veto, gave him the opportunity to conclude – as he thought finally – over commerce and Portugal with the English ambassador, Fanshawe, in late 1665.[100] It was during the opening phase of Mariana's regency, a period of acute disorder and confusion in government, that the faction struggle reached its climax.

The distaste felt for Medina by Philip's widow, shared entirely by her confidant, the Jesuit theologian Nithard, robbed Medina of the longstanding

---

continued

is better attested than that of Haro; for two examples see Marañón, *El conde-duque*, pp. 279, 358. Indeed evidence for the latter relationship seems to rest mainly on Philip's explanation to Sor María in 1647 – 'desde muchacho se crió conmigo', which merely indicates that they were 'brought up' together; Silvela, *Cartas*, i, p. 183.

[98] This union brought him not only the title of count of Oñate (Doña Catalina's husband, Medina's ally, having died in 1658) but also the offices entailed with it. It forged a strong link with the powerful house of Guevara; though (possibly) it weakened that with the Toledo family (dukes of Alba, etc.), of which the deceased count had been a member: see Reglá, 'La epoca', p. 298; Saltillo, 'Don Antonio Pimentel', p. 40; Paz y Melia, *Avisos*, ii, p. 210.

[99] On Caraçena, see Chap. 8, below. On Medinaceli, a redoubtable supporter of the Haros, and captain-general of Andalusia, see PRO, SP 94/45, ff. 99, 109; *consultas* of council of treasury and other anti-English plans, BL, Eg. 332, ff. 22–31; and Medina's rebuke to Philip for countenancing same, 'Quenta del Señor Duque de San Lúcar', April 1665, AGS, 2535. On Peñaranda, see Pfandl, *Carlos II*, pp. 113–15 and the 'Apuntes biográficos' in CODOIN, 84, pp. 563–70.

[100] Negotiations leading to this abortive agreement are described in Stradling, 'Anglo-Spanish Relations', chap. 5.

guarantee of his influence provided by private access to the royal counsels. Worse than this, it meant a volte-face at the top, by which his enemies took over the mainsprings of power once more. Castrillo, Peñaranda, and others of like mind, were appointed to the *Junta de Gobierno* set up under the provisions of Philip's testament to direct the policy of the regency, and were later joined by Nithard, whilst the duke was kept out.[101] They used this position from the outset to undermine Medina's policy. In an operation directed by Peñaranda, attempts were made to intimidate Fanshawe and other English representatives in Spain. The duke's methods and ideas were attacked in the *consejo*.[102] The English negotiations were blatantly sabotaged by Peñaranda and Caraçena in January 1666, when they took steps to ensure that Lisbon would reject the truce offered by Medina, upon which his whole policy depended.[103] When Charles II refused in turn to ratify, and revoked Fanshawe, life was made very unpleasant for the incoming ambassador, Sandwich. The negotiations were then put into commission in a *Junta de Inglaterra*, in which Medina was joined – if that is the right word – by Peñaranda and Nithard.[104] Able in this way to enmesh Medina's policy and preclude its development, the Haros – by now virtually a governing party – also took the decision to launch yet another campaign against Portugal, which was to prove the ultimate and most costly failure.[105] Worst of all, during a great policy-congress in the summer canvassing the opinion of every council and prominent government personality, they asserted that Castile's right to sovereignty over Portugal would be defended 'to the last breath of our monarchy'.[106]

Simultaneously, Peñaranda put forward an alternative plan which threw into relief the party issues. Against the Olivares–Medina strategy of alliance with England and Austria, Peñaranda proposed a link-up with Holland and France, that is to say the revival of the 'Haro policy' implied by the treaty of Münster (in which Peñaranda himself had been plenipotentiary) and the peace settlement with France. On the surface, the idea had a good deal to recommend it. The Dutch were favourably disposed to Spain, and anxious to withhold trading advances in the hispanic world from the English, with whom they were at that moment engaged in war over some cognate issues.

---

[101] Maura, *Carlos II y su corte*, ii, pp. 122, 127; Pfandl, *Carlos II*, p. 137.

[102] *Consulta* of council of state, 23 Oct., *voto* of Medina, 6 Nov., 1665, AGS, E 2535.

[103] *Consultas* of council of state, 8 Feb., 15 April (with enclosures), AGS E 2536. Medina's plan for a 'grand alliance' against France, which he described as 'a thing of paramount importance', and which had been approved over Peñaranda's objections (*consulta* of 3 Jan. 1666, ibid.) was thus shelved. Comments on the duke's predicament in these months can be found in Fanshawe's correspondence, BL, Harl. 7010, passim.

[104] Mapperton, Sandwich MS Journal, ii, pp. 28 et seq.; Royal *cédula* of 17 June 1666, AGS, E 2536.

[105] *Consultas* of council of state, 22 March, 6 April 1666 (and Medina's warning in a further *voto* of 16 March, AGS, E 2536. See also Pfandl, *Carlos II*, pp. 141–42.

[106] *Consulta* of council of state, 20 July 1666, AGS, E 2538.

Both Dutch and French ambassadors in Madrid had previously lent their support to Peñaranda's cause, and now the latter, d'Embrun, offered his master's aid in recovering Portugal, along with protection against England at sea. The offer was, of course, entirely specious, meant purely to disrupt Medina's (and Lisola's) designs for an anti-French coalition.[107]

The debate which now began had the effect of reviving profound divergences in the approach to continental strategy which were by now almost traditional in Spanish policymaking. Medina's insistence on collaboration with the 'flanking' powers of England and the Empire reestablished what might be called orthodox priorities – those adhered to in the most successful periods of Madrid's diplomacy from the very beginning of involvement in European affairs, and only deserted under extreme pressure of events. What undermined its credibility in mid century was the experience of 1640, and above all its association with the disastrous tyranny of Olivares. Whilst the *antiolivaristas* had allowed this strategy to lapse, they had put nothing in its place, and had certainly failed to bring about an improvement in the monarchy's affairs. Peñaranda's attempt in 1666 to enunciate principles from the improvised (and distinctly less than glorious) policies of the Haro period was, despite its personal motivation, at least brave. But though his supporters bitterly condemned Medina's fatalism and surrender, they found themselves in the position of proposing the more revisionist approach to the traditional surface pattern of Spanish policy. In this sense, the duke's case for a radical change of attitudes was strengthened by his ability to utilize tried and well-proven arguments, whilst Peñaranda's effort to preserve the sacred commitment of the dynasty was weakened by the lack thereof. As it proved, Medina was fully able to exploit this paradox.

To many Castilians of a conventional imperial allegiance, Peñaranda's scheme was extremely attractive. For one thing it revived notions of a confraternity between the two great Catholic powers, renewing the ideological passions which still smouldered in so many hearts, yet at the same time offering to submerge the years of Spanish failure, and French ascendancy, in a new phase of equal partnership. This veritable *idée fixe* of Castilian clericalism, with its origins at Cateau-Cambrésis, and still vital during the period of the so-called *Pax Hispanica* (1609–18), had experienced some resuscitation as recently as 1659–60 with the much-celebrated dynastic union and 'perpetual peace' of Habsburg and Bourbon.[108] Verisimilitude was added by the apparent

---

[107] Mapperton, Sandwich MS Journal, ii, pp. 143 et seq. Fanshawe's letters of 15 April, 10 June 1665, PRO, SP 94/48, f. 61; BL, Harl. 7010, f. 282 (see also f. 307). For the development of Peñaranda's scheme, see his memorial of 26 April, 1665, AGS, E 2533.

[108] For the 'ideological' background see J.M. Jover, *1635: historia de una polémica*, (Madrid, 1949) esp. chap. vii. Particular comments are in Domínguez, *Golden Age*, p. 65; H.R. Trevor-Roper, 'Spain and Europe, 1598–1621', in J.P. Cooper (ed.), *The New Cambridge Modern History*, iv (Cambridge, 1970); H. Kamen, *The Iron Century: Social Change in Europe, 1550–1660* (1971), pp. 234–37.

'conversion' of the other traditional enemy, the Dutch, against whom religious animosity had now faded, partly encouraged by the attitudes and behaviour of the ex-rebels themselves. In the aftermath of Cromwellian hostility and persecution from a much-trumpeted ideological motive, currently stimulated by the actions of the Restoration government, confessional rancour against England had by contrast lost little of its force. Points such as these were thoroughly rehearsed in the summer of 1666 by propagandists inspired by Peñaranda's cause, among them the clerical polemicist Arnolfini, who called for a crusade against the heretic English and rebel Portuguese as the hereditary and innate adversaries of every Castilian tradition.[109]

Utterly chimerical and anachronistic as they were in the context of the 1660s, there is no denying the strength, amongst the Castilian 'establishment', of the feelings inflamed by Peñaranda's tactics. Though by no means prone to the type of patriotism they embody, Medina himself could exhibit a degree of self-delusion, induced by residual and ingrained pride in Castilian greatness – for instance in the touching belief that Spain could rally the nations of Europe, and effectively resist French pretensions. To the *Junta de Gobierno*, however, including as it did no fewer than four high-ranking Spanish clerics, his attitude, though perhaps not surprising in a man of such notoriously lax morals, was regarded as a sell-out to heresy and intimidation. It may be suggested that a deeper motive still was present in Medina's enemies, clerical and lay alike, which illustrates the polarization of wider prejudices involved in the Guzmán-Haro vendetta. To both churchman and aristocrat it seems likely that Medina represented the shade of Olivares, whose memory they had no reason to revere. The men who hoped to bring down Medina were in many cases survivors from the 1630s, the same men who had chafed under, and finally toppled, the tyranny of the count-duke.[110] Then, as now, the leaders of church and state in Spain were blessed with an unusual longevity, and the average age of the chief royal servants in this decade was certainly well above seventy.[111] Medina's record as an accomplice of Olivares was not forgotten; they feared and envied his influence and riches; above all they were outraged

---

[109] Several contemporary copies of this treatise are extant in the U.K., an indication of its wide circulation and importance. It is transcribed in the pages of Sandwich's MS Journal at Mapperton (ii, pp. 381–411) and twice in MS vols of the British Library (Harl. 4520, ff. 117–120; Eg. 347, ff. 546–551), in the last instance bearing the title 'Discurso sobre si conviene más a España la liga con Inglaterra o Francia'. Another pro-Peñaranda pamphlet on the same theme is in BN, 1004, erroneously attributed in the general card-index to the count himself. An answer to all these arguments, citing Charles V's celebrated maxim 'guerra con toda la tierra y paz con Inglaterra', is in Mapperton, Sandwich MS Journal, ii, pp. 199–221. Further contributions to the debate can be found in BL, Eg. 347, ff. 552–587; 367, ff. 198–215.

[110] See Marañón, *El conde-duque*, chap. 8. Castrillo, Peñaranda, Medinaceli, Aytona and at least one clerical member of the official governing junta, were original *antiolivaristas*. On clerical and aristocratic grievances in the 1630s, see Domínguez, *Política y hacienda*, pp. 302–6. Medina had once been excommunicated for lack of respect towards the church and its dignitaries, at least according to Reumont, *The Carafas of Maddaloni*, p. 173.

[111] See the estimates (probably from the early 1660s) in BL, Eg. 567, f. 95.

by the prospect of him gaining the office of *valido* which he so deeply coveted.[112] Hatred of the duque-duque-conde (for such he occasionally styled himself in clear imitation of his benefactor)[113] involved also a clash of two different conceptions of government; on the one hand the clerical-grandee oligarchy, loathing monopoly of policy and patronage by an over-powerful favourite, applauding Philip IV's change of heart in the 1640s, the attitude which found its most intense and persistent advocate in Sor María de Ágreda; on the other, the hated single person, dedicated perhaps to abstract and secular ideas of the state, the *politique* inimical or indifferent by turns to the interests of the aristocratic elite who, in the person of Olivares, had led the monarchy to perdition in 1640. With Medina, these latter seemed to threaten an unwelcome recrudescence. In addition, the man who apparently reproduced the main lines of Olivares's policy, who talked so often of reform and material necessity, brought upon himself suspicion from another quarter – the representatives in the *Junta* (again four in number) of the peripheral regions of the monarchy, where the count-duke's deeds were still held in lively execration.[114]

The confrontation of 1666 also indicates that superimposed on all these issues was the ultimate one of the eventual fate of the Spanish monarchy and its ruling dynasty. In spite of the strong deterrent of Maura's contrary opinion,[115] the conclusion that this period witnessed the first round of the politics of the succession problem, both in Madrid and in the other courts of Europe, is one difficult to avoid. The 1660s were, after all, the time of greatest danger to the life of Carlos II, when any number of infantile disorders could so easily have snuffed out his congenitally frail existence. Though speculation on this theme has long been a commonplace of the textbooks, it remains true that its effects were more pressing in the first years of Carlos's reign than at any other time before his final, and childless, decline. Medina was, as we have seen, an avowed, and officially recognized trustee of the Austrian connexion, and frequently condemned France as the inveterate enemy of the house of Habsburg. There is no gainsaying the evidence, either, that the Haro faction was used – not altogether unwittingly – as an instrument of Louis XIV's diplomacy in the Spanish capital. Medina appealed to Vienna a year later in the following terms:

> At present mine is a despised and persecuted voice, and the emperor can only help me by supporting me with the queen and the Father Confessor (Nithard). In this way, we may be able to sustain the interests of the august House of Austria against all the power of the present government. It offends all reason

[112] Medina to Diego del Prado, Nov. 1667, BL, Eg. 338, ff. 470–505. In this letter also, the duke relates a conversation with Nithard in which the former confessed himself 'unworthy and incapable of the *valimiento*', an admission, it must be said, which is distinctly at odds with the rest of the letter.

[113] See (e.g.) BL, Harl. 7010, f. 534; Cánovas, *Estudios*, ii, p. 371.

[114] Soldevila, *Historia*, iv, pp. 351–54.

[115] Maura, *Vida y reinado*, i, 58, cf. Pfandl, *Carlos II*, pp. 113–16.

that those who are declared enemies of the empire should be in command here, whilst true loyalists are despised and excluded ... If Peñaranda's schemes are born of ignorance it is a great misfortune that our chief minister has such an abundance of it, and if from malice, so much the worse.[116]

In this way, therefore, the divisions of interest, policy and even, to some extent philosophy, regularly to be found in Spanish politics, were carried over into the last great issue of the Habsburg period. This element of continuity, so notable a feature of Spanish history in many of its aspects, was provided by the career of Medina de las Torres and the reaction to it of many lesser men.

In this particular phase of the contest, honours were roughly even. Medina failed to impose his view, whilst his enemies failed to stifle his influence. In council, Medina repeatedly warned that France was nearing the end of her preparations for an attack on the Spanish Netherlands, whilst Peñaranda 'wagered his own head that France would never make war on us'.[117] The former, however, killed all talk of a French alliance outright by a manoeuvre which surpassed the cunning even of his major antagonist. For some time, Medina had been intercepting French diplomatic correspondence, and communicating its contents to Lisola and Pötting.[118] In July 1666 he composed a highly-coloured paraphrase in the form of a memorandum from Hugues de Lionne to Louis XIV. This treatise, which Medina and his allies caused to be circulated in informed circles, exposed d'Embrun as a dissembler and Peñaranda's party as, at best, stooges.[119] Their scheme was consequently dropped from the agenda and Medina's basic line confirmed by Mariana.[120] This success was somewhat diminished by the result of the policy-ballot on Portugal, which saw Medina's advocacy of surrender heavily defeated. Only

---

[116] See note 112.

[117] Ibid. The divisions in government described at length in the letter to Diego de Prado were complicated by the growing pretensions of Don Juan José, who was admitted to the council of state in 1666. Thereafter, 'sessions became more like tavern squabbles than the deliberations of an organ of state'; Pfandl, *Carlos II*, pp. 132–33. The prince's interventions were mostly in favour of Peñaranda, who was later to be one of his main supporters. Medina, however, opposed the ambitions of the man who was soon to launch Spain's first ever military *golpe de estado*: perhaps out of respect for Philip's wishes, perhaps because of his knowledge of Don Juan's true paternity, either way because he feared that their fulfilment might lead to a revival of all the old imperial shibboleths. In what was probably his last letter on public affairs he reminded Don Juan directly – and in the circumstances somewhat tactlessly – that he had always promoted his interests 'as if they were those of my own son', but warning him against any attempt on power; Medina ('estando malo') to Don Juan José, (? Nov.) 1668, BL, Eg. 353, f. 452.

[118] Pfandl, *Carlos II*, pp. 116–17.

[119] 'Voto supuesto de Monsieur de Lionny, Secretario de Estado del Rey Luis XIIII de Francia ... Autor es M. Torres', BL, Eg. 353, ff. 33538–33546 (see also 367, f. 217). Lionne himself later accused Lisola of its authorship; Mapperton, Sandwich MS Journal, ii, p. 396.

[120] *Consulta* of council of state, 9 Sept. 1666, AGS, E 2538. An enclosed *parecer* by the count of Fuentes, ambassador in Paris, strongly confirmed the duke's assertions.

three voices spoke in his support, though they included significant figures such as the president of *Hacienda* (Villahumbrosa) and the commander of the non-existent *Armada de Portugal* (Alburquerque, representative of a younger element in government). The conciliar *votos* (with the exception of Medina's own council of Italy), went against him; the *Junta de Gobierno*, including the increasingly important figure of Nithard, supported Peñaranda *nem. con.*[121]

The events of the following spring, nevertheless, made it certain that this decision itself would shortly have to be reversed. Louis XIV's impatience simplified Medina's problems enormously, and by the summer Nithard and even Peñaranda had to face the logic of the situation, with the results already described.[122] The credit for these achievements was, however, withheld from their progenitor. The English treaty was negotiated by a commission, and Peñaranda alone, after Medina's death, arranged the Colonial Peace of 1670. The intensity of animus against the duke was illustrated above all by the Junta's assignment to the marquis of Heliche, son of Don Luis de Haro, of plenipotentiary powers for the conclusion of the peace with Portugal.[123] If only partly for these reasons, no familiar textbook account of this period assigns to Medina de las Torres recognition of his major contribution to the settlement which ended a period of fifty years of continuous war for the Spanish monarchy.

Medina's supporters of 1666, though few in number, were all purely Castilian nobles, few of whom were to be found in the opposite camp. Only a year later, forced to put personal animosity aside, the great majority of its patriarchs finally agreed that Castile had had enough. Over the years, the occasional figure amongst Medina's colleagues had come to sympathize objectively with his fundamental reappraisal of Spain's role and commitments. His enemies, and even Philip IV, were probably able in their more sober and pragmatic moments to see the force of his argument. For all this, it was he alone who realized, and accepted without reservation, that the real enemy of the monarchy was not France, or England, but war itself.

[121] For this collection of opinions, variously dated July–Sept. 1666, see AGS, E 2538, passim. In addition to Medina's, Cánovas printed those of Caraçena and Alba which condemned the former's policy; *Estudios*, i, pp. 354–66. Alba, previously a lukewarm supporter, was heavily influenced by dynastic honour, his ancestor the 'great duke' having been the conqueror of Portugal in 1580. A more loyal figure, Velada, was overruled by his own council, that of Flanders, whilst Ponce de León sent support from Milan, where he was governor (BL, Eg. 2050, ff. 207–9. Nithard's *voto* took the form of a massive quasi-theological treatise under no fewer than 280 heads. The only neutral member of the governing junta was Aytona.

[122] Mapperton, Sandwich MS Journal, iv, p. 146.

[123] Medina was outraged that this important duty should be assigned to a reprieved traitor, but made no mention of his family allegiance; Medina to del Prado, Nov. 1667. In fact, Heliche's conspiracy of 1662 had been inspired by one of Medina's victories in his rivalry with Haro, and the son's determination to gain posthumous revenge for his father; Shergold, *History of the Spanish Stage*, pp. 325–26.

Spanish Conspiracy in England, 1661–63

Spanish intervention in English politics is generally held to be a significant feature of the reigns of Elizabeth I and James I. Although they were by no means the first Spanish ambassadors to use dubious methods of influence, it was upon the figures of Mendoza and Gondomar that were fixed the evocative images of papist conspiracy – profound designs concocted by the shadowy emissaries of the Spanish court, and advanced by plausible traitors at the heart of the body politic. It was certainly during this period of English alliance with the Dutch, and her neutrality in the early stages of the Thirty Years War, that an anxious Spain began to utilize wholesale bribery, contacts with English recusants, and a systematic intelligence network as permanent lines of policy. They were developed particularly as an adjunct to the struggle to prevent the secession of the United Provinces. It was in this period that England's danger was greatest, and here, naturally, historians have concentrated their attention.[1] However, the successes achieved by Gondomar, Zúñiga and their colleagues in this classical era of Habsburg diplomacy encouraged Madrid to continue the practice of covert interference in the domestic affairs of foreign states. Though returns were increasingly disproportionate to outlay, the precarious nature of central government long made such projects a viable aspect of diplomacy. This fact was acknowledged by Louis XIV, who later successfully took up Spanish techniques. Even after defeat by Holland and France, and during the period of withdrawal from her European role, Spain continued to employ all kinds of professional spies in the defence of vital political interests. As before, activity involving such men was especially intense when important European events were taking shape, and/or in time of political crisis within the state concerned.[2] Both these factors were present with regard to England in the years 1659–63. Her uncertain position in the preliminary stages of the peace of the Pyrenees, combined with the emphatic weakening of government after Cromwell's death, led to complicated Spanish intrigue aimed at a separate peace with England, to the discomfiture of France. Following this, when the weak Restoration government sought to strengthen itself by a profitable dynastic tie with Portugal, a new motive for intervention was presented.

---

[1] G. Mattingly, *Renaissance Diplomacy* (repr., 1965); C.H. Carter, *The Secret Diplomacy of The Habsburgs, 1598–1625* (New York, 1964) and many scholarly articles by Albert Loomie, too many to cite in full.

[2] E.g., in England in the years 1598–1603, 1618–23 and 1639–42.

After 1659, Philip IV had transferred all the optimism and tenacity which had marked the struggle with the Dutch to his new mission of crushing the rebellion of Portugal. England now stood between the Spanish monarchy and the achievement of this goal, upon which was concentrated the undivided, but sadly reduced, resources of Spain. The behaviour of the Spaniards in this affair constituted a somewhat pathetic echo of past greatness. It may be regarded, in part at least, as a comment on the condition and effectiveness of the Spanish monarchy after the peace of the Pyrenees.

Cromwell's war with Spain was continued by his son after 1658, and dragged on, increasingly devoid of purpose, through restored Commonwealth and restored Rump. Charles II terminated hostilities soon after his return, but in circumstances which were anomalous. No negotiations took place, and no peace treaty was signed. Instead, a blanket proclamation of peace was vaguely agreed to by both sides. The significance of this fact is often missed. It meant, for example, that many of the deeply-rooted disagreements that had made war possible were left untouched – a situation aggravated by Charles' refusal to restore Dunkirk and Jamaica, the painful evidence of Spanish defeat. The Spaniards too readily assumed that their alliance with Charles, made in 1656, would be to their advantage in this matter, and in much else besides. Charles was later plainly embarrassed by the fact that, although Spain had not contributed to the Restoration, he came to England in 1660 as the professed ally of the Catholic King. Whatever the unpleasant and unsatisfying history of the arrangement, Charles' entourage had been sheltered and supported for four years by Philip IV. Behind him, in Flanders, the young king had left many rash expressions of gratitude and promises of repayment, both written and spoken.[3] The realities of power soon modified these ideas, and in addition serious misunderstandings quickly developed, especially over the interpretation of the peace proclamation. Encouraged by Charles' statements, and those of Henry Bennet, English resident in Madrid, the Spaniards professed not only that the old treaty of 1630, broken by Cromwell, was again intact, but also that Charles should adhere substantially to his 1656 promises, particularly by helping Spain to recover the allegiance of Portugal. The instructions of Batteville, Philip's new ambassador, bade him depend on the goodwill of the royalist party in establishing these principles. Don Luis de Haro, chief minister, who fancied himself the personal friend of Charles and his circle, anticipated few difficulties in progressing from them to a negotiated peace. Few involved reckoned upon the paramount influence of the chancellor. Hyde was not impressed with Batteville or his demands. Under Hyde's direction, Charles within the year had ditched the Spaniards and, going back on his

---

[3] See (e.g.) the unequivocal undertaking made to the marquis of Caraçena, governor of the Spanish Netherlands; G. Warner (ed.), *The Nicholas Papers*, iv (1920), pp. 210–11. Full treatment of Anglo-Spanish exchanges in 1660–61 can be found in R. Stradling, 'Anglo-Spanish Relations 1660–68' (unpublished Ph.D. thesis, University of Wales, 1968), chap. 1. An acute and stimulating general view of English policy can be sampled in the early pages of K. Feiling, *British Foreign Policy, 1660–1672* (repr. 1968).

word, concluded a dynastic and military alliance with the king of Portugal, Alfonso VI.[4] This was the famous Marriage Alliance ultimately sealed by the wedding of Charles and Catherine of Braganza in April 1662. It was adopted in the teeth of Spanish protests, and despite fully competitive proposals from Madrid. The negotiation of the treaty was attended by humiliating treatment of Batteville and other gratuitous affronts to Spanish honour. By it, moreover, not only were all hopes of a peace settlement with Spain disappointed, but England was, on the contrary, pledged to defend Portugal against Philip on the soil of the peninsula itself. The independence of Portugal was to be gained by Charles even if this should entail renewed war with 'the king of Castile'.[5] A further warning for Madrid lay in the knowledge that Charles' decision in this matter had been encouraged by Louis XIV's offers of support. Philip's so recently grateful client had quickly changed masters and seemed intent on cooperating with France in the affairs of Europe. In the following months, indications were plentiful that a new coalition of powers was aimed at depressing the Spanish monarchy beyond hope of recovery.

Between 1661 and 1663 Anglo-Spanish relations remained in a state of severe crisis, verging on war. Much as he feared another embroilment, Philip's patience was at times stretched to its limit.[6] In the summer of 1661, an English squadron sent to take over Tangier was suspected of designs upon the Spanish silver-fleet – an attack which, Batteville claimed, would signal the start of general war. De Ruyter's offer of protection was accepted with alacrity by the Cadiz authorities. Indeed, informed observers believed that a Dutch-Spanish alliance against England and Portugal (with French support) was the likely alignment in any renewal of European conflict. Meanwhile, the refusal to restore the acquisitions of Cromwell's war led to friction both in Europe and across the Atlantic. When Charles began to fortify Dunkirk and reinforce its garrison, the marquis of Caraçena, governor of Flanders, retaliated with a blockade of the port. Incidents in this trouble-spot escalated and, given that both Caraçena and his opposite number, the francophil Lord Rutherford, were soldiers rather than diplomats, it was remarkable that mutual provocation did not lead to an open clash of arms. In the Caribbean, the appointment of Lord Windsor as governor of Jamaica, with uncompromising orders regarding traditional Spanish claims in the New World, stimulated an outbreak of piracy which culminated in the sack of Santiago de Cuba by an English 'privateering'

[4] C.L. Grose, 'The Anglo-Portuguese Marriage of 1662', *Hispanic American Historical Review*, 10 (1930), pp. 230–52. For the Spanish counter-offers, see Haro to Batteville, 28 Feb., Philip IV to same, 31 Jan., 21 March (all 1661); AGS, E 2531, 2532.

[5] This meagre title was given to Philip IV in the text of the marriage treaty, A. Browning (ed.), *English Historical Documents*, viii (1953), pp. 857–59. For the important divergence in interpretation of the peace proclamation of 1660, cf. the English text with the Spanish version, ibid., p. 85; A. Marín et al. (ed.), *Colección de los tratados de paz* . . . (Madrid, 1751), pt 7, i, p. 413.

[6] For a fuller exposition of events noted in this paragraph, see Stradling, 'Anglo-Spanish Relations', i, pp. 55–76.

expedition in late 1662. News of this attack further embittered attitudes in Madrid, and resentment began to mark the attitude of the populace to English residents. Finally, in 1663, came a blow which the Spaniards could hardly bear. The army of Don Juan José, which had been raised only with agonizing expense and effort, was broken and routed at Ameixial, mainly by the onslaught of the English contingent in the Portuguese army. Long before this the Spanish port authorities had begun to take measures of reprisal against English merchants, who, virtually unprotected by treaty, were obstructed on all sides, to the great advantage of their Dutch rivals. Further interruption to English commerce was caused by Philip's decision to prevent the cooperation of England and France in the supply of troops and materials to Lisbon. A well-equipped band of Genoese pirates were hired to infest peninsular waters and prey indiscriminately on English shipping. In 1662–63 the effects on trade were strongly felt and much protested. The despatch of a flotilla under Sir John Lawson to the straits in the latter year was not motivated solely by the clause in the Portuguese treaty which obliged Charles to defend his ally's coast against Spain.

Opinion in Philip IV's *Consejo de Estado* tended to be divided, but the majority accepted that Charles, under Clarendon's guidance, was in effect continuing Cromwell's war. Philip himself, clutching at straws, refused to believe that England's attitude was beyond his influence. During 1661, the deaths of de Haro and of Fuensaldaña, an experienced and moderate statesman, left the king more open to the bellicose suggestions of the hot-heads. The counsellors of war were numerous and influential, although they had the disadvantage of being led from abroad. This leadership consisted of the so-called *ministros del norte*, at Brussels, the Hague, and London. Batteville himself was naturally the most outspoken, but with him the more mature Esteban de Gamarra, long-serving ambassador at the Hague, recommended an offensive alliance with the Dutch, and encouraged his colleague's desire to quit England as a preliminary to reprisals. From Brussels, Caraçena accused the English of open aggression around Dunkirk, and his despatches to Madrid contained mounting demands for war.[7] In the summer of 1661 Batteville began to vent his frustration in other ways. With support from Caraçena, he made contact with leaders of disaffected groups in London, and constructed a cell of agents prepared to work against the Portuguese alliance. His campaign against Clarendon's policy received help from a pressure group of the 'court opposition', in which Bennet and the earl of Bristol were prominent.[8] In Madrid the Venetian resident, noting the strength of feeling against England,

[7] *Consulta* of council of state. 7 June, Gamarra to Philip IV, 13 June, Philip IV to Gamarra, 6 July (all 1661); AGS, E 2531, 2578. See also Caraçena to Philip IV, 15 June 1661; ARB, SEG 268. f. 305.

[8] Batteville to Philip IV, 12 May 1661, AGS, E 2531; Edward, earl of Clarendon, *Continuation of Life* (1759), p. 90; V. Barbour, *The Earl of Arlington* (Washington, 1913), pp. 51–52; K.H.D. Haley, *The First Earl of Shaftesbury* (1968). p. 160.

reported that the *consejo* was ready to place some confidence in the propensity of Charles' subjects for rebellion. Although they gave Batteville's more clandestine operations no official support, Philip's advisers counted on the inexperience of English ministers, and the evidence of the recent past, in assuming that the Restoration government could be shaken, or perhaps even overthrown, by internal disturbance.[9] Batteville's own work along these lines came to an abrupt end in late 1661. After the notorious 'affair of precedence' in the streets of London between the Spanish and French ambassadors, Clarendon instigated accusations of treasonable activity against the former and Philip withdrew him from England. On his way home, Batteville called at Flanders for consultations with Caraçena, and with Cárdenas, his adviser on English affairs.[10]

Philip disapproved of this visit. Other counsels were now coming to the fore in Madrid and, by the time of Batteville's disgrace, the decision had been taken to avoid war with England if at all possible. It was a decision based on tradition and experience as well as pressing financial necessity, but it remained to be seen whether, as in the 1580s, and again in 1624 and 1655, English policy would force Spain's hand. The chief moderate in Philip's government was the immensely wealthy elder statesman, the duke of Medina, who now, in direct opposition to Caraçena and his Madrid allies, began to exert something of the influence formerly belonging to de Haro. Medina's struggle against the war party received support from an unexpected but vital quarter, the king's 'spiritual adviser', Sor Maria de Agreda, who insisted that no new commitment should be allowed to prejudice the reconquest of Portugal, Philip's prior and God-given responsibility.[11] Against strenuous protest in the *Consejo* and the king's own doubts, Medina persuaded Philip to maintain diplomatic communication with England. In the summer of 1662, the king agreed to send an agent, Patricio de Moledi (a servant of the duke), to take up the threads of negotiation in London. Unfortunately, before Moledi could leave, there occurred another adjustment to the balance of influence. Charles' sale of Dunkirk to Louis XIV seriously weakened Medina's arguments. Caraçena was able to regain the initiative, and claimed vehemently that this alienation of Spanish territory was conclusive evidence of an Anglo-French alliance against

[9] *CSPV, 1659–61*, p. 304; *consulta* of council of state, 16 Aug 1661, AGS, E 2531.

[10] Stradling, 'Anglo-Spanish Relations', i, pp. 63–68. Alonso de Cárdenas had been Spanish ambassador in London continuously from 1640–55, accredited in turn to King, Commonwealth and Protectorate. His experience of English politics was therefore considerable, but overinfluenced by its revolutionary phase. He was certain that contacts with Levellers and other dissidents – whose support he canvassed during Cromwell's war against Spain – could work to Spain's advantage. Gamarra also consulted Cárdenas on English issues; see their correspondence in AGS, AEH 476. The Restoration government soon identified Don Alonso as an enemy and associated his name with that of Caraçena in strong official complaints to Madrid; *CSPV, 1659–61*, p. 193.

[11] For Medina's case, see his 'Voto en Materias de Inglaterra'. 23 Feb. 1663, AGS, 2532; and for Sor María's, her letters to Philip IV of 9 Sept. 1661, 13 May 1662, Seco Serrano, *Cartas de Sor María*, ii, pp. 170–71, 178–79.

Spain.[12] For the moment Philip's sense of outrage predominated. Gamarra's diplomatic plans were once more endorsed, whilst, to Medina's chagrin, Moledi's mission was put under Caraçena's control. Thus encouraged, the governor of Flanders began to play upon his king's hopes for a political upheaval in England. By the end of the year he had transformed this passive feeling into an active desire to foment rebellion against Charles II.

Caraçena was already in touch with a group of spies in London (including those previously hired by Batteville), and was making contact with rebellious elements in Ireland. Moledi was now ordered to liaise with the former men and to carry money for their operations and to renew payment of Batteville's 'pensions' at court and in parliament. Although Philip was hereby attempting to allay his own resentments and seeking a substitute for war, he salved his conscience by ordering that the legitimate aspect of Moledi's commission – diplomatic *rapprochement* – should be preserved. In a letter to Caraçena, the king expressly stated that the policies of conciliation and conspiracy were not mutually exclusive but complementary, since a government weakened by internal disorder would be more inclined to compromise in its external relations. He saw Spanish intervention, in addition, as consistent with his Portuguese responsibilities, because it was designed 'to prevent the king of England from succouring my enemies'. The *consejo* agreed and, in the winter of 1662–63 it approved the grant of subsidies to Brussels for the furtherance of conspiracy.[13] The marquis was meanwhile developing his plans. These included the stimulation of armed insurrection in England, but Caraçena exuded greatest enthusiasm over his designs for a simultaneous rising in Ireland, assisted if necessary by an actual Spanish landing. He hoped that the Irish rebels would be able to seduce the garrison of a fortified port on the south coast and hold out until Spanish reinforcements arrived. To this end, he suggested the preparation of an expedition at Corunna. Philip concurred, and issued orders along these lines, even including the supply of arms, Neither Caraçena nor his king was prepared at this stage to consider how the prospect of initial success could be reconciled with the decision to avoid war.[14]

Caraçena had with him in Brussels an experienced and trusted instrument to implement his plans, a native of Limerick, one Ignatius White. Later, as

[12] Caraçena to Philip IV, 21 Feb. 1663, ARB, SEG 273, ff. 179–183; *consulta* of council of state, 8 May 1662, AGS, E 2532. See also Feiling, *British Foreign Policy*, p. 39. Clarendon, indeed, was fully aware of Louis XIV's designs on the Spanish Netherlands, using them as a bargaining counter in negotiations. See the d'Estrades-Louis correspondence for Aug. 1662 in E. Combe (ed.), *The Sale of Dunkirk to the French King Lewis XIV taken from the Letters of the Count d'Estrades* (1728).

[13] *Consultas* of 20 June, 8 Dec. 1662, AGS, E 2532; Philip IV to Caraçena, 24 Oct. and 12 Dec. 1662, ARB, SEG 272, ff. 109, 226; *consulta* of council of state on Caraçena's dispatches, Feb. 1663, AGS, E 2102. Reports from Caraçena's agents in London are scattered in ARB, SEG 272–273, AGS, E 2531, K1387. Some of the Caraçena-Philip IV correspondence is calendared in Cuvelier and Lefèvre. *Correspondance de la cour*, iv.

[14] Caraçena to Philip IV, 13 Nov., Philip IV to Caraçena, 12 Dec. 1662, ARB, SEG 272, ff. 147, 228.

the marquis of Albeville, White achieved some notoriety as an influential member of James II's camarilla. He was the most prominent member of a fascinating family of professional spies who had been variously in the pay of many European princes.[15] In 1662 Ignatius was well-known to the Restoration government. Three years before he had been offered a peerage by Charles, probably in return for a promise to facilitate the Restoration by intrigue in England. Instead, sent over by Caraçena to negotiate in secret for a peace between Spain and the Commonwealth, he stayed on to serve Thurloe, and probably betrayed some of the details of the royalist invasion scheduled for 1659 in conjunction with the Booth rising. In 1660 he attempted unsuccessfully to regain Charles' favour by persuading Caraçena to surrender Thomas Scot, the regicide, for execution. after assuring him of asylum in Flanders.[16] Philip in fact warned Caraçena that Ignatius was too familiar in England for his services to be used on this occasion. The warning came too late, for Caraçena had already sent him, in August, and one of Rutherford's agents in Brussels had send advance notice of his likely employment. In London White met with Moledi, who arrived shortly afterwards. Caraçena did not trust Medina's man and therefore White told him that he had come on official business. Equally suspicious of a fellow Irishman, Moledi nevertheless divined White's true purpose and complained bitterly to Philip that his own position was being undermined. He strenuously supported the argument of his master, Medina, that White's espionage activities would ruin Anglo-Spanish relations for good and asked the king to disown him.[17] White's stay in England lasted some five months, during which he was probably busy in distributing funds and meeting ringleaders. Though details are available of the subsidies entrusted to his care, and their purpose, nothing can be definitely established on this phase of the conspiracy, and we do not know whether Ignatius visited Ireland. Apparently having escaped detection, White rejoined Caraçena who forestalled criticism from Madrid by submitting a report compiled from White's information, which stressed that the political situation in England was too promising to allow the chance of intervention to slip. In this and other ways, Caraçena effectively countered Moledi's objections and asserted that the Irish plotters were afraid of betrayal should the Medina overture prove successful. They had demanded 'his word as a gentleman' that this would not happen before

[15] E.S. de Beer, 'The Marquis of Albeville and his Brothers', *EHR* 45 (1930), pp. 397–408. See also J.P. Kenyon. *Robert Spencer, Earl of Sunderland, 1641–1702* (1958), pp. 136 et seq.

[16] F.R. Routledge, *Calendar of Clarendon Papers*, iv, p. 223; idem, *England and the Treaty of Pyrenees*. (Liverpool, 1953), pp. 28, 117; G. Davies, *The Restoration of Charles II, 1658–1660* (1955), pp. 130–31; C.H. Firth (ed.), 'Thomas Scot's Account of his Actions as Intelligencer during the Commonwealth', *EHR* 12 (1897), pp. 116–26.

[17] Rutherford to Bennet (and enclosures), 18 Aug. 1662, PRO, SP 29/58, ff. 102–105. According to this report, White, 'entertained by this court [i.e. Brussels] . . . for his office of being a spy . . . has gone to see a sick brother . . . or for some other cause, disadvantageous to the king'. In a marginal note, Rutherford carefully drew Bennet's attention to White's name. See also Moledi to Philip IV, 14 Dec. 1662, AGS, E 2532, and cf. *CSPV, 1661–64*, pp. 195, 209.

proceeding with their plans. Soon after, the *Consejo* again considered the marquis' remarks and approved his conduct.[18]

The several optimistic Spanish estimates of the internal situation in England, now being pondered in Madrid, were not altogether fanciful. Throughout 1662 an almost apocalyptic atmosphere of rumour and unrest prevailed. Conversation at court and in the Commons was beset with apprehension as reports of secret meetings, plots and 'conventicles' streamed into the offices of the secretaries of state. Arrests and examinations were filling the prisons and exhausting the magistrates in the localities. Only the king's desperate need for money, which the Portuguese alliance had failed to meet, justified the unpopular sale of Dunkirk, when many had believed that Charles wished to keep it as a possible refuge in case of another ejection from his kingdom. The disbandment of Cromwell's army and the mass sackings of nonconformist ministers, created a potential hotbed of inspired and capable rebels. The bitter disillusionment of many old royalists with the Restoration settlement, the severity of the Clarendon Code, and the confusion caused by Charles' abortive declaration of indulgence, all contributed to the heightening of tension. Government ministers were overworked, quarrelsome and exceedingly fearful.[19] In the summer of 1662, for example, Bennet (though still technically out of office), recommended stiff military precautions to be taken in the provinces. Soon after he succeeded to the senior secretaryship in the autumn, a particularly dangerous plot to assassinate Charles was discovered among the London trained bands. The new year brought no relief. Ireland was seething with discontent. The arch-republican Edmund Ludlow was reported to be everywhere inciting and organizing rebellion. The 'fanatics' were widely believed to have set 3 September – symbolic and evocative date – as their deadline. The apostate Albemarle was to be hanged in an iron cage, and a republican-clerical junto would rule England. Bennet, prepared to risk the consequences, planned to raise new regiments to guard the court and made a new attempt to tighten discipline among the county militias.[20]

In these circumstances, the revelations made to Bennet and Clarendon by a court hanger-on, William Galway, in May, 1663, were at once accepted at face value. Galway's information came from a certain James Tailor, a servant of White, in Brussels, who accused him (White) and the Spaniards

---

[18] For White's espionage payments, see ARB, SEG 168 (*gastos secretos*), ff. 18, 29, 39. For the subsidies taken to England, see the *Tanteo General* of the Brussels government, Nov., Caraçena to Philip IV, 21 March, and *consulta* of the council of state, 10 April (all 1662), AGS, E 2102.

[19] W.C. Abbott, 'English Conspiracy and Dissent, 1660–74', *American Historical Review*, 14 (1908–9), pp. 502–28; M. Beloff, *Public Order and Popular Disturbance, 1660–1702* (repr. 1969), chap. 2; K. Feiling, *History of the Tory Party, 1640–1714*, (repr. 1965). pp. 98–110; and, especially, the comments in D. Ogg, *England in the Reign of Charles II* (2nd edn, 2 vols, 1956), i, pp. 208–10.

[20] Draft Proclamation (? April 1663), PRO, SP 29/72, f. 149; order by Bennet, 5 May 1663, ff. 33–34; *CSPV, 1661–64*, pp. 205–14; *CSPD, 1661–64*, passim.

of plotting rebellion. Detailed evidence was provided by cipher copies of papers, purloined from Ignatius, and enclosed in Tailor's letters to Galway. The design, as revealed therein, was radical and thorough. Charles and the duke of York were to be murdered and strong points in the city seized, while simultaneous risings took place elsewhere. Some centres of sedition were identified, and a written agreement between the conspirators and Spain was cited.[21]

> Our friends in Spain [Ignatius was told] may think that things are not well carried by me; but you may assure them . . . that there is more hope now than ever before, for my party grows stronger every day, and before it be the latter end of August, I do not doubt but to fulfill my promise unto them.

This letter, from a ringleader who was raising support in Ireland and the west country, went on to ask for prompt military aid from Flanders. The writer professed himself 'sure' of the help of the London trained bands and of many of Albemarle's Coldstream regiment. In a code-poem, however, he demanded better terms in his agreement with the Spaniards:

> No, no, thou all of red & *white*[22]
> Thou hast not yet undone me quite,
> For thou hast stolen but half my heart
> Though I must confess the wound doth *smart*
>
> Then pretty life steal no more,
> But let me keep one part in store.
> For half is too much for thee of mine
> Unless I had a greater share of thine.
> ....
> It may chance if I should keep the City
> I might at last be forced to yield
> Not like a coward will I flie
> Nor like a fool will stay to die.

Tailor's ascription of these papers to one 'James Smart' is repeated in the printed *Calendar of State Papers Domestic*.[23] The name, however, is clearly an alias, since the original cipher copy is signed 'Ludlow', and internal evidence strongly suggests that the writer was (or was intended by Galway to be taken

---

[21] Galway's papers are grouped in PRO, SP 29/73, ff. 22–30. They comprise (i) a covering letter from Tailor to Galway, 4 May 1663; (ii) a letter from 'James Smart' to White, 24 April 1663. This is in cipher, deciphered, and with a deciphered copy; (iii) an apparently irrelevant item; (iv) a love-poem, containing a coded message about the plot.

[22] My emphasis.

[23] *CSPD, 1663–64*, pp. 129–30. Here 'Ludlow' is assumed to be the place from which the letter was written, and not the writer's name. Both copies, however, end with the words 'I remain your faithful friend, from Bristol the four-and-twentieth of April, 1663, Ludlow'. The writer, moreover, refers to the place where he is as containing many of his supporters. Bristol had a record of disaffection in this period, in contrast to Ludlow, which was a traditional bastion of loyalism.

as) Edmund Ludlow. Reference is made to the fact that 'Cork and Limerick are sure . . . besides I have engaged several officers who have served under me' in Ireland, where Ludlow commanded before the Restoration. Another regicide, Whalley, and still others who had been associated with Ludlow in his opposition to a 'single person', were implicated in the subsequent correspondence of Tailor.

The idea that Ludlow cooperated with a foreign power, or that he was involved in any sedition in this period, was denied by himself and discouraged by Sir Charles Firth in his edition of Ludlow's *Memoirs*. Firth states that 'not a plot was discovered for the next five years [after 1660] but he was reported to be at the head of it'. Further, 'Ludlow's name was used to decoy men into plots, and freely used by informers to give colour to their lies'.[24] Sound as these statements are, and leaving the Galway case aside, they cannot fully negate the accumulated reports, depositions and oaths of witnesses under examination. Firth, moreover, could not prove conclusively that Ludlow was never in England at this time, and his whereabouts before the end of 1663 have not been definitely established.[25] Unlikely as it may at first seem, there were already precedents for the alliance of Spain with extreme Protestant activists, as the record of Cárdenas' schemes illustrates. It was regarded as more than coincidence by the government, therefore, when soon after Galway's approach, information was received from Brussels that 'Whalley and Goffe were not long since seen to enter de Cárdenas' house'. Coming from a source independent of the initial revelations, and added to the fact that as recently as 1660 White himself had been lodging with Cárdenas, this news tended to confirm suspicions.[26]

At this point, Bennet decided to make investigations in Ireland, sending copies of Galway's papers to the lord lieutenant, Ormonde. Ludlow's letter had forecast imminent action on his behalf in Dublin, and it was believed that a plot recently detected by Ormonde was connected with the affair. Because of the threat to reverse the Irish land settlement, the old Cromwellian interest in Ireland was already disaffected, and vigilance was necessary to prevent Spanish meddling from sparking off a larger upheaval. In view of Ludlow's assertions, a purge of southern Ireland was begun under the earl of Orrery, who quickly found further evidence of Spanish complicity in Cork. Several ex-officers of Ludlow's army were arrested on charges of plotting to seduce the garrison and seize the town. An informant deposed that these men hoped 'that by the help of the Spanish invasion their design would go on well'. Similar evidence also came to light at Limerick, another centre of sedition mentioned by Ludlow.[27]

[24] C.H. Firth (ed.), *The Memoirs of Edmund Ludlow, 1625–1672* (2 vols, 1894), i, p. xiii; ii, p. 329.

[25] For reports of Ludlow's activities in England, see (e.g.) CSPD, 1661–62, pp. 434, 444, 470, 591, 595; ibid., *1662–63*, pp. 12–13, 72, 144. Firth printed a letter, dated December 1663, which states that Ludlow had only recently arrived in Switzerland; Firth, *Memoirs*, ii, p. 483.

[26] PRO, SP 29/74, f. 13; Warner, *Nicholas Papers*, iv, p. 213.

[27] *CSPD(I), 1663–65*, p. 151.

What is mentioned in this deposition [Orrery reported] confirms Ludlow's having agreed with the Spaniard, as his intercepted letter imports . . . (but) if Ludlow thrives no better in his other wicked hopes than in his designs on those garrisons, I daresay the Spaniards will not have much cause to be pleased in his services.[28]

Other ramifications of the Spanish campaign against the Marriage Alliance impinged upon the Irish situation. In Portugal the English auxiliary force was lamentably treated by the government which they had come to save. Their discontent was exploited by Spanish agents, leading to wholesale desertion. The brother of the earl of Inchiquin, their general, was arrested on suspicion of collusion with Spain to sabotage the Portuguese war effort. When he was sent under guard to London, many soldiers, Inchiquin at their head, threw up their commissions and returned home. Soon afterwards, in May 1663, Inchiquin wrote from his Limerick estate that Spanish spies had attempted to recruit his services for a projected uprising. In London, meanwhile, Moledi made contact with Inchiquin's son to the same end.[29] Simultaneously, further pressure was being exerted by Spain in the Mediterranean. Determined to loosen England's hold on Tangier, which he regarded as alienated Spanish territory, Philip IV made an alliance with a local Moorish chieftain. Charles' sparse financial and military resources were further extended when a plot was laid to surprise Tangier but detected by an English double-agent. Despite expensive precautions, the Spaniards nearly succeeded when in June 1664, the earl of Teviot (formerly Rutherford) was killed, and his force nearly annihilated by the Moors. Despite Caraçena's personal satisfaction at this, Tangier held, though only just.[30]

The attempt to uncover details of the conspiracy in England received an apparent reward when it was recalled that Richard White, one of Ignatius' brothers, was in London. Richard was also in Spanish service but had come to England on a quite legitimate mission, to negotiate a contract with the African Company on behalf of the Genoese *asientistas de negros*.[31] Concern over his past record had in fact caused him to obtain a safe-conduct from the duke of York before setting foot in England. Nevertheless, he was now apprehended and 'committed for treasonable practices, close prisoner' to the Tower. His papers were seized, and the house of a wealthy 'Spanish' merchant,

[28] Orrery to Charles II, 6 July 1663, ibid., p. 150. See also *A Collection of the State Letters of the Right Honourable Roger Boyle First Earl of Orrery to the Year 1668* (1742), pp. 69–70. The Cork design, of course, was in precise accordance with Caraçena's plans.

[29] Inchiquin to Bennet, 15 May 1663, *CSPI, 1663–65*, p. 78; memorandum to Oyanguren (secretary of the council of state), 25 May 1663, AGS, E 2578; Historical Manuscripts Commission, *Heathcote MSS*, p. 68. For the affair of the troops in Portugal, see Stradling, 'Anglo-Spanish Relations', i, pp. 122–23. During the 'Yorkshire Plot' – later in 1663 – 'there was a design of inducing the troops returning from Portuguese service to serve as auxiliaries'; Ogg, *England in the Reign of Charles II*, i, p. 209.

[30] Stradling, 'Anglo-Spanish Relations', i, pp. 90–93.

[31] Ibid., pp. 102 et seq.

Alexander Bence, was searched for incriminating evidence.[32] Richard protested his innocence in several letters to Bennet, but suspicion of him seemed confirmed when Spanish diplomatic circles made indiscreet enquiries about him.[33] In any case it was decided to use Richard as a bait to lure Ignatius across the Channel. In council, Clarendon maintained that 'the fellow (Ignatius) is a rogue, and in all plots, yet . . . what is the harm of speaking with him? . . . he may be a knave to those who trust him, and discover all he knows'.[34] The business Richard White was about in London was itself of great importance to the government and court, whose members were for national and personal reasons interested in the welfare of the African Company. These commercial schemes might suffer serious prejudice if Richard were held in confinement, especially when no actual evidence against him had been uncovered. The risk, however, was deemed worth taking to lay hands on Ignatius and, true to the character of his family, Richard was fully prepared to cooperate to save his skin. He wrote to his brother, begging him 'not to stand now upon conditions, leave all to Sir Harry [Bennet]' and to come immediately.[35] According to Tailor, Ignatius was moved to express an intention of meeting this challenge to clear himself. '[But] I cannot believe'. Tailor added, 'that any man that knows himself so guilty . . . can have the confidence to come and justify himself'.[36] Indeed, though he wrote to Bennet, Ignatius made no other move to plead his own case or to save his brother. In June, moreover, Galway produced a third letter from Tailor further exposing Ignatius' dealings with the Ludlow faction.[37] At the same time, Bennet set a thief to catch a thief by enlisting the wanted traitor Joseph Bampfield, who knew Ignatius and his ways, to spy upon him in the Low Countries.[38]

In July there came a surprising intervention. Claims were put forward by Sir Arthur Slingsby which threw doubt on all the evidence provided by Galway. According to Slingsby's testimony,[39] he had suspected Galway of fraudulence for some time. At first he had 'laughed within myself to see such a knavish part so foolishly acted, but now there is much probability that this imposture has abused both my lord Chancellor and yourself'. Slingsby evidently held Ignatius in high regard, and was outraged that a man

[32] *CSPD, 1663–64*, p. 144.

[33] Three letters from Richard White to Bennet, June 1663, PRO, SP 29/75, ff. 48, 76, 88. See also, SP 29/74, ff. 108, 114; SP 94/46, f. 63.

[34] W.D. Macray (ed.), *Notes which Passed at Meeting of the Privy Council between Charles II and the Earl of Clarendon*, (1896), p. 88.

[35] Richard White to Ignatius White, 24 July 1663, PRO, SP 29/77, f. 90.

[36] Tailor to Galway, 11 June 1663, PRO, SP, 77/33, f. 170.

[37] Same to same, 12 June 1663, ibid., 29/74, f. 61. A pass for Ignatius to come to England was issued as early as May; *CSPD, 1661–63*, p. 144. His letter to Bennet unfortunately is not extant.

[38] PRO, SP 84/167, ff. 150–159.

[39] Slingsby to Bennet, 15 July 1663, PRO, SP 29/76 f. 151.

who doth daily vindicate the king our master from the reproaches of the Spaniards ... hath received apparent prejudice by ... a gentleman at court that goes by the name of Sir William Galloway, who has long amused my lord Chancellor with letters of intelligence from abroad, which I doubt not were of his own writing.

Slingsby was so convinced of White's innocence that he went to Brussels to see him, and found the matter, when related, 'so new and strange a thing to him, that after some time I told him ... that he was suspected for corresponding with the fanatics, which he denied with all the imprecations imaginable'. In his turn, Caraçena (no doubt briefed by Ignatius) summoned Slingsby, 'and told me he was sorry to be so much mistaken in England, and protested on his faith and honour that he had no such treaty ... or correspondence in England ... with the king of England's rebellious subjects'. Slingsby had made a point of closely observing Galway, whose behaviour was strange enough in his mind to confirm the vehement denials he had met with in Brussels.[40] There is little reason to doubt Slingsby's good faith, since he was a man of unimpeachable loyalty. His case against Galway, on the other hand, was far from concrete, stemming largely from personal mistrust. The results of his interviews in Brussels could hardly have convinced the government, particularly when Ignatius was known to have a talent for duping the king's less devious servants.[41] More significant, Slingsby was unable to offer reasonable proof that Galway had fabricated his information, and his charges as a whole were not enough to allay a suspicion now supported by reports independent of the Galway-Tailor source. In the circumstances, there can have been little doubt to the government that Spain was developing plans for a rising. As we have seen, such plans existed and were intended to paralyse England, or at least to effect the overthrow of Clarendon. Even before this case had arisen, Caraçena had been identified as a declared enemy of England, and official protests about his activities had been conveyed to Madrid. Whether or not Galway's details correspond accurately with Caraçena's intentions, the latter were, by the use of Ignatius White's services, fairly advanced by the time Bennet received his information, and were certainly geared to reach fruition in the summer of 1663. After this lapse of time, it is perhaps safer to regard Galway's papers as merely amplifying these facts, providing details which in a large number of cases are corroborated elsewhere.

The authenticity of these papers is open to doubts which to some extent tend to support Slingsby's explanation. In the first place the papers exhibit

---

[40] About this time, living conditions in the Tower were made more comfortable for Richard and he was allowed to receive visitors (*CSPD, 1663–64*, pp. 196, 211). He told Ignatius that there was reason to be grateful for Slingsby's advocacy, ibid., p. 281.

[41] See (e.g.) Sir Henry de Vic's gullibility in Brussels; Warner, *Nicholas Papers*, iv, pp. 234, 247, and Clarendon's own first opinion of Ignatius White in 1659, T. Carte (ed.), *A Collection of Original Letters and Papers Concerning the Affairs of England, from the Year 1641 to 1660* (1739), ii, p. 283.

some highly-coloured characteristics of the professional informer's trade. As Oates was to demonstrate, the wider the net of suspicion was cast, the more outrageous and lurid the accusations made, the greater were the chances of provoking genuine discoveries. Galway indeed challenges credibility by the almost hackneyed formula of his revelations. The time-honoured ingredients for a tempting dish are nearly all present – vague references to bodies of men poised to strike, hired assassins, double-agents, secret agreement with a foreign power, codes, ciphers and even love-poetry *à la* the Casket Letters. The papers, in fact, often read like a parody of seventeenth-century conspiracy. Outside them there is only slight evidence of the involvement of Ludlow (or 'James Smart') in the Spanish design, whilst it has proved impossible to identify James Tailor, the 'source' of all Galway's 'information'. Unfortunately, no other relics of Galway are extant, through which his handwriting, spelling, or biographical details material to the case can be investigated. However, Slingsby was certainly correct in claiming that Galway was indigent and desperate for royal favour. He had been on the fringes of the exiled court in Flanders, and could well have gleaned there Ignatius' character, later recruiting him along with the indispensable Ludlow into his story in an attempt to gain preferment.[42] On the other hand, two authorities on the period appear to accept Galway at face value. W.C. Abbott writes, somewhat tentatively, that 'early in May [1663] intercepted letters which seemed to incriminate two brothers, Richard and Ignatius White, and one James Smart, apparently a recruiting officer of rebellion, came into [government] hands, but in spite of the utmost efforts, could not be unravelled'. E.S. de Beer does not dispute Galway's evidence against Ignatius. Neither, however, deals with Slingsby's objections.[43] To sum up: despite certain anomalies, unless Tailor's interceptions were authentic, or Galway was himself betraying the conspiracy from the inside, it would appear to be at least unlikely that the latter could have given such an exact guide to the localities of Spanish intrigue (especially in Ireland), or provided such insight into the policies of Caraçena. These factors helped Bennet and his colleagues to suspend any reservations they may have entertained about Galway. In the circumstances, they can hardly have done otherwise. In any case, and whatever the full truth, Galway's papers are a fascinating document when placed in the context of Anglo-Spanish relations.

[42] *CSPD, 1660–61*, pp. 336, 560; ibid., *1661–62*, p. 30. Galway's knighthood, referred to by Slingsby, was certainly an imposture: a petition of 1661 calls him 'gent.' If, working alone, he invented the conspiracy and forged the papers, merely by the use of acute political observation allied to imagination. Galway must have been an accomplished conman, almost in the Titus Oates class. A more likely explanation of his role, supported by certain inconsistencies of detail in the documents, is that Galway was himself involved in the plot, and betrayed what he knew, producing material which gave correct names and other data, but which were actually manufactured as 'evidence'.

[43] Abbott, 'English Conspiracy', p. 518; De Beer, 'The Marquis of Albeville', pp. 402–3. Both experts accept the implication of Richard White, who in fact on this occasion seems to have been guiltless. Beloff does not commit himself: 'there was even talk of Spanish aid for a projected rising', *Public Order and Popular Dissent*, p. 36.

The affair as a whole reveals the lengths to which Spain was prepared to go in eliminating the problems posed by the Anglo-Portuguese alliance. In concept and implication, this was the most profound intervention in English politics endorsed by the Spanish monarchy since the enterprises of Philip II, yet was made at a time when Spain hardly possessed the capacity to initiate the scheme, let alone see it through to the logical military conclusion. The desire to crush the Portuguese rebellion was the paramount factor in Madrid's reasoning, and the sustained sacrifice made to this end was the main reason for the accelerated pace of Spanish decline after the peace of the Pyrenees. This phenomenon was, however, neither so marked nor so obvious to Europe in 1660–63 as it became at the end of the decade, following humiliating defeats by Portugal and France. The relatively satisfactory settlement with France, and the growing friendliness of Holland, at first freed some Spanish resources and conduced to the illusion that Spain was still a great power. Despite his consciousness of actual weakness, Philip IV was – perhaps naturally – himself a victim of this feeling, and was certainly prepared to pander to it when manifested in the behaviour of his veteran advisers. The habits of imperial power and influence die hard, the more so when (as should be recalled) even in the best circumstances the Spanish monarchy had rarely been more than one step away from bankruptcy.[44] Desperation was mixed with pride in this Spanish reaction to English policy, and later conquered it in the diplomatic surrender, in 1667–70, of nearly all the points of principle and interest for which Philip had fought Cromwell. Once again, as during the heyday of the Counter-Reformation offensive, Spanish attention was focused upon England. The conspiracy of 1663 was the culmination of a minor history of Spanish contacts with religio-political extremists in England, dating back about a decade. Spanish hopes were based upon the feeling, expressed by her statesmen both singly (Caraçena, Cárdenas, Batteville) and collectively (in the *Consejo*), that if the right conditions were recreated England would relapse into a renewal of the civil wars which had excluded her from continental affairs in the 1640s. Indications of such a possibility were present, and not altogether misleading, and the reward of successful action – the easing of English pressure in many spheres on the strained fabric of the Spanish Empire – was well worth the effort. Thus the contacts with Ireland, in an attempt to revive the anarchy of 1641; thus Moledi's attempts to corrupt M.P.s, White's consorting with 'fanatic' elements; and thus – perhaps most significant of all – Batteville's campaign in 1661 to elicit protest against Clarendon's policy in the streets, in the army *and* in parliament. The aims of Spanish diplomats were directly related to the experiences of 1640–42 in England, which Cárdenas had witnessed at first hand. In the 1670s, Louis XIV was to find it equally convenient to base his own English policy on these calculations. As Caraçena

---

[44] Stradling, 'Anglo-Spanish Relations', i, pp. 110; et seq. Lynch, *Spain under the Habsburgs*, ii, p. 124.

put it to Philip IV, Spanish effort and money were spent in the hope 'that all the parties will *reunite against the king*, making one great party'.[45]

The intelligence network at Caraçena's disposal was different both in quality and nature from that of Gondomar. It was much more costly, yet much less reliable or effective. In the earlier period, the sub-diplomacy of Spain was pursued with the aid of an apparatus which possessed a certain homogeneity, a peculiar affiliation to the interests and prejudices of the monarchy. Flemish, Italian and Spanish merchants had then been willing, in return for diplomatic services rendered, to supply information, carry dangerous documents, and otherwise to advance treasonable designs. Such men were now very thin on English ground. In Gondomar's time, too, influential recusants could be relied on to cooperate. After 1660, with the Catholic cause extinguished in Ireland and English Catholicism ruined by its royalist bent in the civil wars, little influence or even sympathy could be raised by the appeal to religion. For Englishmen, in any case, the political edge of such an appeal had become increasingly dull since the 1620s. Spain was therefore forced to turn to the professional spy, to a pool of men who touted for business from any state which would hire them. Often lacking national or religious loyalties, they were expensive and frequently untrustworthy. Madrid also turned to Protestant extremists, men with aims of their own which (especially in Ireland) were entirely odious to their Spanish paymasters.[46] The operations of such agents belong, for the historian, to a twilight world, existing somewhere between the prolix volumes of diplomatic correspondence and complete silence. Since, in the nature of things, written evidence was rarely preserved, it is frequently difficult to observe their movements except, as it were, through frosted glass. Indeed, the historian's problem in evaluating evidence was posed at the time to the king's harassed servants: writing to the duke of Buckingham in October 1663, Bennet himself perceived it:

> How certain soever we morally are of the intended rising, of which we had many concurring informations here from several hands that could not conspire to abuse us, it is very possible you may not be able to produce such convincing proofs as will come home to the inquiry of the law.[47]

In August 1663 Richard White was released from the Tower, upon condition of his leaving England within twenty days.[48] Perhaps Slingsby's testimony had been accepted. At any rate, the influence of Slingsby, and of other businessmen concerned over Richard's mission, must have had its effect. Besides, no evidence against him had ever been found. On the other hand, no proceedings seem to have been taken against William Galway and, in

[45] Caraçena to Philip IV, 12 April 1663, AGS, E 2102 (my emphasis). See also, ARB, SEG 272, f. 303.

[46] See the discussion of Spanish 'political morality' in Stradling, 'Anglo-Spanish Relations', i, pp. 313–15.

[47] T. Brown, *Miscellanea aulica* (1702), pp. 307–9.

[48] *CSPD, 1663–64*, p. 225.

September, the papers and belongings of Ignatius' wife were investigated in London. However, when in January of the following year Ignatius was reported to be plotting fresh mischief with Desborough and others of Ludlow's adherents in the Low Countries, nothing was done. The real crisis for Charles' government had passed with the suppression of the so-called Yorkshire Plot the previous autumn.[49] All Spanish hopes for a new revolution in England had come to nought.[50] The whole affair, like so many of its kind, had petered out.

[49] *CSPD, 1663–64*, pp. 282, 426; ibid., *1666–67*, pp. 145–46; H.G. Gee, 'The Derwentdale Plot, 1663', *Transactions of the Royal Historical Society*, 3rd series, 11 (1917), pp. 125–42.

[50] Relations between England, Spain and Portugal were eventually settled on new foundations by a sequence of negotiations which resulted in the treaties of commerce (1667), Portuguese independence (1668) and colonial relations (1670).

PART III

THE MILITARY RECORD

In contrast to the image of Condé (below, p. 234), this portrait of Francisco de Melo, perhaps understandably, recalls the sober administrator rather than the dashing soldier. (*Biblioteca National, Madrid*)

Catastrophe and Recovery: The Defeat of Spain, 1639–43

As a schoolboy in the 1950s, the present writer dutifully imbibed the received notions regarding the decline of Spanish military power. The Castilian infantry, whose style and pattern was set by the *gran capitán*, Gonsalvo de Córdoba, dominated the battlefields of Europe for nearly 150 years. The steel tips of the puissant pike, along with that other metal, the silver of the Indies, were the mainstay of Spain's supremacy. Then suddenly – so ran the textbooks – a battle was fought at Rocroi, the pike was shattered at a blow, and the power of Spain, like Wotan's authority, was at an end. In this manner a young Siegfried, the prince of Condé, inaugurated 'the Ascendancy of France' and set the seal on 'the Decline of Spain'. Literally and metaphorically a new chapter in the history of Europe had begun. True, it might be noticed, perhaps with mild surprise, that Spain did not actually make peace with France until some sixteen years later: but it was certainly a shock to discover, a good deal later, that the 'invincible tercios' had been beaten on several occasions and, long before Rocroi, even in pitched battle.

In any case, it seemed, on the face of it, incongruous that the Spanish soldier should have survived for so long, when – as everybody knew – Spain had been in full decline ever since the English had dealt with another 'invincible', the Armada of 1588. It was thus difficult to think of Spain as a naval power at all. Her genius was terrestrial, but at least the events of 1588 made the full stop of 1643 more assimilable into a coherent *schema* of decline and fall. Again, it was confusing in later years to read of a great Spanish armada making its way up the English Channel in 1639, more than half a century (so I had been reliably informed) after the Habsburg navy had ceased to exist.

Modern students of the Spanish monarchy should have little difficulty in explaining its survival as the predominant military power in Europe down to (at least) the year 1640. The vast increase in our knowledge of what Dr Brightwell has aptly termed 'the Spanish System'[1] has led to a steady reappraisal, discernible in almost every published work on Spain's military and administrative history since about 1960.[2] What remains unresolved and perplexing is the precise role played in the system's failure by 'the great

---

[1] P. Brightwell, 'The Spanish System and the Twelve Years' Truce', *EHR*, 89 (1974), pp. 270–92.

[2] See Chap. 1, above.

crisis' of 1640,[3] and in particular the meaning and consequences of the two outstanding, and apparently complementary, defeats; those of Antonio de Oquendo's fleet at the Downs (1639), and of Francisco de Melo's army at Rocroi (1643). Were they as final as is still commonly assumed, were they decisive in bringing about political collapse, and do they still deserve reference as appropriate symbols of the breakdown of Spanish hegemony?

With the French entry into the general conflict in the summer of 1635, Spain's strategic problems increased enormously. Her forces and resources seemed already at full stretch, deployed as they were in the Low Countries, southern Germany and Italy, and especially engaged in the maintenance of long and exposed corridors of communication – by land and sea – between these theatres of commitment.[4] France, being situated in the centre of this fragile network, was ideally placed to probe its weaknesses or, if she chose, to attack the dynamo, metropolitan Spain itself. It was partly his awareness of France's strategic advantages which led the conde-duque de Olivares, Philip IV's chief minister, to wrest the initiative from Richelieu and (as he himself put it) to 'stake everything' on a knock-out blow – the joint Spanish–Imperialist invasion of France in 1636.[5] After initial successes, this offensive ran out of steam. Richelieu weathered the storm and by early 1638 was in a position to retaliate. After a feint in the direction of trouble-torn Catalonia, he concentrated his main effort on the Basque country, and invested the important fortress of Fuenterrabía.

The whirligig of war and fortune never spun so furiously as in the frantic exchanges of 1638. The French threatened Milan, assisted by their Savoyard allies, and between them the anti-Habsburg coalition powers achieved a prime target with the capture of Breisach late in the year. With this, the vital link in Spain's Rhineland chain of communications was cut, as it proved for the last time. In his current predicament, Olivares could not consider a serious attempt to repair this shattered flank. It was necessary to preserve, and if possible improve, the other avenue, the seaward passage from the ports of northern Spain to those of Flanders.[6] Besides the threat posed here by the French move across the Pyrenees, the Dutch navy, under its new commander M.H. Tromp, was stepping up its campaign to contain Spanish naval power in the north.[7] Plans were afoot for a large-scale assault on the key ports of Ostend and Dunkirk, possession of which made Spanish maritime logistics

[3] J. Lynch, *Spain under the Habsburgs* (2 vols, Oxford, 1963–69), ii, p. 94.

[4] Essential to this question – and indeed all the issues to be discussed in this chapter – are G. Parker, *The Army of Flanders* (Cambridge, 1972) and J. Alcalá-Zamora, *España, Flandes y el Mar del Norte, 1618–39* (Barcelona, 1975)

[5] J.H. Elliott, *The Revolt of the Catalans* (Cambridge, 1963), pp. 309–10.

[6] Even in late 1636, Olivares reckoned conditions in Germany too unfavourable to permit any further use of the 'Spanish roads'; see 'El Conde Duque sobre lo que se deve disponer para el año que viene de 1637', 1 Oct. 1636, AGS, E 2051, f. 26.

[7] H. Malo, *Les corsaires: les corsaires dunkerquois et Jean Bart* (Paris, 1913), pp. 344–45.

possible.[8] Defence of the sea-lane was vital if Spain was to continue to supply fresh troops and material to the Netherlands, desirable now not so much to defend *las provincias obedientes* themselves as to be able to impede from behind the French designs on the nerve centres of the monarchy in Spain and northern Italy.

Olivares therefore doubled the subsidy earmarked for the support of the highly-effective North Sea squadron, the *armada de Dunquerque*, and began to use it in conjunction with a similar force stationed in Cantabria.[9] Under able and resourceful commanders, these warships registered a series of striking successes. In several expeditions, they ferried 6,000 men to Dunkirk, harried the Dutch attempts to supply by sea the French army in Viscaya, and swept up dozens of enemy prizes into the bargain.[10] Increasingly, the conde-duque began to transfer naval and military resources from the Mediterranean, where French power seemed inert, to the north-western theatre of war.[11] This policy – not to mention that of the Union of Arms – seemed triumphantly vindicated when the siege of Fuenterrabía was raised in August. In a veritable *levée en masse*, supported by a wave of popular enthusiasm, Richelieu's forces were ejected from Spanish soil. A shadow was cast over the victory, since during the campaign the Biscay squadron had been virtually wiped out by the main French fleet, and its admiral. Lope de Hoces, killed at the battle of Guetaria.[12] This significant reversal did not affect the popularity of Olivares, whose stock had never been higher.[13] As one of his staunchest supporters eulogized

> the prudence of His Majesty, and the wise choice of the Conde-Duque as first minister, have brought with them good counsel, complete integrity in the treasury, and the inspiration for valiant deeds of arms.[14]

Not for the first time, Olivares' head was turned by success. In late 1637, in a phrase almost parroted by the king, he had vaguely expounded to the cardinal-infante, Governor of Flanders, the possibility of performing 'some great enterprise at sea' against the power of both Dutch and French, by the

---

[8] See the Spanish intelligence report 'Aviso de la Haya . . . 25 de enero 1637', BL, Add. 6902, ff. 175-78v.

[9] Olivares to the cardinal-infante, 28 Oct. 1637, BL, Add. 14007, ff. 87-90.

[10] *Relacón verdadera de los buenos sucesos y vitorias que ha tenido . . . Don Lope de Hoces* (Seville, 1637). For some fifteen years the armada of Flanders and its privateering auxiliaries had conducted an extremely damaging campaign against Dutch trade and fisheries; J.I. Israel, 'A Conflict of Empires: Spain and the Netherlands, 1618-48', *Empires and Entrepots: The Dutch, the Spanish Monarchy and the Jews, 1585-1713* (London, 1990), pp. 1-41.

[11] The process, which increased in tempo during 1637-38, can be traced in the *consultas* and orders of the war junta and its subcommittees in AGS, GA 1184, 1185, passim.

[12] Alcalá-Zamora, *España, Flandes*, pp. 398-400.

[13] A. Domínguez Ortiz, *The Golden Age of Spain, 1516-1659* (1971) p. 98.

[14] See Virgilio Malvezzi's printed (but untitled) pamphlet in BN, 2370, ff. 339-354v. The immediately anterior volume in this series of *Sucesos de año* (2369) is entirely devoted to a collection of contemporary memorabilia – reports, relations, poems, romances – in celebration of the count-duke and the victory of Fuenterrabía.

concentration of all available maritime resources.[15] This idea was taken up and developed after the interlude of Fuenterrabía. Encouraged by the record of the Dunkirk flotilla in particular, Madrid laid plans for a *gran empresa de armada*, engrossing 'all the ships, money, and men which can possibly be raised'.[16] Initial, optimistic figures were reduced as the time of action approached; but all the same, by August 1639 Oquendo's force comprised over seventy ships and 9,000 Spanish and Italian infantrymen (half as many as sailed with Medina-Sidonia's fleet in 1588), and carried also 3,000,000 *escudos* in silver, a year's payment for the army of Flanders.[17] It was, without question, an amazing achievement in itself, representing to some extent at least a recrudescence of the quantitative standards set during the last years of Philip II. Don Antonio's sailing instructions, however, contained a departure from the tenets upon which Spanish maritime success since 1621, at least in northern waters, had been based. Its contribution to the war-effort lay in surprise attack, privateering and transport, and in the studious avoidance of direct confrontation with the main enemy force. In 1639 Olivares wished to eschew these petty, inglorious and even somewhat dishonourable tactics, and to reassert Spanish prestige by a victory of the kind which had evaded even Philip IV's illustrious forbears. Oquendo, therefore, was to seek out the enemy and draw him into a frontal and decisive struggle.[18] According to the latest authority, an outright and smashing defeat of the enemy had become 'a psychological and material imperative . . . for a nation which had been locked for four years in what would today be called "total war"'.[19]

The result is well-known, indeed depressingly familiar to students of Spain's naval enterprises. After an indecisive engagement in the Channel, Oquendo's fleet was outmanouevred by Tromp and forced to shelter in England's lee – 'the Downs', behind the sandbanks of the Kentish coast – in mid September. There they lay trapped, whilst a prolonged war of words raged in London, until a massively reinforced Tromp attacked suddenly on 21 October, destroying a large proportion of the last armada.[20] Only a year later, another expedition of similar size, despatched (also in 1639) with great hopes of expelling the Dutch from their conquests in Brazil, encountered a tragedy of almost equal dimensions.[21] These two huge operations were the ultimate offensives of any magnitude launched by Habsburg Spain in the attempt to preserve her position in northern Europe and her hegemony in the Atlantic.

---

[15] 'Seria gran cosa . . . dar algun golpe maritimo a Holandeses', Olivares to cardinal-infante, 28 Oct. 1637, above n. 9; cf. Philip's 'es menester que se engruese mucho y que se obre . . . alguna cosa grande contra olanda y francia', to same, 22 Oct. 1637, ARB, SEG 217, f. 361v.

[16] 'El Conde Duque sobre . . . 1637', above n. 6.

[17] Alcalá-Zamora, *España, Flandes*, pp. 89, 429ff.

[18] Ibid., pp. 423–27.

[19] Ibid., p. 406.

[20] C.R. Boxer's inspired account, in his introduction to *The Journal of Maarten Harpetzoon Tromp* (Cambridge, 1938), is still the best available in English.

[21] Lynch, *Spain under the Habsburgs*, ii, pp. 111.

In 1640 the Catalan revolt erupted and the focal point of war switched to the peninsular heartland of the monarchy. During 1642–43 the front lines moved over closer to Castile as French forces poured in to 'assist' the rebellion. Olivares' political career at last broke under the strain, while the king himself donned a breastplate and rode to the front as the supreme exemplar of 'general mobilisation'. With yet another war burning in the rear, along the frontiers of rebellious Portugal, besieged Castile desperately sought relief.[22] For reasons which will become apparent, the governor of Flanders, Francisco de Melo, found himself in 1643 with a strong and confident army, and considerable freedom of manoeuvre. Responding to Madrid's call to take the pressure off Castile, he pushed into French territory and besieged the town of Rocroi. The French army, outwitting Spanish intelligence, made a forced march and trapped the army of Flanders on unfavourable terrain. Faced with a hard-core resistance, determined to die *con espada en la mano*, Condé cut the Spanish pikemen to pieces in an afternoon's work which launched a brilliant career.[23]

The battles were of course greeted with acclamation by the propagandists and pamphleteers of the victorious powers, in the kind of routine celebration which resounds from such clashes of arms in the course of any long and bitter war. The Downs, it is true, was described by one Spanish survivor as 'the worst misfortune which, without the intervention of the elements, the Spanish navy has suffered in history'.[24] As for Rocroi, the seductive prose of Bossuet in his eulogy of 'the great Condé' – 'un jeune prince du sang qui portoit la victoire dans ses yeux'[25] – elevated its status to that of a momentous event of the kind which still, for all the changes of method and emphasis, exercise their fascination upon historians. Rocroi, therefore, 'became the symbol of the decline of a military system which had sustained Spain as a great power'.[26]

During the nineteenth century, Spanish experts fully investigated the central importance of these defeats in the history of Spain's *declinación* and *decadencia*. The military historian Clonard saw the Downs as the key to the seizing up of the Spanish system in its logistical and strategic aspects, a view with which the great contemporary champion of sea-power, A.T. Mahan, heartily agreed. For both, the decadence of Spain's navy was an index of her inability to hold together a geographically diffuse empire.[27] Fernández Duro, whose study of *Armada Española* later complemented Clonard, devoted a chapter to illustrating the importance of Oquendo's defeat, excoriating earlier writers

[22] See (e.g.) Philip to cardinal-infante, 18 May 1641, ARB, SEG 229, f. 84.

[23] C.V. Wedgwood, *The Thirty Years' War* (1938; repr. 1975), pp. 400–4.

[24] J. de Aguilar to J. de Soto, Dunkirk, 15 Dec. 1639, MN, Guillén 1549, ff. 46v–7.

[25] Quoted in J. Boulenger, *Le grand siècle* (Paris, 1911), p. 148.

[26] J.V. Polisensky, *The Thirty Years' War*, (1974) p. 224.

[27] J.M. de Soto, conde de Clonard, *Historia orgánica de las armas de infantería y caballería españolas*, iv (Madrid, 1853), p. 352; cf. A.T. Mahan, *The Influence of Sea-Power upon History, 1660-1783* (n.d. but 1898), pp. 94–95.

who sought to derive comfort from some of its aspects.[28] Meanwhile, and definitively, the eminent figure of Antonio Cánovas del Castillo gave over the second volume of his study of the period to an examination of the antecedents, events and consequences of Rocroi. Though perhaps less unequivocally than Clonard, Cánovas was convinced the battle meant that 'the total decadence of Spanish power was manifest'.[29]

By the time M.A.S. Hume came to write the first modern textbook summary of early modern Spanish history, the significance of the two events was therefore established and beyond question. The Downs, 'ended prematurely Spain's renewed attempt to become a great naval power . . . Spain's hold upon the sceptre of the seas was loosened forever', whilst (with perhaps a suspicion of inconsistency) 'the battle of Rocroy dealt a deathblow to the prestige of the Spanish infantry, from which they never recovered. It was to the Spanish army what the defeat of the Armada (of 1588) was to its navy'.[30] In their classic accounts of the Thirty Years' War, researched and published concurrently in the midst of a similar European crisis of our own times, C.V. Wedgwood and G. Pagès concurred, cogently and unequivocally, with prevailing orthodoxy over Rocroi. For the latter, 'in France, the battle of Rocroi was considered a decisive defeat for Spain, as indeed it was'; to the former, quite simply, 'it was the end of the Spanish army'.[31] Even as late as 1966, an otherwise controversial and revisionist attempt to debunk accepted views of the war could still assert that

> in 1642 and 1643 Guébrier and Condé gained decisive victories over the Spaniards in the Netherlands. The destruction of the largest and last Spanish army in the battle of Rocroy . . . marked the end of Spanish military greatness. Its immediate result was the overthrow of Olivárez and with it, the termination of his aggressive policy.[32]

In the intervening years, a countervailing view was advanced by the distinguished Spanish historian, Antonio Domínguez Ortiz. In 1956 he suggested that Rocroi 'did not have the transcendental significance subsequently attributed to it', and later, in his seminal study of policy and finance under Philip IV, remarked *en passant* that the battle 'did not bring to an end Spanish military power in the

---

[28] C. Fernández Duro, *Armada española, desde la unión de los reinos*, iv (Madrid, 1898), pp. 205–57.

[29] Cánovas del Castillo *Estudios del reinado de Felipe IV* (Madrid, 1888–89), ii, p. 13; cf. Clonard, *Historia orgánica*, iv, 373–75.

[30] M.A.S, Hume, *Spain: Its Greatness and Decay, 1479–1788* (Cambridge, 1898), pp. 242–43, 268.

[31] G. Pagès, *The Thirty Years War* (1939; Eng. edn 1970), p. 208; Wedgwood, *Thirty Years' War*, p. 404.

[32] S.H. Steinberg, *The Thirty Years War and the Conflict for European Hegemony, 1600–1660* (1966), p. 73. There are a number of errors – both of fact and judgement in this extract. A relatively recent Spanish textbook, however, can still glibly repeat Viçens Vives' opinion that 'if any date is significant for the history of a country, that of 1643 is inarguably so for Spain'; M. Avila Fernández et al., *Nueva historia de España*, xi (Madrid, 1973), p. 212.

Low Countries, which was preserved substantially until the end of the reign (1665)'.[33] The deposit of both these statements is clearly identifiable in Lynch's thorough study of Habsburg Spain.

> Rocroi has acquired a legendary reputation as the greatest defeat ever suffered by the incomparable Spanish infantry, and is often taken to mark the end of Spain's military power. But one battle in a war which had already lasted twenty-five years and still had another fifteen to run could not have transcendental significance. There was still plenty of fight left in Spain. Her military effort in the Low Countries did not slacken and ... she managed to maintain her position in the southern Netherlands.[34]

Judgements like these have found an echo in the most recent professional survey of Spain's military record, in which Rocroi is downgraded to 'merely a defeat, similar to those suffered by all the armies of the world'.[35] On the other hand, despite the bland, emphatic nature of such pronouncements, they have thus far remained undeveloped by a process of evidential argument. Their effect has been to strike a note of hesitation and doubt concerning the comprehensiveness and finality of Spain's defeat in 1639–43. The uncertain sound of the trumpet finds a natural response in the ambivalent treatment of the military crisis contained in Parker's trail-blazing logistical examination of the Spanish army of Flanders. He points out that 'not even a defeat as complete as [the Downs] could stop Spain', but later insists that 'the French armies and Dutch fleets cut off almost all contact ... both by land and sea. The supply-routes of the Army of Flanders were all ruptured'. The inevitable result was Rocroi, and 'the end of a legend ... Yet even Rocroi did not end the war'.[36]

Though his own work had stimulated a revival of interest in the maritime aspect of Habsburg imperialism, Domínguez himself latterly implied that the disaster of 1639 was decisive in terms of Spanish strategy, thus agreeing with C.R. Boxer's earlier (if conditional) verdict that 'the last vestiges of [Spain's] power at sea – always excepting the Dunkirkers – had been shattered for good and all'.[37] So far from being 'demythologized', indeed, the significance of Oquendo's defeat has recently been promoted even over the erstwhile glory of Rocroi, by becoming the subject in its own right of an exhaustive documentary study by one of the younger generation of Spanish historians. For Professor Alcalá-Zamora, 1639 represents the failure of a last, supreme effort, based upon a desperate and convulsive sacrifice by dying Castile to obtain an honourable peace and political survival. According to this interpretaion, the defeat at the

---

[33] Domínguez Ortiz, 'Los caudales de Indias y la política exterior de Felipe IV', *Anuario de estudios americanos*, 13 (1956), p. 364; idem, *Política y hacienda de Felipe IV* (Madrid, 1960), p. 64.

[34] Lynch, *Spain under the Habsburgs*, ii, p. 120.

[35] C. Martínez de Campos, *España bélica: el siglo XVII* (Madrid, 1968), p. 113.

[36] Parker, *Army of Flanders*, pp. 78, 261.

[37] Domínguez, *Golden Age of Spain*, p. 99; Boxer, *Journal of Tromp*, p. 67.

Downs was of far greater importance than Rocroi, or (for that matter) than any other setback in Spanish history from the Armada of 1588 to Manila in 1898. It was this, above all, which led to Spain's 'return to the south', to the end of the extrovert 'Spanish Monarchy' and the creation of an introvert Spain, separate and distinct, withdrawn from the mainstream of the European experience.[38]

A decade or so ago the question to be addressed concerning the crisis of 1640 would not have been that of the extent and consequences involved, which seemed well-established, but the apparently incongruous fact that Spain should have been able to resist at all, surrounded as she was by enemies becoming ever more numerous and more powerful, at this stage of her decline. Despite the illumination provided here by much post-war research, Spain's prolonged capacity to absorb punishment, and even to mount what (by the standards of the time) were massive counter-offensives, can still occasion surprise and disbelief. Nevertheless, it may now be timely to progress a further stage in the process of revaluation, and examine the validity of the 'conjuncture of 1640', at least in its military aspect, as the last and decisive crisis in Spain's struggle for power in Europe.

In the late autumn of 1619, a sizeable squadron of twenty-eight royal warships sailed from Cadiz, bound for the East Indies in a bid to prevent further Dutch encroachment on the Portuguese possessions. Not long at sea, it was devastated by storms which sent to the bottom half of the galleons and 4,000 picked troops. 'The loss is very great and much felt here, yet they make show as if they would instantly repair all . . . but for my own part, I think they will hardly be able to do it'.[39] The English ambassador in Madrid who reported thus was, however, wrong. In the early 1620s Madrid devoted much energy to the recovery of the armada, and her maritime establishment expanded rapidly, causing Philip IV to boast (understandably, but somewhat speciously) of the achievement to the cortes of 1623.[40] When in that year Spain's illustrious diplomat, the conde de Gondomar, wailed to Olivares that 'se va todo en fondo' ('the ship is going down'),[41] the *valido* must have felt his correspondent gripped by senile depression. Although Olivares himself was to be similarly afflicted in future years, in 1623 at least the monarchy was demonstrating an unusual command of the European scene. Having thus emerged from the 'conjuncture' of 1618–21, Spain disappeared into another 'interdecennial

---

[38] Alcalá-Zamora, *España, Flanders*, chap. 7 and epilogue.

[39] Cottington to Carleton, 2 Feb. 1620, PRO, SP 94/23, f. 298.

[40] 'La Proposición que el Rey Nuestro Señor mando hacer al Reyno en las Cortes', 6 April 1623, MN, Navarrete 8, ff. 323–332. See also, memorandum for the navy junta, 17 April 1623, BL, Add. 28708, ff. 251–254. The important first initiatives which led to the great recovery of the navy had, in fact, been taken several years before Philip IV's accession; see I.A.A. Thompson, *War and Government in Habsburg Spain, 1560–1620* (1976), pp. 196–99, 295–303.

[41] Quoted in J.H. Elliott, 'Self-Perception and Decline in Early Seventeenth-Century Spain', *Past and Present*, 74 (1977), p. 41.

crisis'[42] in 1628–31, the emergency associated with the war of the Mantuan succession. These critical periods were, of course, accompanied (in ways which were both causative and symptomatic) by economic and fiscal strain. Indeed, it may be argued that 'crisis' was endemic to the monarchy rather than cyclical in nature, with 'structural' dislocation forming a continuous pedal point to political themes and military ostinati.

Be this as it may, in the early 1630s, after failure in the Low Countries and Italy. Madrid decided to put military affairs on a new footing, to tighten up discipline and command organization. In 1632–33 new codes of regulation (*ordenanzas*) were issued by Philip IV, both for 'mis ejércitos' and 'mis armadas', which represented a thorough reform.[43] In this area, as in some others, Spain was not entirely unprepared for the war with France when it began in 1635. To some extent, this administrative shake-up lay behind the string of successes registered by the army, in southern Germany and France in 1633–36, as well as the simultaneous revival of naval power in the North Sea and Mediterranean theatres.[44] The firmer basis it provided may also have helped the monarchy to emerge from the holocaust of 1639–43, if not unscathed, at least with enough left of its resources and strategic capacity – above all, perhaps, morale – to enable it to continue the contest.

What was salvaged in 1639 was a result of the experience of the Dunkirk squadron, recognized by the Spaniards as their elite force, half of which was present in Oquendo's fleet. But the initiative of the admiral himself also contributed to the process. It was Oquendo who shortly after finding himself hemmed in by Tromp, sent the light, fast and well-armed Flemish frigates under cover of night through a passage north around the Goodwins which was too dangerous for the slower and heavier galleons. The Dutch later sealed up this escape route but, in the meantime, the Dunkirkers arrived safely at their home port, thirteen strong and carrying one-third of the infantry (some 3,000 men) and the complete shipment of bullion. 'With this', stated one of Oquendo's staff, perhaps a little disingenuously, 'the object for which this armada was sent was achieved'.[45] The cardinal-infante, Don Fernando, was also impressed.

> Whilst I have no further news [he wrote to his brother in Madrid] I cannot tell how many troops have been landed, nor in what condition . . . But I feel I must

---

[42] The phrase is that of P. Chaunu, who has identified a cyclical series of such crises, linked to the fluctuations in volume of Atlantic trade; see 'The Atlantic Economy and the World Economy', in P. Earle (ed.), *Essays in Economic History, 1500–1800* (1974), pp. 113–25.

[43] See *Ordenanzas del buen govierno de la armada del mar oceano de 24 de Henero de 1633* (Barcelona 1678; facs. repr., Madrid, 1974). For the similar regulations 'para la reformación de la disciplina militar y mejor gobierno de las armas', see Clonard, *Historia orgánica*, iv, pp. 399–405.

[44] A. Van der Essen, *Le cardinal-infant, et la politique européenne de l'Espagne, 1609–41* (Louvain, 1944), p. 327 et seq.; Clonard, *Historia orgánica*, iv, p. 412.

[45] As above, n. 24.

congratulate Your Majesty on the arrival of the squadron, with the considerable supplies of which these provinces were standing in such need.[46]

The success of this operation still left about sixty vessels and 6,000 of the army reinforcements at the mercy of the Dutch. During the attack which followed. Oquendo kept his head, beached a dozen of his command out of range of the enemy fireships and escaped with his flagship and perhaps a dozen others. In early November ten ships were refloated and sent across to Flanders.[47] When the king made a provisional reckoning at the end of the month, he estimated that two-thirds of the infantry had reached Flanders, and that 1,500 had fallen into Dutch hands, with a similar number either killed or as survivors in England.[48]

Philip's figures, it appears, were by no means desperately sanguine. The overall damage, in terms of ships destroyed and precious marine personnel lost, was of course very great; the toll was, perhaps, thirty-five and 5,000 respectively.[49] But although its main task had been so thoroughly frustrated, the enterprise had not fallen far short of its other strategic objectives. The reaction in Madrid was nothing like as furious or gloom-filled as had been the case, ten years earlier, when news arrived of the humiliating disaster of Matanzas. Though naturally anxious for an explanation of the setback, the king ordered a regrouping of forces and promised a full recovery of the maritime situation.[50] In Dunkirk, Oquendo and Don Fernando collaborated on reconstruction, and in early 1640 the former returned to Spain with twenty-four sail ('a strong and well-crewed squadron'), including four new warships built for the king in the Dunkirk shipyards.[51] The admiral was regarded as having emerged with honour; unlike Benavides, the unfortunate victim of Piet Hein's exploit – who had been publicly executed – he did not even lose his command.[52]

Possession of the Flemish ports, and especially the resources centred in Dunkirk, continued to assure the preservation of the sea-link with the Low Countries in subsequent years. As early as the end of October 1639, fresh supplies were reaching Dunkirk from Spain.[53] Between 1640 and the capture of the port by the French in 1646, some 4,000 new recruits were successfully

[46] Cardinal-infante to Philip IV, 15 Sept. 1639, ARB, SEG 223, f. 120.

[47] J.S. Kepler, *The Exchange of Christendom: The International Entrepot at Dover, 1622–51* (Leicester, 1976), p. 65.

[48] Philip to cardinal-infante, 29 Nov. 1639, Cuvelier and Lefèvre, *Correspondance de la cour*, iii (Brussels, 1927), p. 351.

[49] Various modern estimates can be found in Boxer, *Journal of Tromp*, p. 66; Alcalá-Zamora, *España, Flandes*, pp. 454–57; and E. Hambye, *L'aumônerie de la flotte de Flandre au XVIIe siècle* (Louvain, 1967), pp. 66–67.

[50] Philip IV to cardinal-infante, 26 Nov. 1639, ARB, SEG 224, f. 110.

[51] Cardinal-infante to Philip IV, 23 Jan. 1640, ARB, SEG 225, ff. 31–32.

[52] Lynch, *Spain under the Habsburgs*, ii, pp. 74–75; Alcalá-Zamora, *España, Flandes*, p. 456. (Oquendo died shortly after returning to Spain in 1640.)

[53] As above, n. 47.

ferried to Flanders, in exchange for the Walloon infantry needed in Spain, despite the steady augmentation of Tromp's blockading system.[54] By the summer of 1640 Don Fernando's squadron had recovered sufficiently for him to launch one of its periodic, and extremely punishing, attacks on the Dutch fishing grounds off the Shetlands.[55] Flemish privateers continued to inflict serious damage on enemy commerce and, in March 1644, a Franco-Dutch treaty was specifically aimed at the joint reduction of the pestiferous ports of Flanders.[56] Even after the success of these combined operations (Gravelines fell in 1645; Dunkirk in 1646), the point of access was switched to Ostend, communication by sea was maintained, and the 'Spanish system' continued its precarious existence. Though admittedly not on the scale of the 1630s, men and money persistently dribbled into Flanders via this route down to the end of the war, and even in 1668 the traffic was still possible.[57] At the same time, Madrid and Brussels kept up their efficient postal links, and the official correspondence so vital to the exercise of policy showed no lapses in speed or security in later decades from the standards obtaining before 1640.[58] For all these reasons, the funeral of the monarchy was postponed – as it must have seemed to its rivals – to the Greek kalends.

If these facts seem to reduce the significance of the Dutch victory in 1639, it is worth glancing for a moment at the Mediterranean front. Here, in a series of campaigns (to which the Dunkirkers made an invaluable contribution), Spain continued to hold the whip hand. In 1641 Madrid was able to mobilize no less than 128 vessels against the French, and in 1647 the armada proved well up to the task of foiling Mazarin's designs on southern Italy.[59] If, as can hardly be denied, the Downs crushed her aspirations to control of northern waters, Spain remained master nearer home (and, on the whole, in the Atlantic) down to the closing stages of the war.[60]

In the early 1640s, then, the army of Flanders was in relatively good shape, certainly no worse off in most departments than at earlier periods. Though it is true that Madrid gradually realized that supreme priority must be given to the 'home front', the Low Countries were by no means written off.[61] Whilst

---

[54] Cardinal-infante to Philip IV, 28 April 1641, ARB, SEG 228, f. 383; Philip IV to Castel Rodrigo, 6 Feb. 1646, ARB, SEG 235, f. 93. See also Malo, *Les corsaires*, pp. 361–69.

[55] Hambye, *L'aumônerie*, pp. 55–56.

[56] Malo, *Les Corsaires*, pp. 402–3. In 1642, over fifty ships (including twenty-three of the armada) were still operating from Dunkirk, and seven new *capres*, or privateering frigates, were on the stocks; ibid., p. 373.

[57] G. de la Villa to Queen-Regent Mariana, Dec. 1668, MN, Guillén 1291, f. 110. See also Cánovas, *Estudios*, ii, pp. 297–98.

[58] This statement is based on a sample of the correspondence exchanged in the 1650s and early 1660s between Brussels and Madrid, found in AGS, E and ARB, SEG series. See also Cuvelier and Lefèvre, *Correspondance de la cour*, iv (Brussels, 1933), pp. 186–87.

[59] R.C. Anderson, 'The Thirty Years' War in the Mediterranean', *Mariners' Mirror*, 55 (1969), pp. 435–51; 56 (1970), pp. 41–57; Fernández Duro, *Armada española*, iv, pp. 355–74.

[60] Domíguez Ortiz, *Política y hacienda*, p. 64.

[61] *Voto* of Castrillo in the council of state, Dec. 1644, BL, Eg. 340, ff. 108–9.

Castile's forces were bogged down in the defence of Aragonese territory, the strong and confident army of Don Francisco de Melo had great freedom of manoeuvre and the campaigns of 1641–42 went well. Melo was a Portuguese nobleman, particularly anxious for success in order to prove his loyalty and help atone for the attitude of his countrymen towards Castile.[62] In May 1642 he achieved his ambition with the defeat of the French army at Honnecourt. 'Yesterday', he wrote exultantly to Philip, 'God was pleased to grant Your Majesty's army the most signal victory of our times'.[63] The king delightedly concurred, replying in his own hand that 'your services are such that I cannot doubt Our Lord has blessed your endeavours'.[64] The euphoria was justified, for the French left more than 3,000 dead on the battlefield, an equal number fell prisoners, and 500 carts of the baggage train (including the paymaster's chests) were abandoned during the rout. A crack Bourbon regiment, the *Compagnie du Dauphin*, was annihilated. Melo was promptly made a marquis and grandee of Spain.[65]

Few such dazzlingly promising military careers can have been ended so prematurely and abruptly as was Melo's at Rocroi only a year later. The French victory was, to borrow a phrase from another discipline, against the run of play. Like Oquendo's expedition, Don Francisco's invasion of France was an example of the overreach that often comes with confidence and success, rather than a desperate last gamble foredoomed to failure. Whilst wiser heads counselled caution, Melo was acutely aware of Castile's predicament and need for relief in the struggle against rebellion in the peninsula.[66] On the French side, too, Condé's attitude was in sharp contrast to that of his political and military advisers. Honnecourt, the death of Richelieu, and that of Louis XIII only days before the battle – not to mention the uprisings which raged in the rear of the French armies – conduced to apprehension in Paris.[67] But powerful though the army of Flanders was, it had a crucial weakness. Reliance since 1634 on seaward communications ruled out the transport of horses to the Netherlands. Even the insufficient cavalry arm at Melo's disposal was seriously under equipped.[68] As a result, Condé swept them from the field,

---

[62] L. Pfandl, *Carlos II* (Madrid, 1947), p. 22.

[63] CODOIN, 86, p. 36.

[64] Philip IV to Melo, 30 June 1642, Cánovas, *Estudios*, ii, p. 444.

[65] Ibid., pp. 125–36; Hume, *Spain*, p. 267.

[66] Malvezzi to Melo, 11 May 1643, BL, Add. 2845, ff. 233–37; Cánovas, *Estudios*, ii, p. 139.

[67] Boulenger, *Le grand siècle*, p. 147.

[68] Cánovas, *Estudios*, ii, pp. 201–2, which cites Francisco de Melo's opinion that the stronger cavalry arm had been the secret of French success. Deficiencies in this area had not previously been such a tactical weakness, because topographical conditions of war in the Low Countries set cavalry at a discount. During the 'Swedish phase' it became important. By 1633, the cardinal-infante was acutely conscious of the problem; Van der Essen, *Le cardinal-infant*, p. 153. With reference to the general difficulties experienced by Spain in providing cavalry horses (examined in detail in Chap.11, below) it is interesting to note that in the spring of 1643 a vital

continued

leaving the *tercios veteranos* of Castile to fight on stubbornly, unprotected, but disbelieving of defeat – as some reports maintained, for six hours.

> Making a square of their pikes and muskets, they showed no weakness, nor lost time in demonstrating their unity and expertise. The enemy cavalry broke on their resistance, obliging them to bring up their artillery, with which they were battered like a rock, but without causing a failure of composure or discipline.[69]

Only Condé's concession of the right to leave the field in freedom – one forced from him by the onset of night – put an end to the struggle. The monarchy's loss of prestige by defeat was partly compensated by this retention of honour.[70] Moreover, the consequences of Rocroi, both political and strategic, were strictly limited. In the Spanish council of state, the necessity for peace was emphasised, as it had been at intervals for nearly two decades. No special significance was allocated to the battle, and no new diplomatic initiative was launched. As in the case of the Downs, the immediate necessity was to rebuild the army of Flanders – the fixed policy of Madrid to negotiate from strength had not changed with the fall of Olivares.[71] In addition, unlike his distinguished predecessor, the Archduke Albert, who after his complete defeat at Nicuwpoort in 1600 had been replaced as captain general, Melo was not deprived of his command until near the end of a further campaign.[72]

In terms of overall strategy, it is difficult to claim that Rocroi radically altered the balance of power and opportunity in favour of France. In attempting to follow up their victory, the French experienced a serious reverse at Tuttlinghen in Württemberg later in the year – a battle which, though usually credited to the imperialists, was decided by the arrival of a Spanish contingent

---

continued
cargo of saddles destined for the army of Flanders was late in arriving at San Sebastian, and was then held up further by the Dutch blockade of the Dunkirk-Ostend complex; CODOIN, 59, pp. 217–9. On the limitations of military transport via the Channel route, see Alcalá-Zamora, *España, Flandes*, pp. 87–89.

[69] D. Orejón, *Política y mecánica militar para sargento mayor de tercio* (Brussels, 1684), quoted in Cánovas, *Estudios*, ii, pp. 227–28.

[70] *Reputación* and *honor* were related but nonetheless distinct concepts. For their importance in the political behaviour of Philip IV's government, see Elliott, *El conde-duque*.

[71] *Votos* of Oñate, Chinchón and Villahermosa in the council of state on news of Rocroi, 17 June 1643; Cánovas, *Estudios*, ii, pp. 453–67.

[72] Parker states that Melo was 'recalled in disgrace after Rocroi', *Army of Flanders*, p. 282. The assumption is understandable but incorrect. In fact (as Parker himself notes) Melo did not return to Spain until August 1644, when he had completed three years in the governorship – which was the normal minimum for an official of viceregal status. Melo was immediately appointed to membership of the council of state and other important committees by Philip IV. Moreover, the main reason why he was not given a second term of office in Brussels was nothing to do with Rocroi, but was linked to the king's desire to appoint the bastard prince Don Juan José to this position. At fourteen, Don Juan had just achieved his legal majority, which occasion the king marked by officially recognising him as his son; see Philip to Castel Rodrigo, 20 Dec. 1644, CODOIN, 59, pp. 529–30, and Cánovas, *Estudios*, ii, pp. 245–47.

despatched by Melo.[73] Two years later, a Franco-Swedish invasion of Bavaria was foiled by a joint Habsburg army at the second battle of Nördlingen.[74] It is true that both continental and maritime operations remained essentially defensive on Spain's part, at least until the campaign which ended with Condé's repeat performance at Lens (1648). The loss of the Flanders ports, and Spanish defeats on the Aragonese front in 1643–47, may not have taken place if the result of Rocroi had been different, though this is at best speculation and is not, in any case, saying very much. In sum, there is little evidence that either the Downs or Rocroi in itself *vitally* affected the Spanish attitude to the war or their performance in it.

It may be argued, indeed, that more important than either was the defeat of the army sent to put down the Catalan rebellion, at Montjuich in January 1641. This encounter, much less celebrated in the textbooks, *did* bring about a course of events which conduced to the weakening of the Spanish Monarchy's defences. It ordained that the revolt of the Catalans would not be easily suppressed, allowing the principality to secede and, calling on the protection and military aid of Louis XIII, to resist Castile (as it proved) for over a decade. Not only was Spain condemned to a long and debilitating – if ultimately successful – war of attrition within the peninsula; but also the timing of this setback rendered it likely that Madrid would not be able to respond effectively to yet another serious challenge, the almost simultaneous revolt of Portugal (December 1640). In turn, this committed Castile to a further long war – lasting from 1640 to 1668 and this time ultimately unsuccessful – the importance of which in bringing about the final collapse of Spanish hegemony can hardly be overestimated. 'A Montjuich', as Chaunu cogently puts it, 'Olivares a joué et perdu'.[75]

Yet even this significant defeat did not achieve what, in the context of the present discussion, could be construed as a decisive breakthrough for Spain's enemies. Before the end of the decade, the monarchy was enjoying a substantial recovery of its military fortunes. At this juncture, Philip had determined to exploit the opportunities offered by the settlement with the United Provinces (treaty of Münster, 1648) and the worsening domestic situation in Mazarin's France (the Fronde). To some extent, he succeeded in this aim, since Spain turned the tide in the Netherlands and in Catalonia – in the latter case, decisively. Barcelona and Dunkirk were both recaptured in 1652, and the army of Flanders actually took Rocroi itself two years later.[76] It was equally

[73] CODOIN, 86, pp. 156–57; Pfandl, *Carlos II*, p. 45.

[74] CODOIN, 86, pp. 189–90; Wedgwood, *Thirty Years War*, p. 325.

[75] P. Chaunu, *La civilisation de l'Europe classique* (Paris, 1966), p. 109.

[76] Domínguez. *Política y hacienda*, p. 74. The year 1652 was a veritable *annus mirabilis* for Spanish arms, In addition to Dunkirk and Barcelona, the apparently impregnable fortress of Casale in Monferrat, which had provided the core of resistance to Córdoba and Spínola during the war of 1628–30, and had survived Spanish attack on several subsequent occasions, was taken by the marquis of Caraçena; *consulta* of the council of state, 2 Dec. 1652, AHN, E 2815. Two years earlier, the Spaniards had recovered the *presidios* of Tuscany captured by Mazarin in 1646.

remarkable that at Pavia (of all places) in 1655 another Franco-Savoyard attempt to destroy Spain's supremacy in Italy was repulsed with great losses.[77] Finally, in the following year, Condé, now recruited to the ranks of Spain, atoned for his earlier treatment of the *tercios* by leading them to their last triumph, the smashing defeat of Turenne's army at Valenciennes.[78] Spain – or rather Philip IV – failed to take diplomatic advantage, in a mood of quixotic myopia justifiably condemned by Domínguez.[79] After the defeats imposed on the monarchy by the Anglo-French alliance, however, any further chance of negotiation from strength simply disappeared.

It is not in dispute that the 'conjuncture of 1640' represented a serious emergency for the Spanish monarchy. Its intensity was rendered all the greater by earlier 'crises', recovery from which had sapped Spain's strength, leaving scars on 'the Spanish system' and reducing its mechanical efficiency. To revert to a simile very popular with contemporaries, a man who has suffered the shocks of earlier seizures is progressively more likely to succumb to the disease which afflicts him. In the 1640s, as in the tragic period which followed the defeat of the Invincible Armada, military failure was accompanied by rebellion, harvest failure and plague, all further diminishing the material and demographic vitality of the peninsula. Between 1641 and 1646 an angel of death stalked the Habsburg house, depriving Philip IV of his brother, sister, wife and only male heir. As if in sympathy, a wave of mortality swept across all the Mediterranean regions of the monarchy in one of the most prolonged outbreaks of epidemic which lasted from 1647 to 1656. The incidence of population loss since 1599, amongst which must be counted actual military losses – especially those of 1639–43 – had by now drastically impaired the monarchy's capacity to man its defences. Although Castile continued to supply more than its share of conscripts throughout the period of wars with Louis XIV's France (which lasted, with intervals, from 1667 to 1697), from the 1640s on Madrid was searching for new sources of cannon-fodder, in Ireland, Germany and even the Balkans,[80] Meanwhile, a generation of Spanish politicians who had experienced the disasters of the 1640s became convinced that Spain's main priority was to extricate itself from imperial commitments, at least in a European sense.[81]

The attempt to evaluate the consequences of resounding military confrontation of the kind dealt with in this essay is so beset with imprecision and necessarily subjective processes that it is almost a paradigm of the historian's craft. In comparatively few cases are they evident matters of 'fact', clear cut

---

[77] F. Díaz-Plaja, *La historia de España en sus documentos: el siglo XVII* (Madrid, 1957), pp. 330–31.

[78] Anonymous and untitled *relación* of the battle, BN, 2395, f. 203.

[79] Domínguez, 'España ante la paz', pp. 571–72.

[80] A. de Arriola to M. de Revilla, 22 Oct. 1644, MN, Guillén 1291, f. 41; *consulta* of the council of state, 14 March 1656, AGS, E 2087, f. 138.

[81] See Chap. 7, above.

and unambiguous. All the same, when it has become instructive to ask what *might* have happened, if the result of a major battle had been different,[82] it seems all the more necessary to look at what *did* happen, since it was not. The real paradox is that the events of 1639–43, like those of 1588, can tell us more about Spain's strength than about her weaknesses, explaining rather her survival than her decline. In early modern Europe – perhaps unlike earlier and later periods – the complete overthrow and conquest of an enemy, its reduction to the political will of the victor, was not possible for a multitude of reasons. The arbitration of battle was not final nor definitive. Even in the twentieth century, Britain successfully beat off two titanic challenges to her position in the world, but still lost that position and the empire which sustained it. Jutland in 1916, Dunkirk and Singapore in 1940–42, are milestones on the road leading to Suez in 1956 – the time-scale, and much else besides, seems highly analogous to the events here discussed.

Spain's defeat on the field of battle during the crisis of 1640 was in no sense 'decisive', since by this term one understands 'effective in the short term'. During the seventeenth century, the Spanish monarchy was involved in an uninterrupted 'fifty years' War' (1618–68) on many fronts and against many enemies. The Downs and Rocroi took place at only the half-way stage in this epic struggle. That they will continue to be regarded as symbols of Spain's collapse may be, given the nature of our subject, inevitable, but that does not make it any less absurd.

[82] G. Parker, 'If the Armada had Landed', in *Spain and the Netherlands, 1559–1659: Ten Studies* (1979), pp. 135–47.

10

The Spanish Dunkirkers, 1621–48:
A Record of Plunder and Destruction

Following their failure to resuscitate the expiring truce of Antwerp in 1621, Spain and the United Provinces were once again, by definition, in a state of war. In conventional military terms, however, very little happened. In the key fortified towns, garrisons were strengthened, defence works and supplies were attended to; there was some manoeuvring for position by the field armies of both sides. For several campaigns, conditions which might be termed those of a 'twilight war' obtained in the frontier regions which, before 1607, had been the scene of prolonged and bitter exchanges. When, in 1622, something more serious than a skirmish took place, it was fought not between the major protagonists, but by the Spanish army of Flanders against an interventionist force of German mercenaries (battle of Fleurus). The quiet on the western front may be partly explained by Spain's great commitments in Germany at the time, and by the need of Ambrogio Spínola, her commander in the Netherlands, to consolidate his successful occupation of the Rhineland Palatinate.[1] Subsequently, however, Spínola began his programme of operations against strategic objectives, culminating in 1625 in the siege of Breda. Though the surrender of the town was the cause of joyous acclamation throughout the Spanish monarchy, feeling in the central councils of its government was more muted. The evidence suggests that in these quarters, and particularly on the part of Philip IV's chief minister, the conde-duque de Olivares, there was a lack of support for the kind of war represented by Breda. Conviction was growing that its traditional strategy was outmoded and not in line with the best interests of the war effort against the Dutch.

These developments were caused by several factors, of both long – and short – term significance. The Breda campaign itself was viewed with apprehension in Madrid. It was enormously demanding, in terms of men, materials and money, and involved the crown to an unprecedented degree in the raising of war-credits (*asientos de dinero*).[2] It provided the main input to the staggering financial crisis of 1627 which, exacerbated by an acute economic depression and the disaster of Matanzas, triggered off the *conjoncture* which altered the whole course of the Thirty Years War. But such events only confirmed the arguments

[1] C. Martínez de Campos, *España bélica: el siglo XVII* (Madrid, 1968), pp. 81–82.
[2] A. Domínguez Ortiz, *Política y hacienda de Felipe IV* (Madrid, 1960), pp. 19–23.

subscribed to by many Spanish soldiers, politicians, and technical advisers, that conventional warfare in the Low Countries could never bring the Dutch to their knees and was in fact positively counter-productive. Several influential figures had held views of this kind based upon the experience of the 'first phase' of the Flanders wars, since the early years of Philip III's reign. Spínola himself, ironically enough, in large part agreed with them; and they had an influence in the making of the Antwerp truce. Around the time of his advancement to supreme influence in Madrid, Olivares became a firm convert to this belief, and worked consistently to develop his design for a different kind of war – based upon maritime resources, and aimed at the mainsprings of Dutch economic vitality. Accordingly, notwithstanding the Breda campaign, the army of Flanders for the first time relinquished the honour of the military vanguard, and instead provided the anvil for a naval hammer. Not until the major Dutch offensives of 1629–33 was it again involved in serious campaigning; whilst after the entry of France into the war in 1635, both the original combatants were content to observe a kind of unofficial armistice in the landward theatre, which persisted without serious interruption until the final peace of 1648. In complete contrast to the assumptions which have until recently been general concerning the 'second phase' of the Eight Years War, Spain decided to challenge the enemy where he was – at least apparently – strongest, upon the sea, and to a contest over commercial spheres of influence. The greatest land power of the age to a surprising extent transferred its energies to the sea – a phenomenon which can be observed in the Atlantic and the Mediterranean as well as the waters of northern Europe which are the chief concern of this essay.

The beginnings of a reinvigorated naval policy can be traced to the pre-Olivares period. In the years of the truce of Antwerp, dozens of complaints and suggestions were directed to the government of the duke of Lerma on the theme of the general neglect of naval affairs.[3] It is interesting that many of these memoranda were composed by non-Spanish servants of the crown who were inclined to take a more geopolitical view of the Monarchy's affairs than their metropolitan colleagues. Nevertheless, such lobbying coincided with growing apprehension amongst Castilian officials that maritime defences against mounting threats from the Dutch (in the American colonies) and the

---

[3] This paragraph and the next are based (unless otherwise noted) on the following MS material: 'Advertimiento para S.M. y Consejo de Estado año de 1612 de las cosas de Flandes' (Semple), BN, 2348, ff. 13–17; 'Copia de las cartas tocante corsarios y piratas dada en el mes de Henero 1617 años' (Semple), ibid., ff. 531–32; untitled memo by Semple, ibid., ff. 469–73; 'El Coronel Temple [sic] a su Magd. representandole las conveniencias de hazer la guerra ofensiva por la mar a los estados de Holanda y en tierra solo la defensiva' (1619), BL, Add. 14007, ff. 519–523v ; 'Discurso de Don Carlos de Coloma de la forma en que debria hacerse la guerra a los Holandeses' (?1620). ibid., ff. 22–23; memo by Hurtuño de Urízar (Madrid, Feb. 1618), ibid., 36320, ff. 300–302v ; memo by Antony Sherley (Granada, March 1625), MN, Navarrete, ix, pp. 75–124. See also X. Flores (ed.), *Le 'peso político de todo el mundo' par Antony Sherley: ou un aventurier anglais au service de l'Espagne* (Paris, 1963).

North African pirate states (in Mediterranean waters) were grossly inadequate.[4] It was pointed out that the opportunity existed to answer fire with fire, by the use of types of privateering tactics, either in addition, or as an alternative, to rebuilding a fleet of capital ships. An experimental exercise was indeed already being carried out, on a limited basis but with considerable success, against Venetian and Ottoman trading interest in the central Mediterranean.[5] Such had been the growth of Dutch commercial undertakings in almost every direction, accompanied as it was by the atrophy of Spanish shipping and exports, that there now seemed little to lose and much to gain by a resort to economic warfare based upon large-scale privateering activity. The detailed delineation by several experts of the rich, yet exposed and vulnerable trade-routes of the Dutch, which stood in sharp contrast to the close impregnability of their continental defence-system, gave rise to the philosophy of 'guerra ofensiva en el mar y defensiva por tierra'.

In the years immediately preceding the renewal of war with the United Provinces (and expressly in anticipation of that event) a specific programme of maritime/commercial onslaught was elaborated. Among its proponents were Don Carlos de Coloma, a veteran soldier of the Flanders wars, now a senior minister; the experienced administrator Hurtuño de Urízar; the ubiquitous Scots exile William Semple; and the English renegade and advocate of Spanish *Weltpolitik* Antony Sherley. These and other writers recommended what amounted to a 'continental system' for the asphyxiation of Dutch trade, the Dutch economy and, ultimately, Dutch political resistance. For we must be clear that the Spaniards were not merely intent on cheap plunder, nor were they simply aiming at the recapture of an economic position lost since the 1570s. Though these things might turn out to be profitable and successful in themselves, they were in the last analysis means to the end (which remained unchanged) of destroying the Dutch Republic, along with the insidious and widespread danger it represented to the survival of European hegemony and a global empire. Spain, it was suggested, could close the Mediterranean to the Dutch with comparative ease, at the same time embargoing their interests in the Iberian peninsula and prohibiting further commercial contact. Attempts could be made, by the use of river-blockades and other types of harassment, to impede Dutch trade with the continental hinterland – a prospect which later came near to reality with Spínola's capture of several key positions, along with vastly increased Spanish influence amongst the Catholic states of the Empire. More important, however, was to carry the war to the enemy at the sole source of his existence – in the areas of seaborne commerce and (more especially) of fishing. From bases in Flanders and northern Spain, custom-built squadrons of privateering ships were systematically to attack Dutch convoys of

---

[4] See two articles by the late P. Brightwell; 'The Spanish System and the Twelve Years' Truce', *EHR*, 89 (1974), pp. 270–92, and 'The Spanish Origins of the Thirty Years War', *European Studies Review*, 9 (1979), 409–31.

[5] A. Tenenti, *Piracy and the Decline of Venice, 1580–1615* (1974).

merchantmen trafficking with the Baltic or the Indies. Further bases might be obtained athwart Dutch shipping routes in Denmark or in the Scottish islands, either by arrangement or by clandestine use. These latter would be supremely useful for what was considered by most experts as the major undertaking – the destruction by means of surprise raids of the Dutch fishing fleets. The huge aggregations of such vessels which gathered every summer to trawl the shoals of herring around the northern coasts of Britain presented a defenceless yet vital target. Spanish officials and advisers were by now well-informed as to the acute dependence of Dutch civilization upon the matrix industry which fishing represented.

During the opening years of his government, Olivares adopted and implemented in detail the whole of the scheme outlined above. In addition, some time prior to this, a start was made upon the thorough revival of the regular navy, the *Armada del Mar Océano*. Whilst Lerma still held office, the first *asientos* for a programme of galleon-building were made, which went ahead with vigour. By 1622 1,000,000 ducats *per annum* (perhaps some 15 per cent of defence spending) was earmarked for the main armada alone, the *Junta de Armadas* had been revived, and a gleaming new high seas fleet of some eighty sail was in commission.[6] Shortly after Philip IV's accession and the expiry of the truce, this force emerged victorious from its first serious encounter with its Dutch counterpart. This, however, is not the war we are concerned with in this essay. Though the grand classic set-piece exchange of battlefleets retained its importance (particularly in the Atlantic theatre), and remained attractive to strategists (even to Olivares), the European war against the Dutch now devolved upon the considerably less glamorous figure of the privateer. It was a guerrilla war of great bitterness and intensity, made up of a myriad small recurrent incidents and punctuated by occasional acts of ruthless destruction. Though privateering flotillas had been maintained in Flemish ports before 1609, it was only following 1621 that Dunkirk emerged as the headquarters of an official squadron, designed specifically for economic warfare. Moreover, along with Ostend and Nieuwpoort, it became the centre of a new privateering industry which attracted considerable individual capital. In 1622 construction began in Flemish shipyards of a squadron of twenty new frigates. Shortly afterwards Philip IV issued a general call for recruits in a privateering campaign against the enemies of the crown, guaranteeing them excellent material and spiritual inventives.[7] Dunkirk began its rise as 'the Algiers of the North', the major scourge of western European seas – a reputation it was to enjoy in unique and undiminished notoriety for close on a century.

[6] I.A.A. Thompson, *War and Government in Habsburg Spain, 1560–1620* (1976), pp. 196–99; Domínguez, *Política y hacienda*, pp. 19–24.

[7] *La orden que han de guardar los vasallos destos mis reinos* . . . (Dec. 1621, with addenda of Aug. 1623 and Sept. 1624), MN, Varios, ii, pp. 314–17.

As our appreciation of the political importance and strategic context of Flemish privateering (as briefly outlined above) has improved, so also an augmentation of statistical detail has taken place. It may be noted that a reasonably accurate impression of the Dunkirkers' offensive capacity has long been available. In 1913 Henri Malo, the zealous chronicler of their exploits, reproduced a contemporary official table of prize-taking records, covering the years 1627–34 inclusive.[8] For sixty years subsequent commentators have been content simply to repeat these figures.[9] Unlike the assiduous and patriotic Belgian school, Spanish historians were slow to recognize the significance of the Flemish maritime aspect in the renewal of war policy.[10] In the Netherlands, maritime specialists showed little response to Pieter Geyl's comments on this less-than-successful episode in their history. In a study of the Jesuit chaplaincy of the *Armada de Dunquerque*, though he advanced our knowledge of its techniques and organisation, Professor Hambye was not concerned with the assembly and evaluation of statistical data. The same is true of a recent article in which Dr J. Israel, in an otherwise valuable analysis of the maritime-economic dimension of the 'conflict of empires', makes only sporadic and generally impressionistic reference to quantitative factors.[11]

In the past decade, these shortcomings have been energetically tackled in the researches of (appropriately) a Flemish and a Spanish scholar. Considerable additions to our detailed knowledge of Flemish privateering and prizetaking have resulted from the work of Dr R. Baetens.[12] On the questions of the numbers of privateering vessels engaged, and the money value of their prizes, Baetens' extensive tables are illuminating and useful. Still more valuable are his lists of figures which chart the number of prize-takings during the period after

---

[8] H. Malo, *Les corsaires Dunkerquois et Jean Bart* (2 vols, Paris, 1913), i, pp. 333–34. Though Malo correctly transcribed this important document (see Table 1, source 2) as citing the years 1626–34 inclusive, its subscript title clearly refers to the beginning of the re-established Dunkirk Admiralty *at the very end of 1626*. In my own use therefore I have taken its conflated figures for 1626–27 as standing for the latter year alone.

[9] See (e.g.) G. Parker, *The Army of Flanders* (Cambridge, 1972), p. 4 and n. 1; J.P. Cooper (ed.), *The Decline of Spain and the Thirty Years' War, 1609–59* (vol. IV of *The New Cambridge Modern History*, Cambridge, 1971), p. 229; and D. Maland, *Europe at War, 1600–1650* (1980), p. 128.

[10] The pitifully restricted section in Fernández Duro's classic nine-volume history of the Spanish navy, *Armada española desde la unión de los reinos de Castilla y Aragón* (9 vols, Madrid, 1895–1903), iv, pp. 405–14, deals mainly with the Dunkirkers' contributions to the peninsular and Mediterranean campaigns. The special significance of Flanders in this context went unnoticed until the appearance of two pioneering articles: R. Ródenas Vilar 'Un gran proyecto anti-holandés en tiempo de Felipe IV', *Hispania*, 22 (1962), pp. 542–58; and A. Domínguez Ortiz, 'Guerra económica y comercio extranjero en el reinado de Felipe IV', ibid., 23 (1963), pp. 71–113.

[11] P. Geyl, *The Netherlands in the Seventeenth Century*, 2 vols (1961–64), i, 120–23; Hambye, *L'aumônerie*; J. Israel 'A Conflict of Empires' in *Entrepots and Empires* (1990), pp. 1–41.

[12] R. Baetens, 'The Organization and Effects of Flemish Privateering in the Seventeenth Century', *Acta historiae neerlandica*, 9 (1976), pp. 48–75.

1640, and right down to the end of the century. On the earlier phase of the Dunkirkers' activity – so much more important in terms of their relevance to the larger issues of the Spanish war-effort and the Dutch economy – Baetens' work is however less original and less helpful. Here he merely repeats once again the figures published by Malo (giving an aggregate of 1,835 prizes and sinkings in 1627–34) adding some estimates of his own for the subsequent triennium 1635–37.[13] The almost simultaneous appearance of Professor J. Alcalá-Zamora's stimulating study of Spanish naval strategy, set firmly into its 'structural' and economic context, took conclusions on the damage wrought by Flemish privateering a stage further.[14] In particular, Alcalá-Zamora made use of the official report of the Dunkirk Admiralty for the year 1638, in the form published at Madrid the same year.[15] It lists a total of 157 prize units, of which 91 cases specify burthens amounting to 13,000 tons. These figures along with some unofficial (and rather untrustworthy) estimates for the immediately preceding years to be found in various other Spanish sources, somehow lead Alcalá-Zamora to make a 'conservative estimate' of 200,000 tons of enemy shipping captured or destroyed in 1635–38. Baetens' suggestion of 279 *good prize* for the first three of these years (which must be regarded at present as conjectural) would yield a gross tonnage of only 30–40,000 – probably nearer the former. Even allowing for the addition of 1638, and for a (hypothetical) number of sinkings, these two authorities are clearly and seriously at odds concerning the strike-power of the Dunkirkers in the years when, amidst a crescendo of complaints, their depredations had become the most serious political issue confronting the states-general. Alcalá-Zamora, moreover, goes further still in his interpretation. Referring to estimates made by Fernand Braudel of global volumes of shipping in this period, he claims that the Flemish privateers managed to plunder nearly one-third of total European maritime resources, in the space of four years.[16]

Alcalá-Zamora's truly astounding assertion, along with Baetens' more modest proposal, can be examined in the light of information contained in the records of the Dunkirk Admiralty, preserved in the *Archives du Royaume* at Brussels. Both these scholars rightly refer to the unsatisfactory condition of these records for the period in question. Baetens (who has examined them) twice states that there are gaps for the years 1635–41, whilst Alcalá-Zamora (who has not) flatly asserts that 'any statistical exactitude would not be possible in the matter of prizes'.[17] Neither view is entirely valid. The calendar-monthly lists of prize-captures, which were kept in the office of the chief clerk (*greffier*) to the admiralty, seem to me an important source of data, apparently neglected

[13] Ibid., p. 62.

[14] J. Alcalá-Zamora. *España, Flandes y el Mar del Norte, 1618–1639* (Barcelona, 1975), esp. pp. 382–89.

[15] See Table 1, sources 3, 4.

[16] Alcalá-Zamora, *España, Flandes*, pp. 385–89.

[17] Ibid., pp. 76–77; Baetens 'Organization and Effects', pp. 61–62.

by Baetens.[18] Though their information is variable in quality, exactly half of these *somaires des prises* have survived from the decade 1630–39 and provide sufficient basis for a calculated estimation of prize quantities. They are complemented by other registers, some quarterly and some annual (similar to that despatched to Madrid in 1638), against which data derived from the monthly *somaires* can be checked. When collated with yet other (mainly Spanish) sources, these figures permit a statistical analysis of the privateering achievement which both amplifies and modifies recent accounts of the Spanish maritime campaign.

The sixty-one extant *somaires* have their origin in a crisis – part administrative, part financial – which affected the Flanders squadron in 1628–29. Out of this arose a 'reform' of the force, now officially referred to as the *Armada de Dunquerque*. A new and wide-ranging set of operational regulations was issued, superseding those of 1624. Madrid also acceded to the urgent request of the Infanta Isabel (Governess of Flanders) for a separate and exclusive budgeting system for naval subsidies.[19] One of the conditions of the latter was that regular monthly reports should be sent to Spain, covering all activities – whether of the king's ships or the privately-run *particuliers* – which involved a financial consideration.[20] In this way, the *Consejo de Hacienda* hoped to adjust the subsidy according to the fluctuating 'turnover' of the business operated by the *Almirantazgo*.[21] In early 1630 (in fact nearly a year before *Hacienda's* suggestions were finally accepted by the *Consejo de Estado*), the scribes of the *greffier's* office in Dunkirk began to compile the necessary details. Except for a continuous run of entries for the complete years 1633 and 1634, the surviving lists are random, never exceeding a series of four consecutive months in any one calendar year. Another problem is that the entries themselves are erratic in nature, apparently differing according to the practice of individual (Walloon) clerks. Of the type of data about prizes useful to the historian – firm indication of number and of burthen, ports of origin and destination, nature and quantity of cargoes and their respective gross values – only the first category is *invariably* present. These difficulties would severely hinder

[18] ARB, CA 275. From this unfoliated bundle also derives the official table referred to above (n. 8). The lists are all headed 'Somaires des prises et exploits par mer', and are scrupulous in distinguishing between the *armade* and the *navires des particuliers*, a distinction followed here. The records of the Dunkirk Admiralty suffered repeated damage because of the attacks on the port to which its nefarious activities gave rise; see J. Bolsee, *Inventaire des archives des conseils et sièges d'amirauté* (Tongres, 1932).

[19] *Consultas* of council of war, 26 May, 31 Dec. 1630, AGS, E 2044, ff. 43, 122; 'Apuntamentos sobre las quales se podria formar la Instrucción de la Armada' (n.d., ?1631), ARB, SEG 212, ff. 345–346.

[20] 'Tercera Relación de Juan Muñoz de Escobar sobre las cosas de Flandes', AGS, E 2044, f. 40. (The author was a senior accountant in the Madrid treasury.)

[21] 'Primera Relación de Juan Muñoz de Escobar', ibid., f. 38. See also, 'Sobre los medios de poder aderezar y acrecentar la Armada de Dunquerque' (?1630), MN, Navarrete, 8, pp. 167–168v, by Pieter Oppimeer, a Brussels official and businessman.

the gleaning of information which could materially improve our knowledge of European trade or assist our understanding of the financial side of privateering. For the same reasons it would seem (*prima facie*) that these documents are of strictly limited value for the assessment of the *extent* of the economic damage inflicted upon the Dutch. Nevertheless, so significant are these still relatively unexplored topics to the current concerns of the seventeenth-century historian, these records, and others like them may yet be made to divulge vital information. In the meantime the entries permit an exercise which can provide something better than a rough guide to (or 'guesstimate') of the numbers and tonnage of the prizes brought to port, and adjudged to be 'good' by the Dunkirk Admiralty Tribunal, in the decade 1629–38 (Table 1).

Table 1

Estimated totals of numbers and tonnage of enemy prizes brought into the ports of the Spanish Netherlands, 1629–38

	Armada		Privateers		Total	
Year	No. of Prizes	Tons	No. of Prizes	Tons	No. of Prizes	Tons
1629	55	8,470	152	15,808	207	24,278
1630	27	3,782	196	21,088	223	24,870
1631	38	5,582	161	17,212	199	23,064
1632	26	4,388	252	27,204	278	31,592
1633	19	4,210	145	17,196	164	21,406
1634	8	1,114	106	10,042	114	11,156
1635	20	2,100	151	14,834	171	16,934
1636	18	2,604	144	12,972	162	15,576
1637	54	7,804	151	14,238	205	22,042
1638	22	3,962	135	14,568	157	18,530
	287	44,286	1,593	165,162	1,880	209,448

Sources

1. 61 calendar-monthly lists (*somaires des prises* ..) ARB, *Conseils d'Amirauté*, liasse 275.

2. 'Sumaria Relación de la cantidad de presas ... desde ... el fin del año 1626, hasta el fin del año 1634', ibidem. This is the table reproduced in part by Henri Malo (see note 8 to text).

3. *Relación de las presas ... desde principio deste año de 1638 ... Dunquerque 20 abril 1638 ...* (Madrid, printed by Juan Sánchez, 1638). Copy in BN, MS 2369, ff. 78–79v.

4. *Relación de las presas ... desde primero de Mayo hasta último de Diziembre del año pasado de 1638 ... con correo que salió de Dunquerque a los 13 de Henero ...* (Madrid, printed by Diego Diaz, 1639). Copy in BN, MS 2370, ff. 95–96v.

5. *Relación verdadera de las felices vitorias ... desde los primeros de Julio del año pasado, hasta de Marzo de 1638* (Seville, printed by Juan Gómez, 1638). Copy in BL.

6. 'Relación del viage que ha hecho la Armada Real ... enviada al Marqués de Leganés' (1635). *Museo Naval* (Madrid), *Colección Navarrete*, xii, pp. 178–79.

The total of 1,880 such prizes given in Table 1 is, it may be remarked, consistent with the (slightly inflated) figures of 1,500 recorded by the Admiralty for the eight-year period 1627–34. The total tonnage of 210,000 is estimated from a base figure of 71,000 tons recorded for 631 prizes, and cannot be checked against any contemporary computation of total burthens.[22] To these estimates may be added those (considerably less firm) of sinkings on the high seas (see Table 3). These sources indicate that perhaps 500–1,000 vessels (30,000–60,000 tons) were destroyed. From this we may state, with negative caution, that the number of victims of Flemish privateering action in this decade did not exceed 3,000 (300,000 tons).

Table 1 illustrates clearly that the *particuliers* were far more active and successful prize-hunters than the warships of the royal squadron, accounting for nearly 85 per cent of the total number. This disproportion is not quite so marked in terms of tonnage, where the figure is nearly 80 per cent. There are several reasons for this imbalance of achievement. The search for prizes was not the main function of the official squadron, which was allocated several other tactical responsibilities. It was used to convoy the troopships periodically despatched from Spain to replenish the Flanders army.[23] When not thus committed, the armada might support amphibious expeditions striking behind enemy lines.[24] Some of its units were occasionally detached from the home theatre to reinforce the main Spanish fleet in southern waters.[25] Above all, it was frequently engaged in its purely destructive raids upon the Dutch fishing fleet, which (as its advocates had foreseen) had paid enormous dividends since 1625. Indeed, the *Armada de Dunquerque* had become such a superb fighting unit in all respects, that squabbles over its use was a constant feature of correspondence between the authorities in Madrid and Brussels.

[22] See Appendix, p. 232. My figures exclude vessels intercepted and ransomed on the high seas. This was (of course) a common action of the privateers, and clearly involved damage to the enemy, but the sources (at least for the period before 1640) are in my view too sporadic and unreliable to permit quantitative assessment. Baetens ('Organization and Effects') claims to have incorporated ransoms into his prize figures, but in fact his procedure seems somewhat inconsistent. Losses inflicted upon the Dutch were not (it may be mentioned) confined to the totals registered in Dunkirk. The present statistics refer only to captured vessels brought into Flemish ports, plus a small number sold in neutral (mainly English) ports. But in addition privateers operated from the harbours of northern Spain against Dutch trade with France, and (after 1635) against French trade itself; see E. Otero Lana, *Los corsarios españoles durante la decadencia de los Austrias: el corso del Atlántico peninsular en el siglo XVII (1621–1697)* (Madrid, 1992).

[23] F. Graefe, 'Militarische Seetransporte von Spanien nach Flandern (1618–39), *Marine-Rundschau* (1927), pp. 25–33.

[24] In 1636, for example, an attack on Walcheren was made in order to forestall a possible Dutch move against the rear of the army of Flanders during its campaign in France: see CODOIN, 59, p. 66.

[25] In the years following the Dutch success in capturing the Spanish silver-fleet at Matanzas (1628), the Madrid government was desperately anxious to prevent a repetition, and demanded the presence of the whole Dunkirk armada in Spanish waters: see Philip IV's *apostilla* on a *consulta* of the council of state, 15 May 1629, AGS, E 2043, f. 330.

Although the *particuliers* considerably outnumbered the royal warships (between sixty and seventy as opposed to twenty-five to thirty), this advantage was to some degree offset (particularly where prize-burthens are concerned) by the greater size, firepower and general efficiency of the latter. Consequently, when the ships of the armada did bring in a prize, it was usually a more impressive item than the average victim of the privateers. The latter were constantly engaged in the capture of small vessels, such as fishing smacks or coasters, which a royal skipper would either ignore or sink, depending on the circumstances. A factor which reduced the number of captures still further was that the official commanders were instructed to opt for destruction wherever serious doubt existed that a vessel could be safely brought to port.[26] In any case the financial incentives to take risks in this area were much lower for the king's captains than for the privateers. Finally, the *coningsschepen* were generally much better maintained than their auxiliaries, and spent longer periods in dock undergoing repairs and refitting.[27]

The overall figures for the decade reach a peak in 1632 and a trough only two years later. The former, representing 15 per cent of gross tonnage, was due overwhelmingly to the massive haul of 252 made by the privateers in a year when armada returns were beginning to fall away. It is somewhat incongruous, since it comes in a period when only the Dutch merchant marine was a target for legitimate plunder, and when the United Provinces were steadily improving their blockade- and convoy-systems in response to the privateering threat. The sharp decline of 50 per cent (in tonnage) between 1633 and 1634, with the armada's contribution nearly disappearing altogether, seems more explicable. 1634 was the last year in which only one commercial victim offered itself, and the figures may indeed be a result of the very success of previous years, even representing a temporary shrinkage, either in Dutch seaborne trade, or in privateering investment, or both. With the French declaration of war in the early summer of 1635, prospects improved, and by 1637 figures which bear resemblance to those of the early years of the decade had again been attained.

Because of the larger amount of information available, from state sources, about the royal squadron than about the privateers, a more viable interpretation is possible in this limited area. In those years in which the armada was committed to the transport of troops to Flanders the scale of its commerce-raiding operations naturally diminished. Up to and including the Fuentes-Velada expedition of 1636, the commanders concerned were forbidden to make any diversion which might prejudice the primary objective, safe delivery of the *tercios* at Dunkirk.[28] It may be assumed that prize returns for 1634–36 in

---

[26] 'Apuntos sobre las quales se podria former la Instrucción', ARB, SEG 212, ff. 345–346.

[27] On the organisation and technical support-system of the armada, see Hambye, *L'aumônerie*, p. 140ff.

[28] See (e.g.) 'Instrucción al Marques de Fuentes para el viaje que ha de hacer con la armada . . .', 4 May 1636, AGS, GA 3166.

particular were seriously affected by this injunction.[29] In 1637, however, Don Lope de Hoces demonstrated dramatically that the two functions of transport and plunder could be successfully combined, with important effects on prize figures and on the tactical thinking of the conde-duque de Olivares.[30] In contrast to the steady decline of the armada's returns in the first half of the 1630s – a phenomenon which certainly had financial as well as strategic causes – it may be observed that the crisis of 1628–29 had only a delayed effect on them. Alcalá-Zamora, influenced by the outburst of complaints from members of the Brussels government, conveys the impression that the royal squadron languished in the doldrums during these years.[31] In fact, however, it seems that the financial restrictions caused (*inter alia*) by the sudden shift of Madrid's attentions to northern Italy were compensated by the fact that the crown's relative lack of interest in Flanders left its captains free to *faire le course*. In addition to the fact that a substantial profit had been made by the *Almirantazgo* in 1627, giving it an amount of reserve capital, the king's ships were (as it happened) directed in 1629 by Count Waecken, the most experienced and successful commander of the unofficial privateers.[32] It must also be remembered that in 1629–30 the Dutch themselves were heavily committed, to the major land campaign aimed at the reduction of 's-Hertogenbosch, and to the Brazil expedition and the capture of Pernambuco. These factors must have reduced the States' capacity to stem the activities of the Dunkirkers. There is much evidence to argue that privateering thrived when the main naval effort of the enemy was directed elsewhere.[33] In August-November 1639 (for example), when the Dutch concentrated every available vessel on the destruction of Oquendo's fleet, the privateers of Flanders, freed from Tromp's vigilance, had a field day.[34]

Unfortunately, Professor Alcalá-Zamora's treatment of much of this topic is

[29] See the relevant entries in G. Parker's table which charts the sequence and route of reinforcements sent to Flanders, *The Army of Flanders*, p. 279.

[30] *Vuelta a España de D. Lope de Hoces con su armada* (Madrid, 1638), MN, Navarrete 7, pp. 55–55v. Hoces was commander of the Cantabria/Biscay squadron built in the early 1630s as the contribution of those provinces to Olivares' celebrated programme of a 'Union of Arms'. He captured twelve prizes on the outward voyage in September 1637, and a further thirty-two (fifteen of which were sent back to Dunkirk) during the return trip the following March, when his ships were accompanied by twelve Dunkirkers.

[31] Alcalá-Zamora, *España, Flandes*, pp. 286–87.

[32] The sum of 160,000 *escudos* was in the hands of the treasurer of the admiralty at the beginning of 1629, representing the net profit on operations from 27 Jan. 1627 to 31 Dec. 1628: 'Primera Relación de Juan Muñoz de Escobar', AGS, E 2044. Waecken took over from Ribera during the latter's temporary absence in Spain: Malo, *Les corsaires*, pp. 315–17.

[33] This is particularly true of the maritime wars fought by England against Spain, and later France, in the seventeenth century. So much emphasis was consistently placed on large-scale operations in enemy waters that little or no resources were left for commerce protection. For this dilemma, see 'The opinion of several able sea captains to the admiralty commissioners', 9 June 1626, Pepys Library (Magdalen College, Cambridge), MS 2875, ff. 220–222.

[34] Boxer, *Journal of Tromp*, pp. 26–30; Malo, *Les corsaires*, pp. 358-59.

both confused and misleading. He persistently fails to distinguish between the royal ships and the privateers in his description of the maritime-commercial war, a distinction which is germane to the understanding of strategic priorities. In addition his conclusions regarding the important 'reform' of the armada in 1630–31 are, in my view, a misinterpretation. According to Alcalá-Zamora, the discussions in Madrid on this issue were evidence of a renewed interest in the war in the North Sea, which resulted in a 'financial injection' into the Dunkirk Admiralty at the start of the new decade. Consequently there took place 'a new apogee of privateering following 1631',[35] In fact, the 'reform', and the subsequent history of the maritime war should be viewed in the context of an overall strategic situation in which events constantly altered priorities. When Olivares returned his attention to the Netherlands, at the dismal end of the Mantuan War, he did so in a considerably changed atmosphere. The ambitious plans for a strike into the Baltic, coping-stone of his whole North Sea strategy, now had to be shelved (at least for the time being) because of unfavourable developments in Italy and Germany. The early 1630s were marked by more-or-less covert diplomatic exchanges with The Hague, in which suggestions for a renewed truce were under discussion. Signs of political instability in the 'Obedient Provinces' put some premium on these negotiations, which had developed into an official conference by 1632. But the main reasons for the relegation of the Dutch war lay elsewhere. In effect, the decade 1628–37 (almost identical with that which bears the quantitative burden of this essay) was one of shift back to the continental dimension of the war-effort, the Mantuan episode being succeeded by renewed campaigning in Germany (1633–34), and thereafter by the full-scale invasion of France (1636–37) in which the army of Flanders was thoroughly preoccupied.[36]

The Spanish system was thus heavily committed in directions which tended away from the Dutch war and its essentially maritime concerns. The monarchy's increasingly insufficient resources were under appalling strain, despite the extra financial provisions being made by Olivares' government. The Dutch war was now considered as an area of retrenchment, not of additional outlay. In the established military practice of the day, a *reformación* signified a kind of 'economical reform' (what we would perhaps call a 'rationalization') of obtaining organization.[36] In conceding at last to the archduchess's persistent demands for an earmarked and exclusive subsidy for the *Armada de Dunquerque*, the Spanish government was determined to make a virtue of necessity. Far from representing a 'financial injection', the now regularized allowance was conceived as a method of limitation and control, both in a financial and an operational sense. The very fact that the detailed proposals for 'reform' emanated from the *Consejo de Hacienda* seems to give weight to this interpretation.[37] Accordingly (so far as can be deduced from the

[35] Alcalá-Zamora, *España, Flandes*, pp. 325–28.
[36] Parker, *Army of Flanders*, pp. 218–21.
[37] See documents cited in notes 19–21 above.

sparse information available), Madrid's contributions to the armada tended if anything to decrease in amount and reliability in the 1630s.[38] At the same time, Madrid's right to command the use of the squadron for purposes not directly related to the Dutch conflict was strongly asserted, and its ferrying and convoying activities increased steadily after 1630.[39] To speak, therefore, of an apogee of privateering in this decade is misleading, unless it is applied to the exploits of the *particuliers* in 1632 alone. The successful year of 1637 apart, the prize-taking performance of the armada shows a consistent decline from the levels of 1627–29, and (probably) in previous years.

As Spínola himself reminded the commander of the royal squadron in 1626, 'it is vital always to have ships at sea, and particularly while the long nights last, since this is the best time for slipping in and out of harbour'.[40] Winter months were by far the most productive in prize-hunting terms, weather conditions favouring it in many different respects (Table 2). The local topography of Flemish coastal waters, with its continuously shifting maze of sandbanks, compounded the tempestuous climatic environment of the North Sea to make life difficult for Spain's maritime adversaries.[41] In this season, effective blockading of the Dunkirk 'complex' sheltered as it was behind line after line of treacherous shoals, was not possible. Tromp at his most determined and well-supported, in 1637–44, could only cover the period from April to October, and even this was subject to unpredictable interruption.[42] The lesson was learnt the hard way in October 1625, when a terrible storm wrecked a large Anglo-Dutch blockading force, sending to the bottom over thirty of its number.[43] The longer nights, sudden squalls and generally poor visibility at sea rendered the protection of convoys and fisheries, and the detection and pursuit of raiders, far less straightforward than in the (relatively) calmer seasons. In winter, over 40 per cent of prizes were taken, more than twice as much as in summer.

[38] Israel, 'Conflict of Empires', p. 48; Hambye, *L'aumônerie*, p. 143. In 1638, however, *there was* a 'financial injection' as Olivares' thinking returned *a fortiori* to the maritime options, and began to develop towards the ill-fated expedition of 1639: see Olivares to the cardinal-infante, 28 Oct. 1637, BL, Add. 14007, ff. 87–90.

[39] In 1630–32, moreover, the armada suffered serious losses in battle – perhaps as many as thirty units. Although the Flemish shipyards were reaching optimum efficiency in frigate-building, experienced personnel were much more difficult to replace. The squadron's performance in the 1630s was affected; see Malo, *Les corsaires*, pp. 372–73.

[40] Spínola to Ribera, 29 Dec. 1626, ARB, Manuscrits Divers, 3782.

[41] Alcalá-Zamora, *España, Flandes*, pp. 57–59.

[42] Malo, *Les corsaires*, pp. 244–25. So universal was hatred of the Dunkirkers that in 1642 the commander of the English parliamentary fleet cooperated with Tromp against them, contrary to his official orders and neutral role: M.G. de Boer, *Tromp en de Duinkerkers, 1640–47* (Amsterdam, 1949), pp. 162–66.

[43] Alcalá-Zamora, *España, Flandes*, p. 94. The Archduchess Isabel, who was in Dunkirk directing operations, seized the initiative to unleash the aramda on one of its most daring and successful fisheries raids: Isabel to Philip IV, 5 Nov. 1625, ARB, SEG 193, f. 191.

Table 2

Frequency distribution of 161 prizes (20,000 tons) in 1633–34

Tons	Season					
	Spring	Summer	Autumn	Winter	Total	Percentage
0– 50	13	13	7	25	58	36
51–100	4	2	2	13	21	13
101–150	2	4	5	8	19	12
151–200	8	7	9	11	35	22
201–250	3	3	3	4	13	8
251–300	2	0	5	3	10	6
Over 300	1	0	2	2	5	3
	33	29	33*	66	161	
	(20.5%)	(18%)	(20.5%)	(41%)		100%

The entry for *particuliers* is missing for November 1634.

Source: as Table 1, source 1.

Table 3

Dutch vessels destroyed on fishing raids, 1625–37

Year	Month	Number Destroyed	Size of Raiding Force	Commander	Area
1625	October	40-85	12	F. de Ribera	Scottish Isles
1627	May	50	11	C. Jacobsen	Greenland
1627	September	11	5	C. de Waecken	Scottish Isles
1628	?	70–98	?	J. Colaert	Scottish Isles
1632	?	30–100+	?	?	Scottish Isles
1635	August	89	26	J. Colaert	Scottish Isles
1637	August	35–100+	?	S. Rodriguez	English Channel

Sources
1. 'Relation des exploits . . . aux mois de Septembre et Octobre, 1635', C.A.275.
2. As Table 1, sources 2 and 5.
3. Archduchess Isabel to king, 5 Nov. 1625, ARB, SEG 193, ff. 191–91v.
4. E. Hambye, *L'aumônerie*, pp. 23–24, 43–45.
5. J. I. Israel, 'Conflict of Empires', pp. 45–47.
6. J. Alcalá-Zamora, *España*, pp. 203–5, 328.
7. *Cartas de algunos padres de la Compañia de Jesús* (7 vols, Madrid, 1864–65), p. 308.

The relatively low figures for the period March-November recorded in these two years do suggest that blockading was not without effect in restraining the Dunkirkers, despite mounting complaint and protest to the contrary in Holland and Zeeland which was to lead to the wholesale dismissal of the navy high command in 1637.[44] In its prize-hunting aspect at least, the available data constantly demonstrate that privateering as a military/strategic phenomenon moved according to a seasonal rhythm which was exactly the reverse of that associated with campaigning on land. Despite the large numbers of prizes and the important role they played in the economic war against the United Provinces, this did not have the significance for the councils in Madrid which may be assumed. Although anxious to encourage participation and investment in privateering by many other means, the crown itself made no financial contribution towards it, and official influence over its activities in detail was limited. Madrid's fiscal commitment was to the *Armada de Dunquerque*, and the armada (as we have seen) was primarily an instrument of protection and destruction.

Nowhere was the latter function more impressively demonstrated than in the large-scale raiding expeditions against the Dutch fishing fleets. These operations, the planning and execution of which supremely illustrates the talents of the Spanish administration in Flanders, as well as the skill and initiative of Flemish mariners, occasionally led to a veritable holocaust of enemy shipping (Table 3).

In contrast to prizehunting, this aspect of the campaign was confined to the late summer and autumn months, and points up serious weaknesses in the blockading system. Indeed, Fr Hambye states that there were at least fifteen attacks in the quinquennium 1624–28 alone.[45] Unfortunately no official records have survived for this period, and even for the subsequent years there is a shortage of solid and reliable information.[46] All the same, by drawing a considerable number of contemporary estimates together, we can appreciate something of the effort made and success achieved in this quarter. Don Carlos Coloma (amongst others) had always placed great emphasis on operations of this nature as the *sine qua non* of economic war against the Dutch. With the departure of Spínola for Madrid in 1627, Coloma became one of the most trusted advisers of the Archduchess Isabel. By 1628 Olivares himself exhibited close familiarity and enthusiasm with the principles and details involved.[47] In the 1630s the most colourful and successful of royal captains, Jacques Colaert,

[44] Boxer, *Journal of Tromp*, p. 20. In 1635 the expression of grievance over the Dunkirkers' activities seems to have reached a crescendo in the states-general. See the reports of Spanish spies copied in BL, Add. 6902, ff. 179–183v, 188–191v.

[45] Hambye, *L'aumônerie*, pp. 23–4.

[46] 'Hauls' expropriated during attacks on the fisheries were susceptible to exaggerated estimates by contemporaries. I have tried to err on the side of caution in Table 3, and several claims of over 150 sinkings for a single raid have been discounted. Only the figure for the attack of 1635 is attested in the official records of the admiralty.

[47] 'Papel del Conde-Duque tocante de Flandes', 5 July 1628, BN, 2360, f. 73.

became the outstanding exponent of the tactic.[48] Between 1625 and 1637, it is not unlikely that as many as 600 Dutch fishing busses were sunk, a figure which, when added to other recorded feats of destruction in the period, suggests that the overall total of sinkings could have been as high as 1,000. In view of this it may not be imprudent to claim that the Dunkirkers sent one enemy vessel to the bottom for every two which they took as prize.

Perhaps the least surprising statistic which emerges from the Admiralty records is that the majority of prize-victims were of Dutch origin (Table 4). In 1630–34 plus 1638, 234 out of 365 entries in which port of origin is identified hailed from Holland and Zeeland (64 per cent). In the first of these years, Spain was still at war with England as well as France, and by the last France had again been added to the list. These between them accounted for one-third of the prizes. Of course English, French, and German vessels were often taken by the Dunkirkers, even during years of official peace. If such neutrals were found to be carrying Dutch goods, or cargoing war materials to enemy ports, they were sometimes declared good prizes by the Admiralty Tribunal. Equally often, however, they were restored, either because of some technical *desideratum*, or for sound political reasons.[49]

Professor Alcalá-Zamora's reflections on the contribution of the Flemish ports to the Spanish war-effort prompted him to the somewhat euphoric assertion that 'the destructive energy unleashed by the Spanish-directed group (of privateers) against enemy commerce in northern European waters was without question an historical phenomenon of the first magnitude, carried out with implacable efficiency by the most devastating raiding machine, in relative terms, of all time'.[50]

The material dealt with in this essay indicates, it is true, that some of Alcalá-Zamora's suggestions with regard to total figures are wide of the mark. In particular, the estimate of 200,000 tons for 1635–38 is very far from being conservative, and seems rather to be more than a hundred per cent exaggeration (see Table 1). My estimate of 54,000 tons for the first three of these years is, on the other hand, a substantial revision upwards of that suggested by the table

---

[48] Colaert claimed the destruction of 1,000 *buizen* – out of an existing global total of 5,000 – apparently during the 1620s alone. Both figures are wildly exaggerated. As early as 1625, however, Dutch trawlermen were petitioning Brussels to sell them licences to fish undistrubed by the scourge of the privateers, Alcalá-Zamora, *España, Flanders*, p. 202.

[49] See the judicial proceedings over English victims recorded in ARB, Conseils d'Amirauté, 259, passim. Baetens states that English prizes reached a maximum of 19 per cent of the total in 1631, but it seems inherently unlikely, since this was the first year of peace following the Anglo-Spanish war. My figures suggest they reached 42 per cent in the previous year (1630). The data for 1631 are derived from only two monthly lists extant for that year. It may be considered surprising that the overall Dutch percentage here is relatively low. The equivalent English figure is (as it happens) 19 per cent.

[50] Alcalá-Zamora. *España, Flandes*, p. 384.

Table 4

Nationalities of 365 prizes in 1630–34 and 1638

Year	Dutch	French	English	Others	Total
1630	66	7	57	6	136
1631	17	1	0	1	19
1632	35	2	1	2	40
1633	21	7	0	0	28
1634	49	1	11	0	61
1638	46	35	0	0	81
	234	53	69	9	365

Source: As Table 1, sources 1 and 4.

Table 5

Various Privateering Campaigns from 1625 to 1814

Privateering Port(s)	Years	No. of Prizes	Annual average	Enemy
1. Flemish (Dunkirk, Ostende, Nieuwpoort)	1627–38	2114	176	Holland England France
2. English (Channel & North Sea Ports)	1624–30	451	64	Spain France
3. English (as above)	1689–97	483	54	France
4. French (Calais, Saint-Malo, Le Havre, Brest)	1702–13	3180	265	England Holland
5. Flemish (as above)	1702–13	993	83	England Holland
6. Baltimore, USA	1812–14	170	57	England

Sources

1. Table 1, to which the totals recorded for 1627–29 in source 2 have been added.

2. J.S. Kepler, 'The Value of Ships Gained and Lost by the English Shipping Industry during the Wars with Spain and France, 1624–30', *Mariners' Mirror*, 59 (1973), pp. 218–30.

3. G.N. Clark, *The Dutch Alliance and the War against French Trade, 1689–97* (1923), pp. 61–62.

4. J.S. Bromley, 'The French Privateering War, 1702–13', in H.E. Bell and R.L. Ollard (ed.), *Historical Essays, 1600–1750, presented to David Ogg* (1963), pp. 203–31.

5. Ibid.

6. J.R. Garitee, *The Republic's Private Navy: The American Privateering Business as Practiced by Baltimore during the War of 1812* (Middletown, CT, 1977), pp. 243–44.

compiled in Baetens' paper. Nevertheless, despite his failure to consult some important source-material, Alcalá-Zamora's stab at an annual average of *prizes and sinkings* for the 1630s – 250 – is in my view remarkably accurate. In sum, there seems little reason to take serious issue with the Spanish scholar's overall evaluation of the Dunkirkers' achievement. When it is revealed that during over a century of Seville's official trade with the central American colonies (1546–1650), only sixty-two vessels were lost as a result of enemy action, this, and the weakness of the Dutch defence-systems, are thrown into high relief.[51] Equally impressive are the results obtained when we compare the Flemish haul in this period with statistics available in published accounts of other large-scale privateering campaigns in later generations (Table 5).

This exercise illustrates that 'good prize' brought into the ports of Flanders in 1627–38 compares well in absolute terms, and in terms of relative importance (given the steady expansion of European shipping and trade after 1660) appears considerably greater than any similar campaign launched before privateering was outlawed by international treaty in the mid nineteenth century.

For the time being, it remains beyond us to gauge, with any degree of precision, the effect of Dunkirk privateering on enemy economies. Yet while it fell short of some of the grander hopes placed in it, the government of Olivares was surely justified in devoting considerable (and until recently unrecognized) energy and resources to maintaining a naval presence in the North Sea. The modes of warfare adopted seriously discomfited the Dutch, and may have handicapped their economic progress during the second phase of the Eighty Years War.[52] It can moreover be demonstrated in detail that the constant losses of valuable ships, cargoes and personnel in this theatre was a potent factor in persuading the United Provinces to seek a negotiated settlement with Spain, and at times created a dismay which led them to moderate their demands at the conference table.[53] Other authorities have pointed to the severe damage dealt to England's commercial development by Flemish privateering in the two wars of 1625–30 and 1655–60.[54] Down to 1646 (when they captured the port of Dunkirk) at least, the French too suffered a mauling which contributed to the mounting economic distress which lay behind the Fronde. If the index of European economic activity – numbers of vessels engaged, volume and

---

[51] H. and P. Chaunu, *Seville et l'Atlantique, 1504–1650*, vi, pt 2 (Paris, 1956), pp. 876–80.

[52] The second part of this sentence still remains a provisional conclusion. The vigour and number of individual Dutch complaints to the effect that their businesses were vitally affected are impressive but not definitive. Though by one reckoning Dutch trade continued to expand relentlessly during the period 1620–50, its trends are based on the volume and value of insurance business, and thus may actually reflect crisis and even stagnation: C. Wilson and G. Parker (ed.), *An Introduction to the Sources of European Economic History, 1500–1800* (1977), p. 96.

[53] See (e.g.) D. de Saavedra Fajardo to Philip IV, 28 Nov. 1643, CODOIN, 82, p. 6.

[54] B. Supple, *Commercial Crisis and Change in England, 1600–42* (1959), pp. 99–116; R. Davis, *The Rise of the English Shipping Industry* (1962), pp. 26–50.

frequency of trade – can be shown to have resumed a healthy upswing in the period after 1660, the removal of the limitation imposed by the Dunkirkers surely provided at least one of the causative factors.[55]

[55] Prizes continued to be taken in quantity after 1640 but royal interest in the affairs of the Admiralty diminished as military crisis in the peninsula supervened. By 1646, when Dunkirk fell to the French, the armada had been seriously weakened by repeated diversions of its resources to southern waters. Though still nominally in existence as a fighting force, it was used almost exclusively in the Mediterranean, where Spain's greatest need now lay. The privateers were to enjoy a further brief spell of success after the recapture of the port in 1652, and especially against English shipping in the war of 1655–60. But the armada as such – and with it Madrid's naval policy – was finished as a positive counter in northern European strategy. The admiralty was transferred to Ostend following the definitive loss of Dunkirk (1658), but by 1664 it had only four decrepit warships left: AHN, E 107, no.9.

Appendix

A Note on Method

The figures in Table 1 have been restricted to the decade 1629–38, since the detailed *somaires* which survive for the last nine of these years are supported by the printed lists for 1638 (sources 1,3 and 4). In addition, whilst a figure for the number of prizes is available for 1629 (source 2), there is no official evidence whatsoever for 1639. The figures for numbers in 1627–28 were excluded, so as to reduce to some degree the element of hypothesis in the calculations (they have, however, been incorporated into Table 5). As Table 1 stands, therefore, the tonnage columns, and the numbers columns for 1635–37, are based upon detailed information for 61 out of a possible 120 calendar months. The remaining figures (plus that for the total number of prizes in 1638) are not estimates, but the official data given in source 2 (1634 – for which see below – is a special case).

Arithmetical means were calculated and utilised separately for the armada and the privateers, by employment of *all* the data yielded by source 1. Despite the seasonal nature of the 'trade', this method was considered less risky than a computation based on calendar-monthly groupings, since the latter would supply much more limited data and be capable of erratic returns and ephemeral distortion (e.g. the figures for the summer months of 1635, at the entry of France into the war). The means arrived at were (a) Numbers of prizes per month (armada = 2: privateers = 12); and (b) Burthen of prizes per prize (armada = 154 tons: privateers = 104 tons). These figures were then used as coefficients to produce the estimates, as defined above.

The estimated tonnage figures for 1629 – for which no monthly lists exist – are a result of a straightforward application of the burthen coefficients. In six other cases, actual (i.e. incomplete) recorded numbers and tonnage have been augmented by the use of multipliers. For 1633–34, virtually complete numerical data exist, and only the burthen estimate had to be 'built up' from incomplete information. The only major adjustment necessary here was the revision (downwards) of the optimistic *estimate* of 187 privateering captures in 1634 made in source 2. In the case of 1638, the division between armada and privateers of the 157 prizes recorded in sources 3 and 4 was made according to the ratio of 1:6 which all other official sources indicate. Ransoms, recaptures, reclamations, and all other cases in which some doubt existed, were excluded from the calculations.

So long as they are regarded only as *estimates*, it is believed that the only serious weakness in the figures of Table 1 lies in the problem of the prizes recorded in the *somaires* for which burthens were not given. Reason would suggest that these figures were omitted because they were unimpressive and that it is consequently unsound to apply tonnage coefficients to them in arriving at estimates. However, reason would seem to err in a considerable number of individual cases in this category, where the other information provided (such as number of guns, and/or volume of cargoes) indicates a vessel of some note. In any case, the problem is intrinsically insoluble in the context of calculated estimation.

A similar problem occurs with regard to the estimates – which do not pretend to the same level of accuracy – of destructions (see pp. 227–28 of text). Here, it has been assumed that the average sinking was of a relatively small vessel. The multiplier of 60 tons used is of course arbitrary, but was influenced by the fact that as well as many fishing cockleshells and coasters, destructions included hundreds of the type of Dutch deep-sea fishing busses which were of much more solid construction – often well over 100 tons.

The burthen figures actually recorded in the *somaires* are given in *lasts*, a contemporary unit of measurement which was roughly the equivalent of two tons.

In a characteristic French depiction of the battle of Rocroi (1643), the 'great Condé' (then duke of Enghien) is seen in the thick of the fight, whilst the Spaniards flee in disorder or beg mercy from the musketeers.

11

Spain's Military Failure and the Supply of Horses, 1600–60

In Diego de Velázquez's marvellous depiction of *The Surrender of Breda* are displayed the three main elements of Spanish military power at its apogee. They are neatly arranged on the nearer levels of the painting's many perspectives. In the immediate background stands the celebrated line of pikes, which provides the title – *Las Lanzas* – by which the masterpiece is generally known in Spain. They were the unshakeable foundation of strength in battle, and clearly suggest the inexorable weight of human numbers at Spain's imperial command. Closer to the foreground stand the staff officers of the invincible army of Flanders, portrayed quite personally, grouped behind their general, Ambrogio Spínola, marquis of Los Balbases. This is the Monarchy's noble leadership, uniquely gifted in Europe in war and government. But closest of all to the spectator, so close indeed that when viewed (as it were) in the flesh, it seems in its size and movement to demand evasive action, swing the hind quarters of a superb horse.[1] This animal, though doubtless Spínola's own charger from which he has dismounted in order to greet the defeated enemy, is in other respects anonymous, and is rarely the subject of comment. Yet it is, surely, the most impressive of Velázquez's many equine studies, and equally surely does not dominate the Spanish side of this stereoscopic scene by mere accident. Pike, man and horse, the artist seems to be saying, but the greatest of these is the horse.

As a symbol of authority and power, the horse is timeless and universal. By some early civilizations it was actually deified. Later, the riderless horse alone came to represent the physical force of the secular arm in the leisurely recreation of power politics, the game of chess. The animal was germane to the whole chivalric culture of the late middle ages, a creature almost synonymous with hierarchy and caste. As late as Swift's *Gulliver* (1726) it is the metaphorical vessel of a higher grade of being.[2] In early-modern Spain, regard for the horse, if not as a spiritual entity, at least as the essential helpmate of man in war and peace, evidently survived the withering sarcasm of Cervantes in *Don Quijote de la Mancha*. Alongside his creation of *Las Lanzas*, in the 1630s Velázquez executed seven distinct equestrian portraits of the royal family

---

[1] Velázquez's *La rendición de Breda* (c. 1635) is in the Prado Museum, Madrid.

[2] See K. Thomas, *Man and the Natural World: Changing Attitudes in England, 1500–1800* (1983), pp. 100–1.

and of King Philip IV's chief minister, the count-duke of Olivares. Done to the commission of the latter, they adorned the great *Salón de los Reinos* of the new Buen Retiro palace, as part of an overwhelming pageant of civil sovereignty and military might.[3] But at the very moment of this celebration, the reality – in both general and particular – was fading away.

At the beginning of the next decade the Spanish system of military supremacy, having been at war continuously, and on a global scale, for a generation, found itself engaged upon hostilities in some half-dozen different theatres. The annual campaign in the Low Countries was being fought on two fronts since the French declaration of war (1635). The armies of these two main protagonists were locked in conflict in northern Italy. In the Mediterranean, Spain's naval forces faced a further French challenge, whilst in the North Sea and the Atlantic approaches, her armadas continued the struggle with the Dutch. Finally, the political and demographic core of the Spanish monarchy, Castile, confronted its rebel provinces (Catalonia and Portugal) in another two-front war within the peninsula itself. This stupendous conflagration, without exaggeration a total war for millions inside and outside the Spanish system, was in many ways that system's logical conclusion, designed as it was to fight and subjugate in the *conservación* of its dynasty's possessions. But the force and extent of the military pressure which had now built up against the dominions of the Spanish Habsburgs was without precedent in Europe since the demise of Rome. It was, as one official put it as early as 1636, 'a general war greater than any which until now has been waged'.[4] Saavedra Fajardo, the king's envoy to the peace conference in Munster, wrote of 'the earth covered with the flames and smoke of battle, and the fires of Mars obscuring even the view of the Gods'.[5] Indeed even upon Mount Olympus in Madrid a siege mentality developed, with Matías de Novoa describing a monarchy 'inundated with war', and Jerónimo de Barrionuevo 'the ravening wolves who beset us on all sides'.[6] Despite the remarkable resilience of that based upon Castile, no political organization could withstand such an onslaught indefinitely, and the only doubt as to the outcome was the degree of Spain's ultimate failure.

From the moment of Richelieu's declaration of war, the material resources of the monarchy were stretched to breaking-point and frequently beyond. The all-powerful *valido*, Olivares, had prepared with ruthless determination

[3] J. Brown and J.H. Elliott, *A Palace for a King* (1980), p. 141 et seq. In addition, the enormously troublesome and costly equestrian statue of Philip by Pietro Tacca, which today dominates Madrid's Plaza de Oriente, was originally installed (1642) in the prime position in the forecourt of the new palace, ibid., pp. 111–14.

[4] H. de Vallejo (secretary of council of Castile) to archbishop of Burgos, 26 Feb. 1636, BN, 7760/158v. (In all likelihood, however, the expression was coined by Olivares.)

[5] D. de Saavedra y Fajardo, *Locuras de Europa*, ed. J.M. Alejandro (Salamanca, 1973), p. 34.

[6] M. de Novoa, 'Historia de Felipe IV' (part IV), *CODOIN*, 86, p. 185; Paz y Melia, *Avisos de Barrionuevo*, i, p. 181.

for this trial of strength, but by 1640 the shortfalls in almost every important sector of war-supply – from manpower to matchlocks – were critical. 'There is the most urgent lack of all necessities', wailed Olivares, floundering in the wake of the Catalan rebellion,[7] and reference to the *falta de medios* from now on became ubiquitous in the official documentation of every level of the military machine. The rapid thinning in the ranks of Spain's armies led to a frantic search for foreign recruits by the councils of state and war. Attempts were made to hire men *en masse* from Ireland and the Ukraine, and to bring them to bear on the major battle fronts.[8] Agents and contractors spread far and wide in a promiscuous quest for artillery, shot, small arms, powder; ships, masts, oars, rope. Every conceivable kind of military equipment was in demand, and at a premium, in a continent which, during this decade, was at war, *omnium contra omnes*, virtually from end to end.[9]

The supply of horses was no exception to this general famine, but it was nevertheless surprising. Unlike the components of the list just presented, the monarchy was normally regarded as well-endowed in this respect.[10] In 1645, during his grand tour, John Evelyn 'at the Viceroy's Cavalerizzo' in Naples 'saw the noblest horses that I had ever beheld, one of his sons riding the menage with that address and dexterity as I had never seen anything approach it'.[11] Then, as now, Spaniards prided themselves on their horses and horsemanship. The vast aristocratic latifunda of Andalusia and Naples nurtured horses in quantity and quality, and the arabian-type steeds of the southern Mediterranean had always been a feature of Spain's warmaking. In purely functional terms, however, this feature, in the course of the sixteenth century, had become more decorative than essential. At least until the 1620s, when Olivares successfully promoted the navy to equal prominence and status, Spanish military power rested firmly on the infantry *tercios*. These priorities faithfully reflected the nature of the wars which had been fought since the 1560s – either at sea, or in restrictive terrain densely studded with modern fortifications, like Flanders and northern Italy.[12] Though doubtless useful at times, the cavalry arm was rarely the decisive element. In land campaigns the set-piece of siege and march dominated, and in the relatively few cases of pitched battle in open field, the solid forest of pikes and arquebusses, by discipline, experience and numbers, almost never failed to set an enemy's

---

[7] *Voto* of Olivares, Sept. 1640, AGS, E 2055.

[8] See Chapter 12, below, and R.A. Stradling, *The Spanish Monarchy and Irish Mercenaries: The Wild Geese in Spain, 1618–68* (Dublin, 1994).

[9] See (e.g.) *consulta* of the *Junta de Ejecucción* (and enclosures), 7 Jan. 1640, AGS, E 2055; Philip IV to M. de Salamanca, 10 Feb. 1640, AHN, E 963, ff. 168–169 (see also ff. 25, 29, 33); Luis de Haro to Salamanca, 19 Aug. 1645, AHN, E 966, f. 169.

[10] V. Vázquez de Prada, *Historia económica y social de España: los siglos XVI y XVII* (Madrid, 1978), p. 440.

[11] W. Bray (ed.), *The Diary and Correspondence of John Evelyn* (1905), p. 103.

[12] See C. Duffy, *Siege Warfare: The Fortress in the Early Modern World* (1979), pp. 23–24, 58 et seq.

advantage in horse at a discount. No cavalry assault, however rapid in deployment or skilled in manoeuvre, had ever caught the *tercios* napping.

Of course, horses were necessary in considerable numbers for tasks more mundane than the cavalry charge. Many hundreds were employed in the armies of the period for the carting of siege machinery and baggage trains. Over forty were needed to pull and supply each of the largest guns, the 5,600 pounders essential to pulverize an obstinate fortress.[13] But for these purposes the heavy breeds of the northern countryside were commonly utilised as more suitable than the lighter barbaries and jennets reared in the Mediterranean provinces. To return to the cavalry arm, it is notable that over nearly fifty years of the wars in Flanders (1584–1631) a mere 1,029 units were transferred thence from Italy, compared to over 100,000 foot soldiers.[14] It was just as well that cavalry were rarely called upon by Alba, Parma and Spínola, because in any case the problems inherent in transporting horses from the southern regions of the two peninsulas to the cockpits of the north were all but insurmountable. The horse is both a bulky and a hungry animal. Transport by sea was enormously costly and wasteful of space, and the routes across the Alps, especially following the extensive detours made necessary by the closing of the regular 'Spanish Road' around 1600, were daunting. Getting an army successfully across the precipitous Valtelline, or a squadron of troopships safely into Dunkirk, were precious feats in the face of constant enemy harassment. Horses were a distinct liability in the event of attack (especially at sea), and a commodity of limited value at the point of delivery.[15] During the whole of Spain's so-called 'Eighty Years' War' in the Low Countries, cavalry represented only 5.75 per cent of the total number of units so transferred.[16]

The prospect of major war with France in the early 1630s rapidly altered Madrid's attitude to these circumstances. Not long after the end of the undeclared and limited war in Italy (1628–31), which so clearly prefigured a general conflict, Olivares ordered an inventory of the stores of cavalry equipment available in the peninsula.[17] The use of cavalry by the Swedish army on the north German plain was currently attracting attention, since the engagements of Breitenfeld and Lützen had dramatically exposed the weakness in this respect of the German Habsburg and League forces.[18] It

---

[13] The Seigneur de Praissac, *The Art of War* (1639), cited by J.U. Nef, *Western Civilization since the Renaissance: Peace, War, Industry and the Arts* (New York, 1963), p. 242.

[14] The figures are based on G. Parker, *The Army of Flanders* (Cambridge, 1972), pp. 278–79, which provides data on 'Spanish and Italian Troops sent to the Netherlands, 1567–1640'. Here and elsewhere I have assumed that the figures given for cavalry signify both horse and rider.

[15] J. Alcalá-Zamora, *España, Flandes y el Mar del Norte, 1618–1639* (Barcelona, 1975), pp. 87–89.

[16] Figure based on Parker, *Army of Flanders*, pp. 278–79.

[17] Lists of equipment by V. de Frías, Madrid 16 Jan. 1632, BPU, Favre 71, f. 115.

[18] C.V. Wedgwood, *The Thirty Years War* (1957), p. 237 et seq.; J.F.C. Fuller, *The Decisive Battles of the Western World and their Influence upon History* (3 vols, 1954–56), ii, pp. 59–64.

was in the aftermath of these events that the Spanish generals, the duke of Feria and Don Fernando de Austria, who were training armies in Lombardy in readiness to move across the Alps, successively complained of shortages of cavalry horses which could not be made up from resources *in situ*.[19] Though the Swedish army itself was the immediate adversary of both these expeditions (and both in the event prevailed), the flaw was all the more important because the forces concerned were ultimately intended to provide the backbones of two larger armies. These latter, the army of Flanders and an army of the confederate Habsburgs and their allies, along with yet a third based in Catalonia, were intended by Olivares for a wholesale invasion of France. It was evident that campaigning on this scale would involve cavalry activity far exceeding that which Spanish armies normally utilized, especially since the military objective was not to capture towns and territory (as during the earlier invasions of France in the 1590s) but to inflict utter defeat by pitched battle upon the forces of Louis XIII.[20] The logistics of France's wide open spaces were in radical contrast to those of Flanders; and cavalry would be important not only in deciding battles, but for rapidity and depth of penetration, foraging and screening, and also for liaison between the separate invading commands. With an enemy able to move along interior lines of communication, Spain's armies would have to supplant the slow inexorability of their traditional march with something of the mercurial Swedish tactics of movement. In the years between the defeat of the Invincible Armada and his invasion of France in 1591, the duke of Parma had doubled the strength of his cavalry arm. Late in 1633 the marquis of Aytona received orders in Brussels to build up his cavalry department as quickly as possible, and bans were imposed on the export of horses from the Spanish Netherlands.[21] Accordingly, the cavalry component in the army of Flanders increased from 7,648 (10.75 per cent of the total) in 1633 to 14,095 (a record 18.2 per cent) ten years later.[22]

Writing to his envoy in Vienna, the count of Oñate, in December 1634, Philip IV insisted that the joint Habsburg army scheduled to invade central France should be well provided with horses. In his view, the intended ratio of 5 : 1 (infantry to cavalry) was woefully inadequate, and even the suggested

[19] A. Van der Essen, *Le cardinal-infante* (Brussels, 1944) p. 153. In the early summer of 1633, only 1,780 cavalry were available in Lombardy out of a total force of nearly 18,000, ibid., pp. 112–15.

[20] The evidence for Olivares's planning of a multilateral assault on France in 1634–35 is set out in Chapter 5, above. In January 1635 he devoted much of a statement at a meeting of the council of state to outlining a project for hiring up to 20,000 so-called 'cossack' horsemen, who would not only compensate for the Spanish deficiencies in this areas, but also terrorise the French into rapid submission; *consulta* of 16 Jan. 1635, AGS, E 2049.

[21] Aytona to Philip IV, 14 Dec. 1633, BRB, 16149, f. 109v; V. Brants (ed.), *Liste chronologique des edicts et ordonnances des Pays-Bas, règnes de Philippe IV et de Charles II* (Brussels, 1910), p. 46.

[22] Figures based on Parker, *Army of Flanders*, pp. 271–72.

ideal of 3 : 1 probably too weak.[23] It would be preferable, the king argued, even to reduce the overall size of the army (planned as 40,000) in order to be able to afford more cavalry, 'because of the bias in favour of horse in the ranks of our enemies'.[24] In Spain itself, however, it was already clear that whatever the financial rationale, horses were – suddenly and simply – not available. In April 1635, a few weeks prior to the French declaration of war, contracts were still being made for the supply of horses for the army of Catalonia, designed for a diversionary attack upon southern France, and (at least nominally) to be commanded by the king in person. These were to come from the north African *presidios*.[25] But they were not sufficient, and at the same time Philip actually ordered *his ambassador in Paris* to purchase as many horses as he could: 'you are to buy them in the name of the count of Sora, and as his property have them brought to Spain, without letting it be known they are for me in order to avoid problems'![26] The sudden failure of indigenous sources to provide on the new scale of demand was, it seems, a cause of puzzlement in Madrid. At the breeding season of 1633, the king told the marquis of Jódar, one of the many middle-ranking Andalusian nobles whose estates were notable for stud, that 'for some years past the rearing of horses in those parts has suffered a great diminution', and charged him with making enquiries into the causes thereof.[27]

By the time Olivares brought the problem of vanishing horses to the attention of the *Junta de Execucción* in July, 1641, the situation had become crippling.[28] The invasion of France (along with a huge maritime offensive against the Dutch) having failed, Spain was forced onto the defensive, a position exacerbated by successful rebellions in Catalonia and Portugal in 1640. That the armies of Aragon and Extremadura, the main forces confronting the rebels on their frontiers, were desperately short of cavalry can be deduced from the fact that large shipments of horses were on their way from Denmark.[29] At the same time negotiations were proceeding to obtain supplies from Poland, whose king had offered not only a Cossack army of 10,000 for hire but

[23] The ratio of 5 : 1 was that normally prescribed in Spanish armies in northern Europe in these years; see the collection of *relaciones* on the strength of the various component parts of the army of Flanders, BN, 18196, ff. 9–13.

[24] Printed in H. Günter, *Die Habsburger-Liga* (Berlin, 1908) pp. 429–34. As for the army of Flanders, 'we need more infantry if we invade the rebel provinces and more cavalry if we campaign in France', as M. de Salamanca, the Brussels secretary of state succinctly put it in 1637; quoted by Parker, *Army of Flanders*, p. 11.

[25] *Asiento* with the count of Salazar for 400 horses, April 1635, AGS, E 2050, no. 161.

[26] Philip IV to C. de Benavente, 30 April 1635, AGS, E K1425, no. 147. (The title of 'Sora' seems to have been fictitious.)

[27] Philip IV to Jódar, 27 Feb. 1633, RAH, Salazar 934, f. 75.

[28] *Consulta* of the *Junta de Execucción*, 13 July 1641, AGS, GA 1375.

[29] *Consulta* of the council of state, 28 Aug., 1642, AGS E 2522. Alonso de Cárdenas, ambassador in London, had reported the passage of nine ships (?500 horses) through the English Channel in late June.

an additional 6,000 horses for sale.[30] The upshot of the junta meeting was the issue of commissions to a group of agents who were to scour Andalusia for suitable mounts.[31] Meanwhile, there occurred the first defeat in battle which was specifically attributed to an absence of cavalry – the notorious setback of Rocroi (May 1643).[32] The councils in Madrid accepted this, Francisco de Melo's own explanation of the defeat, and an official report noted that although trained cavalry troopers were available, 'the key shortage is that of horses'.[33] Only the duke of Nájera resisted this excuse in the council of state, maintaining 'there is no need to alter the use of cavalry which always brought us victory in the time of his majesty's glorious ancestors'.[34]

As long as the war with France continued, however, this factor played its part in limiting Spain's capacity for resistance. It affected the making of peace as well as the waging of war, for in 1644 Saavedra Fajardo in Münster complained that, whilst he could not manage to despatch a single courier, the French ministers had a stable of sixty horses at their constant disposal.[35] Following the blows dealt to the monarchy's communications network by the loss of Breisach (1638) and the naval defeat in the Downs (1639), it became impossible to supply horses to the Flanders theatre even had the desire to do so existed. But in any case the peninsular fronts now assumed priority, and Madrid concentrated upon filling the gaps in the armies engaged against the Franco-Catalan forces in the Levant.[36] Here, at least, assistance was forthcoming from the Italian dependencies. In six months of 1645–46 alone, 2,000 horses reached Valencia from Naples and Sardinia; this relief made its contribution to the successful campaigns which culminated in the fall of Barcelona and the extinction of the Catalan revolt in 1652.[37]

In this period the horse was an enormously expensive item both to purchase and to maintain. In 1644 a good cavalry mount cost about 45,000 maravedís on delivery, but only two years later this had increased to over 61,000 – more than twice that of a black galley slave and twelve times that of an

---

[30] *Consulta* of the council of state, 18 April 1640, AGS, E 2055, in which the deal with Poland was approved in principle.

[31] Accounts of F. Alonso Lozano et al., 1642–45, AGS, CMC 1969, nos 5–8.

[32] Cánovas, *Estudios*, ii, pp. 201–2. It is possible, however, that the army of Flanders' lack of cavalry on this signal and momentous occasion was due to a shortage of harness rather than horses; see above, p. 208 and n. 68.

[33] 'Papel que se escribió sobre las levas ... y otras cosas', 22 Oct. 1643, RAH, Sal. 1070, ff. 301–310.

[34] Quoted in L. Pfandl, *Carlos II* (Madrid, 1947), p. 42.

[35] Saavedra Fajardo to Philip IV, 4 April 1644, CODOIN, 82, p. 24.

[36] *Voto* of count of Castrillo, Dec. 1644, BL, Eg. 340, ff. 108–9. See also *consultas* of the council and juntas of war, winter–spring 1644–45, AGS, GA 1567.

[37] Admiral of Castile to Philip IV, 5 Feb. 1646, AGS, E 3272, no. 13; Gayangos, *Cartas*, vi, pp. 35, 97, 134.

Irish infantryman.[38] To this outlay had to be added the costs of fodder, shoeing and stabling, leaving aside the equipment of the rider.[39] In these years, demand from the English civil war armies doubtless helped to push up prices, perhaps in Andalusia as well as Flanders. By 1652 Brussels was proclaiming the voluntary donation of a horse for army use as 'preuve la plus certaine du zèle au service du roi'.[40] The crisis eased somewhat later in the decade, when only the Portuguese war provided pressure on Spanish sources of supply. Preparing its army for the major offensive against Portugal in 1659, the government had to pay 51,000 maravedís each for horses which were already saddled and harnessed.[41] During the campaigns which followed on Castile's western frontiers, Philip's armies were comparatively well off in cavalry.[42] In quantitative terms, at least, this factor could not be blamed for the ultimate disasters of the Spanish system and the loss of Portugal (1668).

The failure of horse-rearing in Castile appears to have been coincidental with its demographic losses in the half-century 1600–50, and to have a parallel – though of course not equal – significance amongst the reasons for the overthrow of Spain's European power. To some extent a certain community of causes can be surmised. Expenditure of the Andalusian and Neapolitan products in intensive warmaking was common to both human and equine

---

[38] Account of L. Díaz, recording payment of 445,000 maravedis for eleven horses in Morón de la Frontera, spring 1644, AGS, CMC 1969, no. 5. Two of them were of such poor quality that they had to be returned; *asiento* between P. Pacheco (for the council of the treasury) and A. Piquinoti, 16 Feb. 1646, AGS, CJH 900. For costs of galley-slaves, see *consulta* of the treasury council, 23 March 1640, AGS, CJH 806; for Irish levies, *asiento* between the earl of Berehaven and C. Mayo, 20 Dec. 1647, AGS, E 2523.

[39] A hard-worked horse required at least one pound of grain a day per 100 lbs weight, that is to say above five times as much as the average soldier. According to a French observer, Spanish horses were severely underfed in the early part of the century; Braudel, *The Mediterranean*, i, p. 241. Once again in the mid 1640s they had to compete on unequal terms with human mouths for their barley, since harvest failures were increasing in Spain. Naples, Sicily and Sardinia had to supply feed as well as horses for the Catalan campaigns; royal decree of 29 Sept. 1644, AGS E 3270; Gayangos, *Cartas*, vi, p. 16. The companies of Philip IV's palace guard who escorted him to Zaragoza complained bitterly of the impossible expenses of keeping their mounts fed in the middle of the army of Aragon's headquarters, *consulta* of royal household committee, 12 Aug. 1644, APR, A 2923.

[40] Brants, *Liste*, p. 97. Horses were in desperately short supply in the British Isles during the whole period of the civil wars. When Charles I tried to raise an army to fight the Scots in 1638, they could not be obtained at any price. After 1642 the royalist armies imported them in considerable numbers from the United Provinces.

[41] *Consulta* of the treasury council, enclosing *asientos* with the house of Cortizos for 500 horses for the army of Extremadura, 25 Jan. 1659, AGS, CJH 1108.

[42] The army of Extremadura had 5,000 cavalry mounts in its total of 21,000 effectives in 1657, though the other two (smaller) armies operating against Portugal from Galicia and Old Castile were somewhat worse off; see *Relación de la famosa victoria . . . en la recuperación de la fuerte villa de Olivenza . . .* (Seville, 1657), BN, 2385, f. 140. In the same year it was reported that (apart from Condé's command) only 1,000 cavalry were available to the army of Flanders; 'Relación . . . del exercito de Su Mgd. . . .', AGS, E 3860.

cases, though in the latter (as we have seen) it seems not to have taken place in the ultramontane campaigning, and to have been confined to the period after 1638, when the crisis had already been identified.[43] Being a domesticated animal dependent on human attention and cereal crops, the horse was bound to be affected by the periodic harvest failures which were suffered by Castilian agriculture, particularly the prolonged famines of the 1590s, 1620s and 1640s. To some degree, the horse and its master shared the same destiny. Verily, it might be said, 'that which befalleth the sons of man befalleth beasts . . . as the one dieth so dieth the other: yea, they have all one breath'.[44] Yet other and more particular causes can be identified. These are linked to macroeconomic change in Castile, and to the culture of its urban life and ruling class.

The consummation of Castile's political ascendancy over the whole of the Iberian peninsula in the century before 1580, the simultaneous growth of its cities, and the acquisition of European and Atlantic empires, vastly extended and intensified the use of roads for commercial, administrative and strategic purposes.[45] As late as the 1590s, a spate of road- and bridge-building took place in response to the mushroom population increases of Madrid and Seville.[46] But the roads and tracks which converged upon the capital, linking it with other urban centres, were as generally bad as they were long. Arduous in themselves, especially in extreme weather conditions, they also passed across large semi-arid plains and traversed formidable river and mountain barriers. In the transport of bulky commodities – wool, leather, ore, grain in civilian trade; supplies and equipment in military movement – the horse proved a relatively expensive and inefficient instrument. As a drawer and pack animal, the mule was increasingly preferred as hardier and more docile. Before 1550, it was estimated that 400,000 mules were in use as beasts of burden, and this number certainly increased during the rest of the century.[47] Castile's association of carters (*Cabaña Real de Carreteros*) also increased in influence, which reached a peak precisely in the period 1600–1650. Olivares himself cemented the policy of protection of the carters' privileges when, in safeguarding several different political and strategic interests, he granted them a special court and a *juez conservador* in 1629.[48] The first half of the sixteenth century also witnessed the

[43] But it was nevertheless appalling. In 1641, for example, the marquis of Velada described in graphic terms how deserters from his army on the Dutch frontier – especially Portuguese levies intent on returning home to join the Braganza rebellion – were stealing horses to effect their escape or else killing them in order to impede pursuit; Velada to count of Fontana, 8 July 1641, BPU, Favre 39, ff. 35–40.

[44] Ecclesiastes 3: 19.

[45] Vázquez de Prada, *Historia económica*, pp. 480–87.

[46] D. Ringrose, 'The Government and the Carters in Spain, 1476–1700', *Economic History Review*, 2nd series, 22 (1969), pp. 45–57 (at p. 51).

[47] Braudel, *The Mediterranean World in the Age of Philip II* (2 vols, 1972), i, p. 284, citing A. de Herrera, *Libro de agricultura*. (It is unclear from Braudel's text whether this figure was given in the original edition of 1513 as well as that of 1547.)

[48] Ringrose, 'Government and the Carters', pp. 52–54.

widespread replacement of oxen by mules before the plough, an improvement that helped to stimulate the extension of cultivation and the augmentation of cereal production in response to the growth of population.[49] It is not, therefore, surprising that by the time the famous knight of La Mancha set forth on his travels early in the reign of Philip III, the mule was ubiquitous on the highways and in the countryside of New Castile.

It follows inevitably that the breeding of horses should suffer a decline through this process, since in the great majority of cases mules are produced by the mating of a stud-jackass (in Spanish, *garañón*) with a mare (*yegua*). Whilst the mare carries a mule, she cannot (obviously) be carrying a foal; and the more the volume of trade expanded, increasingly centred as it was on the nexus of Seville and the Andalusian hinterland, the more the mares of the noble stables were engaged in the business of the merchant and the civil servant rather than in their more natural and aristocratic occupation. (In more than one sense might it be said with Quevedo that *poderoso caballero es Don Dinero*.)[50] This threat to the horse had been identified in Andalusia before the turn of the century, according to Braudel, and in 1602 the citizens of Naples were forbidden to employ mules to pull private carriages.[51] In 1638, however, Olivares' government rediscovered it with some surprise, and the king informed the marquis of Jódar that 'it is understood some horse-breeders are permitting the jackass to impregnate the mares (*hechar el garañón a las yeguas*)'. Madrid was evidently anxious to limit or discourage this distressing practice, and the marquis was asked to report on where, and by what licence, he knew it to obtain.[52]

In the breeding of mules we have one important long-term reason why that of horses ceased to flourish as before. But this and the factors earlier mentioned taken together remain insufficient to explain the failure of domestic production to supply Spain's war-needs, a failure which became obvious little more than a decade after the renewal of full-scale conflict in 1621. What turned a serious problem into a critical one was (I suggest) a more concentrated contemporary increase in several horse-intensive leisure activities. These, and in particular bullfighting and hunting, were associated with the sudden efflorescence of the Habsburg court in Madrid, its numbers of personnel, ritual and festivities, in the first quarter of the seventeenth century.[53] Both the hunt (*caza*) and

[49] Braudel, *Mediterranean*, i, p. 426. Herrera gives a figure of 600,000 mules engaged in farming, making a (suspiciously neat) total of one million.

[50] Though traditionally attributed to the contemporary writer Quevedo (1580–1645), this Spanish version of 'money is power' has a much older proverbial history, deriving from a medieval *refrán*.

[51] Braudel, *Mediterranean*, i, pp. 284–5; Vázquez de Prada, *Historia económica*, pp. 440–41.

[52] Philip IV to Jódar, 2 June 1638, RAH, Salazar 934, f. 77v.

[53] On the expansion of the court (and its expenses) after the death of Philip II, see A. Domínguez Ortiz, 'Los gastos de la corte en la España del siglo XVII', in *Crisis y decadencia de la España de los Austrias* (3rd edn, Barcelona, 1973), pp. 75–96. For its culture, Brown and Elliott, *A Palace*, passim.

the bullfight (*corrida*) were originally local aristocratic diversions, small in scale and with important social overtones, but they were taken up to an unprecedented degree by the court of *los Austrias* during the period of the duke of Lerma's *valimiento*. The young Philip III – like his most celebrated subject, Don Quixote – was passionately devoted to the chase, and was followed in his addiction by the burgeoning court nobility. Hardly less devoted than his father to this recreation, Philip IV was also Spain's greatest *aficionado de toros*. Both pastimes received official encouragement – not least from Olivares – on the grounds, no mere rationalisation, that they provided peerless training in the quasi-military skills of equitation, as well as inspiring initiative and courage, essential requirements of a vital warrior caste engaged in the defence of imperial Spain.[54] In contrast to most other aspects of the count-duke's *razón de estado*, this was found to be convivial to the aristocracy of Castile and the people of its cities.

Providing the wherewithal for the royal hunt was the major responsibility of the smaller (though elder) of the king's two coexistent households, the *Casa de Castilla*, and in particular of Olivares' brother-in-law, the marquis of Alcañices, as *cazador mayor*.[55] Under this supervision, three periods of the court's annual season were given over wholly to hunting in the forests and plains of the *patrimonio real*, each of them of eight days duration.[56] Its enjoyment was not confined to the gentlemen of the royal entourage, for the ladies joined in as spectators, and occasionally as participants, like Cervantes' duchess, more forward than her husband to meet the charge of the wild boar.[57] Nor was it limited to these periods alone, or to the court, for what was done by the king must surely be multiplied fifty or a hundredfold in consideration of the nobility, many of whom reserved large tracts of their estates solely for this purpose.[58] The money and attention lavished on hunting lodges and parks under Philip III and his successor provides a special feature of the two

[54] Olivares to President of Castile, 18 Sept. 1631 and his 'Memorial sobre la crianza de la juventud española' (1632–35), Elliott and de la Peña, *Memoriales*, ii, pp. 81–83, 87–98. The context and rationale of Olivares's ideas on this theme receive detailed examination by the editors (ibid., pp. 63–73). For the *valido's* support for bullfighting, expressed in typically brusque and minatory terms to the rector of the Madrid Jesuit college, whose opinion was otherwise, see G. Marañón, *El conde-duque*, p. 681.

[55] The spiralling costs of the hunt led to a move to transfer payment of the *cazadores* from the accounts of the *Casa de Castilla* (where it dominated the budget) to those of the *Casa de Borgoña* which enjoyed an allocation some twelve times greater at c. 500,000 ducats p.a.; see AHN, Hac. 7885, f. 94v. For more precise figures and analysis of the royal household in this and other areas, see R.G. Trewinnard, 'The Household of the Spanish Habsburgs, 1606–65: Structure, Cost and Personnel' (unpublished Ph.D. thesis, University of Wales, 1991).

[56] Justi, *Velázquez*, p. 210.

[57] M. de Cervantes, *The Adventures of Don Quixote*, trans. and ed. J.M. Cohen (Penguin edn, 1950), pp. 693–95.

[58] This avocation did not disappear with the passage of time. In the early years of the present century the dukes of Medinaceli still devoted 15,000 hectares of good farming land to the hunt; P. Vilar, *Spain: A Brief History* (1967), p. 70.

reigns.[59] It was a feature consciously emphasised and recorded by Philip IV, again through the medium of his court painter Velázquez, who worked on a series of portraits of the royal family as hunters – Philip himself, his younger brother Don Fernando, and even his infant heir – in the years 1624–34. During the frantic building programme of the 1630s, dozens if not hundreds of paintings and tapestries were commissioned from the Rubens studio for the royal hunting-places like the Torre de la Parada, all exploiting various mythological aspects of the chase. One of the most popular of all hunting manuals, Juan Mateos' *El Origen y dignidad de la caza*, appeared around this time, and many a contemporary map illustrates that Castile was still replete with bear, boar, stag and wolf.[60] The deforestation of the landscape, which was proceeding apace, made it easier both to concentrate and to pursue these animals in parks like the royal *fincas* at the Pardo (just outside Madrid), Aranjuez (some 40 miles south) and Valsain (near Segovia). Hunting became more systematic and efficient than ever before, as the grand panoramic scenes painted in Velázquez's studio vividly demonstrated, and the king and his *valido* outshone most of their contemporaries in the sport.[61]

If hunting by the court represented perhaps more an organized and intensive revival than a novelty in itself, the reverse was the case with bullfighting. Though of little less antiquity in the peninsula, since it was admired in the ancient Iberians by their Roman conquerors, the *fiesta nacional* was officially recognized and enormously patronized under Philip III and his son.[62] Though not constructed principally, nor reserved exclusively, for this purpose, the Plaza Mayor of Madrid, completed by 1619, became under Philip IV the principal bullring of Spain. The rise in popularity of the *corrida* at this juncture was in every way sensational. The attention of Spain's foremost political philosopher, the Jesuit thinker Juan de Mariana, was drawn to the phenomenon, which in his treatise *De spectaculis* (*On Public Entertainments*,

---

[59] In Nuñez de Castro's celebrated description of seventeenth-century Madrid, we are told that the court spent one month each at the Pardo and Aranjuez, and a slightly shorter sojourn at the Escorial. At all three, much of the time was given over to hunting; *Sólo Madrid es corte* (2nd edn, Madrid, 1669), p. 36.

[60] Mateos' book was published in Madrid in 1634. The Spanish government's *Dirreción general de promoción de turismo* currently (1983) issues a brochure on *Hunting Spain*, in which the availability of these victims (with the exception of the last) is lavishly illustrated.

[61] Philip IV was reputed to have slaughtered well over a thousand of these wild creatures in his lifetime, as well as hundreds of bulls; Justi, *Velázquez*, p. 212. The pursuit of both pastimes is partly explained by Philip III's need to contrast the young and active milieu of his court with that of his deceased father. But the habits had been difficult to eschew even for the moribund king; we are informed – with a little exaggeration – that 'Philip II in the very last days of his life went on a wolf-hunt in the Sierra de Guadarrama' (actually, in August 1597, more than a year before his death), Braudel, *Mediterranean* i, pp. 400–1.

[62] 'Las corridas de toros en el reinado de Felipe IV según documentos originales e inéditos', in A. Rodríguez Villa (ed.), *Curiosidades de la historia de España* (3 vols, Madrid, 1886), ii, pp. 274–345.

1609) he condemned as degenerate and morally corrosive.[63] Little heed was paid to Mariana's strictures. By the time of his death in 1624, the bullfight was almost a weekly event in the capital, and many such occasions were honoured by the presence of the king and of Queen Isabel (the latter not even absenting herself when in an advanced state of pregnancy).[64] The government itself was obliged to take over much of the organization of these events, since places were zealously sought after, and the advantage of a courtier's position, particularly his proximity to the royal balcony, was of some importance to his social standing.[65]

It was during the reign of Philip IV that the earliest manuals of *el arte de torear*, subsequently to become the perennial and most hackneyed genre of Spanish literature, first appeared. These culminated in Gregorio de Tapia's *Ejercicios de la jineta* (*The Horseman's Exercises*, 1643):

> where one can find [in the words of a later commentator] illustrated pictorially the skills of the Spaniards in running the bull with their fiery steeds, and which a few years earlier the court was amazed to witness an Englishman attempting to imitate on his clapped-out nags.[66]

The specific reference here is almost certainly to an incident during the visit of the Prince of Wales and the duke of Buckingham to Madrid in 1623. This unexpected (and unwelcome) six-month sojourn was marked at intervals by extraordinary *fiestas*, at one of which no fewer than twenty-two bulls were despatched.[67] This figure was unusual, though twelve to sixteen victims was not uncommon.[68] At this time, of course, the bull was usually fought from horseback. The power, speed and ferocity of the fighting bull confronted in these spectacles can be gauged from its triumph in combat with a lion, a tiger and a bear in the arena of the Old Palace (*Alcázar*) of Madrid in October 1631.[69] Even in modern times, in a practice which was allowed to persist

[63] A. Soons, *Juan de Mariana* (Boston, 1982), p. 91. Mariana's title and subject-matter were a reference to similar works by earlier Christian writers such as Tertullian and Cyprian. The Vatican had condemned bullfighting in 1567.

[64] A. González Palencia (ed.), *Las noticias de la corte de Madrid en los años 1621 hasta 1627* (Madrid, 1942), pp. 36, 41, 60.

[65] Rodríguez Villa, *Curiosidades*, ii, pp. 298ff, gives lists of place-allocations for a royal *corrida* of 1648. For this purpose a junta met under the chairmanship of the president of Castile himself – sufficient indication of its importance.

[66] N. Fernández de Moratín, *Carta histórica sobre el origen y progresos de las fiestas de toros en España* (Madrid, 1777), pp. 20–22.

[67] González Palencia, *Noticias*, p. 57.

[68] At the *fiestas* of St Isidore (patron of Madrid) in 1639, eighteen animals were butchered in one *corrida*, and several contemporary prints and drawings suggest that this was not a rare spectacle; Pellicer, *Avisos históricos*, ii, p. 17. But the average, at least for fights outside the capital, does not seem to have exceeded the number (six) which became standard in modern times. 'Over two hundred' bulls were put to death in thirty fiestas during celebrations all over Spain for the canonisation of Teresa of Avila in 1615; Rodríguez Villa, *Curiosidades*, ii, p. 279.

[69] Brown and Elliott, *A Palace*, p. 215.

until the fall of Primo de Rivera in 1930, the bull would normally kill the horses of the two *picadores*, so that it may be held certain for the seventeenth century that at least one horse died for every bull.[70] Mariana, indeed, dismissed the defence of the bullfight which pleaded its encouragement of the breeding of fine horses, on the grounds that most of them ended as victims of the *cornada*.[71] The same thing was often true of the chase, especially that of the wild boar, which (in one instance) 'defended himself like a lion and ripped up all the horses'.[72] In the pursuit of stags and wolves, too, horses were regularly ridden to death.[73] The impression is received of the continuous and ritual slaughter of the Spanish horse, not just upon the ever-multiplying fields of battle, but as the casual by-product of the entertainment of a whole society.

Madrid, *corte de la monarquía*, was the scene of continuous festivals in which the horse was an essential participant. The *fiesta* for religious or state occasions, of which bullfighting was a regular feature, was also invariably celebrated by a kind of team-joust (the *juego de caña*) and by interminable processions in which the presence of the court aristocracy and the royal guard was indispensable. 'There was not a single hack in the vicinity of Madrid which did not take part', reported a witness of these events in 1636.[74] The ubiquitous use of horses in Madrid highlights one of the central policy dilemmas of Philip IV and Olivares, which can be observed in nearly every area of their government. In a sense it represents a conflict between *reputación* and *conservación*, the need to defend both the physical dimensions of the monarchy and simultaneously its prestige in the sight of Europe.[75] The court of Madrid had to continue to display itself as the most ostentatious and wastefully splendid in the world, yet also had to supply the resources to resist assailants who were (perhaps unsurprisingly) no whit deterred by the demonstration.

The ingenious *hidalgo* Don Quixote had a suggestion to put to Madrid about the pressing needs of defence.

---

[70] On the killing of horses in the *corridas* of the 1920s, see E. Hemingway, *Death in the Afternoon* (paperback edn, 1977), pp. 63–69.

[71] Soons, *Mariana*, p. 131.

[72] Quoted in Justi, *Velázquez*, p. 212.

[73] In modern Spanish, a phrase which conveys doing something at breakneck speed is a '*a mata caballos*'. A report of 1643 claimed that the regular military training of a cavalryman accounted for two or three animals; 'Papel que se escribío sobre las levas . . .' (above, n. 33).

[74] Gayangos, *Cartas*, i, p. 418. The 440 men of five discrete companies of palace guard were mounted from the king's stables, which came under the *Casa de Borgoña*, and were the official responsibility of Olivares himself, as the king's *Caballerizo Mayor* (Horsemaster General); Nuñez y Castro, *Sólo Madrid*, pp. 128–29. In 1627 the veterinary surgeon in this important department received the substantial sum of 302,000 maravedis for wages and the cost of his materials. We should not derive too positive a conclusion from this, however, since the same man also doubled as chief farrier. Thus the farrier-vet (as is only logical) seems to have been the cavalry equivalent of the notorious barber-surgeon of the tercios; C. Sigoney to the treasury council, 2 Dec. 1628, AGS, CJH 654.

[75] See Elliott, *El conde-duque*, pp. 59–100.

If (His Majesty) were to seek my advice, I would counsel him to take one precaution which is far from occurring to his majesty at present.

Experience has shown (replied the Barber) that nearly all the plans presented to His Majesty are either impracticable or ridiculous, or would do positive harm . . .

But mine (answered Don Quixote) . . . is the easiest and most proper . . . that could occur to any planner's imagination . . . what more is there for His Majesty to do than to command by public crier all the knights errant who are wandering about Spain to assemble at the capital on a fixed day . . . and if they did, His Majesty would find himself well-served at great saving of expense.[76]

However impracticable or ridiculous this *arbitrio*, the flight of Cervantes' fancy stopped on the desk of that inveterate planner, Olivares. In the middle of the 1640 crisis he was moved to adopt an expedient not utterly dissimilar, when in a mood of desperation he decreed the mobilization of the entire knighthood of Castile in the war against the Catalan rebels, in compliance with their immemorial obligations to the crown.[77] Doubtless, *inter alia*, he hoped they would bring their horses with them, in a great saving of expense. In the meantime the native horsebreeding industry was ruined, or at least it lapsed into the situation of most other war-related sectors of the Spanish system – an inability to supply to the numbers and standard required by the state. By the late seventeenth century it was the lately despised English strain of animal which was most admired and sought after, and which was to help win so many of Marlborough's battles.[78] If the magnificent specimen of *Las Lanzas* remained the ideal, *Rocinante* was the more accurate prophecy.

[76] Cervantes, *Don Quixote*, pp. 472–78.

[77] Philip IV to Jódar, 3 June 1641, RAH, Salazar 934, ff. 81–83. See also A. Domínguez Ortiz, 'La movilización de la nobleza castellana en 1640', *Anuario del derecho Español*, 25 (1955), pp. 799–823.

[78] D. Chandler, *The Art of Warfare in the Age of Marlborough* (1976), pp. 53–55. See also J. Thirsk, *Horses in Early Modern England: For Service, for Pleasure, for Power* (Reading, 1978), pp. 24–28.

PHILIPP·S IIII. HISPANIAR· REX·

I. de Courbes F.

IMPERIVM SINE FINE FIDES ASSERTA PARABIT:
ASSERO, ET IMPERIVM,NON MIHLSED FIDEI,

Philip IV. In this engraving, also from the 1620s, the Walloon artist Jean de Courbes depicts Philip in the king's own deeply desired role, as a military hero directing his men in battle. The caption reads: 'The Faith defended will prepare an empire without end. I defend it, and claim the empire, not for myself, but for the Faith.'

12

Filling the Ranks: Spanish Mercenary Recruitment and the Crisis of the 1640s

> We see by experience that great things are done only by princes and republics with
> their own forces, while nothing but disaster comes from the use of mercenaries.
>
> (Machiavelli, *The Prince*)

Spain's struggle for Europe involved limitless liability in terms of resources and belief, of duty and sacrifice. When considering the title theme of the present volume, it seems appropriate not to overlook those who did the actual struggling on a primary level – the field of battle. The armies which were raised to defend the monarchy and its 'Universal Cause' during the prolonged military crisis which dominated the middle decades of the seventeenth century were of dispersed, motley and even exotic origins. During the reign of Philip IV – a long one, in which there was not a single day's respite from war – native-born Spaniards were an ever-contracting minority in the ranks of his armed forces. By the 1640s, less than one in four of the men enlisted under Philip's *banderas* – perhaps 50,000 out of some 220,000 – was a native of the peninsula. Yet we know relatively little about the basic principles upon which foreigners (that is, by far the greater proportion) were recruited and under which they served.

For a proper contextual understanding of the nature of the Spanish Monarchy, various questions need to be addressed. I have already used the words 'Spaniards' and 'foreigners'. What did these terms mean in differential practice when it came to trailing a pike for king and cause? Of course perception of national identity was indistinct and inchoate by modern standards. But, when it came to the barracks square (*plaza de armas*), who were 'Spaniards'? Were all individual Spaniards equal in the ranks of the common soldiers, and were they collectively more equal than others? Were Neapolitan levies considered to be in the same category as Poles or Irishmen, or were there subtle grades of such 'otherness'? Were some non-Spaniards regarded as full members of the Monarchy, in contrast to those who enjoyed only associate status, formed auxiliary cohorts, and were therefore not able to claim '*Civis Hispanus Sum*'? If – as it often could be – national identity was a flexible category, was the same true of confessional allegiance? What role did religion play, especially when the military crisis of the monarchy arrived at its point of resolution in the mid 1640s? To these questions, few unambiguously meaningful answers can be given in the present state of knowledge. In search of some provisional understanding, my review of past musters will concentrate upon the resonances in the Spanish system created by the prolonged battle which may be regarded as the nodal point of the great Franco-Spanish War; the five-year siege of the Catalan town of Lérida in 1643–47.

In 1647 the celebrated English astrologer William Lilly published his predictions for the fate of the various European countries during the year. His view of the Spanish monarchy was both sympathetic and optimistic:

> The Starres have cast their malevolent influence on that brave people for some years: hold up thy head but two years [more], and then hope well; at present I feare more losse unto thee: If the fate of Kings runne as other mens, thy King hath much to doe: yet is not the Monarchy of Spaine speedily determinable; it follows but not precedes; nor shall France rejoyce at thy harmes unrevenged.[1]

Writing about this same year of 1647, Philip IV's chief groom of the wardrobe (*ayudante mayor de cámara*), Matías de Novoa, noted in his journal that:

> Everywhere we are surrounded with anxieties, so that we are never able to draw breath, and our enemies threaten us with ever crueller and more bloody wars, with the aim of finishing us off altogether. Our money is exhausted, or at least we have much less than is necessary.[2]

Spain's fortunes certainly hung in the balance between stars and gods. The year 1647 was – or was to prove – the median year of the great Anglo-French War of 1635–59, from which France emerged as Spain's successor and the leading power in Europe. In the campaign of that year the French army in Catalonia was determined to capture Lérida, which it correctly identified as the axis of victory. The town commanded the main passage leading over the River Ebro, from western Catalonia into Aragon. It lies only 70 kilometres from Zaragoza, and little over 100 from the borders of Castile itself. In the hands of the Franco-Catalan forces, Lérida offered a superb base of operations for Catalonia's war of secession, and an ideal *point d'appui* for a push into Castile. Potentially, it was a dagger pointed at the heart of the monarchy. Almost as soon as they were able to take the offensive, following their crucial victory at Montjuich (1641), the enemy concentrated their forces upon the capture of Lérida. Contrariwise, so utterly critical was its retention that Spain worked desperately to defend it. The council of state even encouraged Francisco de Melo, commander of the army of Flanders, in his plan to ease the military pressure in Catalonia by causing a major diversion on the northern front. The result was Melo's ill-starred invasion of France and his defeat at the battle of Rocroi. The sacrifice of the army of Flanders – and of *reputación* – was all the more painful because it proved pointless, failing to prevent the fall of

---

[1] W. Lilly, *Merlini Anglici Ephemeris: A Modest Prediction upon the present Affaires of Germany, Spaine, Italy, France and United Provinces* (London 1647). The prediction was made in a year which, in the apt words of one recent commentator on Lilly, witnessed 'the zenith of astrological influence in England'; J. Henry in the *Times Literary Supplement*, 4 April 1986.

[2] CODOIN, 86, p. 306 (published as *Historia de Felipe IV*).

Lérida later in 1643. The following year, however, the town was recaptured for Philip IV, following a successful campaign by Felipe de Silva. For three years thereafter it stood as a loyal outpost inside rebel territory, and was thus obliged to endure a more or less permanent state of siege.[3]

Traditionally, the siege is a fundamental trope in the writing of cultural and national identity. Homer's *Iliad*, the earliest serial European history, can be perceived as being prepared with such objectives, being located around Troy and Mycenae, the *polis* under pressure. Many of the great sieges of the seventeenth century were immortalized by tradition, and have likewise provided the subjects of celebrated works of art or literature as well as textbook narrative: from the Thirty Years' War period alone, Breda, La Rochelle, Casale, Magdeburg, Drogheda, even Fuenterrabía, have taken their place in history and legend. Yet in Spanish historiography, despite a certain bias towards the mythology of Numantia, the siege of Lérida has attracted little attention. Perhaps the explanation for this is a reluctance to confront the reality of how close Spain as an entity came to defeat, dissolution and historical oblivion – 'the end of History' – in the 1640s.[4]

In November 1646 the French were again forced to retire from the walls of Lérida, after a seven-month siege. Little wonder that the town came to be a symbol of the monarchy's survival. It dominated the international scene to the point where Mazarin – who was, at the time, struggling to supervise massive French assaults on the Spanish monarchy, in the Netherlands and the Mediterranean as well as the peninsula – decided to award the honour of humbling Lérida to the victor of Rocroi. He calculated that if any general could guarantee this essential breakthrough, it was the Prince de Condé.

The winter of 1646–47 was perhaps the most intense and frenetic period of military preparation which even a society like Castile's, on a permanent war-footing, had yet witnessed. 'For the coming campaign', wrote a court Jesuit in 1645, 'we will assemble a great army of the nations, because our own men value their home life more than duty and glory ... [yet] all the same, the basis of our army will be made up from Castilians.'[5] In fact, only 4,600 recruits (*bisoños*) had been raised in the whole of greater Castile for that year's campaign, compared to twice or more that number which used to be

---

[3] For the military campaigns of the Catalan war, see J. Sanabre, *La acción de Francia en Cataluña* (Barcelona, 1956), passim; and also the contemporary chronicles compiled by M. Parets, *Crónica de los muchos sucesos dignos de memoria que han occurido en Barcelona y otros lugares de Cataluña ... entre los años de 1626 a 1660*, ed. C. Pujol y Camps et al. (5 vols, Madrid, 1890–93), and F. de Melo, *Historia de los movimientos, separación y guerra de Cataluña en tiempo de Felipe IV*, BAE, 21 (Madrid, 1946), pp. 459–535.

[4] The site of Numantia (near Soria) was discovered in the nineteenth century. Because its Celtiberian defenders – the earliest recorded inhabitants of the peninsula to form a widespread community – were believed to have killed themselves rather than submit to Rome, it became a theme of Spanish heroism similar to that of Caradog in Britain, a national paradigm of '*no pasarán*' and 'the last stand'.

[5] Gayangos, *Cartas*, vi, p. 98 (4 July 1645).

reliably provided on an annual basis half-a-century earlier.[6] Accordingly, Luis de Haro was despatched to Andalusia on a recruiting-drive.[7] In the event, his mission was counter-productive. Andalusia was currently undergoing a severe socio-economic crisis, yet its landowners were anxious to demonstrate their loyalty to Philip IV in the wake of the abortive Medina-Sidonia conspiracy. Don Luis, in addition to his personal charm, was politically well-connected in the region. Offers of troops and money from the local aristocracy, which they then had to make good from among their tenants, stimulated an atmosphere of popular grievance and demonstration, which broke into rioting in the village of Lucena in January 1647 and then spread to other Andalusian pueblos.[8] For a time, at least, the prospect of yet another major rebellion had to be faced in Madrid. So acute was the recognition that the coming events of 1647 would be *el momento de la verdad*, that Philip IV chose precisely this juncture to entrust Luis de Haro with a higher degree of power than his other ministers, and made over to him the keys of the *despacho universal*.[9]

As the crisis loomed, the marquis of Leganés, commander of the army of Aragon, was desperate to fill his ranks. He demanded that the whole marine corps (*infantería de marina*) from the armada he transferred from Cadiz and other Atlantic ports for use in the forthcoming confrontation over Lérida, 'in order that nothing be left to chance in a venture of such importance'.[10] Meanwhile, the council of war ordered the commutation of sentences for minor crimes from imprisonment or fines into war-service, while inmates of the prisons of Granada and other towns were forcibly conscripted. At the same time a carrot was placed alongside the stick: the enlistment payment for recruits joining the colours in the lands of Castile was raised from ten to eighteen *escudos* in an attempt to improve recruiting levels.[11]

In 1645 Philip IV convened the Aragonese parliament in Zaragoza, hoping to stimulate the local procurement of recruits. After a year's fruitless bargaining, he complained to Sor María de Agreda, 'I am amazed at the fact that these people do not seem to feel that their homes are any more at risk than if the enemy were in the Philippines'.[12] After months of cajoling and bargaining he eventually persuaded the assembly (*Corts*) to agree to a new levy – but one of only 2,500 men. The printed *voto* of the Estates noted that all the officers

[6] *Consulta* of the war junta, 25 April 1645, AGS, GA 1567.

[7] An account of Haro's visit is in BPU, 82, ff. 106–7. See also A. Soons, 'Cartas sevillanas de Don Luis Méndez de Haro, Noviembre–Diciembre 1645', *Bulletin hispanique*, 92 (1990), pp. 827–35.

[8] For the Andalusian disturbances of 1647–52, see Stradling, *Philip IV*, pp. 199–203.

[9] Serrano, *Cartas de Sor María*, i, p. 91 (10 Jan. 1647). Although conjecture on my part, it seems logical to suppose that it was the king's consciousness of crisis in early 1647 which led to him to relax his earlier resolution against the selection of a chief adviser.

[10] *Consulta* of the war junta, 6 Sept. 1646, AGS, GA 1621.

[11] G. Parker, *The Army of Flanders* (Cambridge, 1972), pp. 45–46.

[12] Serrano, *Cartas de Sor María*, i, p. 70.

would be natives of Aragon: ideally, so should the men, 'if such a number can be found; and if not, then they should certainly be Spaniards'.[13]

If Philip was expecting a *levée en masse* of Zaragoza's citizens, determined to protect nation, property and family against the enemy at whatever cost, his disappointment was understandable. Following the death of his only son, the *infante* Baltasar Carlos, the king came under pressure from his ministers not to risk his life and the future of the dynasty by returning to Aragon for the 1647 campaign. But, as Condé closed in upon Lérida, Philip assured his generals that he would ride to its aid. In the meantime, he told them, 'we will shortly be sending as reinforcements the men who are expected from Ireland, and also the Navarrese levies'.[14] In fact, things were even worse in Navarre than in Aragon. Here, the king's request for a single tercio was rejected by his own *corregidor*, with thinly-veiled threats of violent resistance in Pamplona if Madrid insisted on pressing the point.[15] However, help was forthcoming from another source. As soon as French pressure in Italy was eased by the relief of the fortress of Orbitello in Tuscany (August 1646), 6,000 Neapolitan soldiers were carried to Valencia by the ships of the expeditionary force.[16] In the southern marches of Catalonia they joined an international army – Irishmen, Walloons and Germans – formed around a Spanish nucleus.

To shift the focus briefly away from the epicentre, a multi-directional traffic in troops and arms was a major feature of the North Sea commercial economy for several decades after 1635. Hundreds of Walloons and Germans were ferried from Dunkirk to San Sebastian, the latter being Catholic troops who were raised by contract in the Rhineland and the imperialist lands of south-western Germany. It was not only the petty criminals of Castile who were freed from prison to meet the emergency of 1647. As a sweetener to Madrid during the run-up to final agreement at the peace conference at Münster, the Dutch agreed to release 600 Germans they had earlier captured at sea while en route to Spain: these men resumed their voyage to the peninsula in late 1646.[17]

Continuous transference of its human resources from one front to another enabled the Spanish system, defying all the orthodox logistical rules concerning exterior lines of communication, to plug the gaps which constantly opened up

---

[13] *Voto del servicio que los cavalleros e hijosdalgo hizo a su Magestad en 21 de Octubre 1646*, BN, 2377, f. 416. For Aragon's contributions to the defence of Lérida, see E. Solano Camón, *Poder monárquico y estado pactista (1626–1652): los Aragoneses ante la Unión de Armas* (Zaragoza, 1987), pp. 183–204.

[14] Quoted in Sanabre, *La acción de Francia*, p. 379.

[15] L. Ponce de León to Philip IV, 20 Feb. 1647, AGS, GA 1647. In the following year, the viceroy was obliged to deny that plans had been uncovered for rising in Pamplona, aimed at procuring the secession of Navarre from Spain in imitation of Catalonia and Portugal; see A. Floristán Imizcoz, *La monarquía española y el gobierno del reino de Navarra, 1512–1808* (Pamplona, 1991), pp. 177–78.

[16] CODOIN, 86, p. 247.

[17] *Consulta* of special war junta, 19 Oct. 1646, AGS, GA 1621.

in its ring of perimeter defences. Such demands added further to the space, time and resources taken up by the war effort. In effect, they abolished the winter close season of warmaking, for the relevant months were now filled with the noise of military activity which reached a crescendo in the spring. It was another – and not unimportant – way in which the ordinary soldier had become a full-time professional, with no furloughs and little rest from campaign. It is in areas like this, perhaps, that we may locate the real 'military revolution' of the seventeenth century.

In the spring of 1647 intelligence reported that Condé was not, after all, aiming at Lérida, but instead at the Mediterranean port of Tortosa, with a view to an invasion of the kingdom of Valencia, which might spark off a rebellion sympathetic to France. A stream of orders went out from Madrid and Zaragoza, redirecting various units by land and sea.[18] In the event, Condé made an initial feint towards the south, then suddenly switched his attention west: the investment of Lérida was complete by the end of April. The French ruse had worked, Spain's defences had been pulled out of shape and the situation appeared hopeless. As one of his commanders gratuitously informed Philip IV, 'The whole security of Castile and of your majesty's other kingdoms depends upon the defence of Lérida'.[19]

The only viable solution was the rapid importation of foreign troops on a considerable scale. However, this was a controversial policy. It had long been accepted that Spaniards were indispensable for military use outside the peninsula, as the most reliable and efficient instrument of defence.[20] In 1643 the count of Oñate, veteran survivor from a pre-Olivares period of government, claimed that the reason for disaster at Rocroi had been the low proportion of Spaniards in the ranks. He recommended the immediate despatch of peninsular reinforcements to the army of Flanders.[21] Naturally enough, Melo's successor in Brussels, the count of Castel Rodrigo, concurred with this view.[22] But most royal advisers were reluctant to denude the home fronts of scarce native troops. A congress of ministers and commanders, held at Fraga late in 1644, resolved to give the Catalan war absolute priority in the allocation of resources.[23]

Despite this formal decision, the principle restated by Oñate was never entirely abandoned. Remarkable as it may seem, even after 1640 almost every year witnessed a transfer of native recruits from northern Spain to Dunkirk. As

[18] See (e.g.), the items printed in CODOIN, 96, pp. 390–415.

[19] Quoted in Sanabre, *La acción de Francia* p. 379. (The remark is actually attributed by the author to a 'marquis of Haro', whom I have been unable to trace: a count of Haro was serving in Lombardy at this juncture.)

[20] L.A. Ribot García, 'El ejército de los Austrias: aportaciones recientes y nuevas perspectivas', *Pedralbes: revista d'historia moderna*, 3 (1983), pp. 89–126.

[21] *Voto* of Oñate for the council of state, 17 June 1643, Cánovas, *Estudios*, ii, p. 460.

[22] Castel Rodrigo to Philip IV, 9 Aug. 1644, CODOIN, 59, p. 438.

[23] See the collection of reports and opinions in BL, Eg. 340, ff. 107–113; see also CODOIN, 86, pp. 141–42.

late as February 1646, for example, a force of 3,000 was awaiting transport in Galicia.[24] This represented a luxury which vastly increased the need to replace such men from abroad. During the consultations of Fraga, Haro suggested that the whole diplomatic corps should conduct a systematic search for recruits, to be engaged on almost any terms. 'Such agents [he urged] may be given full powers to make agreements, so that the men they obtain can be brought to Spain with the necessary despatch. The service which your majesty demands in this matter is of such importance that we cannot afford to lose time in its execution.'[25] Another minister went even further, arguing – clean contrary to Oñate – that all Spaniards should be repatriated from Flanders and Italy and mobilized in order to meet the domestic crisis. Even if this were done, he concluded, 'most people agree that by the employment of our native resources alone it will not be possible to maintain armies at the present level'.[26]

The fact was demonstrable by the history of the Spanish system. As early as 1601, Spaniards made up only 26.7 per cent of the Army of Flanders. In 1640, the largest-ever muster in its history recorded the presence of more Spaniards than ever before – yet they now represented only 15 per cent of the total.[27] During his preparations for war against France in the early 1630s, Olivares sent envoys to every potentially friendly court in Europe. They carried instructions to seek permission to raise troops within the host territory and letters of credit to entice local contractors. In 1636 Olivares made another innovation by the hire of an integral mercenary army, under the command of the duke of Lorraine, and a dozen regiments of cavalry belonging to the king of Poland. As a result of these initiatives and deals, even before the revolt of the Catalans began in 1640, almost every ethnic community in western Europe was represented in the armed forces of Philip IV.

It was one thing for foreign mercenaries to serve in the distant northern campaigns, quite another to use them in wars within the Iberian peninsula. This was an emotive political issue which could only exacerbate the already strained relations between the court of Madrid and the local communities. In 1614 a prototype company of wooden toy soldiers had been sent by the Archduke Albert from Flanders to Spain as a present for the young Prince Philip. The gift proved to be a bizarre adumbration: when prince became king, the wood became flesh. In 1631 Philip IV asked his aunt and Albert's widow, the infanta Isabel, governess of the Low Countries, to despatch Walloon

[24] Philip IV to Castel Rodrigo, 6 Feb. 1646, ARB, SEG 235, f. 93.

[25] *Consulta* of a special war junta, Nov. 1644, AGS, GA 1516.

[26] 'Papel que se escribió sobre las levas de espana y otros cosas ... de la posada 22 de Oct. 1643', RAH, 1070, f. 301. Internal evidence suggests this document was not prepared by Castrillo, despite his retaining the special responsibility for troop levies allocated to him by Olivares; see Ruíz de Contreras to Castel Rodrigo, 13 Aug. 1645, AGS, E 2525. A likely candidate is Olivares' intimate aide and factotum, Jerónimo de Villanueva, who had been given a watching brief over Irish policy in the years before the fall of his master and continued to occupy high office for more than a year after that event.

[27] Parker, *Army of Flanders*, pp. 28, 276.

infantry to northern Spain.[28] This move could only justified as a short-term measure. The underlying reasons for the request were the problems of the *Unión de Armas*, and the protracted, problematic negotiations with the Cortes towns for a levy of 18,000 reserves within Castile. The immediate motive was surely the need to suppress the Basque rebellion – which had broken out that year – as rapidly as possible. In the event, no Belgians ever arrived in Spain; the current military circumstances in Flanders, which was under severe pressure from the Dutch army under Henry of Nassau, forbade such assistance, while the Basque insurrection was adequately dealt with by the local authorities.

The first occasion that non-Spanish soldiery operated in the peninsula, since the campaign of annexation against Portugal in 1580, was in 1636, when Italian levies were imported for operations against France on the Catalan frontier.[29] Only the official designation of this particular 'Army of Catalonia' as the personal command of Philip IV, under the formal constitutional provision of *Princeps Namque*, justified this action. However, for some years, Irish recruits had been arriving at a steady trickle to enlist with the army of Flanders – by 1635, according to one authority, nearly 7,000 were mustered.[30] A few years later, some of these men were the first soldiers to arrive in Spain from a northern European source since Charles V's *Landsknechts* in 1521. The Irish tercios of the earls of Tyrconnel (Hugh O'Donnell) and Tyrone (John O'Neill) – 1,200 men in all – were detached from the army of Flanders and transported from Dunkirk to Bilbao. They had been called to help with the relief of Fuenterrabía from the French siege, a campaign to which they made a notable contribution.[31] From then onwards the presence of Irish regiments along the warfronts of the peninsula was ubiquitous.

There was always the fear that the policy might be counter-productive. In 1631 delegates to the Cortes complained that even men recruited within Castile, on their march to the troopships, treated the neighbouring *pueblos* through which they passed 'as if they were the rebel lands of Holland'.[32] It is doubtful whether the Italian soldiery in Catalonia were regarded by the local population, amongst whom they were billetted, as any more alien than their Andalusian (or even than their Leonese) colleagues. Yet the indisciplined conduct of the Neapolitans made a significant contribution to precipitating the peasants' revolt of 1640.[33]

From the perspective of 1647, more recent incidents could be cited in favour of the arguments against importing alien soldiery. In the spring of 1643 several regiments of Walloon and German infantry travelled from San Sebastian to the

[28] Ibid., pp. 3, 30.

[29] J.H. Elliott, *The Revolt of the Catalans* (Cambridge, 1963), p. 330.

[30] B. Jennings, *Wild Geese in Spanish Flanders, 1582–1700* (Dublin, 1964), pp. 7–32, 286.

[31] M. de Salamanca to Olivares, 10 March 1638, AHN, E 962, f. 8.

[32] *Mem[ori]al dado a Su Mag[esta]d para la situación de 18,000 soldados en sus presidios* (?1631), BN, 7760, f. 76.

[33] Elliott, *Revolt of the Catalans*, p. 394.

relief of Lérida. On their march through Aragon, they left a trail of grievances, the details of which (as usual) were much augmented in the transmission. By the time the troops arrived at Zaragoza, fear of their depredations had grown to such an extent that the citizens spontaneously armed themselves and contested the entry of the soldiery, displaying the desperate resolution which Philip IV later found himself wishing they would turn against the enemy. At least fifty soldiers, and (one may suppose) many more civilians, died in the ensuing violence.[34] This shameful incident took place in the same month as the defeat of Rocroi and, since it probably contributed to the failure to save Lérida from the French, the loss of *reputacion* involved was potentially even greater. Later that year, a minister appositely pointed out that the presence of alien soldiery among any community involved the risk of pouring oil rather than water on the flames of rebellion.[35]

In 1647 itself the *arbitrista* Henríquez de Villegas published a treatise which confronted these sensitive issues. He strongly maintained the orthodox view, encapsulated in the nostrum of Machiavelli which stands at the head of this chapter. The *soldado natural* was incomparable. 'It was always the rule of Spanish arms either to conquer or to die, and our warriors would always prefer to die fighting alongside their captains in defence of the fatherland than to admit defeat.' In Henríquez's view, troops should never be employed by *asiento*, since military contractors were mere businessmen, who sought to defraud the crown. Moreover they provided poor soldiers, drawn from places 'where there is little quality of manhood, where our ideas of honour do not exist, men who aspire neither to honour nor to glory'. Even within Spain, Henríquez hinted, there were distinct shades of military worthiness, and outside Castile few could be trusted to serve with complete satisfaction. To this writer, the concept of the *patria* was already familiar and precious; its reputation could only be sullied if it hired foreigners to defend it. In defence of this modern view, he illustrated his rootedness in his contemporary intellectual culture by quoting not only the infamous Florentine but also more ancient and respectable Italian authorities, especially Tacitus's apothegm that foreign mercenaries 'have no knowledge of goodness or any fear of evil'. They were unreliable and indisciplined, given over to plunder, mutiny and desertion – more inclined (as it were) to *vicio* than to *servicio*. If they had to be employed, it must only be in conditions where payment was secure and prompt, and where transgressors were severely punished.[36]

Yet Henríquez's treatise was not as uncompromising as it seems at first glance. It was dedicated to the count of Santisteban, a member of the council of war, and was probably a government inspiration. Its principal motive was to persuade Castilian landowners to relax their opposition to conscription from the villages of their private estates, partly by the scare

[34] 'Sobre los Valones y Alemanes para Cataluña', BN, 9379, f. 1.
[35] As no. 26.
[36] Henríquez de Villegas, *Levas de gente* (Madrid, 1647), pp. 8, 35, 59.

tactics of illustrating the grim alternatives to which continued recalcitrance would oblige the government to adopt. But the onrushing challenge over Lérida meant that the king and his ministers could not afford to wait for Henríquez's arguments to take effect. In April 1647 Philip noted that

> our shortage of men to cope with the present emergency obliges us to obtain recruits from any available source. We must obtain such assistance from the nations most sympathetic to my cause [*naciones más afectos*] since our need is so great that we must leave no avenue unexplored, however difficult it might be, and however poor our chances of success.[37]

Which were the *naciones más afectos*? In the 1630s Olivares had identified two outstanding areas of exploitation. After the *valido*'s fall early in 1643, Philip and his chief advisers – Luis de Haro, the count of Castrillo, and their factional rival, the duke of Medina de las Torres – continued to believe that, of all possible recruiting grounds, Ireland and Poland were the most promising. One report reflected the views of the ruling group in stating that 'it is the Irishmen who are the most attached to your majesty's service, and we must never neglect an occasion to bring them onto the payroll'.[38] In recent years (for his part) Medina de las Torres had been at the centre of an ambitious scheme to employ Polish lancers and Ukrainian 'Cossacks' as regular serving auxiliaries of the monarchy. Spain had never needed to hire Swiss regiments, since her fundamental military proclivity had always been the infantry battalions of the tercios; now – especially in the war around France's northern borders – the need was for cavalry, the specific vocation of the Poles.[39]

Even today, Ireland and Poland are two of the most fiercely Catholic nations. In the seventeenth century, viewed from the cultural centres of continental Europe, orthodoxy of religion was just about the only aspect of western civilization which they had successfully adopted. They appeared to most opinion-formers as marginal, savage, tribal regions, and therefore highly suitable objects of Tacitean suspicion. Neither people, of course, were members of the Spanish monarchy, but – significantly enough – both lacked an indigenous dynasty to provide a focus of sovereignty and allegiance, for which (to some extent) Madrid was a surrogate.

Poland was the largest political entity in Europe (with the exception of France itself) and rich in resources of food and men. Spain had been occasionally dependent upon the former since the last quarter of the previous century, and the recourse to the latter in the final stages of its struggle for hegemony has a certain appropriateness. Olivares' stratagem of hiring 'Cossack' light cavalry (*cosacos*) had been a spectacular feature of the invasion of France by the imperialist army under Count Gallas in 1636. A Madrid Jesuit reported, with undisguised satisfaction, that 'the Poles have advanced to within

---

[37] Philip IV to Castel Rodrigo, 4 April 1647, AHN, E 973.
[38] As no. 26.
[39] See Chapter 11, above.

thirteen leagues of Paris, and burned sixty-three villages'.[40] On this occasion, at least, sensational news does not seem to have been exaggerated; it is not surprising that within France use of the barbarian horsemen was regarded as a kind of war crime. Richelieu's critics made much of the horrors visited upon hapless villagers as a result of the cardinal's war-policy: 'He causes foreigners to complete the pillage that he began in France, and brings seizures, massacres and desolation to all areas that he does not control'.[41]

Two years later, the count-duke encouraged his son-in-law, Medina de las Torres – then viceroy of Naples – to open negotiations aimed at placing the alliance with Poland on a firmer footing.[42] The opportunity arose because of a quarrel between Poland and France over the detention of the king of Poland's brother by Richelieu. Naples was involved mainly because it was intended to devote a proportion of the crown's revenues from the *Regno* to providing the subsidies for the Polish army – a ploy which would avoid difficulties with the *cortes* over the destination of Castilian taxes. Provisional articles for a 'Treaty of Confederation' were drawn up in Naples in the summer of 1639. King Wladislaw was to provide 3,000 cavalry and 6,000 infantry from the royal army, then immediately to raise a further 6,000 'Cossacks'. This force was to be built up to 30,000 by stages, and was to accept the supreme command of Don Fernando, Philip IV's brother and leader of the army of Flanders. Given his chronic shortage of cavalry, Don Fernando was enthusiastic and pressed Medina to finalize the negotiations. As his chief aide put it to Olivares, 'this is the most serious wound that we are able to inflict on France, even though it might cost us much to do so'.[43] The latter was certainly true. The Polish emissary demanded the enormous down-payment of 230,000 ducats – initially to be held in trust in Vienna – and a further 430,000 was to be earmarked from the Neapolitan budget for 1640 to support the army for a whole campaign. Nevertheless, Olivares assured the council of state, 'there can be no better remedy for all our problems than to place these men on French soil'.[44]

The negotiations encountered many difficulties. In managing to avoid confrontation with his own assembly of notables, Philip had not imagined that he might run into problems with not one but two others, which were much further beyond his control. The proposal of the king of Poland was vetoed by the celebrated assembly of the *schlachta* – 'the Republic' as it was called in Spanish correspondence. In any case, as a result of the experience

[40] Gayangos, *Cartas*, i, pp. 409–12.

[41] Quoted in W. Church, *Richelieu and Reason of State* (Princeton, NJ, 1972), p. 378.

[42] See Medina de las Torres to Philip IV, 7 Aug. 1643, BN, 10410, ff. 76–79. This letter, written after Medina's return from Italy, is the source of the information given below, unless otherwise noted. (I am grateful to Dr Robert Frost of King's College, London, for information on the distinctions between 'Poles', 'Cossacks' and 'Ukrainians' and the preferred fighting formations of each.)

[43] M. de Salamanca to Olivares, 12 May 1640, AHN, E 959.

[44] *Consulta* of the council of state, 20 Oct. 1640, AGS, E 2055.

of 1636, when the Polish lancers had caused indiscriminate devastation in their passage across Europe, the Diet prevented the emperor from granting the relevant licences on this occasion. The Spanish ambassador in Vienna, Castañeda, spent 15,000 ducats in bribing members of the Diet, to no avail.[45] Nevertheless, Olivares, Medina and Don Fernando were anxious to persist, especially after events in Catalonia put a premium on the Spanish system's being able to weaken the French push into Spain by mounting a serious attack from the northern fronts. In February 1641 another agreement was reached between Medina de las Torres and the plenipotentiary sent to him in Naples from the court of Cracow.[46] In October 1641, however, Madrid reluctantly decided to shelve the matter, 'since the king [of Poland] can do nothing without the permission of the Republic'.[47] The projected alliance between Poland and the Spanish monarchy was effectively defunct, and therefore the sentimental Polish-French association survived to become a cliché of the history books.

Madrid now switched its main attention back from the easternmost to the westernmost limits of Europe. The Gaelic chieftains of Ireland had traditionally looked to Spain for support against England. Even before Henry VIII sought to impose his Reformation on the Irish, native leaders had appealed to the Habsburgs as an alternative authority. Following the failure of their rebellion against Elizabeth I, and the defeat of the Spanish expeditionary force under Aguila (1601), the so-called 'flight of the earls' brought a dozen Irish nobles and their families to Spain, where they received the patronage of Philip III. Their male dependents enlisted as voluntary rankers (*guzmanes* as they were called) in the ranks of the army of Flanders, and became thoroughly hispanified as courtiers and soldiers.[48] In the late 1630s the sons and nephews of the original exiles were prominent in a series of actions against the French. Praise of Irish courage was heard on all sides – from princes, ministers and experienced *maestres de campo*.[49] Within Spain, their exploits at Fuenterrabía (1638) and Salces (1640) confirmed this high estimation and stimulated demand for their services.[50]

In 1639 Philip ordered direct importation of hired levies from Ireland and during the following year the note of urgency in this demand began

[45] 'Relación de lo que ha cobrado de las letras que ha remitido de Nápoles el señor Duque de Medina de las Torres', RAH, 1053, ff. 407–7v.

[46] 'Capitulación que se ajuste entre el Duque de Medina de las Torres y Alberto Teuleschi . . . en Nápoles a 14 de Febrero 1641', ibid., ff. 401–403v.

[47] *Consulta* of the council of state, 13 Oct. 1641, AGS, E 2056.

[48] S. Ellis, *Tudor Ireland: Crown, Community and the Conflict of Cultures, 1470–1603* (1985), p. 124. M.K. Walsh, *Spanish Knights of Irish Origin* (3 vols, Dublin, 1960–70), passim.

[49] See (e.g.), cardinal-infante to Velada, 10 Oct. 1640, BPU, 38, f. Salamanca to cardinal-infante, 2 Oct. 1640, RAH, 1053, f. 408; Conde Fontana to cardinal-infante, 8 Feb. 1641, AHN, E 957.

[50] 'Gente que habra al presente en Guipúzcoa', BN, 18176, f. 16; *consulta* of the executive junta, 22 Aug. 1641, AGS, E 2522.

to intensify.[51] In 1640–41, stimulated by the rebellion in Catalonia, Madrid made plans for the transfer of the whole of the Irish army (some 10,000 men originally raised on behalf of Charles I by the earl of Strafford) to the peninsula. These strenuous attempts were almost completely frustrated. In the autumn of 1641, moreover, the Celtic Irish began their own rebellion, which threw the whole situation into chaos. It seemed that hopes of further recruitment were dashed – indeed, even worse, some companies actually left Flanders in order to return home to fight with the Catholic Confederation based at Kilkenny. However, this organization needed Spanish support, and in 1642 a bargain was struck in Madrid. In exchange for diplomatic assistance and a financial subsidy, the Irish agreed to grant permission for hire and passage of troops.[52] Philip established a special *junta de dos* to supervise the arrangements. Substantial financial provisions were made and various envoys and agents attempted to expedite the business in the ports of Spain, in Brussels, in London, and lastly in Ireland itself. Despite all this endeavour, results proved disappointing and less than 2,000 recruits disembarked at Spanish ports over a period of five years. By this point, the government was desperate for Irish troops on almost any terms. Haro wrote to one official demanding 'rapid action, for the love of God, in sending us these men, since no other troops we employ here are as useful as the Irish'.[53]

Despite several reviews of the policy and the methods utilized, in which the king personally intervened on more than one occasion, success continued to elude Madrid. In the event, the supreme crisis of 1647 – the siege and final relief of Lérida (April-June), followed by the definitive retreat of Condé came and went with little or no Irish participation. The breakthrough only came in subsequent years, when Catholic and Celtic Ireland was being reconquered by Cromwell and his lieutenants, and the rebel armies were deported *en masse* as a condition of their capitulation. In the quinquennium 1649–53, some 20,000 troops were ferried to northern Spain.[54]

But the military quality of the new arrivals – in effect pressed into service, and already defeated and demoralised – was considerably lower than that of their predecessors. Thousands arrived in a pitiable condition, diseased, starving and often nearly naked. Those who were fit sometimes defied their officers and terrorized the local population. In time the villages of Galicia and Cantabria were exhausted and exasperated by the constant demands of the billet. Even the men disembarking in the Basque ports of Bilbao and San Sebastian had to be quartered across the provincial border in Cantabria, because of regional

[51] *Consulta* of ? the council of state, 28 March 1639, AGS, E 3860; Philip IV to Salamanca, 14 April 1640, AHN, E 963, f. 108.

[52] 'Capítulos acordados con los Diputados de Irlanda' and *consulta* of the junta of state, 9 Nov. 1642, AGS, E 2525.

[53] Haro to Salamanca, 23 Feb. 1646, AHN, E 966, f. 163.

[54] For further detail and information on sources concerning the Irish troops traffic to Spain, see my *The Spanish Monarchy and Irish Mercenaries: The Wild Geese in Spain, 1618–68* (Dublin, 1994).

constitutional exemptions, added to the risks of precipitating fresh outbursts of popular protest so close to the French frontier. Royal officials struggled to maintain discipline, and to appease representatives of irate villagers from Cape Finisterre to the Bidassoa.[55]

Once the Catalan war was brought to a conclusion with the fall of Barcelona in 1652, Philip ordered a fresh round of contracts for Irish troops 'because a goodly number of Irish are needed for the enterprise of Portugal'.[56] As this suggests, the king was now switching his attentions to the Portuguese front, where little more than an extended holding operation had been possible ever since the successful rebellion of late 1640. Early in 1653, indeed, the culmination of Spain's Irish policy was reached when Haro insisted 'it is not possible that more [Irishmen] can ever come than we are likely to need'.[57] As it proved, Don Luis's statement was particularly inopportune. Even as he wrote, desertions were becoming a serious problem.[58] Later that year, hundreds of raw Irish recruits were sent on a major expedition to aid the Ormée rebels in Bordeaux – where most of them went over to the French at the first opportunity.[59] In a scandalous incident, several Irish companies deserted to the enemy on the frontier of Catalonia, while others fled the ranks soon after arriving on the Portuguese front.[60]

The military reputation of the Irish had thus collapsed even before news arrived (in the summer of 1653) that plague was rife in the very parts of Ireland from which the new troops were expected. A moratorium was placed on the whole traffic.[61] At this time, *asientos* were outstanding for around 8,000 troops, and for this reason men continued to dribble into Spain down to 1656. Some regiments continued to serve gallantly on the Portuguese front, but others broke up and were dissipated, their members fleeing to all parts of Spain, pursued by search parties sent out at intervals from major battle-stations to hunt for deserters. To sum up, although Irish regiments were of positive military significance in Flanders and Spain in the 1630s, and certainly made a substantial contribution to the war in Catalonia, the policy as a whole had hardly have justified the effort and the money expended upon it.

A return reference to our opening set of questions indicates – not surprisingly – that the ceaseless task of defending the Universal Cause in arms was not without its paradoxes and anomalies. In the first Irish *asiento militar*, made in 1646, the war junta noted that 'the Irish nation has always enjoyed a place in your

[55] See (e.g.), *consulta* of the war junta, 11 May 1653, AGS, GA 1830.

[56] *Consulta* of the council of state, 1 Dec. 1652, AGS, E 2528.

[57] *Voto* of Haro, 18 Feb. 1653, AGS, GA 1824.

[58] See the *consulta* specified in n. 56, above.

[59] *Consulta* of the navy junta, 4 July 1653, AGS, GA 3337.

[60] *Manifiesto que hizieron los maestros de campo irlandeses que estan serviendo a S.M. . . . en el Principado de Cataluña . . . 29 de Agosto 1653*, BN, 2384, ff. 75–76.

[61] A. Pérez Cantarero to D. de la Torre, 29 June 1653, and *consulta* of the council of state, 21 Aug. 1653, AGS, E 2528.

majesty's armies equal to that of Spaniards'.[62] This was a slight exaggeration, since only in the general regulations revision (*ordenanzas*) of 1633 had the Irish been placed on equal footing with Spanish and Italian troops in respect of pay and conditions of service.[63] However, these regulations were hereafter carefully observed in Flanders and, in musters down to 1665, the Irish usually appear third in the pecking order for receipt of pays, after Spaniards and Italians, but before Walloons and (interestingly enough) Germans.[64] Thus the *soldado natural* of Spain had lost some of his traditional superiority – not to Philip's own Walloon subjects, or those of his Habsburg cousin, but to the bàrbarous, alien Irishmen!

The good discipline and outstanding battle-worthiness of the Irish were two qualities considerably enhanced, in the eyes of Madrid, by a third: they were fanatical Catholics. They came to Flanders and Spain in the care of their native Franciscan padres, who provided not only spiritual sustenance but an essential medium of communication. Their charges were (of course) illiterate and spoke only Gaelic, whereas the clergy of both parties could use the ancient *lingua franca*. The presence of Irishmen in Spain represented no danger to the souls of Philip's subjects – at least in the generality – and thus none to his own. The Catholic orthodoxy of mercenary recruits remained an official prerequisite, so much so that they were sought for in the most obscure places. In 1640, for example, the marquis of Velada, Don Fernando's envoy in London – perhaps with the secret connivance of Charles I – began to contact recusant gentlemen in the provinces to procure volunteers. One of the areas chosen for canvassing was the county of Monmouthshire, where scattered enclaves of the Old Faith still existed.[65] During the Lérida emergency, the Spanish agent in Kilkenny reported that the marquis of Worcester had offered to raise 4,000 'of his own vassals' for Spain – 'though I believe [he added] that the project has little substance'.[66]

Not all the Celtic world was deemed to be suitable for recruitment. In 1647 a proposal for raising men in Scotland received a hostile reception in the council of state. The marquis of Leganés noted 'that nation is obstinately wedded to heresy and cruelty, and for these reasons should be permanently excluded from Your Majesty's service', whilst the count of Monterrey added that (in any case) the Scots were well-known adherents of France. Don Francisco de Melo

---

[62] *Consulta* of the war junta 30 Aug. 1646, AGS, GA 1621.

[63] Clonard, *Historia orgánica*, iv, pp. 399–405.

[64] See (e.g.), the general musters of 22 Dec. 1639, AHN, E 957: and of 19 Feb. 1647, AHN, E 978.

[65] Spanish initiatives in this area were reported to the Short Parliament by a group of Puritan ministers. See, 'El humilde suplicación de Julio Elbrads, Gullermo Roth, Ricardo Walter y Rogero Cradocke, ministros del evangelio en las provincias de Monmouth, Glamorgan, Carmarthen y Brecknock', a translation of their complaint sent by Velada to Brussels (? May, 1640), BPU, 39, f. 305.

[66] *Relación de los servicios de D. Francisco Foisotte en Borgoña, Flandes, Inglaterra, Francia . . .*, BN, 2367, ff. 206–6v.

summed up the feeling that 'only when the supply of Irishmen, Germans, Walloons and Italians fails us should we be forced to consider the Scots'.[67] Yet only three years later, the ex-royalist lowlander Lord Crawford was 'colonel and governor of two Scots tercios serving in the army of Badajoz'.[68] Moreover, despite the pristine rectitude of his councillors, some troops from the *Heimat* of Lutheran heresy were already present in Philip's army of Catalonia. Indeed, it seems that at least one tercio of *alemanes altos*, embarked from Dunkirk in the winter of 1642–43, were among the men attacked by the citizens of Zaragoza in May 1643.[69] Above all, unknown to *Estado*, the king himself had already compromised the principles so piously reaffirmed by his ministers.

Some years earlier, Philip had been forced to concede that Protestants could be enlisted in Flanders. On that occasion he made the rationalization that 'soldiers of a contrary religion are more tolerated in the armies which serve me outside Spain'.[70] As the hour of greatest need in the peninsula itself approached – the spring of 1647 – tempting and timely offers were made to provide Philip with battle-hardened veterans from the Dutch army, only recently his enemies and rebels and still obviously heretics, regiments of which were expected to demobilize in the wake of the negotiations at Münster. Doubtless, Philip consulted a *junta de teólogos* over this dilemma: and it would be fascinating to learn the arguments they put forward. In any case, one deal of this nature was quickly closed.[71] The timing of the decision is interesting, and not only because of the Lérida emergency. Philip ordered that of the 6,000 men involved, only half were to sail for San Sebastian. The other 3,000 were to disembark at Cadiz. In a separate agreement negotiated during the winter of 1647–48, it was arranged that two other ex-Dutch army regiments were also to be landed at Cadiz.[72]

The three occasions when it was decided to disembark men in the south of Spain, rather than at the more logistically convenient northern ports, each coincided with the onset of serious popular protest in Andalusia. Ostensibly,

[67] *Consulta* of the council of state, 12 Oct. 1647, AGS, E 2525.

[68] Royal order of 24 Nov. 1650, AGS, E 2528. It is possible, however, that Crawford's men were Highland Scots, and/or Scots-Irish Catholics from the clans whose homesteads straddled the Western Isles and County Antrim in this period.

[69] 'La quenta de Toribio de Bustamente . . .' (February, 1643), AHN, E 973.

[70] Philip IV to the cardinal-infante, 18 May 1641, ARB, SEG 229, f. 89v.

[71] The king accepted proposals put up by a certain Colonel Norris for 6,000 Dutch veterans; Philip IV to Castel Rodrigo, 4 April 1647, AHN, E 973. At the same time, Lord George Goring's offer to bring 1,500 English royalist veterans to Spain was being pursued enthusiastically; A. Martínez to M. de Salamanca, 30 May 1647, ibid.

[72] Later in 1647, a Spanish enterpriser, Ambrosio Messía, offered to provide two tercios of such troops. This offer took longer to negotiate, partly (perhaps) because the king needed to take advice on the issues involved, partly because the most dangerous period of emergency had passed in Catalonia (though not in Andalusia). In February 1648, nevertheless, a formal contract was agreed: 'Condiciones con que el Coronel Ambrosio Messía se obliga a hazer en holanda una leva . . .', 11 Feb. 1648, AHN, E 973. These men were to be allocated their first payment upon arrival in Cadiz (article 4).

at least, the troops were intended for the Portuguese front. But in 1647 this theatre was dormant and could not provide a genuine military reason for denying three (potentially crucial) tercios to the defence of Lérida. Of course, the order may have been simply a device for splitting up what (after all) amounted to a heretic army into manageable and less dangerous sections. But could Philip also have had in mind the need to cope with the violent disturbances which were, at the exact time of these decisions, spreading throughout rural Andalusia? Did he intend to use Calvinist soldiery to subdue his starving Castilian subjects? Seventy years after the infamous 'Spanish Fury', when mutinous Castilian troops had run amuck amongst the burghers of Antwerp, could there have been a 'Dutch Fury' in Seville? If the nub of this speculation is correct, it would surely represent the most extreme case of the casuistic doctrine of the *verdadera razón de estado* – so-called 'true reason of State' – being used in defence of the Catholic Monarchy.[73] In the event, the contracts referred to above were never carried through; but another, made later that year, stipulated the delivery of 1,000 royalist veterans of the English Civil War, not all of whom were Catholics, also to Cadiz.[74] The evidence of the incidents discussed here does not permit firm conclusions. All the same, it is notable that the only occasion on which foreign troops actually arrived in southern Spain (again at Cadiz) was in early 1653. The enterpriser involved had been issued his sailing instructions at the time of the insurrection of Seville several months earlier. But his men were half-dead Irish refugees, not tough Dutch veterans.[75]

As the marquis of Aytona had informed Philip in 1632, 'mercenary soldiers attach themselves to the army in which pay is most reliable, without taking religion nor nationality into account'.[76] At this particular juncture, Philip was continuing to fight the good fight of the 'universal cause'. He was planning to recapture the most fanatically Protestant community in the world – the island of Zeeland – paradoxically in secret alliance with the Protestant king of England.[77] Twenty years later, thousands of Protestants, including Zeelanders, were in Spanish service. Wherever possible, even when enlisted integrally, heretic regiments were 'reformed' (i.e. broken up) and their members distributed amongst Catholic tercios, diluting their power and weakening confessional resolve. It was customary to impose an oath of loyalty to Philip IV: they became his subjects – technically, at least, full members of

---

[73] On 'Verdadera Razón de Estado', see J.A. Fernández-Santamaría, *Reason of State and Statecraft in Spanish Political Thought, 1595–1640* (New York, 1983).

[74] 'Capítulos . . . con el Coronel Don Thomas Linguen . . .' and royal order of 7 Oct. 1647, AGS, E 2523.

[75] *Consulta* of the navy junta, 1 March 1653, AGS, GA 3337.

[76] Lefèvre and Cuvelier, *Correspondence*, vi, p. 343.

[77] Draft of an Anglo-Spanish treaty of 12 Jan. 1631 (signed between Olivares and Sir Francis Cottington in Madrid), MMG, PHB lb, ff. 105–7.

the monarchy.[78] The conclusion can only be that the Catholic King had at last reconciled himself to ruling over heretics.

Prejudice against mercenaries comes from deep wells in the culture of politico-military elites and is still widespread today. In the long era of the national-liberal state, European commentators continued generally to regard them as an infallible index of degeneration – in this particular case, yet another illustration of 'The Decline of Spain'. Not many years before the French army was humbled by the Prussians in 1870, a French writer drew attention to the use of mercenaries by the Spanish army under Philip IV. Though for different reasons, he came to conclusions broadly similar to those reached by Machiavelli in 1513 and Henriquez de Villegas in 1647: 'A toutes les époques [he asserted] la puissance des mercenaires est le symptôme de l'organisation vicieuse et de l'affaiblissment des societés qui les ont employées.' Spain – it was argued – was not an authentic nation-state, and was therefore foredoomed to failure. In contrast, Richelieu's France fought for the freedom of all European nations, with a genuinely indigenous army; outstanding evidence of national unity and vigour.[79]

In a variety of Spanish sources I have found the noun *nación* used for Irish, Scottish, Walloon, German, Italian – and even Spanish troops. At the other end of the chain of command, Olivares nurtured plans for creating an international ruling class with (what we would call) a common culture, yet at the same time he recognized that ethnocentric differences of *patria* would have to be respected. The Hispanic Monarchy, therefore, at least aspired to what it claimed to be – a comity of nations. In the years covered by this essay, ideas were considered for repopulating Castile with (for example) Irish or Croatian settlers.[80] When an Irish entrepreneur offered to import Catholic negroes for a similar purpose, Philip curtly rejected the idea.[81] Perhaps no Universal Monarchy could ever be quite *that* universal. All the same, during the seventeenth century Spain had been forced to accommodate itself to a Europe of the Nations quite distinct in its fundaments from the one it envisaged – ironically enough, by the very process of resisting this agnostic development to its final breath. Whatever the state of Philip's own conscience, his monarchy had definitively lost its Catholic purity, in terms of subjects as well as resources. Yet we cannot doubt that if the Habsburgs had achieved ultimate

---

[78] See (e.g.), *consulta* of council of state, 28 May 1657, AGS, E 2090.

[79] J. P.–A. Bazy, *Etat militaire de la monarchie espagnole sous Philippe IV: les mercenaires au XVIIe siècle* (Poitiers, 1863), p. 6. Bazy's claim was, of course, absurd – the army of Richelieu and Mazarin employed foreign mercenaries (including thousands of Irishmen) just as freely as that of Francis I had done a century earlier. Moreover, the men raised from within 'national' borders were certainly not the most effective – on which see D. Parrott, 'The Administration of the French Army during the Ministry of Cardinal Richelieu, 1630–42' (unpublished D.Phil. thesis, University of Oxford, 1985).

[80] See (e.g.), CODOIN, 86, p. 326.

[81] Paz y Melia, *Avisos de Barrionuevo*, ii, p. 142; *consulta* of the council of war, 23 Sept. 1652, AGS, GA 3326.

victory in the Thirty Years War, the reconversion of Europe to Rome would have been axiomatic. Such intense ideological paradoxes are not uncommon in history. In our own century, during the Spanish Civil War, the elite troops on the side which claimed to be fighting a Catholic Crusade were African Muslims, while the most feeble were Catholic Irish volunteers. Meanwhile, on the opposing Republican side, fanatical Communist Party officials imprisoned, tortured and even murdered other communists who fought for the pure ideals of the Revolution.

PART IV

CONCLUSION

13

Conclusion: Second Thoughts

In a notorious introduction with the above title, prefaced to the paperback edition of *The Origins of the Second World War* (1963), A.J.P. Taylor answered his critics – several of whom had overstepped the conventions of English academic reticence – by restating his case *a fortiori* and with generous resort to exaggeration. My imitation of Taylor's by-line, while intended as sincere homage to the memory of Britain's greatest polemical historian, is not meant to be ironical. Second thoughts, quite legitimately, may be additional without being alternative. Of course I accept that the historian can exaggerate in order to make a point; but the exercise must be performed overtly and should not become habitual. Upon returning to the essays reprinted above – some of them products of youthful impetuosity laced with arrogance – I was not entirely satisfied that these caveats had always been observed with sufficient care and attention.

The paradox of the art of articles is that they offer the most convenient medium for 'revisionist' history, especially for younger scholars anxious to test new ideas, yet they are rarely subject to the stage of assessment necessary to complete such a test – that is, to public review. Thus all save one of the above essays will receive their first critical notices only as a result of the present compendium. (The exception was greeted in the pages of the Spanish review *Hispania* as 'highly controversial', a judgement which was rather supported than otherwise by its author's refraining from further explanation – a rare occasion on which a Spaniard has outdone English reticence.) In anticipation of a challenging voyage for my *flota de galeones*, the sections which follow represent attempts to brush up the paintwork, to secure the hulls and even to improve the armament of some of the older craft. Despite this, and although I hope (at times) to have been suggestive in argument, I do not expect always to have been correct in interpretation or judicious in emphasis. Of course, historians are never 'right' in any absolute or eternal sense – even if some are more reliable than others. We are, I am glad to say, fallen creatures. The unreadiness is all.

The themes of most of the essays reprinted here received renewed attention in various subsequent publications. In several cases, this has rendered further comment otiose. Relevant to Chapter 2 are various sections in *Philip IV* (1988) and *Europe and the Decline of Spain* (1981); to Chapter 10, *The Armada of Flanders* (1992); and to chapter 12, *The Spanish Monarchy and Irish Mercenaries* (1993).

Chapter 1

The arguments put forward here were amplified, revised, and partly moderated in the course of my book *Europe and the Decline of Spain* (1981). Its attempt to highlight the aspects of 'survival' as against those of 'failure', in the context of Spain's international role, seems to have met with broad approval; at any rate, many textbook surveys of the period have since sought to shift the balance.[1] The emphasis upon comparative factors in understanding the phases of Spain's military failure was also, it seems, not entirely misplaced. Subsequent work on Richelieu's ministry, both in general and in specifically relevant terms, has underlined its importance.[2] I should perhaps record here the sense of surprise which accompanied my recognition of the core political and economic 'weaknesses' of France during its celebrated *grand siècle*: and this particular course was accordingly served up with a little too much relish – a deficiency, perhaps, of *la cuisine Britannique*. In any case we have (I trust) at last escaped from the cultural orientation of 'national histories', and no longer do we take silly fright at the absence of Cartesian rationality, unity, order and 'government' in the political communities of the early modern (or should it be 'late medieval'?) past. This is true even – perhaps especially – in the French connection.

On reflection, however, it must be conceded that there is more, and more subtle, force to the financial arguments for Spain's retreat from European hegemony than I was prepared to admit in 1979. Though the schematic cycles and hemispherical patterns of a Chaunu must still be rejected, Madrid's policymaking was rather more seriously affected by an awareness of financial pressures than I concluded. It was always a supportive element of a case rather than its essence; but the researcher can be too easily misled by the alien, Platonic discourse which surrounds it in the state papers. For example, no two policymakers were more zealous in their Counter-Reformation Catholicism than the Habsburg archdukes in Flanders, Albert and Isabel. Yet in 1605–9 – doubtless influenced by their close friend financier and general, Spínola – they gave money, or rather the lack of it, a high priority when pushing for

---

[1] The most celebrated example is Paul Kennedy's, *The Rise and Fall of the Great Powers: Economic Change and Military Conflict from 1500 to 2000* (1988); see esp. pp. 47–59. In Spain the process began the same year with the relevant chapters in *Historia de España*, vi (Barcelona, 1988), pp. 336–88. A stern critic of my ideas has himself recently perceived that 'even after the revolts of Catalonia and Portugal in 1640, after which Spain's power seemed much less formidable than before, Spain was still the main power in the New World and the principal counterweight to the rising power of France. It was only after the Peace of the Pyrenees (1659) and the humiliating failure of Spanish efforts to reconquer Portugal in the 1660s, that it came to be recognized that Spain was now irreparably weakened and no longer the chief rival to France for the leadership of Europe'; Israel, *Empires and Entrepots*, p. xi.

[2] See (e.g.), J. Bergin, *Cardinal Richelieu: Power and the Pursuit of Wealth* (New Haven, 1985) and D. Parrott 'The Administration of the French Army during the Ministry of Cardinal Richelieu' (unpublished D.Phil thesis, University of Oxford, 1985).

an armistice with the Dutch.[3] With a wider lens we can see that it cannot have been merely coincidence that in 1559 and 1598 (with France) and in 1609 and 1648 (with the United Provinces) peace treaties involving major compromises were concluded in the wake of royal bankruptcies. Even what superficially appears to be the salient exception to this sequence, the *decreto* of 1627, is only deceptively so. Olivares brilliantly exploited the occasion to introduce dynamic improvements in the machinery of international credit available to the crown, and thus to continue the wars.[4] But this actually supports the point, if from the reverse direction. In any case, the year 1628 saw the most intense discussions over a compromise settlement of any phase of the wars between 1621 and 1648.[5] These debates were once again initiated by Spínola and, although they were ultimately inconclusive, the bitterness engendered can be gauged by Olivares' complaints to the king about the marquis of Los Balbases in 1630.

[He] wished to persuade us to conclude the most dishonourable peace which any king has ever made with his own vassals. And since his intervention in Italy he has been able to achieve nothing more than loss of reputation, so that we are now in danger of defeat both in Italy and Flanders because we paid too much attention to his counsels.[6]

In the positive context, as Alcalá-Zamora has pointed out, Spain's phases of military success did sometimes coincide with good runs of silver engrossments at Seville.[7] A good example is 1633–37, which embraced Feria's superb campaign in the upper Rhineland, Don Fernando's march to Flanders and victory at Nördlingen, the crushing assault on France in 1636, and the naval victories spearheaded by the Armada of Flanders. Contrary to conclusions which have so frequently been reiterated – based upon Hamilton's 1934 tables – the second half of this decade was the best phase of general specie imports for forty years.[8] Not surprisingly, it yielded buoyant returns for the crown.[9]

[3] See their correspondence with Madrid on this issue in CODOIN, 42, passim.

[4] J. Boyajian, *Portuguese Bankers at the Court of Spain, 1626–1650* (New Brunswick, 1983), pp. 38–46; N. Broens, *Monarquía y capital mercantil: Felipe IV y las redes comerciales portuguesas, 1627–35* (Madrid, 1989), pp. 26, 35–43.

[5] See above, Chapters 3–6, passim.

[6] 'El Conde Duque de S. Lúcar: voto en las cosas de Italia', ?August 1630, BN, 988, f. 273.

[7] Alcalá-Zamora, *Razón y crisis de la política exterior de España* (Madrid, 1977), p. 27; see also idem, *España, Flandes y el Mar del Norte* (Barcelona, 1975), p. 122. For more contradictory examples from the 1640s, see below, p. 277.

[8] See M. Morineau, *Incroyables gazettes et fabuleux metaux: Les retours des trésors americains d'apres les gazettes hollandaises (XVIe–XVIIe siècles)* (Cambridge, 1985). I have used the material based on this work in J. Lynch, *The Hispanic World in Crisis and Change, 1598–1700* (1991), pp. 280–83. It must be said, however, both that Morineau's figures do not include estimates of the royal share of engrossments, and that the last word has certainly not been written on the quantitative issues.

[9] The following table has been compiled from random contemporary indications collected by the present author. All figures except those for 1633 and 1655 (ducats) and 1639 (maravedis)

continued

Table 6

Silver Imports for the Crown, 1618–55

Date	Amount (in ducats of 375 maravedis)	Source
1618	2,008,837	PRO, SP 94/23, f. 105
1619	1,588,719	Ibid., ff. 249, 260
1626	4,193,153	Ruíz Martín in Elliott and García Sanz, p. 485
1627	2,496,525	MN, Vargas 26, f. 18
1630	1,371,134	Ibid., f. 56
1633	2,597,245	Barozzi & Berchet, *Relazione*, ii, p. 22
1635	3,122,139	BN, 11137, f. 117
1636	2,645,179	Villa, *Curiosidades*, p. 40
1639	2,994,701	AGS, CJH 794
1648	1,762,588	MN, Vargas 24, f. 130
1655	880,000	Paz y Melia, *Avisos de Barrionuevo*, i, pp. 210–13

The medium-term reality – perhaps not sufficiently exposed in 1979 – is that, even by Hamilton's computations, there never was a progressive shortfall of silver in the period when most textbooks assumed such a phenomenon not only to be rampant but also to be the most important single factor in Spain's international collapse. Certainly, poor returns for the crown in 1616–20 caused grave apprehensions in Madrid, but the worst fears of the treasury council and the *Junta de la Plata* were not realised.[10] By 1624, once again, Sir Benjamin Rudyard's assertion in the House of Commons had topical force and validity:

continued

have been converted from *pesos* of eight reales. The figures given by Ruíz Martín for 1626 and 1627 are taken from unpublished Venetian and Genoese diplomatic reports. The latter is exactly corroborated by my source in the Museo Naval. Though incomplete, the series seems to corroborate the totals suggested by Morineau in revising Hamilton's quinquennial averages for total receipts (i.e. royal plus private) for the period before 1660. It seems certain that the royal share was well above Hamilton's figure of 4.7 million ducats during the quinquennium 1636–40.

[10] The reports of the junta from February to May 1621 convey these misgivings volubly; BL, Add. 14017, ff. 8–27.

They are not his great territories which make him so powerfull ... For it is
very well knowne, that Spaine itself is but weake in men, and barren of natural
commodities ... No sir, they are his mines in the West Indies, which minister
fuell to feed his vast ambitious desire of universall monarchy.[11]

Indeed, for almost the whole of the duration of the Thirty Years War
(1618–48), the royal share of silver imports remained – in terms of five-year
running averages – on a plateau of between six and eight million ducats,
despite the appalling losses of some individual years (1628, 1631–32, 1638,
1640).[12] But what should we conclude from the events of the period which
followed (1646–59), precisely that in which, for a variety of reasons, a run
of serious shortfalls actually did occur? The phase 1647–52, which according
to bullionist logic should have provoked its final collapse, instead witnessed
a tremendous energizing of the Spanish system. This began with the repulse
of Condé's determined onslaught on the key Catalan town of Lérida (June
1647) and ended with the capture of the fortress of Casale in Monferrat –
the very redoubt which Spinola's failure to take had provided the occasion of
Olivares' denunciation (October 1652). The latter victory seemed in Madrid
to be a crowning glory: the marquis of Caraçena had succeeded, where others
– besides Spínola – had failed, in conquering a legendary centre of resistance
to Spanish power. The council of state recognized that

there can be no doubt that this victory was attained in spite of a severe shortage
of resources [but also, they added] with such skill and morale among the leaders,
and courage among the men, that it merits every praise. From this victory, Your
Majesty's arms have acquired renewed reputation and yet greater glory.[13]

Even when the system was saturated with silver, military success was by no
means guaranteed. This point was made in the original text but is important
enough to be worth illustrating afresh. The period 1592–1602 – until recently
thought to be the all-time zenith of silver imports – saw no great victories for
Spain. But, after all, this was a decade of multi-fronted war, with resources
stretched over vast regions of commitment. In the 1660s, when (as we now
know) silver returns began to climb back, rapidly to reach unprecedented
heights, Spain could not even manage to reconquer Portugal, even though it
was now able to concentrate its exclusive attention on the Braganza 'rebels'.

In writing my original essay, I was perhaps over-influenced by Domínguez's
Ortiz's assertion that American silver never amounted to more than 10 per cent
of the crown's war budget. In the first place the claim is not strictly correct
and, in the second, the sheer utility of silver collateral considerably exceeded

---

[11] Quoted in J.H. Elliott, *The Old World and the New, 1492–1650* (Cambridge, 1970),
pp. 90–91. These pages also contain a typically balanced and judicious assessment of the role
of bullion in Madrid's policymaking.

[12] E. Hamilton, *American Treasure and the Price Revolution in Spain, 1501–1650*
(Cambridge, MA, 1934), p. 34; J.H. Elliott, *Imperial Spain, 1469–1719* (1963), p. 175.

[13] *Consulta* of council of state, 2 Dec. 1652, AHN, E 2815.

its rateable value.[14] This was true even at the distorted rates of the mid seventeenth century, which at times obliged the crowd to provide a premium of over 100 per cent for every payment it made in *vellón* outside Castile.[15] It was not the absolute but the relative shortage of silver which caused the problem, its diminishing power in the face of the constant multiplication of war commitments and the relentless escalation of costs, especially in the 1630s and 1640s. Indeed – clean contrary to my earlier assertion (see above, pp. 15–16), in 1634 the war lord Olivares *did* summon an alchemist to court. This timeless stereotype was described in suitably stagey terms as 'a foreigner ... whom they say knows how to make silver from the vilest materials'.[16] Despite this revelation, Olivares will continue (rightly) to be regarded as a statesman ahead of his time. Others will perhaps be less honoured in this respect by historians. Three hundred years after Olivares, during another phase of the struggle for the 'universal cause', Francisco Franco commissioned a Swiss chemist to manufacture gold in the laboratories of the University of Salamanca.[17]

On the broader macroeconomic front, to restate my objective in the words of a Spanish colleague, 'all this is not to devalue the importance of economic factors, but merely to relativize them'.[18] I would still see it as important not to concentrate exclusively even on a mix of internal resource failures in explaining Spain's defeat. Of course war is, to a significant degree, dependent on the creation, exploitation and distribution of material resources. In the second and third of these attributes, the Spanish monarchy was *sans pareil* – but this fact was comensurately inimical to success in the first. Nevertheless, the much-vaunted modern methods of analysis and assessment of economic factors do not possess either the quantitative exactitude or the causative precision which they were once assumed to bestow on the historian's calculations. Any disinterested party who has lived through the last thirty years in Britain will (I suppose) admit not only that economics is as irremediably pragmatic a discipline as history (or even alchemy), but also that contemporary government has little cause to feel superior to its prototypes in the effectiveness of economic management. In any case, the cry of '*la falta de medios*', with its accompanying shouts of frustration and moans of despair, echoes from the centre to the periphery of the Spanish system, and re-echoes all the way down its history from 1500 to 1700. It is no more and no less important a reason for the setback at Rocroi in 1643 as for that at Marignano in 1515.

[14] Domínguez Ortiz, 'Los caudales de Indias', p. 335. The formulation I made about the 'peculiar revenue attribute' of the Spanish monarchy had been adumbrated (unknown to me in 1979) by Perry Anderson in his *The Lineages of the Absolutist State* (1974), p. 71.

[15] 'The surcharge has now reached 50 per cent, so that to obtain credit and services to the value of 4,000,000 ducats silver for Flanders, Italy and Catalonia we need to find 6,000,000 in *vellón*'; untitled anon. memo of May 1648, AMAE, 42, f. 212. This complaint actually came soon after a massive deflation of *vellón* in 1647.

[16] Gayangos, *Cartas*, i, p. 117.

[17] See P. Preston, *El Cid and the Masonic Super-State: Franco, the Western Powers and the Cold War* (1992).

[18] Alcalá-Zamora, *España, Flandes*, p. 152.

Chapters 3–6

These essays deal, from several angles of perspective, with the political and cultural interpretation of the great Franco-Spanish war of 1629–59. As well as helping to explain the nature of *Olivarismo* in Spain, this work is concerned with the original generation of structural Franco-Spanish hostility on various levels, conscious and subliminal, individual and collective, and with the imbrication of historiography in its long and polymorphous survival. It seems not inappropriate, therefore, to address the pieces together in one section.

Olivares' resentful mood in 1630 was largely a result of his own disastrous miscalculations over the Mantuan War. The count-duke's determination not to be frustrated in his design for a brilliant politico-military *golpe* in Italy is further illustrated by the fate of the envoy sent to Spain by the duke of Nevers in order, through explanation and apology, to appease Spanish anger. This was Agnelli Maffei, an official based in Casale, who was accredited by Nevers in January 1628. In Milan he was refused an audience with any senior official and was then denied passage for Spain at Genoa by the marquis of Santa Cruz. Eventually, after clandestinely chartering his own vessel, he arrived in Madrid in April – by which time Fernández de Córdoba had marched into Monferrat. Olivares granted Maffei an interview – but only to inform him that his master was required to come in person, cap in hand, to seek the forgiveness of Philip IV.[19] No wonder that most historians concur on the crucial importance of Olivares' Mantuan misadventure: it is one thing to be capricious, another to compound caprice with obstinacy.

Years later, Philip IV did manage to acquire some of the glories of the Gonzaga dynasty. In 1645, around the time that the king revealed his besetting remorse over the Mantuan War to Sor María, 'original paintings by Titian, Pablo Verones and other ancient masters whose work is valued' came onto the London art-market. These had apparently been sold by Duke Vincenzo Gonzaga to the first duke of Buckingham. The Spanish ambassador, Cárdenas, was ordered to put in a bid for them. They were being sold off to help pay the second duke's huge composition fines, imposed to expunge his pernicious royalism; in the event he managed to raise the funds to hold onto this collection.[20] Four years later, the even more splendid gallery of Mantuan masterpieces purchased by Charles I himself were sold off by Parliament. Despite 'the extremely inflated prices' complained of by Cárdenas, Neapolitan revenues were utilized, and the celebrated canvasses (now in the Prado) came to the Buen Retiro for Philip's delectation.[21]

---

[19] R. Quazza, *La guerra per successione di Mantova e del Monferrato* (Mantua, 1926), p. 76.

[20] A. de Rozas to C. de Coloma, 29 June 1645 and *consulta* of council of state, 12 May 1646, AGS, E 2523.

[21] *Consulta* of the council of state, 1 Feb. 1650, AGS E 2526.

Olivares' outburst against Spínola, quoted above, also illustrates his determination to press on with the task of achieving ultimate victory. From this time onwards he regarded Spain as involved in a *de facto* war with France which would be declared *de jure* as soon as it became convenient. According to Leman, 'après le counseil royal de 23 Janvier [1632] la rupture avec la France est même décidée; elle aurait été consommée, si l'Empereur avait consenti a suivre le roi d'Espagne'.[22] In the same month the English ambassador, Hopton, reported that 'they are making here great preparations for a long war'.[23] Later that year, Philip IV explained the policy of *guerra cubierta* to Francisco de Melo, envoy to the republic of Genoa.

> An open war of crown against crown will demand profounder consideration and require many and efficient preparations, so that it is better for now to keep France occupied with diversions in any way we can. I have ordered the marquis of Villafranca to stand by with the galleys of Naples, Sicily and Genoa in order to assist in this policy ... for example in providing help for the cause of Monsieur [i.e. Gaston of Orleans], and your task is to mobilize the Republic in this matter.[24]

By the early summer of 1634, as my essay in the *English Historical Review's* centenary number showed, a scheme of operations had been adopted which, if put into execution, would inevitably have precipitated open war. On 24 July Philip noted:

> Since having seen certain intercepted papers, with details of their designs against Spain, I have decided to send to the *junta de execución* a very urgent order, stating that it is necessary to step up the tempo in all those measures which have been resolved against France.[25]

Indeed, the Abad Scaglia, Olivares' agent at the court of Queen Marie de Médicis (who had taken refuge from Richelieu in Brussels) was insisting that 'the offences given by France are so many that they call for payment – France's reduction to a condition in which she can never offend us again'. Like his compatriot, Prince Thomas, Scaglia sketched out a grand plan of attack, including the capture of Bordeaux by a sea-borne task force.[26] Accordingly, the duke of Cardona, in command of the army of Catalonia, was ordered to join forces with the marquis of Valparaiso in Navarre, preparatory to an invasion of Béarn timed to coincide with Santa Cruz's descent upon Provence.[27]

---

[22] Leman, *Richelieu et Olivares*, p. 101.

[23] Hopton to Juxon, Jan. 1632, BL, Eg. 1820, f. 136v.

[24] Philip IV to F. de Melo, 2 Aug. 1632, AGS, E 3950, f. 136. I owe this and two subsequent references from AGS, E K1425 to Ms Maria Peralta.

[25] *Consulta* of the council of state, 24 July 1634, AGS, E K1425, file, 69–123.

[26] Scaglia to Olivares (1634), quoted in M. Echevarría, *La diplomácia secreta en Flandes, 1598–1643* (Leioa, 1984), pp. 208–9.

[27] Memo to J. de Villanueva, 27 July 1634, AGS, E K1425, file 69–123. This document reiterated an order first issued on 5 July, but which was never carried out.

OLIVARES' MASTER-PLAN, 1634-35

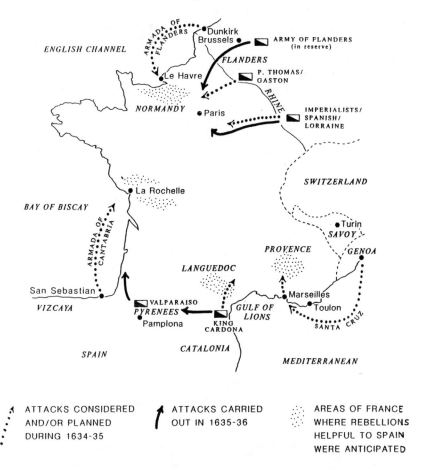

⌃ : ⁚	ATTACKS CONSIDERED AND/OR PLANNED DURING 1634-35	⌠	ATTACKS CARRIED OUT IN 1635-36	⁙⁙	AREAS OF FRANCE WHERE REBELLIONS HELPFUL TO SPAIN WERE ANTICIPATED

Olivares's increasing tendency to dictatorial government resulted from his nagging fear that (as he himself put it), 'time is getting on'. 'We need [he added] to gain every hour and every second we can, and even then we will not reach our goal early enough.'[28] His arbitrary attitudes attracted comment even from supporters, like the Madrid Jesuits, one of whom retailed a story that the *valido* had been contradicted in the junta of state over a renewed confiscation of *juros* dividends, and minister's votes on the proposal were tied at 3–3. Olivares placed his hand upon the insignia of the Order of Santiago embroidered on his doublet: 'By this cross, I say that if this is not done, Spain will be lost.' But his opponent replied, with a similar gesture: 'By this cross, if it *is* done, I say that Spain will be lost.'[29] This incident apparently occurred

[28] 'Papel que dió el Conde Duque al Rey' (1634), BL, Eg. 2053, f. 151.
[29] Gayangos, *Cartas*, i, p. 167.

a few weeks before the French declaration of war (April 1635). A year later –
perhaps a year too late – came the launching of the 'master-plan', when, in the
vivid account of the art-historian Karl Justi, 'the Parisians of 1636 witnessed
from the heights of Montmartre the smoke of the burning villages of Picardy,
which proclaimed the approach of the cardinal-prince and of Thomas of
Savoy'.[30] It is not surprising that when, in the 1640s, French armies occupied
Catalonia, they were not too concerned to discriminate between Philip IV's
rebels and his faithful subjects. In November 1643, the 'most ancient city
of Ampurias' complained 'that the French soldiery rob and mistreat all our
people. Innumerable outrages are reported, and bitter protests are heard on all
sides. The damage they have done in every part of Catalonia is notorious'.[31]

---

[30] K. Justi, *Diego Velázquez and his Times* (1889), p. 196.

[31] Printed flysheet of 2 Nov. 1643, endorsed 'que ha escrit la antiquissima ciudad de
Empuries', BN, 2375, f. 53.

In view of the aggregation of evidence now presented concerning this hypothesis, I cannot
accept J.I. Israel's contention that 'the truth is that Olivares planned no great move against
France in the years 1636–7', *Empires and Entrepots*, p. 184. Of course, during this period the
land war with the Dutch remained on foot. The army of Flanders maintained a field-force on
the northern frontier, defended its border fortifications network, attempted to repulse Dutch
attacks, and, when tactically necessary, undertook certain limited offensive operations. However,
it is my belief that the years after 1634 witnessed a dimunition of the strategic and political
importance of this front, and the promotion of operations against France to priority. In *My
Armada of Flanders* (see p. 89 et seq.) in addition to the present text, more support for this
conclusion is adduced; but also it is demonstrated that the war with the Dutch continued on
a full footing at sea.

Chapter 7

The figure of the duke of Medina de las Torres, whom this essay rescued from obscurity, has now begun to make his mark on textbook treatment of the post-Olivares period. So much so, that on a casual visit to the Prado in 1990, I discovered that the Bernini-style bust of Don Ramiro by Juan Melchior Pérez, which the authorities had earlier refused me permission to examine in its basement exile, had been produced *de profundis* and installed in the main hall (not very appropriately) between Velázquez's two great equestrian portraits of Philip III and Queen Margarita.[32]

A good deal of new material on the development of Medina's political career was incorporated into the relevant sections of my *Philip IV*.[33] As a result of this, along with a number of studies from various hands concerning the Naples viceroyalty, most authorities now accept that his role in government was of considerable importance in the period stipulated by my original essay. However, both inside and outside Spain, experts have been less willing to consider the implications that Medina's career holds for assessment of the roles of Luis de Haro (on the one hand) and of King Philip IV himself (on the other). This reluctance seems so deeply-rooted as to be almost a cultural case-study in itself. As I pointed out in 1976, no less an authority than Cánovas del Castillo concluded a century ago that Haro's ministry was markedly different in nature to that of Olivares, and that (at best) the former was *valido* only in a highly qualified sense. Reluctance (especially in Spain) to register these facts stems – it seems to me – from the profounder issue which lies behind it: a residual resistance to the idea that Philip IV had a mature character and real political ability, and did not need a dominating favourite. Strange though it may seem after generations of inveighing against 'the Black Legend', many Spanish intellectuals are determined to cling to the comforting images of seventeenth-century *decadencia*, perhaps fearing that Spain can never become superior again if she abandons the stimulus of her complex inferiority, perhaps because of an ideological tendency to nurture the myth that Spain failed because of *olivarismo's* crazy European crusade, coupled with its abandonment of the traditional regional consensus. Despite this, and despite their caution over revising a nostrum as old as the history textbook itself, few authorities would still see Haro as the straightforward successor to Olivares in the *valimiento*.[34]

Medina was a Guzmán of the ancient stock, descended by tradition from the bodyguards of Visigothic kings – the *gutmannen*.[35] Paradoxically, this uniquely distinguished provenance was never quite enough to eradicate the

---

[32] The bust is Prado General Catalogue no. 254; the label gave its subject the erroneous personal names of 'Don Gaspar de Guzmán y Acebedo'.

[33] See esp. pp. 107–17, 246–68.

[34] See (e.g.) Lynch, *The Hispanic World*, pp. 162–63.

[35] 'Solar de los S[eño]res Guzmanes de León', AHPC, CEM 33, ff. 52–3v.

feeling – in his own mind, perhaps, as well as the jealous minds of others – that he was an interloper. Certainly, he was able to seize the opportunities provided by Olivares' patronage with both hands. Wherever he went and throughout his long career, he made enemies just as easily as his father-in-law, and with a seeming indifference even greater. As a result of the Carafa marriage, those enemies came to include Olivares himself. The *valido* freely expressed dissatisfaction with Medina's conduct as viceroy and the latter began (more mutedly) to reply in kind.[36] Moreover, Don Ramiro may have carried his response to advice ('make your own reputation, and do not rely upon my remaining in a position so subject to sudden change') to lengths not intended by its originator. Medina's accumulation of power can be gauged by a list of his titles and offices made in 1641.

> Señor Ramiro Phelipe Guzmán, Duque de Medina de las Torres, Marqués de Toral, Marqués de Monasterio, Conde de Parma, Conde del Cole, Conde de Baldeón, Señor de las villas y montañas del Valle de Corueno, Sumiller de corps de su Magestad Catholica, Gran Chanciller de las Indias, Teseroro General de la corona de Aragón, Comnedador de Valdepeñas, Capitán de los 100 continos de la guardia de la persona real, castellano de Castel Novo de Nápoles, virrey lugarteniente y capitán general del Reyno de Nápoles.[37]

Thus Medina saw himself as successor in the *valimiento* – perhaps even as the agent and/or beneficiary of some 'sudden change' in Madrid. He was physically, and in terms of personality – if not in those of ability – very much on the Olivares scale. This probably helped to persuade Philip to hold back from awarding him the ultimate prize. I suspect, moreover, that the seven years of Medina's separation from the king did, in practice, have a partially eroding effect on the bond of their friendship. Don Ramiro returned from Naples in 1644 flushed with success, with a hardened ambition, huge personal wealth and the crude political instincts of a Camorra boss. His behaviour as convener of the council of Aragon in the late 1640s illustrates a determination to obtain deference and recognition which was obsessive even by the standards of his caste.[38] Philip had been matured by quite a different set of circumstances, by failure (even humiliation) by the debilitating pangs of conscience and by a series of agonising bereavements. Medina's rampantly amoral lifestyle and his experiences of married life rendered him hardly *simpático* on issues which had come to concern the king rather more than the pursuit of sexual and artistic diversions. Such concerns were catered for, not only by Sor María and by another conventual confidante, Sor Luisa,

---

[36] See (e.g.) Olivares to Don Fernando, 19 Feb. 1639, Cuvelier and Lefèvre, *Correspondence*, ii, p. 290; Medina to Philip IV, 20 Feb. 1641, RAH, 1053, ff. 403v. 405. The latter refers cryptically to the need to attack 'the cancer which is beginning to fester in the principal organs of Spain, such as the head and heart'.

[37] Given in the preamble to his agreement with the Polish envoy, RAH, 1053, f. 401v. It modestly fails to include Medina's private Neapolitan titles acquired by the Carafa marriage.

[38] Information kindly provided by Dr Patrick Williams.

but also by the marquis of Aytona, a deeply religious and sensitive soldier-statesman of the younger generation.[39]

In the 1650s Medina's access to funds, household offices and political experience brought him a faction-following which became, in effect, a kind of semi-official 'opposition' to the Haro (junta-based) 'cabinet'.[40] The Haro group was seen by Philip as heir to Olivares, at least in the sense that it held the line against the constant pressure of the traditional *grandeza*, providing royal government with a senior civil service which was largely free of aristocratic influence. The signs are that, for all his regrets about the degree of power he had alienated to Olivares, Philip wished to preserve the tightly-knit and professional intra-governmental teams, positioned and trained by Don Gaspar, in order to avail himself of their services in a more direct manner. In terms of what I have called 'the balance of faction', Medina and Haro had partly differing – but also partly overlapping – areas of authority and influence. Whether they also had sincere differences over policy is impossible to establish, certainly in any convincing detail. Medina's concern for the domestic situation perhaps began as a mere political tactic, a cynical attempt to take advantage of the fact that Haro was responsible for management of the war-policy. But this policy itself was that of Philip, and not of Don Luis. Haro worked intensively to make the Madrid peace conference of 1656 a success. In any case, Medina carried these priorities over to the following decade, when he himself had the foreign affairs 'portfolio'.

[39] For Sor Luisa, see J. Pérez Villanueva (ed.), *Felipe IV y Luisa Enríquez Manrique de Lara, condesa de Paredes de Nava: un epistolario indédito* (Salamanca, 1986). Aytona's friendship with the king, dating from the years of Philip's *jornadas* to the Catalan war, remains at present unexplored. He was reported to be the only lay person who stayed at Philip's bedside in the latter's last moments, 'hablándose en materias de espíritu'; 'Relación de la enfermedad y muerte del Rey . . .', BN, 12952, f. 4.

[40] 'Both inside and outside the council of state, he captained the opposition'; Maura, *Carlos II y su corte*, i, p. 30.

Chapter 8

This, my first publication in history, is also the only chapter to have been quarried entirely from the work carried out for my Ph.D. thesis, 'Anglo-Spanish Relations from the Restoration to the Peace of Aix-la-Chapelle, 1660–1668', completed in 1968, which remains unpublished.

Years later at Simancas, searching a bundle of miscellaneous addenda to do with English affairs, I came across the records of a council of state meeting which definitively established the link between Spain, Edmund Ludlow and the conspiracy scares of 1662–63. Early in 1662 Spain's governor-general in Flanders – Caraçena, victor of Casale – reported that the English Presbyterian party, outraged by the return of bishops to the House of Lords, had determined on violent protest. From his exile hideout in Geneva, Ludlow sent word to Brussels, stating his intention of responding to the request of certain conspirators to take up residence in one of the Channel ports, so as to be ready to cross and take command of a rebel army when the signal came. Given the state of mutual (if covert) hostility existing between Spain and England, Ludlow wished to ascertain whether he could rely on Spanish aid in such an eventuality. Caraçena's main interest lay in the opportunity which this alliance offered of recovering the port of Dunkirk, then garrisoned on King Charles's behalf by a force of ex-Cromwellian soldiers.[41] The council, comprising Medina de las Torres, the marquis of Velada, and the dukes of Alba and Terranova, reacted positively:

> Since Your Majesty has so few means by which to strike back at England, or to make war officially, we have felt it necessary to dissimulate as much as possible, and avoid open hostilities. Yet considering the provocative actions of that king [Charles II] we fear that it will not be possible to delay an official declaration for much longer ... In everything he reveals his vast and dangerous designs against us. Therefore we are justified in taking action which may divert and prevent such intentions, and nothing is more efficacious in this respect than to stir up trouble, within the kingdom, which will make impossible any adventures outside it.
>
> We recommend that the initiative of General Dodololo [sc. Edmundo Ludlow] should be encouraged. A further point in its favour, is that the Presbyterian party is struggling for freedom of conscience in England, an aim which is most laudable, for once the public exercise of the Catholic religion is allowed, it will be the best means of returning that people, one day, to the full obedience and membership of the Roman Church.

---

[41] Caracena to Philip IV, 5 Jan. 1662, AGS, E 2099. A marginal note explains to Philip that 'this General Dodololo is not one of the chiefs at the present parliament, subordinate to the king, but a leader of the parliament which overthrew the [previous] king and executed him'. Looking back, my original failure to discover this document seems a blessing in disguise. I would never have had the courage to reveal details of a conspiracy led by General Dodololo to the sober readership of the *English Historical Review*.

It should be done as recommended [Philip decided] but in such a careful way that the king of England can never know, since it might go badly for us should he discover anything before we are in a position to declare war.[42]

A decade earlier, when he was chief parliamentary commissioner in Ireland, Ludlow had dealings with Richard White of Limerick. The latter approached the commissioners for licence to transport the surrendered remnants of Catholic armies which had opposed the Commonwealth, to serve as mercenaries in Spain.[43] Once he received clearance from Madrid, it would have been logical for Caraçena to put Ludlow in contact with the White brothers, who in person, and/or through their extensive commercial and political contacts, were able to liaise between Ireland, England, the Spanish Netherlands and Spain itself. In his list of 'secret expenses' for the London embassy, later submitted to the Madrid treasury, Baron Batteville claimed the disbursement of £2,577, 'for an extraordinary business of which your majesty has knowledge'.[44] In not even confiding details to paper in these circumstances, this assiduous (if somewhat undiplomatic) ambassador certainly obeyed Philip's keynote instructions to the letter.

On the Spanish side, all concerned may have been following a will-o-the-wisp. Without question, Edmund Ludlow was Public Enemy Number One for the Restoration government in the early 1660s (and for some time thereafter). There seems a strong possibility that the affair was an elaborate ruse, planned in Whitehall, and intended to tempt Ludlow away from the protection of Switzerland, bringing him within the compass of an English snatch-squad. After all, only a year or so earlier, Ignatius White himself had successfully organized the abduction of another exiled regicide, Thomas Scot, who was picked up in Brussels and given a one-way ticket to Marble Arch.[45]

---

[42] *Consulta* of the council of state, 29 Jan. and royal *apostilla* of 4 Feb. 1662, AGS E 2099. The council was certainly excited by the prospect of recovering Dunkirk. For the importance and strategic situation of the port of this time, see my *Armada of Flanders*, esp. pp. 144–50, 229–30.

[43] Parliamentary Commissioners to Speaker Lenthall, 6 May 1652, C. McNeil (ed.), *The Tanner Letters: Original Documents and Notices of Irish Affairs in the Sixteenth and Seventeenth Centuries* (Dublin, 1943), p. 358. For the context, see R.A. Stradling, *The Spanish Monarchy and Irish Mercenaries: The Wild Geese in Spain, 1618–68* (Dublin, 1994).

[44] Batteville's accounts as ambassador in London (1660–62), AGS, CMC 2985, no. 13.

[45] C.H. Firth (ed.), 'Thomas Scot's Account of his Actions as Intelligencer', *EHR*, 12 (1897), p. 117.

Chapter 9

As one commentator suggested at the time, this contribution may well have contained 'an element of special pleading'. Originally appearing simultaneously alongside 'Decline or Survival?', it was intended to complement and illustrate its partner's hypotheses by concentrating on two familiar case-studies, the battles of the Downs and Rocroi. In some respects, it seems, this exercise proved only too successful; I recently encountered the remark of an examination candidate that 'Stradling has shown how important was the Spanish rout of the French at Rocroi'! In fact, my aim (once again) was to relativize the catastrophe, not to minimize it, in the context of explaining how Spanish military power was able to recover and survive. To the extent that the military emergency is actually wished away, Spain's achievement in surviving it appears less worthy of remark and attention. In the commentary which follows I have largely left aside the maritime dimension of the 'catastrophe', which is much further amplified in my book on *The Armada of Flanders* (1992).[46]

One impression conveyed by the 1979 text may have been slightly mis-leading. What happened at Rocroi was regarded very seriously at the time, and even the heroic comportment of Castile's 'poor bloody infantry' did little to assuage the loss of *reputación* sensed in Madrid. Don Luis de Haro, losing no opportunity to attack a rival, sought to blame Medina de las Torres, suggesting that the background reasons for the debacle lay in the viceroy's failure to supply Flanders with subsidies (and Polish mercenaries) from the Naples *asistencias*. He hinted that some kind of inquiry into the setback was under way.

> From the defeat of Rocroi have resulted the grave consequences which we have feared for so long. The original decision to invade France was a very strange one [*notable resolución fue aquella*] and nobody seems to be able to account properly for the military or political reasons why it was taken. I confess openly to you that it is a matter which I never bring to mind without great melancholy.[47]

These remarks were addressed to the marquis of Velada, the experienced second-in-command of the army of Flanders, who had been chief *aide-de-camp* of Don Fernando (the cardinal-infante). Philip IV had always feared that the latter, who led his troops from the front, might be killed in battle. Early in the year of his untimely death (as it happened, from 'natural causes'), Don Fernando himself asked his brother to consider the problem of how the Netherlands were to be governed in that eventuality. He put forward the names of Prince Thomas of Savoy and of a promising protégé of the count-duke's, Francisco de Melo, count of Barajas.[48] Melo had proved himself

[46] See esp. pp. 96–118.

[47] Haro to Velada, 17 Nov. 1643, BPU, 39, ff. 88–89. These papers of the Favre collection comprise assorted material relevant to the tours of duty of Antonio Sancho-Dávila, 3rd marquis of Velada, in Flanders and England (1636–43).

[48] See *consulta* of council of state, 17 Jan. 1641, AGS, E 2056.

an accomplished administrator (in Sicily) and diplomat (in Genoa), but had not yet won his military spurs. His name had been first canvassed for a senior post in Brussels some years earlier; one jealously barbed opinion was that

> he is a splendid gentleman and very clever – but Portuguese, and perhaps a little green for the job he aspires towards. He makes so much of the count-duke my master's favour, that one would think he has enough credit for His Excellency to make harps sound in the meadows in his praise.[49]

When the council of state met to respond to Don Fernando's request it was in the immediate wake of the rebellion in Lisbon. As a result, the question of Melo's national allegiance – and also, perhaps, that of his source of patronage – was even more sensitive. Olivares felt obliged to concede that Melo would have to be thoroughly vetted before further promotion.[50] Yet even when it proved, in the upshot, that it was Prince Thomas, and not Don Francisco, who had been harbouring a scheme to transfer his services to the enemy, the situation was still not resolved in the latter's favour. In July 1641 Philip named a contingency commission, including Melo and Velada – 'to whom collectively I give power and authority to act as my sovereign lieutenants in those provinces' – as *pro tempore* replacement for his brother.[51]

Despite this interim decision, Melo was nominated as sole governor and commander-in-chief shortly after Don Fernando's death in October 1641. If – as seems likely – the count-duke had insisted upon the appointment, then the following spring, in Melo's first campaign, his patron's confidence was spectacularly rewarded. Utterly obscured from the view of most textbooks by the excessive smoke and noise from nearby Rocroi, Honnecourt was a victory such as Don Fernando himself had never achieved in this theatre – in which even the coveted prize of the 'white lily' standard of the house of Bourbon, never before lost, was captured from the *compagnie du dauphin*.[52] The triumph was all the more welcome since it came when Philip IV was in the saddle, *en route* to his first campaign against the French on Catalonia. Melo's contribution had made the king's task – specifically the relief of Lérida – that much easier, since it was expected that the French would now be forced to divert resources away from the campaign in the peninsula.

A sadder and wiser man following Rocroi, Melo was at pains to point out that the record of the army of Flanders under his leadership was both generally successful and had been achieved despite an asphyxiation of resources. He referred in detail to the fact that his predecessors had enjoyed much larger subsidies from Spain, yet still managed to lose vital

---

[49] F. de Galarreta to M. de Salamanca, 6 Oct. 1637, AHN, E 962, f. 63v.

[50] *Consulta* of 17 Jan 1641 (as above n. 47). The others present were Cardinals Borja and Spínola, the marquises of Mirabel and Santa Cruz, and the count of Castrofuerte.

[51] 'Copia del Poder que Su Magd. da a las Personas que van nombrados en el para el gobierno politico de los estados del Pais Bajo . . .', 19 July 1641, BPU, 38, ff. 88–91.

[52] CODOIN, 86, p. 37.

strong-points. Don Francisco stated that in 1642 the receipts of his military treasury had slumped badly. Despite this, in addition to Honnecourt.

> we took Lens and La Bassé, hitting the enemy so hard that he was obliged to abandon Gebrian into the bargain. We lost nothing ourselves, and indeed the enemy was unable even to trespass for one yard upon Your Majesty's territory. As a result, the king of France was obliged to retreat from his move towards the Spanish frontier.[53]

During 1643, however, aid from Spain had fallen away dramatically to a total of only 1,250,000 escudos – little over a quarter of that received only two years earlier – with the predictable result. Doubtless in response to Haro's inquiry, Melo did not neglect to add some other reasons for his disaster at Rocroi. Above all, in his own defence he could plead that he had been encouraged both from Madrid and by his senior colleagues to seek once more to take the pressure off the Catalan front. In September 1642 Velada had reported the general state of the army to be surprisingly good 'considering that we have invaded and beaten the enemy and marched almost 300 leagues back, in good order throughout'. The marquis acknowledged that another diversion in 1643 should be the priority, for the same reason: 'to draw the king of France back from our Spanish borders'. However, he added that the exercise was fraught with risk; the army of Flanders had to operate on three fronts, and the state of supplies from Spain was already giving cause for concern.[54] When the time arrived, Velada had apparently changed his mind. He now advised his chief to await political developments within France, since the death of Louis XIII was expected imminently. If he was to invade France, Melo might alienate potentially pro-Spanish interests and even force them into a patriotic common front. Velada added that

> I cannot forbear to tell your excellency that I am apprehensive about the army which you have at your command. It seriously lacks discipline, and I fear it might prove too brittle if called upon to stand up to a pitched battle.[55]

---

[53] 'Memoria para el Snr Marq[ue]s de Castel Rodrigo sobre materias de hacienda ... Valenciennes a 30 de Sept. de 1644, Don Fran[cisc]o de Melo, Marqués de Tordelaguna', ARB, SEG 90bis, ff. 328–30. Melo recalled that his royal predecessor had received nearly 5,000,000 escudos subsidy in 1640 and over 4,500,000 in 1641.

[54] 'Papel que el Marqués mi Senor dió al Snr Don Fr[ancisc]o en Nuevofosse a 15 de Settr 1642', BPU, 39, ff. 268–69.

[55] 'Voto que el Marqués mi Señor dió al Senor Don Francisco en Lila a – de Mayo 1643 sobre el manejo y empleo de las armas de Su Magd el mismo año', ibid., pp. 271–76. The missing digits in the title-date and some unusual corrections to the text of this *voto* may be taken to indicate that it (and perhaps the document cited in n. 53) was prepared in response to an official enquiry (or *visita*). If this is the case, they may not faithfully reproduce the advice tendered on the occasions in question. Notably, Velada seems to have back-tracked from his September assessment of the state of the army. But, of course, armies could often undergo serious deterioration during winter months; that of Flanders was no exception.

Concurrently with Velada's opinion, Melo was the recipient of almost identical advice from another close associate of Olivares, who happened to be in Brussels, Marquis Virgilio Malvezzi. In his view, internecine strife in France was likely to be serious enough to save Melo the trouble of an active campaign in 1643. Melo should do nothing to discourage such developments, he added, since 'the saying is very old and very true that fear of attack from outside is the best remedy for any internal disorders'.[56]

Given the inauspicious circumstances sketched out above, why did Melo decide to ignore advice from such experienced and distinguished counsellors and to push ahead with the invasion of France? This, surely, was the 'notable resolución' of Haro's letter to Velada. Perhaps the triumph of Honnecourt had gone to Melo's head. After all, he had begun in Spain's service as an impoverished squire with no fortune nor great family connection. In terms of military glory, the raw *bisoño* of 1642 had become a grandee and Spain's most famous soldier in one fell swoop. For all this, the probably answer is that in May 1643 Melo placed more importance on his standing strategic instructions from Madrid – that is, on his obligation to help relieve the pressure on Lérida at all costs. Mixed with this, perhaps, was anxiety that his own career (following the disgrace of his protector, Olivares) would not survive accusations of dereliction of duty on such a vital score.

Don Francisco need not have worried on the latter count. King Philip remained grateful to the victor of Honnecourt, and ensured – whatever the result of Haro's inquiry – that Melo was not treated as a scapegoat. On the contrary, he was welcomed back to court, took up membership of the council of state, and played a major role both here and in the council of war until his death in 1651.

---

[56] Untitled memo dated 11 May 1643, BL, Add. 28452, ff. 233–37. Like Velada, Malvezzi seems to have had access to unusually reliable forecasts concerning the demise of Louis XIII.

Several of the arguments made in this section were first advanced by Cánovas del Castillo at various points in his *Estudios*, ii, and later taken up by the great German scholar Ludwig Pfandl in his superb study of *Karl II von Spanien* (Munich, 1940). The later was translated into Spanish as *Carlos II* (Madrid, 1947); see, in particular, ibid., pp. 22–28.

Chapter 11

Like that of the Castilian infantry which he commanded, Melo's personal courage at the battle of Rocroi had helped to salvage something from catastrophe – if it was only material which became the stuff of future legend.[57] Yet at some point, the commander-in-chief was obliged to make his escape, abandoning to their fate more junior functionaries, such as one who fell into the enemy's hands whilst trying to protect his papers. The victim of this incident, so evocative of the archetypal Spanish *papelista*, was Pedro del Vaus y Frías, *oficial mayor* in the military paymaster's section, with special responsibility for the cavalry.[58] Given the relative absence of horses, Don Pedro was perhaps not terribly overworked: indeed his capture on the battlefield suggests that he may not even have possessed the means of his own escape. As material in this chapter (and in Chapter 9) illustrates, not only was the army of Flanders crucially light on its cavalry component because of the shortage of horses but, even if the mounts *had* been available, the saddles for them were not. Whatever the general strategic position and/or the immediate financial resources of Melo's army, and whatever conclusions Madrid's inquiry may have arrived at, it can be argued in time-honoured style that for want of a nail the battle was lost.

The equestrian crisis in the Netherlands had been building up for some time. There was one input to it, however, which I had not fully registered in 1984. It was customary after a pitched battle for the men of the winning side to cut up and cook the cadavers of the day's cavalry carnage – it provided a splendid celebratory feast such as that enjoyed by Estebanillo González after the victory of Nördlingen in 1634.[59] Seven years later, during the campaigns immortalized in Snayers' canvasses, the desperate subjects of his studies reached such a pitch of starvation that they crept upon their own horse-compound at night and despatched the healthy animals, the quartered quadrupeds promptly disappearing into the scattered cauldrons of the camp. This particular intelligence comes from Velada, whose force was guarding the Dutch frontier. Velada also reported that his cavalrymen had not been paid since the previous September; his chief stableman had been without funds for twenty-two months and only had six horses left.[60]

The situation within Spain gave even more cause for concern. In 1635 the loss of three transport vessels carrying horses from Naples was a grave blow to Olivares's hopes for rescheduling the projected military landing in southern

---

[57] Velada, in his own account of Rocroi (presumably submitted to the inquiry), paid tribute to his chief's valour on the day; see BPU, 39, ff. 277–82.

[58] Testimonials for Vaus y Frías, July 1648 and March 1649, BL, Add. 22503, ff. 23, 26.

[59] N. Spadaccini and A. Zachareas (ed.), *La vida y hechos de Estebanillo González, hombre de buen humor* (2 vols, Madrid, 1978), ii, p. 312. Notably enough, Estebanillo also later commented upon the absence of Spanish cavalry at Rocroi, ibid., p. 470.

[60] Velada to Fontana, 8 July 1641, BPU, 39, ff. 35–40.

France.[61] By 1641, Olivares was demanding that Medina de las Torres provide 9,000,000 ducats, 12,000 troops *and* 2,500 horses from the kingdom of Naples, for deployment in that year alone.[62] A few years later, the viceroy of Valencia noted that no horses (nor mules) were available to keep the royal posts going. He ordered that the men in charge of posting-stations within his jurisdiction should simply confiscate any animals they felt suitable, compensating owners 'with what is the normal price, making no concessions to the rate of demand'.[63] It is hardly surprising that not a single horse from the large Danish shipment which called at an English port (probably Gravesend) in June 1642 could be spared for the army of Flanders.[64] The more the 'conjuncture' of Rocroi is considered, the more it seems to be the logical outcome of the military emergency within the peninsula, which in turn hinged upon the fate of the redoubt of Lérida, and upon the decision (formalized in 1644, despite Rocroi) to give the Catalan war supreme priority in the allocation of resources.

In Madrid in 1652 the French traveller Brunel noted that 'the wars have made horses very scarce and dear in Spain'. He was commenting on the bizarre custom at the Spanish court that 'no man ever mounts a horse the king hath once made use of'. Medina de las Torres had recently sent the most beautiful horse in his stables for the king to ride in the forthcoming procession to the church of Our Lady of Atocha, where a *Te Deum* was to be sung for the recapture of Barcelona. Philip, mindful of the said custom, sent the animal back to its owner with the comment 'it would be such a pity'. 'And indeed', Brunel added, 'no horses are so little rid as the king's, which almost burst with fat'. Philip himself had recently made a present of twelve of them to Queen Christina of Sweden.[65] Contrary to appearances, this was not simply another demonstration of plenty for the purposes of maintaining *reputación*, but may be considered an investment of some foresight. After her abdication, the convert Christina was to prove a stalwart ally in the raising of resources for the defence of the Spanish monarchy.[66]

Like most other princes of his epoch, Philip had a keen appreciation of horses. The main public memorial to him in present-day Madrid is the enormous equestrian statue, cast by Pietro Tacca from Velázquez's sketches,

[61] Hopton to Coke, 19 June 1635, PRO, SP 94/37, f. 191.

[62] Villari, *La rivolta antispagnola*, p. 139.

[63] Duke of Arcos to Jurats of Alicante, 16 Aug, 1644, AHMA, Alm. 5/17, f. 59. My calculations of prices paid for army mounts in the 1640s and 1650s have been confirmed by later investigation in the bundle of *tanteos* returned by the commission of 1644 (in AGS, CMC 1969); and by 'Punto en razón de la compra de veinte caballos que su excelencia por su órden mandó comprar en ésta ciudad y provincia . . .[por] Simón de Mena', 27 Sept. 1658, AHPO, caja 144.

[64] *Consulta* of council of state, 28 Aug. 1642, AGS, E 2522.

[65] A. de Brunel, *A Journey into Spain* (London, 1670), pp. 97–98. The various psycho-sexual connotations of this custom are intriguing – particularly in this instance; see the discussion (in Chapter 7, above) concerning the paternity of the alleged royal bastard, Don Juan José.

[66] See Paz y Melia, *Avisos de Barrionuevo*, ii, pp. 201, 211.

which stands in the busy square fronting the royal palace.[67] In 1624 the king ordered Juan Gómez de Mora, now known as a fine architect, but then being addressed merely as the foreman in charge of palace refurbishments, to 'construct, with the greatest care, a new wooden enclosure in the park [i.e. the Casa del Campo] for the horses, so as to protect them from casual maltreatment'.[68] Yet the king himself casually rode horses to death in the hunt and watched whilst they were gored to death in the bullfight. The English royalist envoys in 1649 witnessed seventeen bulls killed in the Plaza Mayor during a *corrida* to celebrate Philip's wedding to Mariana of Austria; just one of these was able to 'hurt very dangerously eight goodly horses'.[69] Doubtless the poor of Madrid obtained scraps of the latter whilst the court enjoyed the culinary results of the former.

The most affecting spectacle for the modern sensibility, at least vicariously, remains the killing of horses in war. As I began my essay by pointing out, in the painting of the seventeenth century the magnificence of the war-horse is meant to contribute to the overwhelming image of human triumph. This was often done in imitation of Titian's *Charles V at Mühlberg*. *The Cardinal Infante at Nördlingen* by Rubens and Van Dyck's *Charles I* are good examples. But in Velázquez's *The Count-Duke of Olivares on Horseback*, through the arch formed by the body of the rearing charger, we are able to discern one of the prices that had to be paid: a battlefield scarred by dead and dying horses. When Lewis Milestone made his famous film of *All Quiet on the Western Front* (1930), he felt able to include all the gory details of man's inhumanity to man which Remarque had chronicled in the novel; but he felt it unwise to include the scene where horses are dying noisily during a bombardment, doubtless in case audiences could not cope with it.

[67] For the history of its commission and original installation, see Brown & Elliott, *A Palace for a King*, pp. 111–14.

[68] 'El pagador Juan Gómez destajo', 13 Dec. 1624, APR, Admin. 5207.

[69] W. Edgman's diary of the royalist mission to Madrid, Oxford, Bod., Clarendon 137, f. 22.

Index